Walking
Raddy

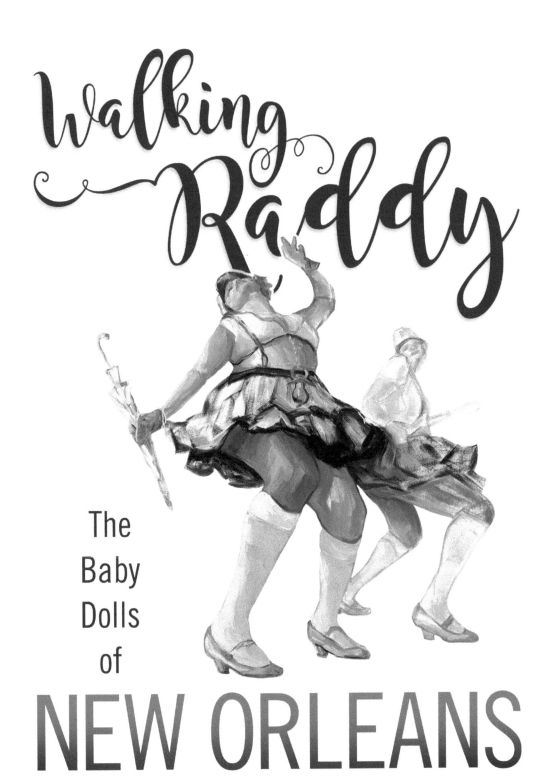

Walking Raddy

The Baby Dolls of NEW ORLEANS

Edited by **Kim Vaz-Deville**   Foreword by **Karen Trahan Leathem**   Afterword by **Tia L. Smith**

University Press of Mississippi / Jackson

www.upress.state.ms.us

The University Press of Mississippi is a member
of the Association of American University Presses.

First printing 2018
∞

Library of Congress Cataloging-in-Publication Data

Names: Vaz, Kim Marie, editor. | Leathem, Karen Trahan, writer of foreword.
Title: Walking raddy : the Baby Dolls of New Orleans / edited by Kim Vaz-Deville ;
foreword by Karen Trahan Leathem.
Description: Jackson : University Press of Mississippi, [2018] | Includes bibliographical
references and index. |
Identifiers: LCCN 2017054503 (print) | LCCN 2018000678 (ebook) | ISBN
9781496817419 (epub single) | ISBN 9781496817426 (epub institutional) | ISBN
9781496817433 (pdf single) | ISBN 9781496817440 (pdf institutional) | ISBN
9781496817396 (cloth) | ISBN 9781496817402 (pbk.)
Subjects: LCSH: Carnival—Louisiana—New Orleans. | African American women—
Louisiana—New Orleans. | African Americans—Louisiana—New Orleans. | New
Orleans (La.)—Social life and customs.
Classification: LCC GT4211.N4 (ebook) | LCC GT4211.N4 W35 2018 (print) | DDC
394.2509763/35—dc23
LC record available at https://lccn.loc.gov/2017054503

British Library Cataloging-in-Publication Data available

Contents

ix   Foreword

xi   Introduction

3   **"I Know My Ancestors Are Happy"**
A Conversation with Merline Kimble
—Megan Holt

7   **"True Doll Stories"**
A Conversation with Cinnamon Black
—Kim Vaz-Deville

Claiming Their Own Mardi Gras

21   **Fighting for Freedom**
Free Women of African Descent in New Orleans and Beyond
—Jessica Marie Johnson

31   **Geographies of Pain, Geographies of Pleasure**
Black Women in Jim Crow New Orleans
—LaKisha Michelle Simmons

45   **Protectors of the Inheritance**
Black Women Writers of New Orleans
—Violet Harrington Bryan

Black Women and Carnival Performance Traditions

61   **Women Maskers**
Critics of Social Issues
—Pamela R. Franco

75   **Operationalizing "Baby" for Our Good**
A Critical Cultural Commentary on Early Twentieth-Century Songs about Women as
    Baby and Baby Doll
—Melanie Bratcher

89   **From the Bamboula to the Baby Dolls**
Improvisation, Agency, and African American Dancing in New Orleans
—Jennifer Atkins

109   **Is the Unruly Woman Masker Still Relevant?**
—Kim Vaz-Deville

Memoirs and Musings

141   **How the Baby Dolls Became an Iconic Part of Mardi Gras**
—Kim Vaz-Deville

167   **In Memory: Uncle Lionel Batiste (February 11, 1932–July 8, 2012)**
"Colorful in Life—Rich in Spirit"
—Jerry Brock

189   **Baby Doll Addendum and Mardi Gras '49**
—Jerry Brock

195   **Dancing Women of New Orleans**
Mardi Gras Baby Dolls
—DeriAnne Meilleur Honora

203   **Reinvention**
Miss Antoinette K-Doe and Her Baby Dolls
—Rachel Carrico

213   **The World That Antoinette K-Doe Made**
—Rob Florence

223   **Sass and Circumstance**
The Magic of the Baby Dolls
—Daniele Gair

Visual Artists Respond to the New Orleans Baby Dolls

235   **John McCrady's "Southern Eccentric" Regionalism**
"Negro Maskers" from the *Mardi Gras Day* Series of 1948
—Mora J. Beauchamp-Byrd

261   **Culture-Building and Contemporary Visual Arts Practice**
The Case of "Contemporary Artists Respond to the New Orleans Baby Dolls"
—Ron Bechet

273   **Beyond Objectification and Fetishization**
Telling the Story of the Baby Dolls through the Visual Arts
—Sarah Anita Clunis

285   **Contemporary Artists Respond to the Baby Dolls**
Artists' Statements

285   Ann Bruce
288   Phillip Colwart
290   Keith Duncan
291   Marielle Jeanpierre
293   Ulrick Jean-Pierre
295   Karen La Beau
296   D. Lammie-Hanson
298   Meryt Harding
301   Annie Odell
302   Ruth Owens
305   Nathan "Nu'Awlons Natescott" Haynes Scott
307   Gailene McGhee St.Amand
309   Charles Lovell
310   Steve Prince
312   Vashni Balleste

315   Afterword
321   Acknowledgments
323   Contributors
333   Index

Foreword

Over the last two decades, the Baby Doll tradition has gone from an obscure, almost-forgotten practice to a flourishing cultural force with strong historical documentation. When the Louisiana State Museum opened its permanent Mardi Gras exhibition at the Presbytère in 2000, it featured a new Baby Doll costume made by Miriam Batiste-Reed, which had been created for a demonstration at the New Orleans Jazz and Heritage Festival. Because of an accident, Batiste-Reed—recognized a number of times in this volume as a pivotal Baby Doll elder—never got to show it off in person, but it was put on display at the festival. The pink satin, lace, and tulle dress was an artifact, produced to illustrate a dying art and later installed in a museum case.

What happened to the Baby Dolls next is a perfect example of the ever-evolving landscape of carnival in New Orleans. As this book shows, the Baby Dolls revived, starting with Antoinette K-Doe's group in 2004 (schooled by none other than Miriam Batiste-Reed) and spreading to other women, who took a century-old practice and reinterpreted it for a modern age. As the centennial (according to one of the origin stories) of the Baby Dolls approached, scholar Kim Vaz-Deville and New Orleans Society of Dance Baby Doll Ladies leader Millisia White proposed an exhibition at the Louisiana State Museum, scheduled to coincide with the publication of Vaz-Deville's book, *The "Baby Dolls": Breaking the Race and Gender Barriers of the New Orleans Mardi Gras Tradition*. Thrilled that this long-neglected aspect of carnival history would finally get the recognition it deserved, we jumped at the chance to collaborate with such expert guest curators. The exhibition, *They Call Us Baby Dolls: A Mardi Gras Tradition*, featured costumes and other memorabilia loaned by Baby Dolls and their families, vintage photographs, Antoinette K-Doe's costume from the museum's collection, and other items.

This in-depth exploration of the Baby Dolls would have been remarkable enough, but it was only the beginning. Community interest resulted in further explorations of the tradition, including the 2015 exhibition Contemporary Artists Respond to the Baby Dolls at the George and Leah

McKenna Museum of African-American Art. Then came this volume, a wide-ranging interdisciplinary collection of essays and art, demonstrating the impact of this significant segment of the New Orleans carnival universe. How did this happen? The answer emerges from the contributors to this volume, who situate the Baby Dolls in historical context and tease out the layers of meaning in their history as well as contemporary practices. If it can be boiled down to one thing, it would be this: the power and allure of "walking raddy." As many of the essayists remind us, the Baby Dolls fashioned a look from their own experience and popular culture, but ultimately it was their performance in public space that cemented their place as carnivalesque icons. In the early years of the twentieth century, they defied the Jim Crow's "geographies of pain," as delineated by LaKisha Simmons. Like the women of Trinidad and Martinique described by Pamela Franco, they asserted control over their sexuality in a ritualized public setting. "Walking 'raddy,'" as Jennifer Atkins points out, was a "flamboyant display of claiming one's space and body." While today's context differs from that of the early twentieth century in important ways, African American women—who make up the preponderance of Baby Dolls—still struggle to assert their "performative identities" against myriad interpretations that would deny both their agency and their pleasure. As Kim Vaz-Deville asks, "Is the unruly woman masker still relevant?" The response is positive, as Baby Dolls continue to expand the tradition, embracing the possibilities for Mardi Gras, that sacred day for performative masquerade, and extending the Baby Doll ethos throughout their lives.

This collection has much to teach us about Mardi Gras in New Orleans. It shows how lines of gender and race have intricately shaped this ritual, both in the past and today. And it clearly demonstrates how the spirit of carnival emanates from the grassroots, from people who passionately dedicate themselves, year after year, to assuming identities, dancing in the streets, and walking raddy for all the world to see.

—Karen Trahan Leathem

Introduction

Oh, we dressed out. One year, we dressed out as clowns, and so if you passed our house, you saw a porch of clowns. It was a big thing. It's a family thing. We have our house on Claiborne and St. Bernard Avenue. Everybody knew they could pass over there. She'd say, "You want a beer, baby? Come on in here." Oh, my God, we'd prepare. All of the family members would bring a dish. We had music blasting from inside the house. The church people would come. Everybody knew it was Claiborne and St. Bernard Avenue, right there. Henrietta was there, and she's throwing down. We still do it. We don't do it at the level that they did it, when her, my uncles and everybody was alive. We were little kids, and everybody came, and we'd sit on the porch. We owned that, and everybody knew.[1]

I came across the obituary of Henrietta Hayes Warrick, who had passed away "unexpectedly at the age of 91" on Monday, March 17, 2014, and had been "a member of Baby Dolls dance team in the thirties and forties." I wondered if this was the informal krewe tradition of the iconic Mardi Gras practice. I printed out the obituary and filed it. Two years later, pouring over the meticulous records amassed by Henrietta Warrick, I learned that she was the beloved daughter of her father, Sherman Hayes. Her birth certificate recorded her as the illegitimate issue of 20-year-old laborer Sherman and 16-year-old Viola Armstread, both of New Orleans. In a November 14, 1958, letter sent to Emma in New Orleans by Warrick while visiting San Francisco, 36-year-old Warrick instructed Emma to tell her father to meet her at the train station in two weeks' time at 4 or 4:30pm. Among her papers was a note he had written to her on plain paper, the lines drawn himself, on which he wrote:

Daughter,
Roses are Red,
Violets are Blue,
No One Knows,

Henrietta Warrick. Reproduced with the permission of Jenestaer Horne.

Henrietta Warrick. Reproduced with the permission of Jenestaer Horne.

How Much I Love
You.
From Your
Father

Her hand-scripted obituary for her father revealed that their love lasted until his death at the age of 87 and that her mother, whom he married, preceded him in passing. The records revealed what Jenestaer Hayes Horne, her sister 38 years her junior, told me as she left the precious archive for me to review: Henrietta, affectionately known as "Sister," was deeply loved and deeply loving.[2]

The story of how Warrick's home at the corner of black Mardi Gras central, North Claiborne Avenue, became the gathering place of her family and community, runs through Toulouse Street in the French Quarter, where she was renting a home. She and her friends, including a male cousin who was a musician, paraded in the Quarter as the Baby Dolls with a little band. They sashayed around the area and would stop at bars to get her favorite, scotch and water.

Henrietta Warrick (center) Mardi Gras Day. Reproduced with the permission of Jenestaer Horne.

She loved being a Baby Doll and she loved Mardi Gras. Her uncles belonged to the Zulu Social Aid and Pleasure Club, and during WWII, one served as the Big Shot, a key character in the krewe's tableau. She never missed the annual ball, even sitting at the king's table as an uncle held the position one year.

She moved to Claiborne Avenue, at first renting a house and then accepting, with her husband Joseph Warrick, the offer of their Italian American landlord to buy the house across street. Her move to that street was purposeful. Not only was it a thriving economic center for the African American community, it was where African Americans produced Mardi Gras for themselves, barred as they were from Canal Street, white elite krewes, and most entertainment establishments. From her porch, Henrietta, her father, mother, sister, and a host of relatives and friends, including and unapologetically, gay ones, observed the fete.

> While many whites celebrated Mardi Gras in the French Quarter, or further upriver along St. Charles Avenue, thousands of black revelers crowded Claiborne Avenue, lined with make-shift stands which sold all sorts of food and drink, while itinerant musicians entertained. Impromptu parading by black "Indian" tribes who bore little resemblance to Native Americans could be found throughout. "Marching bands" of as few as two musicians could readily attract "second lines" of black maids and porters dressed as baby dolls or movie stars, while ordinary black longshoremen and other unskilled workers were often masked as cowboys or gangsters.[3]

All the ornately suited black "Indian" tribes passed in front of their home. The wide oak-tree-lined neutral ground provided ample park-like space for picnics. Zulu, the only African American parade, meandered around the area as they stopped at local businesses[4]. In 1950, there were 150 businesses in the area[5]. People got around largely by foot, meaning that given the culture of sitting on the porch or banquet, sitting on the 'neutral' ground (the space between two sides of a street), waiting at bus stops, and easy access to restaurants, entertainment, essential services and shopping (such as, The Capital Theater, LaBranche's Drug Store, People's Life Insurance, Two Sisters Restaurant, Albright's Sewing Machine Shop, Gilbert's Toy Store, and Elite's Drug Store[6]), the ties to the community were constantly reinforced. Families had lived in the neighborhood for generations. No paper, debris, or trash was allowed to accumulate, but that would soon change.

The couple purchased their home in 1968, ironically at the dawn of the neighborhood's destruction. The Federal Aid Highway Act of 1956 was passed with the intention of providing highways for the army to defend the country against foreign invasions. This stated purpose was quickly seized upon by city and business interests and sped up the drift of capital from downtown to suburban areas. Nationwide, "white flight," as it was colloquially called, developed as more people of color came to dominate city centers and whites moved to the edges of the cities and industries and conveniences emerged to serve them. Two interstates through the downtown of New Orleans were proposed, a Riverfront Expressway overtaking the French Quarter and one through the heavily African American community of the Sixth and Seventh Wards, on North Claiborne Ave. The Riverfront expressway had major local support of the business and legislative class, but nation-wide resistance and threated law-suits helped to defeat the proposal.[7] On the other hand, the African American community was embattled in struggles of integration. The Congress for Racial Equality and the National Association for the Advancement of Colored People were preoccupied with desegregating schools and businesses, leaving little energy for action and event reflection on the dramatic change the proposed interstate would impose on the local black economic engine. More succinctly stated,

> There were people protesting the bridge being built in this neighborhood, but it was just the minority. This is white versus black, black versus white. And in the South, if you're black, you're not going to win. So this is something white folks want, that's what they got.[8]

The case against the Riverfront Expressway was made on the basis of preserving areas of historic value. It resulted in a major victory, raising the issue of heritage preservation as a consideration in transportation appropriations. The freeway would have affected Jackson Square, and the argument made was that the French Quarter was the nation's heritage. The issue of whose heritage (often coded as white heritage) is to be preserved was a national one. Eric Avila writes that "high above (and sometimes below) the landscape of human activity, the freeway removes the driver from social contact. For many, the freeway is a safe passage through the ghetto or barrio that (by design, many would argue) maintains the social distance between separate and unequal worlds."[9]

The elevated freeway that tore through homes, businesses, and the center of the thriving community was completed in 1969. The havoc on the community was swift; property values declined, businesses closed or moved, residents were scattered throughout the city, the beautiful throughway with its ample community gathering space destroyed. Crime, blight, rage, and sorrow came to settle there. Always an independent-minded woman, even though Henerietta marched in rallies for civil rights with Jenestaer's mother, Dorothy, she resolutely and steadfastly refused to vote even as the backlash against the city's notorious segregated grip resulted in black elected officials. She had no faith in the system. In spite of the many conversations, "All she would say was, 'It doesn't matter whether I vote or not. They're going to put in who they want anyway,' and that was that."

On a day like any other in 1970, Warrick said goodbye to her husband who left for work as a longshoreman. She went off to her own job as a cook for a Catholic school. Later that day she would learn that her husband who had diabetes had suffered a massive heart attack as he picked up his co-worker to head for the docks. Horne remembered that day with sadness as her mother, ten years younger than Warrick, informed her of the sad news beginning with, "We have to go by Sister." Horne described her sister as a woman who

> said what she meant, and she meant what she said. She was very, feisty, and she would cuss somebody out. She carried a gun. She believed in self-protection. She wasn't afraid when her husband died. She was broken by it; but she was going to make sure that everything that he had wanted for them occurred. After her husband died, she never remarried. She said she was not going to ever let anybody else live in his house. She never remarried and she stayed in that house the rest of her life.

Warrick's determination to live the life she and Joseph imagined for themselves is revealed in the records of contracts made to improve their property and in the ledgers she maintained of regular and timely payments for legal, mortgage, and burial debts, and her visible and cele-

Still dancing at 90. Henrietta Warrick on the porch of her North Claiborne Avenue home, October 5, 2012. Reproduced with the permission of Jenestaer Horne.

brated role as the family matriarch. She also recorded the genealogy of her large extended family. Baptismal certificates of godchildren and those she helped raise, Western Union telegrams from San Francisco and sympathy cards received on the occasion of the death of her husband, death certificates of immediate family members, Old Testament-like lists of names of ancestors and their dates of death, and more chronicle the life of a 91-year-old woman who in spite of her age, was expected by her kin, to live on and on.

What can the study of women's participation in Mardi Gras traditions tell us about restrictive gender norms, creative methods of subverting them, or unintentional reinforcing of gendered racial stereotypes? How did a "masking" practice (that is, to costume on Mardi Gras day) founded and perpetuated by women and men who had the lowest social status in their city—living before women gained the right to vote—emerge as an expected part of black Carnival that was revered by some and reviled by others but nonetheless survived to the present day? How has a practice steeped in inauspicious beginnings, in which the Baby Dolls flaunted every norm of Victorian respectability by smoking cigars and lighting them with money they had tucked in their garters, dancing in the street to bawdy rhythms, and the shameless claiming of the spotlight wherever they traveled on Mardi Gras day, experienced a renaissance in the 21st century, piquing the interest of members of all walks of life in New Orleans and beyond? Who are current day Baby Dolls and why are they committed to this tradition? This anthology answers these questions through explorations of the socio-historical context of segregated lives, concepts of street masking performances, profiles of Baby Doll groups, and the meaning of this embodied practice for those who perform it.

A special feature of this anthology, in addition to the scholarly essays, are artist statements regarding their work on documenting and being inspired by the tradition. Visual artists created work specifically for the exhibit *Contemporary Artists Respond to the New Orleans Baby Dolls*, held in 2015 at the George and Leah McKenna Museum of African-American Art in New Orleans. Through their visual productions, the artists consider issues of segregation, such as the second line carvings of those whose lives are constructed within 'segregational entitlement' as expressed in the work of Nathan Scott; appropriation of masculine signifiers such as women's smoking of cigars depicted in the work of Ulrick Jean-Pierre; and the rejection of shaming of sex workers as seen through the street photographer of Kim Welsh as she documents the current day Storyville-era tableau performance of the Treme Million Dollar Baby Dolls. This volume is polyvocal and the data it presents is diverse. Scholars draw on interviews, theoretical perspectives, archival material, and historical assessments to create empowered epistemologies about women's cultural performances that take place on the streets of New Orleans. Personal narratives of immersive experiences provide passionate testimony of the impact of the Baby Dolls on their audiences. Artists use their tools to ferret out the meaning of the tradition as it stimulates their imagination. By being brought closer to a tradition through study and getting to know the maskers, the artists have come to understand their struggles and the way the tradition helps to revitalize spirits.

The Baby Dolls are groups of black women and men who used New Orleans street-masking[10] tradition as a unique form of fun and self-expression against a backdrop of legal and social racial discrimination. Wearing short dresses, bloomers, bonnets, and garters with money tucked tight, they strutted, sang ribald songs, chanted and danced on Mardi Gras Day and on St. Joseph's feast night. Origins of the Baby Doll masking practice are disputed; one view situates the tradition as having begun in the city's black vice district before leaving the district to become imitated and innovated by others throughout the city. Some contend that the practice was the brain child of Sixth and Seventh Ward Afro-Creole families and neighbors such as the Batiste family of the Golden Slipper/Dirty Dozen tradition and the Phillips family of the Gold

Digger tradition, influenced by the rise of vaudeville acts and popular songs lauding women dressing and behaving as little girls. The practice emerged around 1912 and, while it waxed and waned, has endured to the present day.[11]

The Baby Doll maskers dressed in sexually revealing clothing and danced bawdily in the streets. It was a scene that was both shocking and titillating to carnival revelers, both black and white in the early twentieth century[12]. The Baby Doll maskers became an established part of black Mardi Gras and this scholarly attention adds to that which has been offered to the mostly male-dominated traditions of the Mardi Gras Indians, the Skeletons, the Zulu Social Aid and Pleasure Club, and black Carnival music. The aim of the anthology is to provide multidisciplinary background and context on the Baby Doll tradition and examine the contemporary relevance of this aspect of New Orleans's cultural heritage.

Claiming Their Own Mardi Gras

The three chapters making up this section set the foundation for an exploration of the 'politics of respectability' which lays at the heart the life circumstances of men and women who masked as Baby Dolls from its inception. The pall of the transgressive sexuality performed publically by women has made the Baby Doll tradition one of the last to be 'redeemed' among the black Mardi Gras traditions, especially among the middle class and adherents to respectability politics, though the positive sanctioning not only by middle and upper-class blacks, but by white New Orleanians for the Mardi Gras Indians and the members of the black-face masking group of the Zulu Social Aid and Pleasure Club fetes are more recent historical development (Trillin, 1964, 1968, 1998). The path from neighborhood and community revelry to iconic status representing the way the city and tourism industry professionals market New Orleans to outsiders began, according to cultural historian Maurice Martinez with his film documentary, *The Black Indians of New Orleans* (1976).[13] The film is recognized as a definitive sociological and cultural examination of The Yellow Pocahontas, led by Big Chief Allison "Tootie" Montana, and The White Eagles, led by Big Chief Gerald "Jake" Milon, as they prepare their "suits," practice their song traditions and parade in their communities on Mardi Gras day. The film was screened widely outside of New Orleans and around the world. He next credits musician Bo Dollis and the Wild Magnolias' musical performances in Europe under the direction of the Quint Davis, now of Festival Productions Inc.–New Orleans. The 1970s saw a surge of important recordings

by the Wild Magnolias and another important gang, the Wild Tchoupitoulas, led by the tribe's big chief George Landry and his relatives, the
Neville Brothers. Not only were they in demand for stage performances
as musicians but for appearances outside black Indian ritual contexts
at cultural events such as the New Orleans Jazz and Heritage Festival.
Photographer Michael Smith's books, notably the 1994 *Mardi Gras
Indians*, brought these stunning and relatively obscure artful creations
to a wide audience.

The growing recognition of black Mardi Gras traditions developed
during the period of African Americans' increasing interest in their
African heritage, normalization of pride in ideas about "black power,"
and an increasingly empowerment-minded group of black city council
members led by Dorothy Mae Taylor, who sought to outlaw discrimination in elite white male carnival krewes with a 1992 city ordinance[14].
The Zulu Social Aid and Pleasure Club had survived community and
activist critiques against their black-faced masquerading to emerge in
the 1990s with a large and well-connected all-male membership. In 1993,
the club began staging the arrival of their king by boat on Lundi Gras,
(the Monday before Mardi Gras) at Woldenberg Park with a greeting by
the then-second black mayor of the city. By this time, the Baby Doll tradition had virtually disappeared. The Baby Doll maskers, much fewer in
number and still connected to working class backgrounds, have lagged
in being recognized. The origins of the tradition in the vice district and
the 'freedom' allowed to women in carnival seasons to engage in boda-
cious sexual suggestiveness have been conflated and the ambivalence of
the tradition lingers. Since the publication of my book, *The "Baby Dolls":
Breaking the Race and Gender Barriers of the New Orleans Mardi Gras
Tradition*, the accompanying exhibit of costumes, historic photos and
ephemera at the Louisiana State Museum unit The Presbytere, and the
visual arts exhibit at the George and Lean McKenna Museum of African-American Art, the impact on awareness, appreciation, and serious-
ness with which the tradition is being regarded has improved.

In her chapter, "Fighting for Freedom: Free Women of African Descent
in New Orleans and Beyond," Jessica Marie Johnson outlines how during
the eighteenth and nineteenth centuries, enslaved and free women of
color played a vital role in the city's commerce and in its cultural development. Her chapter traces the changes in opportunities for women of
color in New Orleans, from the beginning of the French slave trade in
the Gulf coast in 1719 to the control of the colony by Spain in 1769 and
ultimately to the transition to American rule in 1803. Johnson shows that
enslaved women "labored as spiritual and health practitioners (including
at Charity Hospital), domestics, laundresses, cooks, and vendors, as well

as in gangs on plantations." Free women of color found ways to amass fortunes by investing in "land, homes, and stores, [b]y buying, selling, and renting real estate, or by purchasing and leasing slaves," and like enslaved women, they participated in the robust street vending market. Both groups "initiated and fostered the development of an Afro-Creole Gulf Coast culture, visible today in contemporary foodways, musical, and spiritual practices." This chapter offers a historical overview of New Orleans's women of African descent through 1912.

LaKisha Simmons's "Geographies of Pain, Geographies of Pleasure: Black Women in Jim Crow New Orleans" draws on the author's work with archival sources—including court documents, newspaper reports, police records, and delinquency home records and interviews of women who grew up in New Orleans between 1930 and 1954, a time period that witnessed the peak of Baby Doll masking activity before it began to wane. The chapter explores "sexuality in the lives of African American girls living in New Orleans during the late Jim Crow period," examines "interracial sexual violence, which many black girls experienced and most feared," and explains "how girls negotiated between the pressures to live up to standards of purity with simultaneous racist representations of black women and girls as sexually promiscuous."

New Orleans women writers are a vanguard in reviving and preserving traditions of the history and culture of the region, its love of family, community, and music, as Violet Harrington Bryan discusses in "Protectors of the Inheritance: Black Women Writers of New Orleans." Recognition of the centrality of blues and jazz and remembrance of the ancestors and religious traditions are also essential themes. This chapter explores the issues affecting the lives of New Orleans's women of African descent through an exploration of the work of writers: Alice Dunbar-Nelson, Sybil Kein, Mona Lisa Saloy, and Brenda Marie Osbey. For example, Mona Lisa Saloy grew up in New Orleans, playing games with the other children in the Seventh Ward—traditionally thought of as an Afro-Creole stronghold of the city. Her discussion of color, an important intra-racial subject, and what many of the community felt about the surprising marriage of her parents—a light-skinned Creole man to a "chocolate"-complexioned woman—prepares readers for the discussion in the fourth section of the book on the so-called "brown paper bag test" that dominates the Baby Doll portraiture of visual artist D. Lammie-Hanson. The focus on the Afro-Creoles of the Sixth and Seventh Wards lays the groundwork for understanding one of the most prominent families involved in the masking tradition: Alma and Walter Batiste and their children and the Phillips family and their descendants who still mask today and the family memoir by Derianne Honara.

Black Women and Carnival Performance Traditions

How are we to understand early masquerade dress aesthetic and performance of dispossessed and disenfranchised black women in New Orleans and the Caribbean where Carnival traditions were prevalent? Pamela Franco's "Women Maskers: Critics of Social Issues" offers a foundation and historical reference for women's masking styles to address this question. Black women's Carnival performances are shaped by their social and political conditions and the cultural memory of their African and colonial pasts. Franco notes that "to fully understand women's masking style one must look at their lives and socio-political concerns." As oppressed people, women were barred from mainstream "public avenues to respond to the issues that affected their lives." Their response was to appropriate "carnival when all eyes would be on them. They applied one of two approaches to their costume and performance styles: the sartorial body and the unruly woman. They controlled both approaches. The sartorial dress provided black women a space to respond to the common appraisal of them as grotesque and unladylike. The unruly woman was a much more physical and confrontational approach. 'She' permitted black women to be outrageous in their response to those social issues that degraded them." Franco's chapter looks at the sartorial body (the *Martinican*) and the unruly woman (the Baby Doll) and the decision of contemporary women to continue to comment on their social conditions by exposing their bodies.

When the Baby Doll masking tradition began, the song "Oh You Beautiful Doll" written by A. Seymour Brown (1911) and "Pretty Baby" created by New Orleans native Tony Jackson (1912 or earlier) and other similarly titled songs were part of the new and popular ragtime music. Jackson's rag was especially written to accompany sensual erotic dancing that characterized entertainment in the "District," a legal area for engaging in activities associated with "vice." Most of the black women who resorted to prostitution came from hardscrabble families and situations. The desire to be special to someone, in fact to be treated like a baby doll, was a pervasive one for women left to their own devices to survive. African American blues singer Bessie Smith wrote and performed the song "Baby Doll" not only to "get her loving all the time" but to "ease her mind." On the other hand, songwriters objectified black women in the lyrics they crafted. In "Operationalizing 'Baby' for Our Good: A Critical Cultural Commentary on Early Twentieth Century Songs about Women as Baby and Baby Doll," Melanie Bratcher explores early twentieth century songs about women as babies or dolls which can serve to further contextualize Baby Doll masking practices in the early phases of its development.

Jennifer Atkins's chapter "From the Bamboula to the Baby Dolls: Improvisation, Agency, and African American Dancing in New Orleans" places the Mardi Gras dance performances of the Baby Dolls in the context of dancing and its connection to Mardi Gras activities among various social classes. It traces the historical roots of black dance and the impact of women's growing ability to provide for themselves and demand self-autonomy on women's social dancing. The chapter focuses on the ways African American dance customs in the city validated the meaningfulness of their lives, reaffirmed their bonds with one another, and actuated an internal and physical strength even as they coped with discrimination and disenfranchisement. As Atkins states, "for the Baby Dolls, this agency mitigated, even if only to a small extent, the racism and misogyny they experienced in daily life. Dancing became a meaningful tool for confronting and negotiating deeply embedded societal challenges through upbeat celebrations and smart movement exchanges that expressed personal sentiments and attitudes while galvanizing a community." The chapter affords readers the background to appreciate the costuming of the maskers: the 'shake baby' dresses, the ruffled bloomers, and the continued practice of "showing their linen"—clothing designed to joyfully show off the posterior in vigorous dance moves.

The Million Dollar Baby Dolls were New Orleans Black Mardi Gras's original unruly women. Unruly women are characterized by their "too muchness": too much fat, too much noise, too much physicality, too much political or worldly ambition, too much of whatever exceeds the normative standards of femininity (Glenn, 2000). The Golden Slipper social group, consisting of family members and friends who were not associated with prostitution, still enjoyed the bawdiness of singing sexually suggestive songs and pushing the proverbial decorum envelope on "Old Fools Day." The Baby Dolls continued as the iconic "unruly women" (even when men masked this way) up through the period of integration (circa 1950s) as the practice began to wane. The Baby Doll masking tradition has been enjoying a resurgence in the millennium. Given the opportunities of black women in New Orleans to parade in organized 'krewes' and 'walking groups,' this chapter addresses the question, "are the Baby Dolls still relevant today as unruly women?"

Memoirs and Musings

Reflecting its African influence, black music is made in response to those who will be dancing to it. The idea of "looking audiences," people who watched and listened to musicians without participation, is a European and Eurocentric style of cultural interaction. The varying groups of Baby Dolls of New Orleans can be distinguished to a certain extent by the music and the musicians they are connected to. "How the Baby Dolls became an Iconic Part of Mardi Gras" traces the history of the Baby Dolls through their connection to songs, bands, and musical genres. This chapter was originally published in the 2015 Mardi Gras edition of *Offbeat Magazine* and is adapted and expanded for inclusion in this anthology.

Jerry Brock, the co-founder of WWOZ radio, which is a community radio station focused on local New Orleans and regional music, has published an alternative guide to Mardi Gras traditions. He has been following the black musical productions and cultural and religious traditions of New Orleans since the 1970s. Originally published in *The Jazz Archivist*, his articles included in this volume are "In Memory: Uncle Lionel Batiste (February 11, 1932–July 8, 2012): "Colorful In Life—Rich In Spirit" and "Baby Doll Addendum and Mardi Gras '49." Brock is committed to telling the story of Lionel Batiste's family, whose parents were the most well-known of all Baby Doll maskers. Brock argues that the origins of the tradition popularly believed to have roots among prostitutes is overemphasized and lacking in sufficient evidence to be credible. He argues that it is an unlikely origin because Batiste's mother, a married woman and officer in a strict religion, participated in the tradition and was not a prostitute. Instead, he emphasizes the aspects of early twentieth-century popular culture that would have influenced women to adopt this playful costume. His affection for the Batiste family and devotion to telling their view is evident. The Batiste siblings, with their guidance of new Baby Doll maskers in the twenty-first century, are important conduits of the transmission of the tradition. The Batistes were key to the revival of the tradition Antoinette K-Doe and her friends organized in the years immediately preceding Hurricane Katrina.

In her article, "On Thieves, Spiritless Bodies, and Creole Soul: Dancing through the Streets of New Orleans," first published in *TDR/The Drama Review* and adapted for this anthology, Rachel Carrico chronicles her introduction to the street performance traditions of New Orleans noting divisions along race and class lines. As a white woman, she discusses how she straddles those divides through her participation in the women's dance groups that have a relationship with Mother-in-Law lounge owner, the late, Antoinette K-Doe. She writes "the lounge also served as the seminar room, sewing station, and boudoir for the Ernie K-Doe Baby Dolls, a Mardi Gras marching group spearheaded by Miss Antoinette in 2004. The K-Doe Baby Dolls were one example of a revival of a masking and marching tradition of New Orleans black carnival that dates back, at least, to the early 1900s, but had dwindled to scant visibility by the late twentieth century. The K-Doe Baby Dolls emerged from the Lounge each Mardi Gras morning until Miss Antoinette's death in 2009. Miss Antoinette's K-Doe Baby Dolls came out 40 strong on Mardi Gras day in 2004: older, younger, black, white." K-Doe launched the first integrated group of Baby Dolls in the history of the tradition. In "Reinvention: Miss Antoinette K-Doe and her Baby Dolls," the author charts the development of the Ernie K-Doe Baby Dolls and their central role in reviving the tradition.

Rob Florence has immortalized Rhythm and Blues singer Ernie K-Doe and his wife Antoinette, founder of the Ernie K-Doe Baby Dolls, in his dramatic work. In his play, *Burn, K-Doe, Burn!*, Florence follows the rise of the self-proclaimed "Emperor of the Universe" from his early success as a chart-topping R&B singer with songs like "Mother-in-Law" during the golden age of rhythm and blues in New Orleans. His success would not last and Ernie sank into alcoholism, homelessness, and obscurity. The play also traces his rescue by life-long fan and second wife, Antoinette, who helps revive his career and to reconnect to the community in New Orleans and beyond. Ernie died in 2001, but Antoinette kept the lounge going herself. She provided a shelter for newcomers to the community and fans of local music. As a publicity stunt, she commissioned a life-sized effigy of Ernie that not only was enthroned in the lounge, but would appear with her at events. After the storm, the Mother-in-Law continued its signature role of as place to feed, nurture, understand, abuse, or eject patrons, whichever seemed to her to be appropriate. Florence, in the comedy, *Katrina: Mother-in-Law of 'Em All*, has hurricane survivors tell their stories to each other with his widow overseeing this salutary, spirit-lifting experience. Florence's "The World that Antoinette K-Doe Made" consists of his personal impressions and experiences on his life as a member of K-Doe's circle and many of these involve the people who masked as Baby Dolls.

Daniele Gair explores the *joie de vivre* experienced by contemporary Baby Doll maskers, dubbing it "Sass and Circumstance: The Magic of the Baby Dolls." In contemplating the embodied song, dance and costuming spectacle of cultural traditions that are performed on the street, she concludes that the performativity of the tradition is a "spectacular gem of brazen authenticity hidden among the cheap plastic of Carnival commercialism." Her chapter demonstrates that "maskers have existed as sublime examples of self-determination, uplift, and women's power even when black women were considered lowly." Reflecting on her experience of meeting Baby Doll maskers and masking herself with the Baby Dolls on Mardi Gras 2015 in preparation for the visual art of the show "Contemporary Artists Respond to the New Orleans Baby Dolls," her chapter captures the pleasure of transgressive gender prowess in all of its complexity and timelessness.

Visual Artists Respond to the New Orleans Baby Dolls

Mora Beauchamp-Byrd examines in "John McCrady's 'Southern Eccentric' Regionalism: *Negro Maskers* from the *Mardi Gras Day* Series of 1948" the artist's drawing of "Negro Maskers" published in the 1948 work *Mardi Gras Day*, featuring the art of McCrady and collaborating artists Ralph Wickisier and Caroline Durieux. It is the only known visual arts representation of New Orleans Baby Doll masqueraders until the second decade of the twenty-first century. Beauchamp-Byrd demonstrates how McCrady's *Negro Maskers* is deeply influenced by the 1938 photograph of Baby Doll masqueraders taken by Bradley Smith, a *Life Magazine* photographer and a founder of the American Society of Magazine Photographers (renamed the American Society of Media Photographers, or ASMP). Her chapter orients the lithograph within the context of McCrady's life and work to situate the chapter's "detailed formal analysis of *Negro Maskers*, with its stylistic references to El Greco and Mannerism, the paintings of American Regionalist Thomas Hart Benton, and the dream-like aesthetics of symbolism" to illustrate how Negro Maskers demonstrates his project of 'the southern strange.' Beuachamp-Byrd argues that McCrady worked to differentiate the south from other parts of the United States and in so doing established "a complex genre of Southern Regionalism, marked by a reliance on highlighting the "eccentricities" of Southern life." It was the work of a man of his time presenting an image of the Baby Dolls of New Orleans as prostitutes without reference to their life circumstances.

The exhibit "Contemporary Artists Respond to the New Orleans Baby Dolls" has involved the contemporary visual arts community in a dialogue that examines the meaning and relevance of traditional cultural forms in contemporary times. Now past its 105th year, the Baby Doll tradition is as important today in its meaning and interpretation of present day issues as it was in 1912. In "Culture-Building and Contemporary Visual Arts Practice: The Case of 'Contemporary Artist Respond to the New Orleans Baby Dolls,'" exhibit co-curator Ron Bechet explores how this exhibition offers newer ways of engaging in conversations about contemporary issues that emerge in examining the Baby Dolls: issues of resilience, independence, feminine identity, and the emergence of the meaning of artists and performances collaborations in today's visual art practice.

Sarah Clunis demonstrates in "Beyond Objectification and Fetishization: Telling the Story of the Baby Dolls through the Visual Arts" that visualized in a myriad of ways by the contributions of the various artists to the exhibition "Contemporary Artists Respond the New Orleans Baby Dolls" the Baby Doll maskers' Mardi Gras performance is collectively seen here as an activated, vibrant, kinetic site of empowerment for African American women and men. In the show, the viewer is treated to a number of different artistic receptions of the Baby Dolls—from ornate quilted textiles to vibrant photographic realism. The artists capture the Baby Dolls' paradoxical performance which combines a feminine ideal type and a wanton display of bodily pleasure. The artists demonstrate how the Baby Dolls craft their identities through their costuming, accessories, chanting and dancing and also through careful juxtapositions of both physical manifestations of womanly sensuality and ideal virginal girlhood full of purity and innocence. They convey through their work how the Baby Dolls use their feminine theatricality to facilitate a relationship with their neighborhood audience while they also affirm their own womanly self-assertion and exciting bodily display. Through depicting their aggressive female sexuality coupled with a defiance of women's gender restrictions, the art of this show mimics the Baby Dolls performance of struggle, of protection, of seduction, and of normative transformation. Following Clunis's chapter are artists' statements about what draws them to the tradition and how it has influenced their work.

African American New Orleanians have used their cultural practices of second-lining, costuming and masking to respond to large group social trauma of enslavement, of Jim Crow legislative and social disenfranchisement and state-sanctioned endangerment of their lives and the property destruction and loss of life, displacement, media and governmental disrespect and other crises stemming from the levee breaches following Hurricane Katrina in 2005 (Vaz, 2011). Today's Baby Doll maskers continue a tradition of one of the first street women's masking and walking groups in the United States whose significance rests in their joyful and unabashed defiance of prescribed gender roles during the annual Mardi Gras fete, claiming public space and a collective voice proclaiming through their performance their right to social citizenship.

NOTES

1. Interview with Jenestaer Horne, September 20, 2016.

2. My book on the tradition of the Baby Dolls was the 2016 selection of the Young Leadership Council's One Book One New Orleans project. On August 15, 2016, at the project's kickoff, Loyce Alexander told me her cousin had been a Baby Doll. A few minutes later, she showed me the photo of Henrietta Warrick in her Baby Doll garb sent by Manuel Bernard, Henrietta's cousin. I called Manuel and he put me in touch with Jenestaer Horne.

3. Cassimere, Raphael (February 12, 2013). A brief, racial history of Mardi Gras, *The Griot*. Accessed at http://thegrio.com/2013/02/12/a-brief-racial-history-of-mardis-gras/

4. An analysis of the parade routes from 1927 to 2010 demonstrates their interconnection with business and residences, as they changed annually and crisscrossed numerous streets, until after 1969, when the parade was officially recognized, and it conformed to a scheduled, pre-announced route. Rhonda Castillo, "Claiborne Avenue in the Treme: Re-Claiming Neutral Ground." PhD dissertation, University of Illinois at Urbana-Champaign, 2011.

5. Laine Kaplan-Levenson, 'The Monster': Claiborne Avenue Before and After the Interstate," May 5, 2016. http://wwno.org/post/monster-claiborne-avenue-and-after-interstate

6. Elie, Lolis, "Planners Push to Tear Out Elevated I-10 over Claiborne," *The Times Picayune*, July 11, 2009. Accessed at http://blog.nola.com/news_impact/print.html?entry=/2009/07/photos_for_iten.html

7. Laine Kaplan-Levenson, "The Second Battle of New Orleans." Accessed at http://wwno.org/post/second-battle-new-orleans?nopop=1

8. Laine Kaplan-Levenson, "The Monster," May 5, 2016.

9. Eric R. Avila, "The Folklore of the Freeway: Space, Culture, and Identity in Postwar Los Angeles," *Aztlán: A Journal of Chicano Studies* 23, no. 1 (1998), 25.

10. As Cherice Harrison Nelson points out, these are not "street cultures" but cultural traditions that take place on public streets. Personal communication, July 12, 2016.

11. Vaz, 2013.

12. Burns, 2006, and Kinser, 1990.

13. Personal communication June 5, 2016. Martinez named his film as being about "black Indians of New Orleans." The term "Mardi Gras Indian" may have come into existence in the early 1970s with the founding of the New Orleans Jazz and Heritage Festival in 1970 and subsequently appeared in the academic literature beginning around 1973.

14. Flake, 1994; Gill, 1997; Stanonis. 2006; and Vennman, 1993.

BIBLIOGRAPHY

Burns, M. 2006. A Note on the Baby Dolls. In *Keeping the Beat on the Street: The New Orleans Brass Band Renaissance*, Pp. 93–94. Baton Rouge: Louisiana State University Press.

Flake, Carol. *New Orleans: Behind the Masks of America's Most Exotic City*. New York: Grove Press, 1994.

Gill, J. *Lords of misrule: Mardi Gras and the Politics of Race in New Orleans*. Jackson: University Press of Mississippi, 1997.

Glenn, S. *Female Spectacle: The Theatrical Roots of Modern Feminism*, Cambridge: Harvard University Press, 2000.

Gotham, K. F. *Authentic New Orleans: Tourism, Culture, and Race in the Big Easy.* New York University Press, 2007.

Kinser, S. *Carnival, American Style: Mardi Gras at New Orleans and Mobile.* Chicago: University of Chicago Press, 1990.

Stanonis, A. J. *Creating the Big Easy: New Orleans and the Emergence of Modern Tourism, 1918–1945* (2006).

Trillin, C. "The Zulus." *The New Yorker* 40, no. 18 (June 20, 1964): 41.

———. *Mardi Gras, The New Yorker.* March 9, 1968, 138–44.

———. New Orleans Unmasked. *The New Yorker.* February 2, 1998, 38–43.

Vaz, K. "How Wounded Healers Help: A Culture-Specific Response to Recovering from a Natural Disaster." *VISTAS online* (2011). Retrieved from http://counselingoutfitters.com/vistas/vistas11/Article_93.pdf.

———. *The "Baby Dolls": Breaking the Race and Gender Barriers of the New Orleans Mardi Gras Tradition.* Baton Rouge: Louisiana State University Press, 2013.

Vennman, Barbara. "Boundary Face-Off: New Orleans Civil Rights Law and Carnival Tradition." *TDR (1988-)* 37, no. 3 (1993): 76–109.

Walking Raddy

"I Know My Ancestors Are Happy"

A Conversation with Merline Kimble

—Megan Holt

Recently, One Book One New Orleans project leader Dr. Megan Holt sat down in Congo Square with Merline Kimble—mother, grandmother, civil rights activist, and founder of the current incarnation of the Gold Digger Baby Dolls. Kimble talked about her family's role in the history of the Baby Dolls and what inspires her to keep masking year after year.

MH: How long have you been masking, and how long has your family been a part of the Baby Doll tradition?

MK: When I was a child, Uncle Lionel [Batiste] and his family were Baby Dolls, and after they stopped, there were no more Baby Dolls until I started in 1978 or '79, when Lois Andrews (Trombone Shorty's mother) talked me into it. After Katrina, we came back in '07, and we've been out every year since, even that year it was so bitterly cold.

But the history goes way back. In the 1100 block of Dumaine, my great-grandparents, an African American woman and a German Jewish man, raised seventeen kids, thirteen of whom were boys. One of the girls was my grandmother, who masked as a Baby Doll. She raised my mother at 1405 Dumaine, and my mother raised me in the 1400 block as well. I raised my daughter and grandchildren in the 1500 block. So, we had six generations in about five blocks. My grandmother and grandfather were Baby Dolls back when the sidewalks were made of bricks; they called themselves the Gold Digger Baby Dolls, and I took that name to honor them when I started masking. Women and men masked as Gold Digger Baby Dolls. They masked until 1942 or '43. The war was going on, and most of the male Gold Diggers were drafted. They drafted my grandfather, even though he had eight children. That's what ended the original Gold Diggers. Most of the women didn't want to come out without their husbands. My grandmother always said that being a Baby Doll was one of the best times of her life. It makes me proud that she lived long enough to see us mask.

I want to set the record straight here. Not all the original Baby Dolls were prostitutes. My grandmother certainly wasn't. Far from it. The Baby Dolls were a Mardi Gras club. Before all these all-women groups you see today, the Baby Dolls were the first ones. The Baby Dolls actually kept the men away from Storyville on Mardi Gras Day, so the Storyville prostitutes started masking to draw the men back toward that area.

MH: Your grandparents' pictures are in [Dr. Kim Vaz-Deville's book, The Baby Dolls: Breaking the Race and Gender Barriers of the New Orleans Mardi Gras Tradition], right?
MK: Yes, and that's the grandfather that got drafted, right up front [on page 105].

MH: I heard that Mardi Gras Day 2017 was a special one for you and your family. Can you tell me a little bit about what took place?
MK: We'd brought out our banner on Mardi Gras Day, the Gold Digger Baby Dolls banner. We never had a banner before. It was blessed in the church the Sunday before Mardi Gras day. A descendent from each family in the original Gold Digger Baby Dolls masked with us. Just like in my grandparents' day, we had both women and men masking. My aunts, uncles, cousins, nieces, and nephews came in to be with us Mardi Gras Day. My uncle was our grand marshal. We also brought back some of the old styles of dress, like the shake baby and the shimmy dress. The shimmy dress is made like a shift dress, but with ruffles on the bottom. So when you hear those old songs saying "shake your shimmy," they mean to shake the bottom of your dress.

MH: What does it feel like when you mask as a Baby Doll?
MK: When I put on my Baby Doll costume, I feel free. And it's important to feel free as a woman. I do things as a Baby Doll that I would never do in real life. I might hike up the back of my dress and show the ruffles on my bloomers. I would never normally do that, but when I'm a Baby Doll I just might! It's about freedom and fun, and women especially need that kind of freedom.

MH: How do you feel about the way that masking as a Baby Doll has grown and changed since you started your group of Gold Diggers?

MK: Well, you never know. When I'm gone, and the other women doing it now are gone, it might die out like it did in the 1940s. But then the children who are growing up now might remember us and say "let's do it again." The children masking as Gold Digger Baby Dolls right now love it. They are all smiles when they put on their costumes.

After the Gold Diggers, the first group to come out after us was the K-Doe Baby Dolls [founded by Antoinette K-Doe]. We went down to where they were to see them. As of last year, I know of nine different sets of Baby Dolls. We have Baby Dolls in the Seventh Ward, Baby Dolls in the Ninth Ward, Baby Dolls Uptown, Baby Dolls in the Treme. My main goal when I started was to have Baby Dolls all over the city, and I've done that. I know my ancestors are happy.

MH: Do you have a favorite memory of all your years as a Baby Doll?

MK: That would have to be the first year I came out. We went to my aunt's house, where my grandmother was. The family had kept our plans to mask as Gold Digger Baby Dolls a secret from her. I told my cousin to put on a second line song, and then we came in and danced in a circle around my grandmother's chair. We were dressed in all colors that year, and I was all in white. When I came back around to see my grandmother's face, she was laughing and crying at the same time! She was a strong, powerful woman, and I had never seen her lose control like that before. It scared me a little. I asked my grandmother if she was okay, and she just stared at me. She said "It's amazing that you're standing here in front of me in white. That's the last color I paraded in. We wore white because the men were going off to war." And she laughed and cried some more. She saw us for many years after that, but that first time was really special.

"True Doll Stories"

A Conversation with Cinnamon Black

—Kim Vaz-Deville

ith her finger on the pulse of New Orleans's past and present spiritual and cultural heritage, I asked Resa W. Bazile, who is best known as "Cinnamon Black," about the meaning of the Baby Doll tradition, about the modern revival of the tradition, about the impact of white women maskers on the tradition, and what she sees as the future of the practice.

Cinnamon Black is a cultural ambassador, an entertainer, second queen in the Fi Yi Yi Mandigo Warriors Black masking Indian tribe, a Voodoo practitioner and reader at the New Orleans Historic Voodoo Museum in New Orleans, and a cultural consultant for documentaries, film industry projects, and media outlets such as ESPN, SPIKE TV, Travel Channel, and fusion.net. Cinnamon is a former producer of "New Orleans Live," which aired on the cable access station NOA-TV. She has danced with N'kafu Traditional African Dance Company and Casa Samba, a Brazilian dance company, both based in New Orleans. She has been featured in commercials for products such as Turbo Tax and most famously in the Rouses' grocery chain Mardi Gras commercial, which airs annually. Cinnamon has had cameos in *NCIS New Orleans* and HBO's *Treme* and Oxygen channel's *Bad Girls Club*. She is regularly booked for events through "French Quarter Productions" and "Bespoke Private Tours." She masks as a Baby Doll of the renegade style.[1] Cinnamon has masked with the Gold Digger Baby Dolls and the Ernie K-Doe Baby Dolls, she has masked with family and sister groups, and she has founded several groups of Baby Dolls: The New Orleans Baby Dolls (now defunct) and the well-known Treme Million Dollar Baby Dolls.

Below is a record of our conversation, divided into thematic sections with editing to remove repetitions.

Origins of the Revival of the Baby Dolls

KV-D: Why have you begun to change your costume? It's become much more detailed.

CB: The masking tradition has always been somewhat of an underlying competition where one group wants to look better than the other. According to Sylvester Francis, founder of the Backstreet Cultural Museum, our style is more of the Million Dollar Baby Dolls than the regular Dolls in the Treme. "Uncle" Lionel Batiste agreed. I started off with the Gold Diggers. Before being invited to join the Gold Digger Baby Dolls, I had my own childhood group which was called the Rag Dolls, which disbanded after high school. I was eager to find another group. One day, while visiting with the neighbor elders Ms. Antoinette K-Doe, Lois Andrews, and Merline Kimble at the Mother-in-Law Lounge, the subject came up, and we were all excited. Ms. K-Doe spoke up and said if we bring them back and they come out of her club, they will be the Ernie K-Doe Dolls. This caused an uproar from the other women. They felt violated by her demand. "K-Doe was not a jazz musician" said one, and the other said, "my grandmother was a Baby Doll during her early years. She was a Gold Digger. She's still one so that is what I am. That's what I am going to be."

Later that evening we resumed the matter to bring back the Dolls to the street and exchanged ideas about costumes. We decided to ask "Uncle" Lionel's sister, Miriam Batiste Reed, to show us what the dress and bloomers should look like. Ms. K-Doe's club was in the Seventh Ward, and we were from the Sixth Ward. We overlooked the tradition of staying within our wards for the moment. That same night we went to see Ms. Merline's grandmother, Louise Recasner Phillips, who was about ninety years old. She immediately named her dolls, Gold Diggers. We enjoyed hearing her stories of what it was like in her time of masking. I wanted to be a Gold Digger because they knew how to dance; but the K-Does had the business network. I was with both groups and decided to go renegade. Eventually, the groups began to develop different tastes in costumes. I began to put my own special additions. I wanted style.

The group separated also because of a racial conflict and with that we had two groups that had evolved. I liked that the Gold Digger Baby Dolls, but they wanted to dress homely to me. I was young and into name brands. I needed some style and heels. They allowed me to do what I did, to put my own flavor to it. It evolved into what it has become today. It started off with ruffles and satin. They allowed me to add lace. They told me stories about how many rows of lace you have on your butt showed how long you had been out there. Every year I started adding another row of lace. I have not just one row of lace; my suits have maybe three or four, four or five rows of lace. They told me that the lace showed prosperity and money. My great-grandmother told me that little girls love lace. The girls back then who shimmied would shake fringe, tassels, and some even had miniskirts or culottes.

Back then Baby Dolls just didn't come out like they do now. They didn't come out every festival. They didn't come out every Super Sunday. They came out on special occasions, that is what made them special. They came out for Mardi Gras and maybe once or twice a year and that was it. That's how I was able to become an Indian as well because I only came out twice a year, then I had eight other months of the year that I could do some other type of activity. So I started following them. At first they only accepted me at practice, but it took time to actually get invited into a tribe. And I tried and I tried and I tried and I tried. That's why when I see the Baby Dolls putting feathers on, I wonder how they do that. It took me fifteen years to be accepted by the Indians to be able to do that. You just don't do that. You just didn't put on a suit, according to history and according to culture, and become this. You have to earn it. And you earn it through participating in society. You just didn't put the suit on, you had to be invited in. So when I got the opportunity to become an ambassador then I had the opportunity to decide how I wanted the suits to go. I wanted the suits to be inviting to young girls. And so I started to add more lace to it, little trim, to make it look more appealing to the eye.

KV-D: What are the 18 accessories of the Baby Doll suit?
CB: Let's count them. The gloves. The stockings. The shoes. The bloomers. The pacifiers. The bottles. The bib. Optional sippy cup if they're super thirsty. The bonnet. The skirt, if you don't have a dress. The top. The vest. The belt. That's thirteen. The garter. Handkerchief. The umbrella/parasol. And you normally would have optional earrings, rings and necklace. Some of them do carry a purse. You would do a pair of shorts under your bloomers in case your bloomers bust.

The Lingering Stigma on the Tradition

KV-D: Why is it important for this tradition to continue?
CB: From my understanding, it was a women helping women type of thing. Some of the women wore many hats. Some were seamstresses by necessity of taking care of the family. They were seamstress. They knew how to take care of the business of the house and manage the

money. They didn't have time to do nothing else but work, work, work, work, work. This was the opportunity for women to take a breath, talk to another woman, maybe find out a secret or something between the two to share that can help the other. They exchanged ideas and let their hair down and had fun. They did creative things in the community that meant something. It wasn't just about butt shaking. I want to make sure that this is something that you can pass from generation to generation where women can help one another through ideas, through activities and demonstration while being a respectable woman throughout the whole darn thing.

Back then the reputation was that you didn't want to really do be a Baby Doll because it was kind of sultry. People said they are prostitutes that are doing that, and you don't want to follow in their steps. That was how it was when I was a child. How we looked at it. But t I enjoyed dancing. I had a little ballerina music box and I used to watch ballerina dance and I watched dance programs on television, and it was more interesting than the cooking show for me. It didn't really make a difference what people said to me. I just felt what I felt.

I had heard the bad stories but I wanted to do it. I wanted to figure out how we can erase the bad stories as well to make it strong again because if you look at the history, Uncle Lionel's mother was a minister. She did other things besides and she was a Baby Doll too. She was a respectable woman. I met Ms. Merline Kimble's grandmother; she was a respectable woman. This almost ninety-year-old lady told me, "Everybody wasn't hos. We were families. You see that picture, you see police officers, all the other people with the little pots and the drums and the sticks." They made their music the way they could. But they were not all hos. They were families that did this.

We had our own Carnival because there was a time when there was segregation going on in our cities. Mardi Gras was practiced at the same time as Carnival was. It had its good and it had its bad part. Just like all the good things and you hear bad things too. We have a tendency to listen to more and remember the bad things than we do the good things. So they have good Baby Dolls. They had good families out there as well as the prostitutes. So my whole idea was what can I do to make this culture survive? What would make another woman look at and say hey, "I want to be a part of this. I want my children to be a part of this." Only thing that makes it last is with entire families. You look at a child and you see the mother doing it. You say well hell, that's what's real to me, that's what's familiar to me. That's how we pick our mates. Well, if you're going to grow up in a bad home, it's possible you will pick a bad mate with bad habits. We do this as a religion. Subconsciously, we do it every day without thought. We spend all our money. It's like a bad cocaine habit. We spend all our money on it. Sometimes people ask, "How much does your suit cost?" I say, "I don't know, somewhere in the thousands." I know that that button there cost me ten dollars. I'll buy a particular material that is expensive. It's just in my soul, in my spirit. I want to protect it. I want to make sure that other women look at it and say, "Hey, I want to be a part of that." I know if I were to stay with the prostitute thing, it would get back to where it had become. Women would shy away from it; they wouldn't want their children in it. They wouldn't have the support of their friends and family because a lot of times we don't want to support prostitutes in their endeavors.

KV-D: Why do Baby Dolls show their bloomers?
CB: That's bad girls. Bad girl moves. That fits the ward, whether it is the sixth or the seventh. If I go to the Seventh Ward, I couldn't show my bloomers because Ms. Antoinette did not like it. It was different in the Sixth Ward where they knew how to party. Men were being so funny about the bloomer thing that I found big joke underwear. Ms. Lois and I wore over to the Mother-in-Law and posed for a photo and a reporter published it. That made Ms. K-Doe mad.

White Women as Baby Dolls

KV-D: White women's participation in the tradition has been controversial. Why is that?
CB: Everything you do in life you have to have a reason. Everything has a cause and an effect. Because I have the opportunity to be an ambassador, I look back, and I did some bad things and I did some good things. The thing that I regret was allowing some white people to get into it after the storm. I'm not prejudiced. I don't know how else to say it. I'm not prejudiced. I have some white people in my family and as best friends and sponsors. An elder asked me "What are you doing? They're going to take it from us and we aren't going to make any money." I said "It's like a woman thing. Women want to do this and we could exchange ideas. We could network, they could let us in their business, we could get in the white areas and they can come in ours." He said yeah, "but this is our culture. They don't let us in Rex. You can come in and serve them. You can come there and monkey shine for them. You can come there and dance. But you won't be at the table. You won't be recognized as a member. They can bring their money and connections, but in the end, they're

going to take the culture from you. It's going to become their culture. It's no longer going to be ours."

You see, when they wouldn't sell us insurance so we had benevolent societies. When the jazz[2] funeral first began it was just for musicians and their friends and their families. Funerals were held in the living rooms of homes. The band would escort you from your house, take the body to church, and to the burial site. This home-going celebration only occurred in certain parts of New Orleans. It wasn't until after Katrina that we noticed how other races were beginning to claim our culture. It's a part of us. We did this because we were not able to buy burial insurance. We had to find a way to bury our dead. By this time, we had European girls from the Westbank and Carrollton and even Haiti who wanted to be Baby Dolls. But I had the hardest time trying to get black women interested because of the red light district stories. It left everyone feeling that they had to be bad or sultry. One day I looked on Facebook, and a young lady was in Switzerland doing a gig. A European lady dressed like a Baby Doll with an umbrella in one of my costumes that I made that she probably copied, making three thousand dollars a show, with a man looking like a three-way brass band. Then I understood what he meant. They're going to be able to look at the pictures and show their grandchildren and say this was our culture. This wasn't their culture. And our history will be disappeared and it will no longer be there.

It was not a city culture as it's becoming now. It was a black thing. The only time we saw white folks was on Mardi Gras day and Super Sunday and maybe four or five at a second line parade. But we see so many now, and our history is disappearing. So I backed up from European girls. you see it was rough because no one was in town. I got whoever I could, but I realized I was wrong. I was not doing this thing correctly. I made a mistake. I was not culturally correct, so I did not call them for rehearsals or shows, and they eventually faded away.

Now years later this prophecy came to be right before my eyes. I was in the French Quarter and heard a traditional brass band. I said, Oh, that must be somebody I know. I got excited and ran outside. It was a European band, but that wasn't surprising. What surprised me most was a white girl coming down the street in a grand marshal outfit. I had never seen this before. Who invited her in? What social group did she belong to, or who was she related to? In getting to this culture, you have to get it by blood like the Allison Montana family. Or, you had to get invited in and be socially accepted. You weren't supposed to just put on an Indian, Baby Doll or Bones and Skeleton suit if you were not a part of the culture.

We are of African, Afro-Creole, and Caribbean decent, so we move in a spiritual and tribal way. We work in an ancestral way. So the elders will pick the colors, or they'll tell you, you should wear this color, or they'll ask you what color you feel in your heart or how does your spirit feel, and they'll allow you to wear that. Today, Baby Dolls will come out in different colors. Back then, the material truck would come by. A lot of them would pick up a bolt of material from the truck and they would make a suit for everybody from that one bolt so everybody would have the same color. As time passed and when I got my own group only then was I able to pick my own colors. Now the girls ask me what color I think they should wear and I'll ask them—what is your nature, or what has been your experience? You have to be you.

You couldn't just put on an Indian suit if you weren't in a tribe. They would tear it off you. You couldn't put a Baby Doll suit on unless you were invited. Now things have begun to be watered down a bit. And as an ambassador, I have to make sure that I do the right things at the right time. May God help me, protect me, and preserve the culture.

Future of the Tradition

KV-D: Where do you think the tradition is going?

CB: It's unfortunately going very commercial. A lot of people are starting to clone our traditions. Now you have so many people doing the second-line and the Baby Dolls. We had the Caucasian Baby Dolls, they're now the Pussy Footers and the Camel Toe Steppers. The Caucasians will work with people we don't like to work with. Whereas the Caucasians, they'll work with people who they don't like just to make a club work. They have a tendency to be professional and say well, I don't really like that person, but I know I'm here for this common goal to make this organization go forward. And you'll see it in the men with the shorts on, the 610 Stompers. There's a whole bunch of them. I'm pretty sure all of them don't like each other. We have a tendency to look at the trees and forget the forest, to focus on the individual and not on the group. We focus on what we aren't getting instead of focusing on the culture and the evolution of the tradition. It's hard to get our women to work together, for some strange reason. They take it too personally. Because it's only a club; it's just an organization. It's a way of life. It's how we live. We do this in our city. It reminds me of back when Hurricane Katrina came and all our families were all over the country. The government decided they were going to give them a check for $2385.00. When our people got the check, you know what the first thing they did with it? You think they would have found a house or an apartment. They should have been looking for a place to live, right, because they were living in shelters. Our people went out and bought radios, barbeque grills and were sitting in tents and barbequing and playing music. Unbelievable, right? A church put 250 people out because they couldn't understand us. It is the way we live here, that music, that New Orleans sound, that second line sound. That's what makes us go from point A to point B when we don't have that money. That music, that second-line, that's our religious medicine. That's our antidote. If you're from here, then you understand why the people did that. That's how we get by. So the second-line, the music helps us get by. We have something to look forward to. There is a brighter day. There is a reason why we're here. The women working together, they'll be able to share ideas. Once they develop a relationship with each other.

KV-D: Has it been easy to develop these relationships?

CB: It's going to be a hard task, but I'm not going to give up. It's going to happen eventually. One way or another, it's already happening. My dream is to have women all over doing this thing, even though they're not speaking to each other. But now a fire has been ignited. I saw a young lady Baby Doll Chocolate.[3] I was so proud. It was like "Oh, my God, it's like a little baby." I saw it on the internet. She said, "Look, I've got my own organization. It's the Baby Doll club and I'm stepping out and I'm going to invite more women." I was like "Okay, yeah." So if we keep making it that way, we erase the stereotype that it is only for prostitutes. They can talk to their sisters to get the answer rather than waiting for a man to tell them how to do it. Somebody out there that can show you how to sew a button. There might be somebody out there show you how to make your curtains if you don't have the money to buy it. Or they can show you how to get a sheet and cut it up and design it and make it into a curtain. Because that's what the whole idea of making a suit is about, not just putting that suit on. That suit is showing you how to fix your children's pants so you don't have to spend $40 to get them altered.

Really that's what it's supposed to be about—exchanging that way. Most of the women are mothers and grandmothers. These ladies have houses. They have to learn how to develop economically. Before she died Ms. Antoinette K-Doe wanted to have a health fair and to teach women things they don't get in books or no one is telling them at home. This is the New Orleans Women's club. That's what they're supposed to be. It's so hard to get it there, but eventually it's going to come. One day Ms. K-Doe's health fair going to come. One day maybe we'll have Christmas Baby Doll ball. They'll be able to wear their formals and they'll be able to give out awards for the different groups for the year's "bests"—best dance gear, the most photogenic of the year, the most community out-reach. I want to make sure it's not just throwing down and shaking it like it's hot. There must be a way that we can give that to the other women and keep it growing.

KV-D: What are those things that are needed to make it survive?

CB: This reminds me of the time Ms. Merline, our Baby Doll elder, would fuss at me. I was so excited to wear that Doll suit till it didn't take much to convince me to put it on for any reason! "Y'all supposed to come out only twice a year!" she would scream. "What are you doing out here? Baby Doll is a special thing. You are making it common!" I thought she was being mean. I'm doing me, but sad to say now, I understand. I'm glad that you are putting this together, because there are certain traditions that should stay in order to keep the culture there, to make it survive, to keep it strong like it was. There's certain things that you shouldn't do, that you shouldn't do.

The fact is that we have certain times we come out was special. We have to make sure that we keep the tradition: how we dress; when we dress; how we talk; when we walk; and where we walk. We want to try not to venture too far off into what we think personally it should be. I feel that in a way I did that and it was wrong. But then in another way, everyone puts their own twist on everything. When a new administration comes in, they're going to bring their own ideas. But most of all, I just think that it's important that we write the book and let people know what was traditional and what wasn't. That way the next generation will look on us say okay, to bake bread I need eggs, butter and milk. I'm not going to substitute it with the imitation butter because it's not going to make the watery cake rise properly.

KV-D: Are Baby Dolls now beginning to mix with the Indians?

CB: Yes, we are now, and each Indian group is now saying they want to have their own dolls, which is okay. But it will change history. It will become a new story. But when a new group comes out, they should still go to the older groups. When I came out, I went and found all the elders I could find for advice. When a group came out, we all brought glasses and we broke glass on the street. That was a symbol of us accepting them to the real world—away from the school to the street, because that's what's real on the streets. So when new groups come out, they should seek out the elders and ask for their blessings and their acceptance and say, "Hey, this is who we are. We would like to come and join you guys." The elders would then turn and say, "Okay, you can go to the streets and these are the rules of how you play this game."

KV-D: What do you mean when you say that's what's real on the streets?
CB: There is a wide range to do this thing. You can't do the same things on the street that you do on the stage, and vice versa. So you have to understand when you're getting into this art, what it applies to. You can't wear the same thing on a traditional Mardi Gras day that you can wear for a show because it has the traditional thing that is expected to be seen. You can't for instance, wear a corset for Mardi Gras because that's not the show. Traditionally, you wear the satin suit. Come out with your Baby Doll pacifiers and things of that nature. It's just like other traditions. When you get married and you go to church, traditionally the woman will wear the white dress and she'll go down the aisle. Why all of a sudden would you want to change it with women wearing red and the purple dresses? It's going to lose its specialness, its essence—what made it so wonderful from the beginning and why you wanted to do it. So, I'm really afraid so much of the girls doing too much of their own thing.

I look at Ms. Merline looking at me. It's because the next generation is going to look at that and eventually is going to be lost. There will be no special Baby Dolls. It will just be a costume in a costume store that anybody could pick up. Once it becomes so common, it's no longer special. Just like the Indians, when they showed HBO's *Treme* crew how to make their suits, the next season the production staff started making the suits and not the real masking Indians. Before you know it, in the next five years, you're going to have suits coming from China. Now these guys are making their suits costing as much as $10,000. You're going to start being able to get them off the internet for $120. We have to follow the cultural rules and protocols to keep the tradition alive, to keep it in its rightful place.

So, with the Baby Dolls, we want to keep it special, because that's what makes it so wonderful. We want the girls to know when to come out. I come out sometimes with the Indians but I also come out as a Doll. But then, I'm part of a tribe. Just because someone is doing something, doesn't mean that everybody can do it. Because see, I'm coming from a different background and a lot of them don't know that. I come from Casa Samba. I belong to an African dance club. You might see me on the African stage. I'm married to a musician who has a reggae band. You may have seen me perform last year at the New Orleans Jazz and Heritage Festival in his reggae band. So they get confused when they see me different places and they think because I'm one that Baby Dolls do all the things that you see me doing. Not knowing that I'm an actress or entertainer; that's why I'm doing all this. So everybody out here putting on a Baby Doll suit is not an actress. So they all may not get hired with the Indians or they all might not get hired. I'm a trend setter. I guess then I have to be careful what I do. There are few women that were Baby Dolls that hung out with the Indians. The rest of them didn't do that. So I guess we all choose our path to which we want to go. But I'm so glad that you're writing this book so people will know which path to choose and why I chose the path that I chose. My path might not be right for everybody.

But the traditional way of a Baby Doll is to come out once for Mardi Gras and a couple of times special for shows during the year. Baby Dolls don't come out to funerals. Not every time somebody died you got a Baby Doll at a funeral. Why? What's the purpose? Are you just trying to be seen or are you carrying a tradition? The purpose is to carry a tradition. When do we come out? We come out when we're invited out. Or if a Baby Doll passes or someone passes who had an affiliation with the Dolls. But we don't come out to everything dressed as a Doll. Sometimes we wore t-shirts, arm bands, or special social attire.. When they see me at the Indian funerals, I'm coming there because I'm a part of the Indian group. I've been accepted into a group. So now we have Indian groups and they want to start having their Baby Dolls.

So I will say my influence of being a Baby Doll changed that in the tradition. My influence of being a Baby Doll and also being a part of the other clubs allowed me to see design in a different manner. I use marabou, stones, and gimp to cover my mistakes in making my costumes. Once when I was making the costume, I sewed something crooked on the seams. I put that trim on top and it made it look smooth. So that's where the use of the trim came from. That's where the bloomers came in because I knew that when I was dancing I may hold my dress up for fun to show my layers. The camera, may catch my dress up, so I will put the marabou on the bottom. But that didn't come tradition. That is a personal effect that the girls are thinking of. So for us too. My artistic abilities, that's where those things came from. It was not part of the tradition. It has now become part of the tradition I guess by me.

I am not the oldest in the tradition, but I am the oldest in practicing the tradition. Ms. Merline and Ms. Miriam Batiste Reed are the oldest in the tradition. But I also have much respect for the older Baby Dolls. We presently have Ms. Eva (Tee-Eva) Perry, who is the oldest entertaining Doll. She's performed for President Bush in the White House with Mr. and Mrs. K-Doe along with Geannie Thomas, a dancer. We have men, Mr. Al "Carnival Time" Johnson, a New Orleanian who wrote and sings the song "It's Carnival Time" and Mr. Ricky "Spyboy" Gettridge of Fi Yi Yi masking Indians. It's good to be associated with the elders. We need them to help us remember when.

I have to find a way to do things where the girls keep it traditional in the Baby Doll things, but we only come out at certain times of the year.

We wear our bloomers underneath there so that we don't look whorish. We look like little girls, like Ms. Merline said, going out, dressed up. I found that I started putting the sheer on top of my material because my mother is a fashion designer. But that's not traditional. Traditional is the satin and lace. The other stuff just came through, how would you say, game and to see if others would follow. They have kept it going. Now everything is decorated: the gloves, the shoes, and the hair. I decorate the inside of the umbrella and the handle. I wanted to make it interesting for them.

NOTES

1. Read about and see a video of Cinnamon in "Baby Doll Tradition Remains a Rich Part of New Orleans' and Mardi Gras Culture" by Kathleen Flynn and accessed at http://www.nola.com/arts/index.ssf/2015/03/mardi_gras_baby_doll_tradition.html.

2. For African Americans in New Orleans, bands accompanied the procession of mourners to the cemetery with sorrowful dirges followed by more upbeat tempos and dancing after the internment. This custom existed before the invention of jazz.

3. Shannon Paxton, founder of the Wild Tchoupitoulas Baby Dolls.

Claiming Their Own Mardi Gras

Fighting for Freedom

Free Women of African Descent in New Orleans and Beyond

—Jessica Marie Johnson

New Orleans's social and political terrain was and is motley. The struggle to define freedom and black citizenship occurred in a city made up of Africans, Afro-Creoles, and Anglo-Blacks; Republicans from the North, Unionist Democrats and die hard Confederates from across the South; Irish, German, and Jacobin French immigrants and expatriates; enslaved Africans and people of African descent born in the Americas; and free people of African descent born free, recently emancipated, or freed after 1863 as a result of the Civil War. Of these, those with the most at stake were free and enslaved women and children of African descent.

During the eighteenth and nineteenth centuries, enslaved and free women of color were central to New Orleans's life and the formation of black community. Beginning in 1719, with the arrival of the first French slave ships to the Gulf Coast, enslaved women were forced to labor in gangs on farms and plantations, and as domestics, laundresses, cooks, and health practitioners for white, black, and indigenous residents of New Orleans, including at Charity Hospital. Where they could, and because of out-migration and high mortality rates among French and other European settlers, enslaved Africans attempted to transform forced labor into hired out, paid labor opportunities. Some became vendors, selling food items in the street and on the levee or leveraged healing skills for supplementary income. Participating in frontier-exchange economies or trade with Native American groups around New Orleans was common. And where and when they could, enslaved women purchased their freedom or gained their freedom as the aides, domestics, nurses, and, at times, as the consorts or children of men in French employ.

The majority of ships arriving during the French period embarked from what is today Senegal and Gambia, and in a relatively short period of time (20 odd ships between 1719 and 1731, with only one more in 1743), significantly influencing the culture, politics, and social structure that enslaved and recently freed women of African descent created on the Gulf Coast. The sudden and condensed period of African arrivals, supplemented by an intermittent but protracted periods of transshipment slave trading between the Caribbean, Anglo-America, and coastal outposts, initiated and fostered the development of an African-influenced Gulf Coast culture. Described by some historians as Afro-Creole, this culture is visible today in contemporary foodways and expressive, material, and spiritual practices—including the vibrant and rich Baby Doll tradition.[1]

After Spain seized control of the city in 1769 and instituted *coartación*, a legal process allowing slaves to purchase their own freedom from their owners, even if the owner resisted, women and children of African descent predominated among slaves legally freed from bondage.[2] This occurred despite the tendency of enslaved populations to be weighted towards men. As slave importations increased and slaveowners sought enslaved men for labor on lower Louisiana's rapidly expanding sugar plantations, the numbers of the enslaved grew. At the same time, as a result of *coartación* and loosened restrictions on manumission, it was during the Spanish period Africans and people of African descent found the greatest opportunity to secure their freedom. Women played a crucial role as the population of enslaved and free people of color developed. As free persons, free women of color could and did accumulate wealth and invest in property—land, homes, and stores. By buying, selling, and renting real estate, or by purchasing and leasing slaves, free women of color guaranteed themselves a regular income. Enslaved and free women of color also labored in markets and as street vendors or hired themselves out as general labor. Enslaved and free women of color raised families and participated in communities formed through Catholic rituals of baptism, marriage, and by standing as godparents. Whether enslaved or free, women of African descent did not hesitate to express their sense of justice if they believed themselves wronged. Women from Perine Dauphine to Jaqueline Lemelle engaged in a long and broad tradition of women of African descent challenging slaveowners, employers, colonial officials, and each other in the courts to secure stolen persons as well as property, defend their freedom or secure manumission, mediate business conflicts or property exchanges, and settle personal disputes.[3]

Just as it was not surprising to find enslaved and free women of African descent using the courts to defend their own, it was also not surprising to find that women of African descent moved across a broad geographic space. The interconnectedness of the ports—from New Orleans to Mobile, from Havana to Cap-Français, from Gorée and Saint-Louis to Pensacola and Charleston—gave slaves and free people of color in one place access to those in the others. From the 1720s, free and slave persons circulated between Atlantic ports, seeking new opportunities and escaping threats. Women of color could be found, migrating from Martinique to New Orleans in search of kin or absconding from the Gulf Coast to Havana to escape undesirable husbands. By the end of the eighteenth century, New Orleans emerged as the hub of a rich Atlantic world filled with women of African descent who owned property, navigated complicated kinship relations (many of them across status), and who demanded their rights from colonial and national officials.

A shift occurred during the first decade of the nineteenth century, as free women and children of African descent found their way to New Orleans, predominating among people of color caught in the 1809–1810 expulsion of French refugees from Cuba escaping the insurgent conflagration that would come to be known as the Haitian Revolution.[4] Adding their resources and skills to New Orleans's existing free population of color, free women of color came to manage a significant proportion of property and wealth attributed to that community as a whole. In a survey of over nine hundred property records generated between 1794 and 1866 and catalogued by the Collins C. Diboll Vieux Carré Survey at the Historic New Orleans Collection, close to 435 involved exchanges of property by or between free women of color just within the boundaries of the French Quarter.[5]

After the acquisition of Louisiana by the United States, opportunities and rights accrued by free people of color began to close down. Over the course of the American period, first territorial then state legislatures placed manumission in the hands of elected officials, canceling *coartación* and diminishing opportunities for freedom accordingly. Upon becoming a state, Louisiana prohibited free men of color from access to suffrage, a sign of things to come. The acquisition of Louisiana also opened the South to an in-migration of Anglo-American slaveowners from the Chesapeake and Low Country, precipitating the rise of a heavy domestic slave trade routed through New Orleans. The city became host to the busiest slave market in the United States—even as it was also home to the largest free black population outside of the North.[6]

In 1811, a failed slave revolt, arguably the largest slave insurrection in North America, sufficiently terrified state political and military officials into ameliorating their attack on the free population of color.[7] Despite official distrust of free blacks, who they feared would be willing and well positioned to aid or incite further slave revolt, others argued free people of African descent were more likely to protect the city against black insurgents than join rebels. In 1812, Governor W. C. C. Claiborne mustered free men of color militias to relieve white troops at the Battle of New Orleans during the War of 1812, and did so despite resistance to men of African descent bearing arms. By 1830, however, growing anti-slavery agitation from across the country frightened lawmakers into passing and attempting to pass measures against all non-whites within Louisiana's boundaries. One of the more infamous was the 1830 registration act which required all free people of color who arrived in the state after 1825 to leave and all those who arrived before 1825 to register at cost or risk fines and imprisonment. Subsequent laws required recently manumitted slaves to leave the state within a certain number of days or "extended the privilege" to existing free people of color to select a "master" and voluntarily become "slaves for life."[8] Meanwhile, manumission remained in the hands of the state legislature, which persisted in denying access to freedom despite petitions sent by slaves—many of whom continued to arrive in the city to be sold to planters along the Gulf Coast and across the Cotton South.

In the face of outright repression and everyday antagonism, life for enslaved and free people of color in New Orleans grew extremely difficult. After 1836, real estate owned by free people of color dropped by 32 percent.[9] At the same time, New Orleans's antebellum black community fought to survive and do more than survive—to create legacies that would last generations, to protect community members and kinfolk, and to build as much lived autonomy as possible even in a city of slaves. Despite manumission restrictions, during the 1830s and 1840s, a third of manumission petitions originated from free people of color, many in the form of formal requests to free kinfolk from slavery. Among free women of color, women like Saint-Domingue refugee Marie Couvent, who passed away with enough property to endow a school for orphans, continued to accumulate wealth and property when and where they could.[10] Others created institutions to support women of African descent. In 1842, Henriette Delille, with Juliette Gaudin, both free women of color, founded Sisters of the Holy Family, a confraternity for women of African descent.[11] Business women of color across the city owned dry goods stores or operated boarding houses, including laying-in homes, brothels, and taverns. Others, like Eliza Potter, labored in the beauty industry as dressmakers and hairdressers. Some women, like Rose Nicaud, sold coffee, pralines, and other food items.[12] Others, like Rose Herera, Rosalie Vincent, and Rosalie's daughter Elizabeth Dieudonné, all three of whom arrived in New Orleans via the migration from Saint-Domingue, survived slave trading and everyday violence as best they could, watched their children kidnapped to the Caribbean, and waited until war, federal military might, and the changing laws of the nation could give them the opportunity to demand justice for themselves and their progeny.[13]

The outbreak of the Civil War, Union occupation, and the rise and fall of Reconstruction governments in the South did more than broadcast slaves' demands for freedom. These events—and enslaved and free people of color's role in them—crystallized a debate over freedom's meaning by clarifying what was at stake. No longer free people of color and slaves, the numbers of black residents swelled as former slaves migrated to Union-occupied New Orleans as contraband and remained post-emancipation as freed people. In the aftermath of emancipation, as former slaves sought to rebuild families, claim land and livelihoods, and escape the clutches of recalcitrant former masters, freedom meant more than a signature on a piece of paper. It meant the right to protect and claim kin, as Rose Herera attempted to do when her former mistress kidnapped her newly freed children to Cuba.[14] It meant choosing, as some formerly free women of African descent did, to participate in the work of building a post-slavery New Orleans. While some formerly free families of African descent withdrew and avoided identifying with former slaves, education and the education needs of freed women, men, and children created opportunities for other women of African descent to create ties across a very complex community. Women like Mrs. Margaret Adams, who wrote letters to the American Missionary Association on behalf of "colored parents" of New Orleans protesting the AMA's treatment and education of their children, or Edmonia Highgate, who arrived in New Orleans from New York to teach newly emancipated men, women, and children and became principal of the newly christened Frederick Douglass High School, stepped forward to help redevelop the city.[15] In New Orleans, one of the gains of Reconstruction, if brief, included the desegregation of the city's schools, a profound change made possible as a result of the work of black women teachers in the city.

Unfortunately, the legacy of slavery continued well beyond the ratification of the Thirteenth Amendment. Slavery's afterlife showed itself in laws restricting labor options, land purchase, residence and mobility. It re-emerged in police harassment and in courts, newspaper portrayals of black residents, and a white public accustomed to violating the space, property, and rights of black people, and empowered to exert extralegal violence on black citizens and call it justice. Violence across the South led to the death of hundreds of black residents and white sympathizers as anti-Republican, pro-Confederate white mobs attempted to drive out and take down Reconstruction governments. The Mechanics Hall Riot (1866) and the Battle of Liberty Place (1874) in New Orleans, and the Colfax Massacre (1873) in Grant Parish, Louisiana, demonstrated the extent to which many whites resisted black self-determination in Louisiana.[16] By 1896, when the Supreme Court ruled against a light-skinned man of color descended from Saint-Domingue refugees named Homer Plessy who, in an organized campaign led by interracial civil rights groups like the Comité des Citoyens, argued that state laws like the Separate Car Act were unconstitutional, the resurgence of white segregationist control over state and city government appeared to be complete.[17]

Meanwhile, an image of New Orleans as a city of interracial vice gained new life in the second half of the nineteenth century. Boosters and businessmen, as well as travelers, local color essayists, and novelists like George Washington Cable, published narratives of New Orleans lauding it as a site for illicit sex, lascivious women of color, and unlimited play in the form of dancing, gambling, and other amusement. For those managing the city's pleasure economies, attracting curious and titillated tourists from across the country with such stories filled an economic need. In 1897, a city ordinance created Storyville, a racially divided redlight or vice district. Sex workers were required to reside within the bounds of Storyville. It was a district created in the "back of town," a multi-racial working-class area of the city, adjacent to Congo Square and a stone's throw from the French Quarter, the Central Business District, and what is now the historic Tremé neighborhood. Storyville became a place known for dancing, gambling, alcohol consumption, and more, but it was also a neighborhood where residents lived, worked, and resisted the racial violence of the city.

For most women of African descent in the city, there was no fitting into the manufactured and racist booster stereotypes of the tragic mulatta or strange quadroon, but there was little they could do to avoid or protect themselves from them. Without question, many women of color navigated the city by practicing a culture of dissemblance or what Darlene Clark Hine has described as the "appearance of openness" within a practice of silence and secrecy, particularly around issues of sex, sexuality, and sexual violence.[18] In New Orleans, some wealthier widows and married women of color, many descended from French and Spanish-speaking free people of color, formed their own societies. However, as was true across the South, few women of African descent, including married women, had the luxury of refusing to labor outside the home. Those who attempted to do so often worked from their homes as laundresses, dress-makers and designers, or as cooks and used their homes as an economic base by taking in boarders.[19] For many others, work as teachers, domestic servants, or general laborers forced them to move throughout the city and confront daily threats of harm.

Life in the segregated city required care and creativity, and black women also worked for and profited from the vice economy. Some labored as sex workers, as servers, managers or owners of bars and saloons, operated boarding houses where sex work occurred, and otherwise participated in the vice economy of the city. For these women, race, class, and gender impacted their work and play. For example, the Blue Books that circulated as guides to Storyville's brothels allowed madams of either race to advertise for clientele but did not include sex workers who worked from "cribs" or one or two-bedroom homes, many of whom were women of color.[20] Color differentiations also impacted how sex workers in the books could be ranked, with the highest ranking of "tenderloin 400" often going to white or light-skinned women. Lulu White, one Storyville madam, described herself as the "Handsomest Octoroon," using the well-circulated fantasy of New Orleans women as lighter-skinned, mixed-race, and sexually available to her advantage.[21] In 1912, when a group of black women gathered to form the Million Dollar Baby Dolls, a new masking society that intended to dress, dance, and take over the streets on Mardi Gras Day, their determination to take pleasure in play drew on a long tradition of black women gathering together to support each other socially, financially, and emotionally, despite the institutional pressures against them.[22]

As black New Orleans women entered the twentieth century, the rich diversity of New Orleans's black female population reflected broader intra-racial tensions as well as productive fusions. From the city's founding, women of African descent who arrived on the Gulf Coast from West Africa and West Central Africa, as well as the Caribbean, were forced to labor in the desperate swampy outpost that would become New Orleans. Differences between women based on free status, place of birth, and wealth shifted in importance as slavery rose and fell. However, key features of black women's lives, including strategies for resistance and survival in New Orleans, remained constant. Through French and Spanish dominion and into the American period, through the demographic shifts caused by the reopening of the African slave trade, the Haitian revolution, the domestic slave trade of the American period, and, finally the Civil War and Reconstruction, women of African descent continued to create new lives for themselves, support each other through kinship networks, build intimate bonds, and establish propertied legacies for their descendants to pass on. The Baby Dolls' emergence in the twentieth century was part of this legacy and longer history, one revealed in fits and starts as scholars scour for voices of women lost in time. Recovering these voices is critical, particularly to those of us living in a twenty-first century that appears to have slipped back in time, with black communities denied the right to protection, safety, and a life free of intimidation and bloodshed and black women subject to a resurgence of dangerous stereotypes better left in travel missives of the postbellum South.

NOTES

1. Gwendolyn Midlo Hall, *Africans in Colonial Louisiana the Development of Afro-Creole Culture in the Eighteenth Century* (Baton Rouge: Louisiana State University Press, 1992).

2. On coartación see Kimberly S. Hanger, *Bounded Lives, Bounded Places: Free Black Society in Colonial New Orleans, 1769–1803* (Durham, NC: Duke University Press, 1997); Alejandro De La Fuente, "Slaves and the Creation of Legal Rights in Cuba: Coartación and Papel," *Hispanic American Historical Review* 87 (2007), 659–92.

3. Jessica Marie Johnson, "Death Rites as Birthrights in Atlantic New Orleans: Kinship and Race in the Case of María Teresa v. Perine Dauphine," *Slavery & Abolition* 36, no. 2 (April 3, 2015): 233–56; Virginia Meacham Gould, "Urban Slavery, Urban Freedom: The Manumission of Jacqueline Lemelle," in *More Than Chattel: Black Women and Slavery in the Americas*, edited by David Barry Gaspar and Darlene Clark Hine, 298–314. Bloomington: Indiana University Press, 1996. See also Kimberly S. Hanger, "Protecting Property, Family and Self: The 'Mujeres Libres' of Colonial New Orleans," *Revista—Review Interamericana* 22, no. 1 126–50 and Hanger, *Bounded Lives, Bounded Places*.

4. Paul F. Lachance, "The 1809 Immigration of Saint-Domingue Refugees to New Orleans: Reception, Integration and Impact," *Louisiana History* 29, no. 2 (1988): 109–41. See also Emily Clark, *The Strange History of the American Quadroon: Free Women of Color in the Revolutionary Atlantic World* (Chapel Hill: University of North Carolina Press, 2013). On the Haitian Revolution see Laurent Dubois, *Avengers of the New World: The Story of the Haitian Revolution* (Cambridge, MA: Harvard University Press, 2005).

5. Collins C. Diboll Vieux Carré Digital Survey <http://www.hnoc.org/vcs/>. Accessed March 9, 2015.

6. Walter Johnson, *Soul by Soul: Life Inside the Antebellum Slave Market* (Cambridge, MA: Harvard University Press, 1999). See also Erin Greenwald, "Purchased Lives: New Orleans and the Domestic Slave Trade, 1808–1865," exhibition, Historic New Orleans Collection, New Orleans, LA, 2015.

7. Robert L. Paquette, "'A Horde of Brigands?' The Great Louisiana Slave Revolt of 1811 Reconsidered," *Historical Reflections* 35, no. 1 (March 15, 2009): 72–96; Glenn Conrad, "Summary of Trial Proceedings of Those Accused of Participating in the Slave Uprising of January 9, 1811," *Louisiana History* 18, no. 4 (1977): 472–73; James Dormon, "The Persistent Specter: Slave Rebellion in Territorial Louisiana," *Louisiana History* 18, no. 4 (1977): 389–404. For a review of the literature on the revolt seee Nathan A. Buman, "Historiographical Examinations of the 1811 Slave Insurrection," *Louisiana History: The Journal of the Louisiana Historical Association* 53, no. 3 (2012): 318–37.

8. For these and other laws, see Judith Kelleher Schafer, *Slavery, the Civil Law, and the Supreme Court of Louisiana*, Louisiana State University Press, 1997. See also Acts of January 17, 1859, of Fourth Legislature of Louisiana (effective March 17, 1859), 2nd

Sess., Act No. 275 §§1–4 at 214 (1859), cited in "The Significance of Race: Legislative Racial Discrimination in Louisiana, 1803–1865," Bill Quigley and Maha Zaki, *Southern University Law Review* Spring 1997, FN 312. My thanks to the anonymous reviewers for this citation.

9. Loren Schweninger, *Black Property Owners in the South, 1790–1915* (Urbana: University of Illinois Press, 1997), 81: "The number of property owners in the city dropped from 855 in 1836 to 642 in 1850 to 581 on the eve of the Civil War, a total decline of 32 percent."

10. For more on antebellum free women of color and the community as a whole, see Virginia Meacham Gould, "In Full Enjoyment of Their Liberty: The Free Women of Color of the Gulf Ports of New Orleans, Mobile, and Pensacola, 1769–1860," PhD dissertation, Emory University, 1992; Judith Kelleher Schafer, *Becoming Free, Remaining Free: Manumission and Enslavement in New Orleans, 1846–1862* (Louisiana State University Press, 2003); Shirley E. Thompson, *Exiles at Home: The Struggle to Become American in Creole New Orleans* (Harvard University Press, 2009). On Madame Couvent herself, see Elizabeth C. Neidenbach, "'Mes dernières volontés': Testaments to the Life of Marie Couvent, a Former Slave in New Orleans," Transatlantica. Revue d'études américaines. American Studies Journal, no. 2 (October 10, 2012). http://transatlantica .revues.org/6186.

11. Virginia Meacham Gould, "Henriette Delille, Free Women of Color, and Catholicism in Antebellum New Orleans, 1727–1852," in *Beyond Bondage: Free Women of Color in the Americas*, edited by David Barry Gaspar and Darlene Clark Hine, 271–85 (Bloomington: Indiana University Press, 1996). See also M. Shawn Copeland, *The Subversive Power of Love: The Vision of Henriette Delille*, Paulist Press, 2008. Mary Bernard Deggs, Virginia Meacham Gould, and Charles E. Nolan, *No Cross, No Crown: Black Nuns in Nineteenth-Century New Orleans* (Indiana University Press, 2002).

12. Michael A. Ross, *The Great New Orleans Kidnapping Case: Race, Law, and Justice in the Reconstruction Era* (Oxford University Press, 2014); Chanda Nunez, "Just like Ole' Mammy Used to Make: Reinterpreting New Orleans African American Praline Vendors as Entrepreneurs," PhD dissertation, University of New Orleans, 2011; Lisa Ze Winters, "'More Desultory and Unconnected Than Any Other': Geography, Desire, and Freedom in Eliza Potter's a Hairdresser's Experience in High Life." *American Quarterly* 61, no. 3 (2009): 455–75; Eliza Potter, *A Hairdresser's Experience in High Life* (Cincinnati, OH: 1859); Judith Kelleher Schafer, *Brothels, Depravity, and Abandoned Women: Illegal Sex in Antebellum New Orleans*, Louisiana State University Press, 2009.

13. Adam Rothman, *Beyond Freedom's Reach: A Kidnapping in the Twilight of Slavery* (Cambridge, MA: Harvard University Press, 2015); Rebecca J. Scott and Jean M Hébrard, *Freedom Papers: An Atlantic Odyssey in the Age of Emancipation* (Cambridge, MA: Harvard University Press, 2012).

14. Rothman, *Beyond Freedom's Reach*.

15. Patricia Brady, "Trials and Tribulations: American Missionary Association Teachers and Black Education in Occupied New Orleans, 1863–1864," *Louisiana History: The Journal of the Louisiana Historical Association* 31, no. 1 (January 1, 1990): 14–15; Edmonia Highgate's letters to Rev. Strieby in Sterling, Dorothy, ed. *We Are Your Sisters: Black Women in the Nineteenth Century* (W. W. Norton & Company, 1984), 297–300. Highgate resigned her post as principal of Frederick Douglass High School rather than teach in a segregated school district. Sterling, *We Are Your Sisters*, 300.

16. LeeAnna Keith, *The Colfax Massacre: The Untold Story of Black Power, White Terror, and the Death of Reconstruction* (Oxford University Press, 2008); Lawrence N.

Powell, "Reinventing Tradition: Liberty Place, Historical Memory, and Silk-Stocking Vigilantism in New Orleans Politics," *Slavery & Abolition* 20, no. 1 (1999): 127–49. On Reconstruction in New Orleans and Louisiana, see also Eric Arnesen, *Waterfront Workers of New Orleans: Race, Class, and Politics, 1863–1923* (University of Illinois Press, 1994); Justin A. Nystrom, *New Orleans after the Civil War: Race, Politics, and a New Birth of Freedom* (JHU Press, 2010); John W. Blassingame, *Black New Orleans, 1860–1880* (University of Chicago Press, reprinted 2008).

17., Joseph Tregle Jr., "Creoles and Americans," in *Creole New Orleans: Race and Americanization*, edited by Arnold R. Hirsch and Joseph Logsdon (Louisiana State University Press, 1992), 131–85; Joseph Logsdon and Caryn Cossé Bell, "The Americanization of Black New Orleans, 1850–1900," in *Creole New Orleans: Race and Americanization*, edited by Arnold R. Hirsch and Joseph Logsdon (Louisiana State University Press, 1992) 131–85; Arnold Hirsch, "Simply a Matter of Black and White: The Transformation of Racial Politics in Twentieth-Century New Orleans," in *Creole New Orleans: Race and Americanization*, edited by Arnold R. Hirsch and Joseph Logsdon (Louisiana State University Press, 1992), 262–319.

18. Darlene Clark Hine, "Rape and the Inner Lives of Black Women: Thoughts on the Culture of Dissemblance," in *Hine Sight: Black Women and the Re-Construction of American History* (Bloomington: Indiana University Press, 1997), 290.

19. Arthé A. Anthony, "'Lost Boundaries:' Racial Passing and Poverty in Segregated New Orleans," in *Creole: The History and Legacy of Louisiana's Free People of Color*, edited by Sybil Kein (Baton Rough: Louisiana State University Press, 2000).

20. Pamela Arceneaux, "Guidebooks to Sin: The Blue Books of Storyville," *Louisiana History: The Journal of the Louisiana Historical Association* 28, no. 4 (1987): 397–405.

21. Emily Epstein Landau, "Hidden from History: Unknown New Orleanians, Louisiana Division, New Orleans Public Library (online Exhibit)." Accessed July 30, 2015. http://nutrias.org/exhibits/hidden/hiddenfromhistory_intro.htm; Emily Epstein Landau, *Spectacular Wickedness: Sex, Race, and Memory in Storyville, New Orleans* (Baton Rouge: Louisiana State University Press, 2013). Alecia P. Long, *The Great Southern Babylon: Sex, Race, and Respectability in New Orleans, 1865–1920*, Baton Rouge: Louisiana State University Press, 2005.

22. Kim Marie Vaz, *The "Baby Dolls": Breaking the Race and Gender Barriers of the New Orleans Mardi Gras Tradition* (Baton Rouge: Louisiana State University Press, 2013). See also essays in this volume.

Geographies of Pain, Geographies of Pleasure

Black Women in Jim Crow New Orleans

—LaKisha Michelle Simmons

For black women living in New Orleans at the dawn of the twentieth century, the pain and trauma of living as a "colored" citizen in a Jim Crow world took place on the geography of the modern city. The Million Dollar Baby Dolls, and the black female communities that danced and paraded on the streets during Mardi Gras, responded to a definition of New Orleans's landscape as "white only": they turned painful geographies into pleasurable geographies.

As historian Tera Hunter has explained, "Modernization and Jim Crow grew together in the New South."[1] The histories of southern cities as diverse as Atlanta, Miami, Charlotte, Houston, and New Orleans demonstrate how segregation was tied to progress, not simply to tradition. Jim Crow grew and prospered alongside the development of urban space, technological innovation, new industries, and consumer cultures.[2] In 1890, Louisiana passed the Separate Car Act, forcing "colored" citizens to sit in separate railroad cars. This act eventually lead to the Supreme Court case, *Plessy v. Ferguson* in 1896, that enshrined "separate by equal" into American law and is widely cited as the birth of legalized segregation in the American South. By 1902, New Orleans began a vast modernization project. Citizens enjoyed newly paved roads, sewage, draining systems, water purification, and updated streetcars. The brand-new streetcars included signs that read "for colored patrons only" to demark the white from colored sections. In the 1920s, city planners, businessmen, and boosters further developed sections of the city and improved Canal Street by adding newly paved streets, electric street lights and public restrooms, transforming the street for shoppers and *flâneurs,* cosmopolitan city dwellers who leisurely explored urban space.

However, city planners and business officials specifically excluded black New Orleanians from modernization projects. The new public restrooms installed to improve Canal Street only served "the white people of New Orleans."[3] By including racial segregation in city modernization projects, city officials and businessmen defined who belonged on the street, freely enjoying the city, and those who did not.

Writer Langston Hughes noted modernity's effect on Jim Crow cities: "It is in the South that black hands create the wealth that supports the great cities—Atlanta, Memphis, New Orleans, where the rich whites live in fine houses on magnolia-shaded streets and the Negroes live in slums restricted by law . . . It is in the South that hate and terror walk the streets and roads by day, sometimes quiet, sometimes violent, and sleep in the beds with citizens at night."[4] As Hughes explains it, the racial regulation of urban space, white supremacist violence on the streets, exploitation of black labor, and black inequality in the modern city defined southern modernization and southern wealth.

For black women and girls navigating Jim Crow New Orleans, this segregated geography was built around a "racial-sexual domination."[5] In the urban geography of Jim Crow, white citizens and white police officers insulted, excluded, and abused black women and girls. Black New Orleanians experienced suffering on the newly paved streets, in movie theaters and on the bustling streetcars and buses. One black commentator investigating Jim Crow streetcars for *The Crisis* magazine, noted Jim Crow's attack on black women's dignity and femininity: "The general treatment accorded to Negroes on the 'Jim Crow' cars by the subalterns of the road is discourteous, rude, and humiliating. Such treatment renders travel for the girls and women of the race extremely distasteful and hazardous."[6] This investigator pointed specifically to the lack of respect afforded to black women in Jim Crow spaces.

Pain and Trauma in the Jim Crow Streets

In oral history interviews, black women who lived in Jim Crow New Orleans consistently point to the lack of respect women faced when navigating the city's landscape. Clarita Reed explained: "It wasn't easy. You just got hardened to it. You always expected an insult."[7] Everyday geographies could be full of physical danger and verbal abuse. White abuse forced black women and girls to think about bodily control within urban geography and the various spaces where they were most likely to expect harassment. This was an embodied experience: "of becoming a body in social space."[8] Black women knew that modern New Orleans functioned as a site of insult: while shopping, on buses, streetcars, trains, in cars, and on the street itself (paved roads and sidewalks). These encounters underscore the urban character of gendered racial violence during segregation. Furthermore, it did not matter what kind of woman you were—young, elderly, educated, and working women all had to carefully navigate space and think carefully about the vulnerability of their bodies.

Cases of assault on the streets highlight the ways in which bodily vulnerability defined black womanhood and girlhood in New Orleans. In one 1936 case, a white grocery store clerk attacked a seventy-one year old black woman, who worked as a domestic in a white home. The elderly woman went to the store to buy ham. After the white clerk gave her leftover pieces for full-price, she protested. The store clerk "rushed enraged from behind the counter and knocked her to the floor, ordering her to 'get up and get out.'"[9] The store was located across the street from Straight College's former building.[10] The area was known as a place where black New Orleanians experienced street harassment, despite being near black institutions such as Straight (later the colored YWCA) and Albert Wicker Junior High School.[11] The newspaper article reporting the attack at the grocery store noted the location and that the store was "patronized by quite a few members of the Race." The elderly woman's white employer came to her defense by going to the store and confronting the clerk. The white employer commented on his maid's character and emphasized that she "had always been an ideal servant."[12] This woman was not protected by her age, respectability or her dedication to her employer. Instead, she was a victim of senseless racial violence on the streets of New Orleans. In the Jim Crow racial order, she was forced to work as a "servant" in white homes as well as expect "insult" or attack on the streets.

In 1944, thirteen-year-old Hattie Louise Williams was also attacked at a grocery store. Williams was walking by a downtown corner store when she accidently stepped on freshly laid asphalt. The grocery store owner insulted her and physically abused her.[13] These two stories—one of an elderly woman, the other of a junior high school student—reveal the violence of segregation. Both women's bodies and lives were devalued by the Jim Crow system, unless they were put to specific work (as a servant, for example). Here age as a category of analysis helps underscore the inner workings of Jim Crow violence because "Americans have used chronological age to construct race, gender, and sexuality."[14] Black girls and elderly women were denied phases of life that might be deemed "innocent" or "defenseless." White supremacists in the city did not see black girls or black elderly women as fully human, as developing through stages of life that required any extra care, respect, or consideration.

Just as age did not protect black citizens from racial violence on the Jim Crow streets, nor did maintaining a commitment to "respectable" behavior. In 1945, for example, "highly respected," forty-two year old dressmaker Beulah Jones encountered the danger of Jim Crow space. A white man assaulted Jones on the street as they both attempted to board the Galvez Street bus. The man was angry because Jones simply walked in front of him. He yelled, "What do you mean, getting in front of a 'white' man?" He then proceeded to hit Jones over the head, causing bleeding. The altercation continued when the two boarded the bus, and Jones attempted to protect herself from the man's blows. Jones's experience on the Galvez Street bus functioned as a reminder that something as simple as walking could offend white men on the streets. Black women did not have the freedom to walk or board a bus without worrying about the politics of race and the politics of space. The African American newspaper, *The Louisiana Weekly*, pointed to this injustice, highlighting the regularity of such attacks against black women in the city: "Another American citizen was subjected to brutality on one of the infamous Galvez Street buses of the New Orleans Public Service."[15] By using the word "citizen," *The Weekly* attempted to emphasize black New Orleanians' lack of rights in the communal space of the Jim Crow city—especially ironic in the 1940s at a time when the United States was fighting against racism abroad.

Beulah Jones routinely encountered racism on that particular bus. A couple of years earlier all of the black passengers riding the bus, including Jones, were arrested and accused of causing a "disturbance" by the bus driver. *The Louisiana Weekly* described the arrest as "Nazi-like." Jones's multiple encounters with regulated Jim Crow space demonstrates the daily insults black women faced on the streets of New Orleans. Indeed, Jones surely learned that she had to be careful about how she spoke to whites, how she walked while near them, how she sat and rode a bus, and the way her body took up space. Such carefulness when thinking about one's body in urban space was a regulatory feature of Jim Crow life for black women.[16]

In all of these assaults, New Orleans police rarely protected or defended black women and girls. Instead, the New Orleans police department was known for their cruelty towards African Americans in the city.[17] As historian Leonard Moore explains, "Police brutality has been an integral part of the black urban experience."[18] In New Orleans, African American protest against police brutality often centered on the desire to protect black women's bodies and respectability. In one notorious instance, Charles Guerand, an off-duty police officer, attempted to rape and then killed fourteen-year-old Hattie McCray in 1930. Despite protests from some members of the black and white community, and a guilty conviction for Guerand, the police department never questioned a culture of violence that led to the murder.[19] Prompted by a 1948 case where police arrested a ninety-two-year-old black woman for "cursing a policeman," activist and newspaperman C.C. Dejoie, Jr. argued that New Orleans's "police officers are as sadistic, rude, brutal, down right thoughtless and lacking in the high and fundamental qualities of good law enforcement principles and techniques as any who ever received salaries from taxpayer's money."[20] In 1957, a black northern visitor to the city, Bonnie Overton, a Chicago mother, experienced police brutality firsthand while on vacation. While in New Orleans, the police pulled over a car in which Overtone was the passenger. The New Orleans police officers found the gun she carried for safety in her purse, "struck her in the face and then jammed the gun into her stomach." The officers took off her shoes, tore off her jewelry and mink shawl, stomped on it, and told her, "No nigger woman has any business with a mink stole." The officers continued to beat Overton, stomping on her feet, punching and kicking her.[21] Bonnie Overton's visit to New Orleans reveals how black women had to think about the possible racial violence they might endure, even while in search of pleasure.

White supremacists in the city attempted to control black women's bodies through the organization of modern space. Segregated streetcars, busses, entertainment spaces and shopping reinforced notions of second-class citizenship and black inferiority. But racial violence on the street also controlled black movement. Black women and girls were forced to think carefully about where they were safe, if they might offend some white man, white woman, or police officer, and if their body might be viewed as offensive.

Searching for Pleasure in the Jim Crow City

Despite the violence and trauma of Jim Crow life, black New Orleanians sought spaces of freedom. How did black women find pleasure in Jim Crow geographies? How did they sustain themselves and their communities? As feminist theorist Judith Butler contends, "What makes for a livable world is no idle question."[22] Asking these questions highlights issues of justice, humanity, and sexual autonomy. As we have seen, black women's bodies were not defined as fully human by whites in the city. Black women and girls declared their humanity and reclaimed their bodies time and again by seeking out pleasure in the city's geography.

Dancer at Dew Drop Inn, 1954. Courtesy of the Ralston Crawford Collection of New Orleans Jazz Photography, Hogan Jazz Archive, Tulane University.

Black women resisted white definitions of black bodies and Jim Crow space by moving, dancing and performing in public—on the same streets where they had to carefully watch where they stepped. Black women danced at jazz clubs, on street corners, and at Mardi Gras. Geographer Katherine McKittrick argues that black women continually "think, write, and negotiate their surroundings as place-based critiques or respatializations."[23] By dancing in public, black women and girls performed in their surroundings, reclaiming the urban space of the city. They gave way to a free body, one not fully hemmed in by Jim Crow dictates; thus, they remade the city itself.[24] In this way, black women were able to let go of the careful, controlled body of their daily lives.

The barrooms and nightclubs, where so many young women found these spaces of freedom, were not sanctioned by black middle-class respectability politics. Some black New Orleanians found these spaces sordid and low-class. In an oral history interview, Florence Borders recalled her mother's disapproval of such entertainment: "I imagine that Rampart Street [where many bars were located] would have a greater

Dancer at Tijuana Club, 1951. Courtesy of the Ralston Crawford Collection of New Orleans Jazz Photography, Hogan Jazz Archive, Tulane University.

appeal to people who lived in a style that would not be attractive to middle-class blacks. My mother, for instance, did not go in barrooms. I don't think she called herself middle class, but she did call herself a lady. And she would not have considered it appropriate for anyone who wished to be called a lady to go into a barroom, no matter what kind of barroom it was."[25] Some of these bodily performances contradicted middle-class black New Orleanians' ideal black female body: a respectable body that remained sexually pure and protected from Jim Crow violence. Dances in barrooms and jazz clubs represented a performing body that embraced sensuality and fun; such sensuality seemed dangerous to some parents. These conflicts within the black community highlight contests for space, and disagreements over the definitions of proper behavior for black women and girls.[26] But in these spaces black women were able to take up space and to perform pleasure—instead of a demure, shrinking body, black female performers' bodies embraced audaciousness and expansiveness. Simply taking up space in the Jim Crow landscape represented a radical act. These geographies of pleasure served to create a new space for black femininity—a new way of inhabiting the body in the Jim Crow city. Urban geographies of pleasure, then, countered the trauma of racial and gender violence.

A series of images from white photographer and artist Ralston Crawford, archived at the Hogan Jazz Archive at Tulane University, underscores the respatializations and pleasure geography of Mardi Gras,

Million Dollar Baby Dolls, and dancing for black women and girls. In these images we see pleasure geographies at work. Ralston Crawford, an outsider to New Orleans, was obsessed with the black music scene and folk culture of the city. To capture images of New Orleans music, he explored segregated black spaces, revealing the intimacy of black cultural life.[27] In his work, we see how black women and girls were able to take over the street and reclaim segregated space. In doing so, they proclaimed, "This, too, is my New Orleans." When read alongside the violence of everyday life and the pains of Jim Crow geography, these images serve as a reminder that black women were always speaking back to dominant notions of black female inferiority. Images 1 and 2 show dancers at two local clubs: The Dew Drop Inn and the Tijuana Club. At these clubs, musicians, shake-dancers, and black queer performers in drag entertained partygoers. One oral history informant, jazz musician Tony Bazley, remembered the performer, Juanita, from Image 1, saying, "She danced with fire and was from St. Louis." Bazley's description underscores the dancers' performance as both big and bad—nothing could be more dramatic than dancing with fire (both a literal and figurative fire).

Barely visible in Image 2 is the audience taking in a dancer's performance. A woman sitting in the background, dressed in a long skirt, the proper fashion of the day, watches at a nearby table. The clubs and barrooms represented a place of freedom for the performers and the audience. Young black women who went to these clubs, despite the warnings of their parents or pastors, gained an opportunity to dance, sing, and find a bodily freedom outside of Jim Crow, even if they were not at the center of the stage or in the risqué clothing of the performers. In another image from Hogan Jazz Archive, a group of young women in longs skirts and "proper" attire, clap and cheer along as black queer performer Lollypop Jones entertains the crowd.[28]

Ralston Crawford's photography also shows the freedom black women and girls found on the streets of New Orleans during parades and Mardi Gras—dancing and masking on the Jim Crow landscape. Images 3 and 4 show women dressed, most likely as Baby Dolls, dancing along the street. These photographs were later used as advertisements for the Caledonia Club, a nightclub in the heart of the Tremé that catered to a black audience.[29] In Image 3, the woman dancing in the street, in Baby Doll outfit, is in full ecstasy, with a smile and a cigarette in her right hand as people line up on the sidewalk and stand on their porches to watch. Her demeanor demonstrates the audacity of Baby Dolls and other black women performers who opposed black respectability culture.

In Image 3 and 4, black girls line up to watch the Baby Dolls perform in the street, and in Image 4, one of the women has a toddler, dressed up

Dancing in the Street, 1953. Courtesy of the Ralston Crawford Collection of New Orleans Jazz Photography, Hogan Jazz Archive, Tulane University.

Dancing in the Street with Baby, 1953. Courtesy of the Ralston Crawford Collection of New Orleans Jazz Photography, Hogan Jazz Archive, Tulane University.

Young Girl and Boy Dancing on Table, 1959. Courtesy of the Ralston Crawford Collection of New Orleans Jazz Photography, Hogan Jazz Archive, Tulane University.

in a matching, miniature baby doll outfit. As highlighted before, black girls learned early to control their bodies in segregated space. Black writer Margaret Walker remembered the lesson she was taught as a child in New Orleans, "Before I was ten I knew what it was to stay off the sidewalk to let a white man pass otherwise he might knock me off. I had had a sound thrashing by white boys while Negro men looked on helplessly."[30] But in these images we see that black girls also learned of the sensuousness of the performing body, of finding space to live and let go. Crawford's photography often shows black children populating the sidewalks, observing the dancers, playing instruments, and joining in on the fun. These spaces of freedom were open to the children of New Orleans, just as black women performers created them. In watching and participating in these performances, black girls learned movements that might counteract the painful geographic lessons they also learned each day; just as the baby Baby Doll who danced with her mother, inherited black performance culture. Another Crawford photograph, of a party in Algiers, New Orleans, [Image 5] highlights black girls' enjoyment and participation in pleasure geographies. A young girl dances on a table with her friends and family watching. The crowd of children and adults smile and clap along. This image is remarkable for the joy and pleasure it imparts. These images remind us that despite Jim Crow's regulatory features, black women and girls found spaces of pleasure and freedom.

Here, between the space of pain and the space of pleasure, we see the important work of black Mardi Gras and the Million Dollar Baby Dolls. As Kim Marie Vaz has poignantly explored in her work, the Baby Dolls enacted a sense of self separate from the racist narratives of the Jim Crow South, and also separate from black middle-class respectability narratives that might also constrain black women's movement in space.[31] These women took over the cityscape and remade it anew, even if for fleeting moments. In this way, they worked hard to "make for a livable world."

NOTES

1. Tera W. Hunter, *To 'Joy My Freedom: Southern Black Women's Lives and Labors after the Civil War* (Cambridge, MA: Harvard University Press, 1997), 98.

2. For some examples see: LaKisha Michelle Simmons, *Crescent City Girls: The Lives of Young Black Women in Segregated New Orleans* (Chapel Hill: University of North Carolina Press, 2015); Hunter, *To 'Joy My Freedom*; N.D.B. Connolly, *A World More Concrete: Real Estate and the Remaking of Jim Crow South Florida* (Chicago: University Of Chicago Press, 2015); Karen Benjamin, "Suburbanizing Jim Crow The Impact of School Policy on Residential Segregation in Raleigh," *Journal of Urban History* 38, no. 2 (March 1, 2012): 225–46; Thomas W. Hanchett, "Race Shapes the New South City," *Journal of Urban History* 26, no. 2 (January 1, 2000): 259–66; Grace Elizabeth Hale, *Making Whiteness: The Culture of Segregation in the South, 1890–1940* (New York: Pantheon Books, 1998); Tyina Steptoe, *Houston Bound: Culture and Color in a Jim Crow City* (Berkeley: University of California Press, 2015).

3. "Report on Public Comfort Stations," June 9, 1931, New Orleans Association of Commerce Minutes, University of New Orleans, Earl K. Long Library, Louisiana Collection and Special Collections.

4. Langston Hughes, "Going South in Russia," *The Crisis*, June 1934, 162.

5. Katherine McKittrick and Clyde Woods, *Black Geographies and the Politics of Place* (South End Press, 2007), 4.

6. T. Montgomery Gregory, "The 'Jim-Crow' Car: An N.A.A.C.P. Investigation, Part III," *The Crisis*, February 1916, 197–98.

7. Clarita Reed, interview by Michele Mitchell, tape, June 24, 1994, *Behind the Veil*, John Hope Franklin Collection, Duke University.

8. Kathleen Canning, "The Body as Method?: Reflections on the Place of the Body in Gender History," *Gender and History*, November 1999, 505.

9. "71-Year-Old Race Woman Attacked in Store; Mob Threatens Dixie Clerk Accused of Act: Mob Threatens Clerk For Attack On Woman, 71," *The Chicago Defender* (National Edition), October 31, 1936.

10. Straight College later became Dillard University

11. Simmons, *Crescent City Girls*, 67.

12. "71-Year-Old Race Woman Attacked in Store; Mob Threatens Dixie Clerk Accused of Act."

13. "13-Year-Old Girl Beaten by White Grocer," *The Louisiana Weekly*, February 12, 1944, Amistad Research Center, Tulane University.

14. Corinne T. Field and Nicholas . Syrett, *Age in America: The Colonial Era to the Present* (New York City: NYU Press, 2015), 4. For more on age as a category of analysis, see the introduction to Simmons, *Crescent City Girls*.

15. "Bus Victim Is Notified to Be in Court Feb. 16," *The Louisiana Weekly*, January 27, 1945.

16. Simmons, *Crescent City Girls*, 25–55.

17. Ibid., 56, 93–107; "Accused of Speeding, Is 'Beat Up,'" *The Louisiana Weekly*, February 22, 1930; Leonard N. Moore, *Black Rage in New Orleans: Police Brutality and African American Activism from World War II to Hurricane Katrina* (Baton Rouge: Louisiana State University Press, 2010), 5–7.

18. Moore, *Black Rage in New Orleans*, 6.

19. Simmons, *Crescent City Girls*, 109–15.

20. Moore, *Black Rage in New Orleans*, 24.

21. "Chicagoan Tells Beating by New Orleans Police," *The Chicago Defender* (National Edition) (1921–1967), December 7, 1957.

22. Judith Butler, *Undoing Gender* (New York: Routledge, 2004), 17.

23. Katherine McKittrick, *Demonic Grounds: Black Women and the Cartographies Of Struggle*, 1st ed. (Minneapolis: University Of Minnesota Press, 2006), xix; Simmons, *Crescent City Girls*, 199–204.

24. Black women's resistance to racial dominance on the streets of New Orleans was not new to the Jim Crow era. In a Spanish colonial attempt to control the bodies, beauty, and sexuality of gens de couleur and to restrict plaçage (white male relationships with free women of color), governor Esteban Miro enacted a law commonly called the "tig-non law" of 1786. He attempted to regulate free women of color's bodies by forbidding them to adorn their body in jewels or fancy dress and required them to cover their hair with a handkerchief. Free black women resisted these laws by making beautiful what was supposed to be plain: the handkerchiefs. As Lisa Ze Winters explains, "That free women of color appeared, at least in a public way, to at once embrace and resist the tignon law is important because these women's actions articulated a performance of femininity inextricable from their specifically gendered, racialized experience as women of African descent in a slave society." Lisa Ze Winters, *The Mulatta Concubine: Terror, Intimacy, Freedom, and Desire in the Black Transatlantic* (Athens: University of Georgia Press, 2016), 77–82, quote on page 80.

25. Florence Borders, interview by Kate Ellis and Michele Mitchell, June 20, 1994, *Behind the Veil*, John Hope Franklin Collection, Duke University.

26. For more over contests for space within the black community, see Elsa Barkley Brown and Greg Kimball, "Mapping the Terrain of Black Richmond," in *The New African American Urban History*, ed. Kennith W. Goings and Raymond Mohl (Thousand Oaks: Sage, 1996), 66–115.

27. Ralston Crawford, Curtis Jerde, and John H. Lawrence, *Music in the Street: Photographs of New Orleans by Ralston Crawford* (New Orleans: Historic New Orleans Collection, 1983), xi.

28. Ralston Crawford, "Audience at the Dew Drop Inn," Photograph, 1952, Box 3 #32, Ralston Crawford Collection, William Ransom Hogan Jazz Archive, Howard-Tilton Memorial Library, Tulane University.

29. For more on Caledonia Club, see J. Mark Souther, *New Orleans on Parade: Tourism and the Transformation of the Crescent City* (Baton Rouge: Louisiana State

University Press, 2013), 127; Matt Sakakeeny, *Roll With It: Brass Bands in the Streets of New Orleans* (Durham: Duke University Press, 2013), 27–28.

30. Margaret Walker, "Growing Out of Shadow," in *How I Wrote Jubilee and Other Essays on Life and Literature*, ed. Maryemma Graham (New York: The Feminist Press at City University of New York, 1990), 4.

31. Kim Marie Vaz, *The "Baby Dolls": Breaking the Race and Gender Barriers of the New Orleans Mardi Gras Tradition* (Baton Rouge: Louisiana State University Press, 2013).

Protectors of the Inheritance

Black Women Writers of New Orleans

—Violet Harrington Bryan

ew Orleans's black women writers are particularly interested in using and preserving traditions of the culture of New Orleans, its love of family, community, and music as contexts for their writings. Re-creation of blues and jazz and remembrance of the ancestors and religious traditions are essential themes. The writers and their characters are proud of themselves, their family, and their heritage. They know and feel who they are. They love their surroundings, including the plants and flowers that they grow in their gardens and the food that they cook. But mainly they love and protect their families—the men that they love, the children that they raise, and the friends that they share life with, their history, and stories of the past.

Alice Dunbar-Nelson, born Alice Ruth Moore in New Orleans in 1875, joined the literary world early in her career. At twenty years old, she published the first of her two books of poetry and short fiction, *Violets and Other Tales* (1895). She followed with her second book, *The Goodness of St. Rocque and Other Tales* (1899).[1] Both books were stories and poems of Creole life in New Orleans, where race was not defined, but subtly suggested. She also wrote stories about immigrants to the city and about the changing and complex roles of women in society in such stories as "Tony's Wife" in *The Goodness of St. Rocque*.[2] As I remarked in my book *The Myth of New Orleans in New Orleans Literature*, Dunbar-Nelson's future husband at that time, the well-known African American poet Paul Laurence Dunbar, said in a letter to her, "Your determination to contest [George Washington] Cable for his laurels is a commendable one. Why shouldn't you tell those pretty creole stories as well as he? You have the force, the fire and the artistic touch that is so delicate & so strong."[3] Alice

Dunbar-Nelson probably knew *Old Creole Days* of George Washington Cable (1879) and his novels, such as *The Grandissimes* (1880) and *Doctor Sevier* (1882), better than she knew the contemporaneous works of white women of New Orleans at the turn of the century, such as Grace King and Kate Chopin, but the works of the women writers, both black and white, are similar in many ways. Grace King had just written her history *New Orleans: The Place and the People* (1892) and her romantic tales, such as "Bonne Maman" (1886), "Madrilene, or The Festival of the Dead" (1890), and "The Little Convent Girl" (1893), published first in *Harper's* and *Century* and then in King's *Tales of a Time and Place* (1892) and *Balcony Stories* (1893). However, King's stories of complex race and gender situations and the tragic mulatta were comparable to many of Dunbar-Nelson's early tales. Kate Chopin's tales, such as "La Belle Zoraide," and "Neg Creol," and the much more well-known "Desiree's Baby" (from *Bayou Folk*, 1894 and *A Night in Acadie*, 1897), also deal with the tragedy of race and dismissal, but also with the marginalization of gender and the struggles of women to find their voice.

In her early stories, Dunbar-Nelson usually camouflaged the matter of race. She mentioned race only indirectly in such phrases as "dusky-eyed," "the small brown hands," "the wizened yellow woman," "dat light girl," or she mentions place names that were usually associated with people of color, such as Rampart Street or "the lower districts," in the story "A Carnival Jangle." In the 1890s Dunbar-Nelson's story "Little Miss Sophie" (in *Violets*) would have been read as a typical story of tragic heroism, a tale of a young woman whose lover has rejected her but whom she still loves and will do anything to save, a story comparable to Cable's *Madame Delphine* or "'Tite Poulette."[4] But Alice Dunbar-Nelson was revising the image of the free woman of color. Little Miss Sophie in the story by that name accepted that she had lost the white man that she had loved in a placage relationship to a white woman that he married. She heard his friends after the wedding say how sad it was that their friend would not have any money for his new household, that he needed to show his family signet ring to the lawyer to receive his part of the inheritance, but he had had "some little Creole love-affair some years ago, and gave this ring to his *dusky-eyed fiancée* [my italics]."[5] But Sophie had traded his ring in at a pawn shop to get money to save her father from an illness, and now resolved to work her hands off sewing day and night to buy the ring back again, and get it back to him, only she had worked so hard that she died that Christmas Day clasping the ring in her hands. The sentimental story informs the reader about the dangers of placage arrangements and the determined persistence of the Creole woman, even though she had no gain in the transaction except for her pride and sense of integrity.[6]

Jordan Stouck points out how Alice Dunbar adds to the tale of the tragic mulatta by also showing how the white male subject, Neale, is also a hypocrite in the social tradition and the Creole woman wins out because of her moral superiority:

> As the simultaneously diminutive and formal title suggests, the narrative moves in two directions, containing identity through the violently divided figure of the tragic mulatta and yet implicitly reproaching the white male subject who benefits from such actions.[7]

"A Carnival Jangle," another short story published in both *Violets* and *The Goodness of Saint Rocque,* adds to the readers' insight into the mulatta's role in the New Orleans Carnival. The protagonist, who is portrayed as the quiet young mulatta, Flo, would have been much better off that beautiful Carnival day if she had stuck with her original unmasked group of young friends, but she decided to accept a young "Mephisto's" invitation to go with him to enjoy the Carnival. He tells her, "Flo, you're wasting time in that tame group."[8] Details about the city of New Orleans and descriptions of characters lead the reader to imagine that this young man carries Flo into a more treacherous part of New Orleans, "the lower districts." After an old lady costumer on Toulouse and St. Peter Streets, a small, elderly lady, with *yellow,* flabby jaws and neck like the throat of an alligator, sells Flo a masquerade that suits her out as a troubadour, she and the Mephisto move on to Washington Square and Elysian Fields. In the square, the two friends meet a troupe of Mardi Gras Indians who are ready to battle each other. One of the "chiefs" notes to a friend that his enemy has just come dressed up as a troubadour. He takes his sword and attacks the troubadour, Flo, who is not at all the young man that he looks like. The masquerading has led to the murder for no reason. Dunbar-Nelson has disguised whether Flo and the young man, the Mephisto, are of color or not. But the yellow skin of the costumer, the presence of the Black Indians, we assume, and the reference to "the lower districts" all point to the idea that they are persons of color. Dunbar-Nelson did not think that her works would have been published if she had been more direct about race and ethnicity.

After moving to Brooklyn, New York, Alice Ruth Moore and Paul Laurence Dunbar met and secretly married in 1898. Their tumultuous marriage ended in 1902 after four years of marital horrors.[9] Dunbar-Nelson went on to teach at Howard High School in Wilmington, Delaware, where she taught and continued to write, including plays that were performed by her students. One drama and operetta, which was recently discovered by Lurana Donnels O'Malley, was called *An Hawaiian Idyll* (written and performed in 1916).[10] In the drama, she worked with the popular subject of Hawaiians, who were popularly conceived in the early twentieth century as parallels to African Americans. Both groups were the subjects of oppression by their colonizers, who stole the strength of their bodies for labor as well as for their resilience. The missionaries and the planters in Hawaii, like the landowners of the American South, manipulated black people in America and the natives of Hawaii to make them their subjects. While she was teaching, Dunbar-Nelson secretly married another teacher, Arthur Callis, and divorced him when he left for medical school. Dunbar-Nelson later married Robert J. Nelson, a journalist with whom she co-edited the newspaper *The Wilmington Advocate.*

In her life in Delaware, she continued to publish poetry and fiction as well as articles in the newspaper, particularly her columns "As in a Looking Glass" and "A Woman's Point of View" (later called "Une Femme Dit"), which dealt overtly with matters of race and gender. She also published other plays and became an active advocate of anti-lynching and a member of the Republican Party. Her later writings were edited and published by Gloria T. Hull's in her 3-part edition of *The Works of Alice Dunbar-Nelson* (1988). In her later writing done in the North, while she was married to Nelson and while she was an activist for women's suffrage and for anti-lynching, her writing became more race-conscious. She wrote the stories "The Pearl in the Oyster "and "The Stones of the Village" and such politically conscious poems as "I Sit and Sew" and "April is on the Way" (1927). She was in touch with people who were active in the Harlem Renaissance, such as Georgia Douglas Johnson, and she kept a diary, which openly revealed her lesbian relationships ad her political and social connections. Gloria Hull published her diary in 1984 as *Give Us Each Day: The Diary of Alice Dunbar-Nelson.* She wrote the essay "Brass Ankles" about her experiences as a child and young adult who suffered greatly from both darker black people and whites for the false intentions people attributed to her just because of her light complexion. Of course, in her diary, she also points out how much she also credited herself for her attractiveness because of her color and how much she looked down on many others for being too dark.[11] Dunbar-Nelson's problems with color and acceptance intra- and inter-racially caused her many difficulties with finding and accepting her identity all her life.

Three poets of New Orleans who have continued to pass on the traditions, language, and folklore of New Orleans are Sybil Kein, Mona Lisa Saloy, and Brenda Marie Osbey. Sybil Kein (born Consuela Marie Moore in New Orleans in 1939) is a poet, dramatist, and scholar, whose major interest is to preserve and re-create the history, folklore, and language of the Louisiana Creole culture in her creative and critical work.

In Kein's first volume of published poetry, *Gombo People* (1981), each poem was written in both Louisiana Creole and English. The second, expanded edition, published in 1999, includes more English sections, examples of her music publications, such as *les gardenias et roses*, references, and scholarly articles on Louisiana Creole culture. The word *gombo*, which means *okra* in one of the African Congo languages, and is the name of the popular Creole soup of many ingredients, including okra, has been changed to the more Americanized version of the word, "gumbo" in the title of the later edition. Sybil Kein points out that: "This spelling is used to emphasize the "Americanness" of the culture within its old world charm as reflected in the different "ingredients" of this text. Also included here with the literature are essays and bits of folklore. In the second edition of the book of poetry, she speaks confidently about the increased popularity of Creole studies in America and the study of the subject of *creolite* internationally since the publishing of the first edition of *Gombo People*.[12]

The life of the Creole in Louisiana is one rich in family, religion, and good times, including food and wine, and "love everywhere," as Kein ends many of her poems in *Gombo People*. Kein's women characters tend to be peppery in voice and attitude; they are quick to voice their opinions. The bold life of the Creole woman can be seen, for example, in the spirit and language of poem VIII of the section of the book called "The Nine Rites of the Creole":

> They had a very good life,
> She [the new wife] says, but don't break those China cups!
> Everybody better have a good time, because
> Her Charlie didn't like anything sad.[13]

Family and community work hand in hand under the leadership of New Orleans women, from behind the scenes, of course.

Many of the characters in her next volume of poems, *Delta Dancer* (1984), are historical subjects that express themes of slavery, color, and miscegenation. Her third volume of poetry is *An American South* (1996). In addition to poetry, she has recorded several albums of original songs and traditional Creole songs, including *Serenade Creole* (1987), *Creole Ballads and Zydeco* (1996), *Maw-Maw's Creole Lullaby and Other Songs for Children* (1997). Along with her publication of poetry and music, Sybil Kein has become a leader in the preservation of Creole literature, music, and history. Her volume of essays *Creole: The History and Legacy of Louisiana* begins with Alice Dunbar-Nelson's essay "People of Color in Louisiana."[14]

Mona Lisa Saloy, New Orleans poet and folklorist, is professor at Dillard University and director of creative writing. Her first book of poetry, *Red Beans and Ricely Yours* (based on Louis Armstrong's usual closing of his letters), was published in 2005, shortly before Hurricane Katrina violated the city so unmercifully. For her first book, she won the T. S. Eliot Prize for Poetry. She published her second book of poetry, *Second Line Home*, in 2014. Her poems of growing up in New Orleans describe playing games with the other children in the Seventh Ward, matters of color (an important intra-racial subject), and what many of the community felt about the surprising marriage of her parents—a light-skinned Creole man to a "chocolate"-complexioned woman. Her love of family, the community, and the city of New Orleans shows through in all of her poems. The speaker of "I Had Forgotten the Loud" says,

New Orleans leaves a honey taste in my mouth.
The cracked boulevards and weeping willows
shade bare front porches/and call her children home.[15]

In the first poem of her book *Red Beans and Rice*, "Word Works," Saloy points out consistent themes of her poetry: her writings are "a gumbo of culture"; they picture the many colors of New Orleans Creole community and their folklore, language, foods, and racial and socio-economic environment. "Folks all colored / from pale and yellow / to midnight blue-black."[16] While Saloy's poetry is partly autobiographical, she is also a folklorist and linguist and draws a lively picture of Creoles in New Orleans and their behavior and beliefs. Saloy grew up, in the Seventh Ward, the traditionally Creole ward of New Orleans. She joyfully describes her life as a child in the Seventh Ward of New Orleans, the foods and gatherings, the games that she played with her cousins, the Catholic Church and its training and catechism, the calls of the vendors, the milk man, and the French Market, the mother's work at the Haspel Brother's suit factory and her father's work in the cigar factory, the community's music and crafts, shotgun houses, gardens, and Carnival. Even though there was racism, and plenty of it, there was still family, community life, and fulfillment.

Of course, there is a recognition of sickness and death and the plague of racism but with a sense of humor, as in Saloy's signature poem, "The N Word," in which she professes her right to use the N word if she pleases, for with her usual sense of humor, she says:

So, I hope that no card-carrying
African American, or no stamped, certified,

Colored, or Negro is ever insulted
cause I call a nigger *my nigger.*"[17]

Saloy is more serious in her repeated discussion of the dead or death and dying. As Brenda Marie Osbey makes clear in much of her poetry, New Orleanians have "a peculiar fascination with the dead."[18] Saloy discusses visiting the city of the dead and the grave of Marie Laveau, Voodoo priestess, and others in her poem "The Last Mile."[19] But the grief she felt at her mother's sudden death when she was almost sixteen and her father's move into Alzheimer's were unrelieved sorrow, which is clear in her poems, such as "Missing Mother"[20] and "The Day Alzheimer's Showed,"[21] and in her many poems about the killer hurricane Katrina in her second volume of poetry. Saloy's poems give the reader a living portrait of the city of New Orleans and its Creole community.

Another poet of New Orleans, who is particularly well-regarded among contemporary literary scholars is Brenda Marie Osbey (1957–), Poet Laureate of Louisiana from 2005–2007.

Brenda Marie Osbey is the author of five books of poetry.[22] She writes primarily narrative poems set in the Treme district of New Orleans and surrounding parishes and bayous.[23] Her landscape is, however, more internal than physical. Her mission as a poet and historian is to remember the past and re-create it for others. Using blues, call-response rhythms, ring games, and hoodoo traditions and ceremonies, she develops recurring characters of her poetic community. Her characters are also engaged in finding grace or healing through the community and the knowledge of their ancestors.

In her essay "Why We Can't Talk to You about Voodoo," Osbey counts herself among the Faithful and gives only certain highlights about Voodoo traditions to the serious people who are interested in knowing more about the religion to help themselves and understand the lives, writings, prayers, and traditions of friends and relatives. So much of the understanding of Voodoo by outsiders is from the commercial Western world of film and popular culture, but Osbey points out the importance of the ancestors as our protectors and our source of continuity and healing. She confirms that

> There are really three kinds and realms of being: this Living, the Dead, the Yet-to-Be-Born. Throughout our lives, we continually seek wholeness and healing, restoration, the way to the Land of the Dead, the path to the City of the Ancestors. Such is the Community of the Faithful. Whenever we sit or stand or dance or otherwise turn in the circle, we affirm that continuity and claim our place in it.[24]

She also points out that women are the leaders or "Mothers" of the "Deep Work" of the Voodoo religion.

Women in Osbey's poems serve all these functions. They are workers, as in the poem "Alberta (Factory Poem/Variation 2)."[25] The setting is a New Orleans suit factory of the early twentieth century. She calls it Solomon's Factory, although Haspel's Factory is better known and is mentioned by Mona Lisa Saloy in her poems. The speaker's grandmother is one of the women working there, so busy sewing that she and the other women had no time for lunch or to go to the bathroom or even to have babies in their homes. Her grandmother once helped her baby sister abort a child in the bathroom, flush him down the toilet, and return swiftly to her work. The men looked from the mezzanine down on the women who were standing and sewing on the upright sewing machines. The women sang together to keep each other going, and, while at home, they passed on their knowledge about embroidery and making pillowslips and dresser scarves to their grandchildren, who would lead the sewing activities in the future. The poem gives a clear idea of the patriarchal society that these women lived through and the beliefs in hard work and perseverance that they passed on to their daughters and granddaughters.

The women of the city also had to find time to express their desires and their griefs. In the poem "Desire and Private Griefs," the speaker writes about her love for a man named Sterling, a man she loved all her life, but could never marry; now, after many years, he is dead. "It was a dangerous affair from the beginning," he told her. But they continue to meet, even when they both begin to grey and grow old. She travels to travel to many places, alone. "I send him gifts—/my fingernails/twists of hair from the nape of my neck/scarves I find in Trinidad and Algiers."[26] She goes to his funeral, but quietly. They never married. They were probably Catholic and could not have a second marriage. So she wears gray instead of black and has her hat cocked to the side:

> She turns only after the others have done so—
> a private grief that does not surface
> she leaves alone.[27]

The women of Brenda Marie Osbey's poems are often devotees of Hoodoo, sometimes "readers" or members of prayer groups, and family members who bury the dead. They take care of the ancestors, who protect them in turn. The narrators of "Faubourg Study No. 3: The Seven Sisters of New Orleans" narrate a very detailed story of spiritualism and psychic reading. The epigraph of the poem is a blues riff from "the quintessential blues mama." It reads:

Take me to the edge of town
there ain't nothing left for me here
I said walk me to the edge of town, baby
ain't nothing for me here no more.[28]

The 13-part narrative poem tells the story of seven sisters who move into the Faubourg Treme in the city of New Orleans from their home in rural St. John the Baptist Parish after their mother died. The youngest sister, Eulalie, or Baby Sister, has been called to come to the city and practice her very strong knowledge of Hoodoo. Her sisters came with her, and people came from all over the country to consult Baby Sister. When people began to see how she was able to read their minds and bless or heal them, they came from all over, from Bay St. Louis, Mississippi, to Detroit and the West Coast.

By the end of the poem, the Seven Sisters have died; but others have taken their place. The young woman Josefina is brought to the house to get to know the seven sisters and she becomes a close acquaintance of Baby Sister. She becomes knowledgeable of all the signs and truths of Hoodoo and feels herself called to take her place when Baby Sister dies. When a young reporter and photographer comes to the house to find out more about the religion and the worshippers, Josefina calls her *daughter,* but warns her of the journey that she seems to be moving toward and gets in touch with her family member Ava Lee, who sings the blues at the new club on Rampart, *Anybody's Place.* Blues and jazz are at home with Hoodoo and other spiritual thought in Osbey's poetry. Throughout her poetry Osbey uses the multilayered effect and antiphonal sounds of blues and jazz. We hear the sounds and words of Nina Simone, Thelonious Monk, Roberta Flack, and many musicians of the late twentieth century music and the music of the streetcars.

Musical scholar Vijay Iyer has analyzed the relationship between jazz and much African American narrative

Musical meaning is not conveyed only through motific development, melodic contour, and other traditional musicological parameters, it is also embodied in improvisatory techniques. Musicians *tell their stories, but not in the traditional linear narrative sense; an exploded* narrative is conveyed through a holistic musical personality or *attitude.*[29]

"The Seven Sisters" poem ends with *Daughter* chanting:

i want to walk a little further
along the shallow water

i want to live a little longer
with my dangerous dream.[30]

Remembrance of the community's cultures and traditions is an essential theme of African American women writers of New Orleans. Black women writers also recognize the language, music, food, and geographical environment so essential to the city of New Orleans. While they are always aware of race, color, and the influences of the past, the city's black women writers are predominantly interested in the living environment and community. They recognize the important role that women play in remembering the traditions and spirits of the ancestors and passing them on to family and friends of the present.

NOTES

1. Alice Dunbar-Nelson, *The Works of Alice Dunbar-Nelson,* vol. 1, ed. Alice Dunbar-Nelson (New York: Oxford UP, 1988). *Violets and Other Tales* (Boston: The Monthly Review, 1895), and *The Goodness of St. Rocque and Other Stories* (York: Dodd, Mead and Co., 1899).

2. Dunbar-Nelson, "Tony's Wife," *Works*, vol. 1, 19–33. All of the following works of Alice Dunbar-Nelson will be from *The Works*, edited by Gloria T. Hull, unless noted.

3. Violet Harrington Bryan, *The Myth of New Orleans in Literature: Dialogues of Race and Gender* (Knoxville: University of Tennessee Press, 1993), 70. George Washington Cable (1844–1925) wrote *The Grandissimes* in 1880 and a number of stories and novels about race and Creoles of New Orleans. He also wrote about the demand for civil rights in the New South after the Civil War. His attitudes toward these subjects made him an enemy of many white Creoles, and he moved to Northampton, Massachusetts, in 1885.

4. George Washington Cable, "'Tite Poulette," *Old Creole Days* (New York: Scribner's, 1879) and *Madame Delphine* (New York: Scribner's, 1881).

5. Dunbar-Nelson, "Little Miss Sophie," *Works*, vol.1, 45.

6. Emily Clark, *The Strange History of the American Quadroon.* Chapel Hill: University of North Carolina Press, 2013. Clark argues that the term *placage* to describe the liaisons between free women of color and white men was first used by E. Franklin Frazier in his book *The Negro Family.* It was not a term, she says, used in antebellum society in New Orleans. The practice grew with the immigration of Haitians into New Orleans during the Haitian Revolution in the late eighteenth century.

7. Jordan Stouck, "Identities in Crisis: Alice Dunbar-Nelson's New Orleans Fiction." *Canadian Review of American Studies* 34.3 (2004), 280.

8. Alice Dunbar-Nelson, "A Carnival Jangle," *Works,* vol. 1, 77.

9. See Eleanor Alexander, *Lyrics of Sunshine and Shadow: The Courtship and Marriage of Paul Laurence Dunbar and Alice Ruth Moore* (New York: New York UP, 2001).

10. Lurana Donnels O'Malley, "Alice Dunbar-Nelson's *An Hawaiian Idyll* as Hawaiian Imaginary," *Comparative Drama* 47, no. 1 (Spring 2013).

11. Dunbar-Nelson, "Brass Ankles Speaks," *Works*, vol. 2.

12. Sybil Kein's two editions of her first book were *Gombo People: New Orleans*

Creole Poetry, Limited First Edition, 1981, and *Gumbo People*, Expanded Edition (New Orleans: Margaret Media, Inc., 1999).

13. Sybil Kein, "Neuf Rites de la Vie Creole," VIII, *Gombo People,* 71.

14. Alice Dunbar-Nelson, "People of Color in Louisiana," *Creole: The History and Legacy of Louisiana's Free People of Color*, ed. Sybil Kein (Baton Rouge: Louisiana State UP, 2000), 3–41.

15. Mona Lisa Saloy, "I Had Forgotten the Loud," *Red Beans and Ricely Yours* (Kirksville, Missouri: Truman State UP, 2005, 20.

16. Mona Lisa Saloy, "Word Works," Red *Beans*, 3–4.

17. Mona Lisa Saloy, "The *N* Word," *Red Beans*, 99.

18. Brenda Marie Osbey, "Peculiar Fascination with the Dead," *All Saints*: *New and Selected Poetry* (Baton Rouge: Louisiana State UP, 1997), 25–33.

19. Saloy, "The Last Mile," *Red Beans*, 99. See Barbara Rosendale Duggal, "Marie *Laveau: The Voodoo Queen Repossessed,"*, *Creole: The History and Legacy of Louisiana's Free People of Color*, ed. Sybil Kein (Baton Rouge: Louisiana State UP, 2000). 157–78.

20. Mona Lisa Saloy, "Missing Mother," *Second Line: New Orleans Poems*, Kirksville, MO: Truman State UP, 2014,

21. Mona Lisa Saloy, "The Day Alzheimer's Showed," *Second Line*, 45.

22. Brenda Marie Osbey is the author of *Ceremony for Minneconjoux,* 1983; *In These Houses*, 1988; *Desperate Circumstances, Dangerous Woman*, 1991; *All Saints: New and Selected Poems*, 1997; the libretto, *Sultane au Grande Marais: A Tale of Rebellion and Resistance* (Osbey, 2000); and *History and Other Poems*, 2012.

23. Brenda Marie Osbey, "Glossary of New Orleans Ethnic Expressions, Place Names, and Characters," *All Saints: New and Selected Poems*, 127. Osbey defines the Faubourg Treme as "the first suburb of the original city of New Orleans (Vieux Carre), settled in the 1710 by free Black, and now part of downtown New Orleans.

24. Brenda Marie Osbey."Why We Can't Talk to You about Voodoo." *Southern Literary Journal* 43.2 (Spring 2011): 11.

25. Brenda Marie Osbey, "Alberta (Factory Poem / Variation 2," *All Saints*, 15–19. All other Osbey poems in the text are from this volume.

26. Osbey. "Desire and Private Griefs," 9.

27. Osbey, "Desire and Private Griefs," 10.

28. Osbey, "Faubourg Study No. 3: The Seven Sisters of New Orleans," 39.

29. Iyer, Vijay, "Exploding the Narrative in Jazz Improvisation," *Uptown Conversation. The New Jazz Studies.* Ed. Robert G. O'Meally, et al. New York: Columbia UP, 393–403.

30. Osbey, "Faubourg Study No. 3: The Seven Sisters of New Orleans," 53.

BIBLIOGRAPHY

Alexander, Eleanor. *Lyrics of Sunshine and Shadow: The Courtship and Marriage of Paul Laurence Dunbar and Alice Ruth Moore*. New York: New York UP, 2001.

Brosman, Catherine Savage. "Depictions of Popular New Orleans Culture by Mona Lisa Saloy and John Kennedy Toole." *Arkansas Review: A Journal of Delta Studies*. MLA Bibliography. May 2, 2015.

Bryan, Violet Harrington. *The Myth of New Orleans in Literature: Dialogues of Race and Gender*. Knoxville: University of Tennessee Press, 1993.

Cable, George Washington."'Tite Poulette." *Old Creole Days*. New York: Scribner's, 1879.

———. *The Grandissimes*. 1880. Rev. rd. New York: Scribner's, 1907.

———. *Madame Delphine*. New York: Scribner's, 1881.

———. *Doctor Sevier*. New York: Osgood, 1884.

Chopin, Kate. *The Complete Works*. Ed. Per Seyersted. Baton Rouge: Louisiana State UP, 1969.

Davis, Thadious. *Southscapes: Geographies of Race. Region, and Literature*. Chapel Hill: University of North Carolina Press, 2011.

Dunbar-Nelson, Alice. *The Works of Alice Dunbar-Nelson*. Ed, Gloria T. Hull. 3 vols. New York: Oxford UP, 1988.

———."Brass Ankles Speaks," *Works*. vol 2.

———. "Little Miss Sophie." *Works*, vol. 1. 137–52.

———."Tony's Wife." *Works*, vol. 1. 19–33.

———. "People of Color in Louisiana." In *Creole*: *The History and Legacy of Louisiana's Free People*. Ed. Sybil Kein. Baton Rouge: Louisiana State UP, 2000. 3–41.

Iyer, Vijay. "Exploding the Narrative in Jazz Improvisation," *Uptown Conversation*. The New Jazz Studies. Ed. Robert G. O'Meally et al. New York: Columbia UP, 393–403.

Kein, Sybil. *Gombo People: New Orleans Creole Poetry. Limited First Edition*, 1981, and *Gumbo People, Expanded Edition*. New Orleans: Margaret Media, Inc., 1999.

———."Neuf Rites de la Vie Creole: VIII." *Gombo People*. 71.

———. *Creole: The History and Legacy of Louisiana's Free People of Color*. Ed. Sybil Kein. Baton Rouge: Louisiana State UP, 2000.

King, Grace. *Balcony Stories*. 1892. Ridgewood, NJ: Gregg P, 1968.

———. *New Orleans: The Place and the People*. New York: Macmillan, 1895.

Lowe, John, "An Interview with Brenda Marie Osbey." *Southern Review* 30.4 (Autumn), 1994. Academic Search Complete. April 25, 2015.

O'Malley, Lurana Donnels. "Alice Dunbar-Nelson's An Hawaiian Idyll as Hawaiian Imaginary. *Comparative Drama* 47.1 Spring 2013. Academic Search Complete. May 11, 2015.

Osbey, Brenda Marie. *All Saints: New and Selected Poems*. Baton Rouge: Louisiana State UP, 1997.

———. "Ceremony for Minneconjoux." *Callaloo Poetry Series*, 1983, UP of Virginia, 1985.

———. *In These Houses*. Wesleyan UP, 1988.

———. *Desperate Circumstances, Dangerous Woman*. Story Line P, 1991.

———. *Sultane au Grande Marais: A Tale of Rebellion and Resistance* (libretto). Osbey, 2000.

———. *History and Other Poems*. St. Louis, MO: Time Being Books, 2012.

———."Glossary of New Orleans Ethnic Expressions, Place Names, and Characters." *All Saints*. 123–27.

———."Why We Can't Talk to You about Voodoo." *Southern Literary Journal* 43.2 (Spring 2011).

———. "Alberta (Factory Poem / Variation 2." *All Saints*. 15–19.

———. "Desire and Private Griefs." *All Saints*. 6–10.

———. "Faubourg Study No. 3: The Seven Sisters of New Orleans." *All Saints*. 39–53.

Saloy, Mona Lisa. *Red Beans and Ricely Yours*. New Odyssey Series. Kirksville, Missouri: Truman State UP, 2005.

Saloy, Mona Lisa. *Second Line Home: New Orleans Poems*. Kirksville, Missouri: Truman State UP, 2014.

———. "I Had Forgotten the Loud." *Red Beans*, 20.

———. "Word Works," *Red Beans*, 3–4.

———. "My Daddy V," *Red Beans*, 45–46.

———."The N Word," *Red Beans*, 95–99.

Siegel, Allison. "Brenda Marie Osbey and the Blending and the Blending of Christianity and Hoodoo in New Orleans." *Literary New Orleans: An Exploration of the Geography and Culture of New Orleans.* Posted April 28, 2013. April 20, 2015.

Stouck, Jordan. "Identities in Crisis: Alice Dunbar-Nelson's New Orleans Fiction." *Canadian Review of American Studies* 34.3 (2004). 280.

Black Women and Carnival Performance Traditions

Women Maskers

Critics of Social Issues[1]

—Pamela R. Franco

In the 1960s and 1970s, at the height of the American feminist movement, women's performance art exploded. Women artists, predominantly white, turned to performance as a confrontational new medium that provided a forum to critique a patriarchal society that marginalized and devalued them and also to reinterpret the discourse on women's sexuality. For example, Ana Mendieta's *Untitled (Rape Scene)* (1973) was a bloodied response to the brutal rape and murder of a nursing student at the University of Iowa, Hannah Wilke's *Super-T-Art* (1974) critiqued Christianity's traditional suppression of women by representing herself as a female Christ, and Carole Schneemann's *Interior Scroll* (1975) presented the female body as a source of knowledge and experience. In each performance the (exposed) female body is central to the women's attempt to re-inscribe themselves as subjects and agents of knowledge and power. By foregrounding the female body these performance artists were "challenging the very fabric of representation by refusing that [patriarchal] text and posing new, multiple texts grounded in real women's experience and sexuality."[2]

For black women, these types of performances were not particularly original or inventive. Since their enslavement and sexual violation at the hands of Europeans, they have been using their bodies to respond to insidious images of black women created by whites. Frequently described as ugly, immoral, lascivious, and grotesque, black women had to find a strategy to respond to the diatribe, the negative portrayals, and to save their sanity. They used the one thing that they controlled but which ironically was also the site of personal violation: their bodies. Thus, the centrality of the female body in performance was not novel in black women's public or festive performances as it was for white women performance artists. The historical experience of slavery and the mistreatment of their bodies, very early, spawned a counter narrative in which black women attempted to reclaim and re-inscribe their bodies. In the very public arena of festival, Carnival, they took control by composing commentary on society's mistreatment of them and the violation of their bodies through a particular style of masking. In this way, black women's Carnival performances took on the tone of autobiography. The following discussion of the *Martinican* and the *Baby Doll* can help us understand and appreciate how and why black women used masquerading as autobiography and political commentary.

I came to the study of black women masking traditions in a roundabout way. I started off wanting to study Trinidad Carnival's traditional masques. In 1988, I traveled to my native Trinidad and became enthralled with such male characters as the *Midnight Robber, Indian, Stickfighter,* and *Pierrot Grenade.* Realizing that these characters were no longer at the center of the contemporary Carnival, I decided then that I would like to study their history and performance styles. I saw well-intentioned individuals attempt to revive the earlier Carnival *mas* characters.[3] One person organized a street parade through the streets of Port-of-Spain, the capital city, on the Friday preceding Carnival Tuesday. Another introduced *Viey La Cour* (old yard) on Carnival Sunday that highlighted a parade of the aforementioned characters. As the local newspaper explained "There you will see masquerade in authentic Carnival costumes."[4] Watching these exemplars of a bygone era, there was a feeling of nostalgia and I quickly decided to be part of the effort to preserve this cast of masquerade characters and their performance styles.

By 1991, when I entered graduate school, I had settled on a dissertation topic, a historical and performance analysis of Trinidad's traditional *mas* characters. However, as I began my research, I quickly realized that the "timely" resurrection of the traditional characters was not as innocent or altruistic as it first seemed. In fact, this revival was at the center of a public debate on the authenticity of the contemporary Carnival which, by the way, was overly subscribed by women maskers. Labelled as "traditional," the male characters wore the mantle of authenticity. Tradition, with its connection to the past and the aura of legitimacy, is often used as a synonym for truth, the genuine, and the authentic. Newspaper articles, editorial comments and letters to the editor laid out the binary that underpinned the discussion. The contemporary Carnival, the antithesis of the traditional *mas*, highlighted women maskers, scantily dressed and engaging in a highly sexualized dance known as "wining."[5] This perceived perversion positioned the contemporary Carnival on the opposite end of the spectrum from the traditional *mas*. With the latter posited as traditional, the fully clothed body, stylized choreography and boastful speeches of the male-centered traditional *mas* became markers of Carnival's authentic or true self.[6]

The (in)authenticity debate led me to ask the question, what was women's masking history? What was their performance style? Was characterization important to their *mas* choices? Was there a tradition of women's *mas* styles? Why did women maskers prefer to highlight their bodies? Why did they prefer sexy dancing and not bombastic self-aggrandizement speeches like the *Midnight Robber*? Without an analytical model that considered and valued gender in the formation of authenticity/traditional *mas*, it was virtually impossible to counter a male-centered model of authenticity. It looked like black women's masking and performance styles were without tradition; therefore, without history. Looking at the contemporary *mas*, I could not identify the clues to discern women's masking tradition. Later in my research I realized that the clues were there but I could not read or interpret them. With a new focus, I began my research. I turned to the nineteenth century and Trinidad's colonial history for answers.

In the early decades of the nineteenth century, race and class dictated the place and style of women's masking styles. White, upper class women were prominent in private masquerade balls. They also paraded in the streets within the confines of decorated carriages. Pre-emancipation, enslaved black women were prohibited from taking part in the street festival.[7] They dressed up and performed at Carnival drum dances. Post-emancipation, blacks took to the streets and introduced their unique masquerade style to the local Carnival. Following in the footsteps of their West African ancestors, men were the primary participants who disguised as women and fictional or mythological figures. Sidney Mintz and Richard Price (1976), in their discussion of the transference of culture from the African continent to the New World, tell us that Africans were unable to bring their cultural institutions to the Americas. Instead, they brought memory of cultural practices and value systems.[8] The peculiar circumstance of slavery coupled with the absence of native institutions precipitated the creation of new rules/lores and revisions of old ones to accommodate the harsh reality of slavery. The inclusion of black women as public masqueraders was a divergence from the West African model that privileged men disguised as Other, be it woman or animal. In nineteenth century Trinidad, with few examples of West African women's public masquerades to provide a suitable model, black women incorporated elements from the popular dance societies—dressing up, dancing, and singing. Initially, they did not wear masks, which were still the domain of men as it was in their ancestral lands. However, with the passing of time, subsequent generations overcame this taboo.

These stylistic differences in black women's and men's Carnival performances and disguises are instructive. It is clear that black men preferred the West African style of masquerading. Black women, on the other hand, did not favor disguising as fictional or mythological characters. Instead, they preferred to use their bodies to respond to societal ills that degraded or dismissed them. The "freedom" and presumed safety of Carnival allowed black women to create a public voice to vocalize their concerns. With few avenues to respond to the issues that affected their lives, the women took advantage of the public nature of Carnival when all eyes would be on them. They applied one of two approaches to their costume and performance styles: the sartorial body and the unruly woman. They controlled both approaches. The sartorial dress provided black women a space to respond to the common appraisal of them as grotesque and unladylike. The unruly woman was a much more physical and confrontational approach. "She" permitted black women to be outrageous in their response to those social issues that degraded them. For the remainder of this paper I will look at the sartorial body (the *Martinican*) and the unruly woman (the *Baby Doll*). With these characters I lay the groundwork for my argument that black women's early masquerade dress aesthetic and performance are the foundation and historical reference for women's *mas* style in the contemporary Trinidad Carnival.

Dressing Up and Looking Good: The Sartorial Body

From the Latin word for tailor, sartorial refers to distinct dress style. It also conjures up images of taste, personal style, sumptuousness, and distinction. Here, I am using sartorial to describe sumptuous dress and jewelry that allude to wealth, real or imagined, class, and power. The sartorial aesthetic was made up of three major components—a layering of sumptuous cloth, a profusion of jewels, and decorated headdresses. Together they created a dazzling and radiant image.

The constant drudgery, humiliation, and, above all, violence, both physical and sexual, meted out by planters, their wives, and other administrative and governmental personnel enabled the stereotyping of black women as troublesome, lascivious, grotesque, and unclean. Confined and limited in their grueling daily work schedule, the women took liberties in their leisure activities. No longer "dirty" and "grotesque," black women basked in the opportunity to create an alternate self-image, one that reinvented them as "ladies," exemplars of the Victorian feminine ideal. They opted for an elaborate yet distinct sartorial style what I have defined elsewhere as "dressing up and looking good."[9] Generally, "dressing up" refers to the donning of specific clothes that are socially and culturally recognized as different from everyday attire, and that help to mark an event or occasion as special. On these occasions, participants are transformed. In this sense, "dressing up" can be understood as a form of masquerading. "Looking good" is the visual effect or aesthetic of dressing up. It garners visibility for the wearer. "Dressing up" also affords black women opportunities to construct new realities, recover personal histories and, if necessary, to make reference to a bygone era. In essence, "dressing up," a seemingly benign style of masquerading, allowed black women to be visible, not as objects, but as agents and producers of meaning in their Carnival performances.

The nineteenth century *Martinican*[10] is a prime example of the sartorial body. The term was a popular designation for two dress styles: the *a la jupe* and *la grande robe*.[11] The former was a skirt and blouse ensemble. The latter was a more formal gown with a train that was often draped and tucked into the waist to reveal an elegantly decorated underskirt. Although the *Martinican* was a New World creation, the components, sumptuous materials, billowy skirts, jewelry and shoes and stockings, were associated with the upper classes. So, in an attempt to counter the insidious categorization of their bodies and behavior, black women transformed themselves as "ladies" using the sartorial aesthetic of the contemporary upper class women's dress style. This dress aesthetic worked for them on two levels. First, it created a spectacular sight, which garnered everyone's attention and second, it exhibited a distinct style of dress that distanced black women from the insidious images created by white elites.

While some may interpret black women's appropriation of the dress aesthetic of the upper classes as a classic Carnivalesque inversion, from low to high, I am positing another reading. Black women's adoption of the upper class dress aesthetic was a performative strategy to reclaim and re-inscribe the black female body. As Michel Foucault has observed "the body is the inscribed surface of events."[12] In other words, the body is not simply a static being. It is shaped and valorized through its experiential relationship with history. For example, in the early nineteenth-century, whites' salacious imagining of the black female body was based on its involuntary participation in the slave trade and plantation culture. Black women, veering from a prevalent perception of the degenerate and highly sexualized black female, tried to distance themselves, albeit temporarily and symbolically, from the repeated violation of their bodies. Through a combination of large billowy skirts and underskirts, black women transformed themselves by covering up their shapeliness and highlighting a dazzling and somewhat benign body.

Employing the dress aesthetic of the upper classes, black women also "re-positioned" themselves as members of the leisure class. The sumptuousness of dress style alluded to wealth and social status and negated the women's quotidian life of physical work and hardships. Alison Lurie (1981) helps us to understand what black women were hoping to achieve. She notes that "to put on someone else's clothes is symbolically to take on their personality."[13] In other words, the meaning socially embedded in clothes is passed on to its wearer. This is not to say that a wearer cannot give new meaning to a garment. Even so, the original meaning is often at the root of the reinterpretation. In the case of black women's appropriation of upper class women's dress style, the weightiness and cumbersome nature of the skirts required them to modify their gait. No longer able to walk fast and brisk as laborers did, black women created a novel self-image that freed them from manual labor. Of course, the response from the upper classes was not salutary. Nevertheless, black women's re-positioning of themselves as members of the upper classes was a bold and disruptive act.

The Unruly Woman: The Case of The *Baby Doll*

Elsewhere I have written about the *unruly woman* in Trinidad Carnival.[14] As a festive and literary character, the *unruly woman* was a site for social commentary. Historian Natalie Zemon Davis contends that the festive play with the *unruly woman* widened behavioral options for women within and even outside of marriage. In some cases it sanctioned riot and political disobedience for both men and women.[15] Generally, the *unruly woman's* performance included loud and boisterous speech, inflammatory language, and erotic gestures. However, as Davis further explains, the festive "play with the concept of the *unruly woman* is partly a chance for temporary release from traditional and stable hierarchy; . . . it is also part and parcel of conflict over efforts to change the basic distribution of power within the society."[16] In other words, the *unruly woman* challenges hegemony. However, because "she" is a festive character, the *unruly woman* is often exempt from any responsibility or accountability for "her" subversive actions. The absence of accountability makes this character very desirable for female maskers because "she" provides them with enormous latitude to push the envelope of transgression.

To the nineteenth century white plantocracy, for whom race was a principal signifier of deviance and unruliness, the black woman and the festive "unruly woman" collapsed into one becoming almost indistinguishable from one another. This racialized equation effectively modified Davis's *unruly woman*. "She" was no longer simply a festive character. Instead, "she" had become interchangeable with poor, black women. And as such, was subject to the island's unofficial laws, particularly those pertaining to race, class, and gender. Despite the festive and topsy-turvy nature of Carnival, Davis's assertion of the *unruly woman's* exemption from accountability and responsibility did not always apply to black women's festive performances. In late nineteenth-century Trinidad, "unruly" women were frequently arrested and incarcerated, and some even faced deportation to their native countries. In spite of the harsh responses, black women continued to engage the *unruly woman* as social critic. The early twentieth century *Baby Doll* is a prime example.

The character of the *Baby Doll* appears to be popular in Carnivals/Mardi Gras in francophone colonies or territories and societies with a deep French footprint. In nineteenth century Martinique Carnaval, for example, the *en bébé* character was a popular women's masquerade. According to traveler and researcher Lafcadio Hearn, "this costume comprises of only a loose embroidered chemise, lace-edge pantalets, and a child's cap . . . As the dress is short, and leaves much of the lower limbs exposed, there is ample opportunity for display of tinted stockings and elegant slippers."[17] At Carnival time the women paraded often in the early morning parades. Beyond parading, we know very little about their performances or how the character evolved.[18] In the former French colony of New Orleans, Baby Dolls generally wore variations of the "short satin dresses, stockings with garters, and bonnets."[19] Reportedly, the Baby Doll tradition began in 1912 with the Million Dollar Baby Dolls. In the following years several versions of this character would emerge, for example, the social and pleasure club Baby Dolls. New Orleans Baby Dolls fall into two categories: the sexy Baby Dolls ("babes") and little girl Dolls ("the toy").[20] Their preferred performance style was dancing and singing bawdy songs. As Kim Vaz tells us, the women "were known for 'walking raddy'(a kind of strut that would end with the steps needed to 'shake on down').[21] Their performance repertoire included club and street dances like the "naked dance," cakewalk, foxtrot, second line, and black bottom.

In Trinidad's Carnival, this character most likely was imported by Martiniquian immigrants who relocated to the island after the French Revolution. In the late nineteenth century there are reports of men and women parading in women's nightdress, sometimes short and frilly.

There is no reliable evidence that supports the notion that these maskers called themselves "baby dolls," although the costume was similar to the Martiniquian *en bébé*. The term "Baby Doll" would appear much later, in the early decades of the twentieth century. By the 1930s, the Trinidad *Baby Doll's* performance had morphed from a procession or street parade into an outrageous skit in which "she" attempted to locate her baby's daddy for child support. "Her costume was that of a gaily dressed doll: bonnet tied under the chin, a frilled dress reaching to her knees, colored cotton stockings, and strap shoes."[22] Black women maskers carried a doll cradled in their arms as they searched for the baby's father. Very often, the women approached men randomly and in a loud public shaming accused them of being the baby's father and scolded them for not taking care of their children. This public shaming was done in front of and for the benefit of an audience, many of whom would egg on the mother by also shouting derogatory remarks at the "father." Sometimes, a "policeman" character would approach the accused father requesting that he comply with the mother's wishes. To defuse the situation, the men, now totally embarrassed, would "pay off" the *Baby Doll* just to keep her quiet and also to get rid of her. After receiving a few coins, the "mother" then moved on to another man and repeated her performance.

In a 1988 interview with renowned Carnival bandleader, Stephen Leung described this *mas* genre as "beggin *mas*." According to Leung, the goal of this character was to extract money from the viewers. Some of the popular "beggin mas" characters included the tailor, doctor and street sweeper. As playwright Errol Hill explains masquerade characters like "doctors, nurses, tailors bailiffs, surveyors, policemen, street sweepers, even thieves . . . extorted money from passersby for work that they ostensibly performed on behalf of their victims."[23] For Leung, this *mas* was popular with the men and women of a lower socioeconomic background and it provided an opportunity for them to supplement their meager income. The association of money with women's carnival performance was certainly not restricted to Trinidad. In New Orleans, the Million Dollar Baby Dolls carried money in their garters. Theirs was a flashy display of wealth, real or imagined. It was not uncommon for the women to throw money at the onlookers. According to Vaz, some prostitutes who masked as Baby Dolls would turn tricks during the street parade. The reference to money in New Orleans indexed black women as successful entrepreneurs. In Trinidad, money suggested the underemployment of black women and the need to supplement their income.

The Trinidadian *Baby Doll's* performance, searching for and shaming her baby's father, categorized her as promiscuous and immoral. Not only was she an unwed mother but she did not know the identity of her baby's father. This implied that the mother had slept with numerous men, a hint at prostitution; therefore it was impossible for her to know the identity of the baby's father. "Promiscuous" and "immoral" are terms that have been used to describe black women in the Americas and Caribbean. During slavery, the black female body was a sight/site for white men's desire and domination. In twentieth-century New Orleans, the *Baby Dolls* were subject to the same derisive name calling. Kim Vaz tells us that the women lived in an area described as a "quasi red light" district, located close to the notorious Storyville, also known as Back o' Town. Many were sex workers and those who weren't would easily be classified as such because of the neighborhood in which they lived or their association with prostitutes in the district. In fact, their self-naming as *Baby Dolls* is a reference to the appellation that their pimps used to address them.

Another reading of the Trinidad *Baby Doll* is based in the notion that the conventional female attribute is that of gatekeeper of society's moral and ethical values. Thus, she symbolizes the virtuous and all that is good in society. Motherhood best exemplifies this ideal. Apart from biology, motherhood is also a culturally, historically, and sociologically defined concept with "each society ha[ving] its own mythology, complete with rituals, beliefs, expectations, norms, and symbols."[24]

In the Caribbean, according to feminist writer Elaine Savory Fido, "motherhood is . . . viewed as a most important role for women by both men and women."[25] Janice Lee Liddell, writing on the representations of mothers in Caribbean literature, states that "the image of mother—giver and nurturer of life: teacher and instiller of values and mores—has indeed become the most persistent of Caribbean archetypes."[26] Author and literary critic Gordon Rohlehr proffers motherhood as "part of an ideology of control which was/[is] designed to deny women the possibility of successful movement beyond the home and family."[27] Thus, motherhood confines and limits women in non-domestic or other professional pursuits. It reaffirms the old adage, women's place is in the home.

With the trope of motherhood in mind, the *Baby Doll* was more than a "beggin *mas*." She could be interpreted as a dedicated mother, the antithesis of the promiscuous woman, seeking the best for her child. Although her child was born out of wedlock, nonetheless, she overrides the stigma by re-presenting herself as a caring mother who would do everything in her power to ensure her child's safety and wellbeing. Therefore, she was not going to let the father abdicate his responsibility to take care of his offspring.

The popularity of this character in the 1920s and 1930s may have been due to the new laws pertaining to child support and protection for unwed mothers. In Trinidad and Tobago, new legislation purportedly made it easier for unwed mothers to take errant fathers to court, under the Bastardy Ordinance, which was revised and expanded in 1925, for child maintenance (support). The Bastardy Ordinance was on the books in the nineteenth century, however, the law was ignored. It was probably not enforced to protect the reputation of upper class, white males who fathered children outside of their marriage.[28] The 1927 Legitimation Ordinance No. 8 among other things allowed the Courts to seek financial compensation for children from their delinquent fathers. In order to collect child support, mothers needed to provide documentation of the place and date of marriage. This was a problem. If the child was born out of wedlock, a marriage certificate would not be forthcoming. In addition, documentation was needed to prove the date of the child's birth, disclose the status and residence of both parents, and verify the occupation of the father.[29] For many women, it may have been challenging to collect all of the pertinent information, especially the father's occupation and residence. Men unwilling to pay child support would not provide the correct information or possibly lie making it difficult for women to make their case. With little recourse, some mothers turned to the streets. This time they would be heard and fathers *would* pay up.

The third reading of the Trinidadian *Baby Doll* revolves around the 1941 U.S. naval base on the island. Earlier in the century, World War I servicemen flocked to New Orleans's infamous Storyville to seek the sexual services of the white and mixed-race women of New Orleans. Baby Doll masker Beatrice Hill, who lived and worked in "Black" Storyville boasted that the presumably white servicemen preferred the "brownies," that is, darker-skinned black women. The closeness of both parts of the District to the naval base led to the end of Storyville as a segregated residential area for sex workers.[30] In a segregationist New Orleans, white servicemen in the area would have visited Storyville where the light-skinned octoroons worked. In Trinidad, however, the U.S. presence caused quite a stir. In the 1940s, the U.S. occupied a naval base on the island. The presence of servicemen affected the lives of the local citizens. Men and women readily reported for work on the military base because the wages were higher than that offered by local industries. One area that saw exponential growth was the sex trade. Brothels, bars, and clubs cropped up everywhere in Port-of-Spain, the capital city. The famous calypsonian Lord Invader's "Rum and Coca-Cola" (1943), appropriated by Morey Amsterdam[31] and later popularized by the Andrew Sisters, is a critique of the romantic/sexual relationship between local Trinidadian women and U.S. servicemen. The Mighty Sparrow, in his 1956 "Jean and Dinah," relishes in the dilemma facing local women/prostitutes with the departure of the servicemen. They were now at the mercy of the local "saga boys." In the 1940s the blond-haired and blue-eyed "babies" that the *Baby Dolls* carried were now associated with the fallout of the Trinidad-U.S. naval troop sex trade. Since the majority of military men were white, the "baby" would have been interpreted as the bastard offspring of this opportunistic encounter. Unlike the 1930s, when the blonde-haired, blue-eyed doll was one of convenience and availability,[32] in the 1940s it became one of exploitation, economics and politics. In her Carnival performance, the *Baby Doll*, having lost the U.S. servicemen's financial support, was left with little recourse. So, "she" took to the streets seeking aid from the local men by accusing them of being the father of her child. By the 1950s, amidst a burgeoning black nationalist, anti-colonial climate, the *Baby Doll* masquerade declined. It would be in the 1980s, with the resurrection of traditional masquerade characters in response to the contemporary female-dominated maskers, that the *Baby Doll* would return to Carnival. This time "she" was passive, a shell of herself; however, the memory of her radical performance persists.

Conclusion

The *Martinican* and *Baby Doll* characters provide us with a baseline for discussion of black women's employment of presence and performance to voice commentaries on their lives. The former tells us that black women/female maskers loved to dress up and look good. They employed a sartorial body to garner the public's attention and reverse insidious suggestions that black women were grotesque and lascivious. The latter facilitated commentary and critique on personal or societal issues that affected black women's lives. In the contemporary Carnival, the sartorial and unruly bodies are conflated. They are not separated as they often were in earlier periods.

To understand the masking style of contemporary women maskers, one must consider the following: first, this generation of female maskers is very comfortable in their skin and they do not view semi-clad bodies as degrading or demeaning. In Carnival, their preference for the bikini underscores this point. Second, social media has opened up vistas of other Carnivals and women's non-festival performances, many of which are centered in the female body. Third, these maskers constitute a well-traveled group. They participate in a global economy including fashion trends. The less-is-more dress aesthetic is not lost on Trinidadian women. Fourth, female maskers live in a more secular world; therefore, religious tenets are not a factor in their masking choices. Fifth, reputations are not damaged by women's Carnival dress style or performance. Women are not playing *mas* to gain respectability as their earlier predecessors did. Sixth, today's women maskers are well-educated, mostly tertiary education and beyond. They have disposable income which enables them to dictate their costume silhouette. These six items are critical in creating a social context for women maskers' preferred style of masking.

Within this context, contemporary female maskers have redefined the sartorial and unruly bodies. Now, the former is a well-toned body, makeup and nice hairstyle (which is refreshed throughout the day), pretty colors, non-characterization, and the bikini as the foundation garment. The latter resides in women's performance of wining. Many of the women whom I have interviewed described wining as "freeing up." The gyrating, semi-clad body puts sex and women's sexuality, symbols of their oppression, up front. Why? They have witnessed an increase in rapes and reports of domestic violence and agonized over abysmal conviction rates. Carnival offers women a public opportunity to 'rectify' this situation. They do this by marginalizing men. Thus, it is not uncommon to see women wining with other women. The woman-on-woman wining is often framed in a gay/lesbian context. While there is some validity to that interpretation, the majority of the women are not gay. So, what could be prompting this type of performance? I believe women are attempting to re-define themselves as the ones in control of sex and their sexuality, or, at the very least, have a strong voice in those matters. While the *Martinican* de-sexualized her body with voluminous skirts, today's women maskers flaunt their bodies. While the unruly woman/*Baby Doll* relied on a public shaming of men, the contemporary female maskers, as critics, symbolically shame men for their inability to perform sexually and judicially. Carnival is shaped by contemporary social, political, and cultural histories. To fully understand women's masking styles, one must look at their lives as they intersect with socio-political issues. The contemporary women maskers, like their earlier sisters, are commenting and responding to the world as they experience it.

NOTES

1. For an in-depth look at the issues covered in this paper, refer to Pamela R. Franco, "Dressing Up and Looking Good: Afro-Creole women in Trinidad Carnival." *African Arts* 31, no. 2, 1998, 62–67, 91, 95–96; and Pamela R. Franco, "The Unruly Woman," *Small Axe* 7, March 2000, 60–77.

2. Jeanie Forte, "Women's Performance Art: Feminism and Postmodernism," in *Performing Feminisms: Feminist Critical Theory and Theatre*, ed. Sue Ellen Case (Baltimore and London: The Johns Hopkins University Press, 1990) 254.

3. The term *mas* is an abbreviation of the word masquerade. It is the preferred form that Trinidadians use to describe Carnival masquerade.

4. *Trinidad Express*, February 12, 1990.

5. Wining is the gyration of the hips and pelvic area.

6. See Pamela R. Franco, "The Invention of Traditional Masques and the Politics of Gender," in *Trinidad Carnival: The Culture Politics of a Transnational Festival*, eds. Phil W. Scher and Garth L. Green (Bloomington: Indiana University Press, 2007) 25–47.

7. In the nineteenth century, Carnival was multidimensional. Each ethnic/cultural group celebrated in a different way. Pre-emancipation enslaved blacks had a limited presence in the street festival. Sometimes their masters allowed them to parade in the street. The colored middle class were allowed to organize fancy dress balls and parade in the streets, however, they needed governmental permission to do so.

8. Sidney W. Mintz and Richard Price, *The Birth of African American Culture: An Anthropological Perspective* (Boston: Beacon Press, 1992) 7.

9. Pamela R. Franco, "Dressing Up and Looking Good: Afro-Creole Women in Trinidad Carnival," *African Arts* 31, no. 2, 1998, vol. 7.

10. This anglicized spelling is used to describe the dress or costume. When referring to a person or a citizen from Martinique, the term Martiniquian is used.

11. The *a la jupe*, also known as *chemisette et jupe*, was a bodice and skirt ensemble. Draped to the side and tucked into the waist, the skirt revealed a *jupon* or underskirt. The *grande robe*, the more formal attire, was based on the French *douillette*. Like the *a la jupe*, the skirt was draped, rolled and tucked into the waist, revealing an elaborately decorated underskirt. Both styles incorporated a *foulard* or scarf which was draped around the shoulders. In what can be called an "act of cultural bricolage" black and mulatto women fused bits and pieces from the region's major ethnic and colonial groups. Using an assemblage technique, they combined European-manufactured cloth, scotch plaid, madras, printed cotton, or sumptuous materials like silk, damask, muslin, and lace, which they draped, rolled, and tied in the mode of the West African woman's wrapper. A profusion of jewelry, a fancy headtie or hat, and shoes and stockings completed this ensemble.

12. Michel Foucault. "Nietsche Geneology and History," in *The Foucault Reader*, ed. Paul Rabinow (New York: Random House, 1984) 83.

13. Alison Lurie, *Language of Clothes*. (New York: Random House, 1981) 24.

14. Pamela R. Franco, "The Unruly Woman" *Small Axe*, vol 7, March, 2000, 60–77.

15. Natalie Zemon Davis, *Women and Culture in Modern France*, 131.

16. Davis, 131.

17. Lafcadio Hearn, "La Verrette and the Carnival in St. Pierre, Martinique," in *Harper's New Monthly Magazine*, vol. LXXVII, June–September 1888, 740

18. This is possible because very little research has been done in Martinique primarily because the texts are in French.

19. Kim Marie Vaz. *The "Baby Dolls": Breaking the Race and Gender Barriers of the New Orleans Mardi Gras Tradition*. (Baton Rouge: Louisiana State University Press, 2013), 8.

20. Vaz, 2.

21. Vaz, 14.

22. Errol Hill. *The Trinidad Carnival: Mandate for a National Theatre*. (London: New Beacon Books, 1997 [1972]), 108.

23. Hill, 88.

24. Shari L. Thurer, *The Myths of Motherhood: How Culture Invents the Good Mother*. (Boston: Houghton Mifflin Company, 1994), xv.

25. Elaine Savory Fido, "Freeing Up: Politics, Gender, and Theatrical Form in the Anglophone Caribbean," in *Gender in Performance: The Presentation of Difference in the Performing Arts,* ed. Laurence Senelick (Hanover: University Press of New England, 1992), 283.

26. Janice Lee Liddell, "The Narrow Enclosure of Motherdom/Martyrdom: A Study of Gatha Randall Barton in Sylvia Wynter's *The Hills of Hebron*," in *Out of Kumbla*, eds. Carole Boyce Davies and Elaine Savory Fido (New Jersey: Africa World Press, 1990), 321.

27. Gordon Rohlehr *Calypso and Society in Pre-Independence Trinidad* (Port-of-Spain: Gordon Rohlehr, 1990), 225.

28. Under a new title—Ordinance Relating to the Protection of Children and Young Persons, Industrial Schools and Orphanages, and Juvenile Offenders—in the 1920s this law granted adults the responsibility for the safety and wellbeing of their children.

29. Information on the Legitimation Ordinance No. 8 was obtained from the *Trinidad and Tobago Revised Ordinances*, 1950. vol. VIII, 68.

30. Vaz, 61.

31. Morey Amsterdam was a radio comedian in the United States. On a 1943 visit to Trinidad, as part of a group to entertain the U.S. troops on the island, he heard Lord Invader's *Rum and Coca Cola* calypso. He liked it and wrote new verses using the song title, melody, and salacious content. In 1944 Amsterdam tried to apply for copyright of the calypso with himself as the lone author. He was unsuccessful.

32. Prior to the 1960s there were relatively few black dolls. I remember in the 1950s, my sister receiving a black doll as a Christmas present from her godmother. The doll was purchased in New York.

Operationalizing "Baby" for Our Good

A Critical Cultural Commentary on Early Twentieth-Century Songs about Women as Baby and Baby Doll

—Melanie Bratcher

n a conversation with a black male poet regarding how men might employ the word "baby" to refer to a woman, my consideration of male perspective was deepened, particularly regarding women as men's possession.[1] There are cultural variants, gender inconsistencies, and socio-economic factors that play out in the simple term, "baby." What becomes of great import is how that term ultimately empowers a female.[2] If empowerment cannot be churned out from the term, then it is of no use to anyone as a referent to women[3]. I flesh out some lyrics from the 1890s through 1922 that refer to women as "baby," "doll," or "baby doll." I explore and explain some cultural intersections in the usage of these terms and contextualize the potential and power of the culture that the Baby Dolls wielded, as it relates to song lyrics.

A Brief Overview of Conditions That Birthed the Baby Dolls

At a time when black women had relatively less power than anyone in the United States, the New Orleans women's club, The Baby Dolls, organized in an effort to provide a sort of protection for some of the most disenfranchised humans in America. Initially made up of black women who sold sex, the most literal type of prostitution, these women used the asset that was used against blacks to socially control them.

In a Christian nation that enslaved human beings, propaganda that purported the lasciviousness of black people gave rise to fear of black men and created fear in black women about their virtue and their value.

"Act XII," the Jamestown, Virginia, Colonial Law passed by the Virginia House of Burgesses in December of 1662, declared, "The child bears the status of the mother." This fueled the fathering[4] of black children by white males and enslaved black females to populate plantations with free labor. Black females, the breeders, were a boon for many whites.

It was a bust for blacks; black women were reduced to busts, to mildly put it. Black women became valuable more because of their reproductive parts and consequently less valuable than before because of the less-than-human status conferred upon them by virtue-defining dehumanizers. What a crossroads from which to sojourn.

Propaganda that could reach masses of people by means of entertainment, what is called "Art" in the Occident, was strategically employed. Some two hundred years after "Act XII," the socialization of humans in the West, informed by scripted strictures of the most brutal holocaust or "Great Disaster"[5] perpetrated against humans, left little room for black women to carve out prosperous space.

The so-called "oldest profession in the world" was a viable option for some who understood that you have to do what you have to do until you can do what you want to do. Dire circumstances in which to survive, let alone thrive, painted the landscape across which some brave black women traveled. Hard choices were made in an extremely harsh environment.

The Sound of Music

There was no "saline consciousness" for people of African descent who were forcibly brought to the Western Hemisphere some four hundred years ago. They brought with them sound. They were stripped of material possession and human rights. Sound, however, was not dismantled.[6] It kept them or at least their spirits alive.

Vocalization, singing, and speech were all steadily employed to tell tales, provide instruction and social commentary, liven ceremony whether secret or public, and aid in work. Black folks had their own uses for propaganda although it often included racist and sexist nomenclature.[7] There was, however, potential for restructuring and repurposing those demeaning naming practices.

The advent of the phonograph in the 1880s was a beacon for mass production and selling of recorded music. Where live music performance could not go, records could. Of course, only the very few with monetary wealth could afford them, so they were able to further entrench themselves in profiteering human subjugation via amusement and entertainment. To partake, from a distance, in some practices of Black folks' survival aesthetic, was a hoot.

In the lyrics, particularly those created and mass produced at the turn of the twentieth century, can be found a spectrum of living conditions, life choices, expressions of fear and faith, the mundane and the sacred, and sadly, limited options for defining black human existence. For black people, the sound of music aided survival. For others it was amusing and entertaining, not unlike the bodies and body parts of black women. From a sample of African American sheet music, consider some of the following song titles that describe black women as "Baby":

"Baby Loo: A Negro Ditty of the Tenderloin"—1898
"I've Lost Ma Baby"—1899
"Ma Baby Girl"—1899
"Ma' Rag Time Baby: Original Rag Time Song"—1899
"My Hannah Lady, Whose Black Baby Is You?"—1899
"My Little Zulu Babe"—1897/1900
"That Brown Skin Baby Mine"—1898
"She's My Warm Baby"—1897
"The Warmest Baby in the Bunch: Ethiopian Ditty"—1897
"Yer Baby's A Comin' to Town: A Song and Chorus"—1896
"Hello! Ma Baby"—1896, 1899
"Virginia, Ma Baby: An Ethiopian Episode"—1897
"I Couldn't Stand To See Ma Baby Lose"—1899
"I Got My Baby Back"—1898

The sound of music reflected creations by both black and white composers. The sounding out of particular lyrics recreated a destruction of a people's humanity, thereby promoting a severely burdened pathos. However, the sounding out of the same lyrics also set up the potential for a reconstruction of a people's ethos. At the center were the black female body, the black woman, and the disfigured feminine. The cost of the sound of some music has yet to be repaid. There are some old roads still in need of repair and new roads that must be paved—sojourn.

In the Key of Black and White

"The Warmest Baby in the Bunch: Ethiopian Ditty" was written by George M. Cohan when he was nineteen years old. He is described as a flamboyant and talented luminary, a fiercely patriotic man. A prominent writer in the Tin Pan Alley network, who for a short time wrote in the minstrel tradition, he perpetuated a racist and sexist tradition that at best merely objectified African Americans and, at worst, maliciously dehumanized them.

That "lesser of two evils" spectrum was typically executed in the manners and subtle phrasings expected by navigators of polite society. In other words, it was acceptable to create deleterious imagery about African Americans, especially black women, as long as it was done in the name of patriotism. The result in any case was mass promotion of ignorance.

On American soil, many whites perpetrated a horrific xenophobia against blacks in a genre of music generally referred to as "ethnic characterizations." These songs were popularly known as "minstrel songs," "Ethiopian ditties," and "coon songs." These kinds of songs fueled the institutionalization of racism in mainstream America through racist lyrics with stereotypical imagery—a mass socialization in sound ensued.[8] Popular music was largely played in traveling shows and various kinds of parlors across the country. Its popularity grew with the development of recorded music, which in the late 1800s only wealthy people could afford.

The nascent wax cylinder record was scarce and too costly for most Americans to purchase.[9] Initially written mostly by white males and performed by whites in blackface, these "songs of racial stereotype" also promoted gender stereotypes. The imagery of the lyrics and the imagery performed in live shows reinforced prevailing negative ideas about people of African descent and about women.

Cohan's 1897 song "The Warmest Baby in the Bunch: Ethiopian Ditty" was "a moderately successful hit in the popular 'coon song' genre . . . [and] was all the rage" (The Parlor Songs Academy 2004). His song certainly promoted ignorance in the name of humor. Humor about and mockery of the contrived social stations to which blacks were relegated were powerful tactics used by polite society to maintain social control. Social control is facilitated by the construction of social restrictions and starts with defining a person or people.

The options with which people could define and imagine black female existence were extremely limited. Black females were doubly if not triply objectified and dehumanized by whites and blacks alike. The confines imposed on the portrayals of black females enforced a heinous kind of social restriction. While the social ideal of black womanhood was situated within the confines of the "Cult of True Womanhood," it was understood that black females could not achieve the status of "true woman": "lady." She was restricted to roughly four images, four ways of being defined, and none of them celebrated her existence as a female and woman or human. Rather, imagery was used to qualify her as sexually appealing or not, a sexual object. Cohan's song reinforces this kind of thought restriction, thereby promoting the continuation of ignorance that created such dichotomization.

In the first verse we are introduced to the extremes of the spectrum into which a female, in general, could be defined:

> You're well acquainted with the Highborn lady,
> You might have heard of Hot Tamale Sal,

As the verse proceeds, a third option of female existence is introduced. This woman is neither cold nor hot. She is warm but still a wench who is up to something and you may not be able to believe what you see:

> But there's a wench that makes them all look shady,
> You've got to take your hat off to dis gal,
> You'll all be dazzled when you see dis member,
> You'll think that you've been drinking nigger punch,
> The steam comes from her shoes in cold December,
> For she's the warmest baby in the bunch.

The image suggests that her physical beauty is intoxicating; her physicality is alluring to those who see her. However, the reference to "nigger punch" belies any reference to the beauty of her blackness. She is denigrated in the sense that she can only be seen as beautiful because one has imbibed some sort of Africanized (meaning lowbrow), exceedingly potent alcohol. You have to be drunk to find a black woman beautiful, in this case.[10]

In a twist, her presence and appearance knock you out. It is akin to being punched, like a sneak attack that leaves a person victimized and cheated. However, she is also referred to as "dis member," presumably a body part—she is dismembered.

Next, the chorus of the song promotes envy, a divisive state of being. Women will be jealous of this woman who is "the warmest in the bunch" because she dawns expensive jewelry and a lethal style of dress. Jealousy about someone's accouterment promotes materialism,[11] a divisive economic tactic. The majority of blacks in the late 1800s were poor, and promoting materialistic envy easily fueled the desire to acquire money by any means, legal and illegal, moral and immoral. Would this be the template for future black music? The chorus lyrics bemoan high-risk activities, signify imagery of female as sex organ, and turn this black woman into a high priced object.

> When they see her coming, all dem wenches take a chill,
> Diamonds glist'nin' all around and style enough to kill,

Her steady feller broke a crap game,
Down in Louisville,
And buys her chicken ev'ry day for lunch.
"Come Seben!"
Dreamy eyes that sparkle and she rolls them mighty cute,
Colored gemmen say that lady cert'ny is a "beaut,"
"Go broke," dat she's a hot potater
She's a red-hot radiator,
She's the warmest baby in the bunch.

She has nice things because her man is a gambler, a dice thrower. Illegal and potentially life-threatening hustles for money are inadvertently, and perhaps not so inadvertently, promoted. In this song we see precedent for songs that report "facts" of street life today.

Gambling, a major part of street life, is a prospect for acquiring money in order to look wealthy. This is a testament to the economic restrictions that African Americans were made to endure. A vast majority of black people were forced into sharecropping in the late 1800s, so it is not far-fetched that additional means of earning money were deemed necessary by some. An ill effect of illegal means of financial gain lingers in the mass incarceration of black people we witness today.

This "warm" woman's man buys her chicken for lunch, every day. Short of saying fried chicken, the reference to poultry is laden with racist "humor." Descriptions of her move toward objectification: "red-hot radiator"—a reference to cars, in this case a car part. Then she is completely kicked out of the animal kingdom of which humans are a part, and reduced to vegetation—a "hot potater,"—a hot potato.

If the dehumanizing references to her are not enough at this point in the song, the second verse attributes her with sorcerer's powers, making her something or someone to be feared. The reference to "wizard" that follows could certainly speak to pejorative lore about African spiritual practices. Consider the lyrics that hint at the misused allusions to "Voodoo[12]/Hoodoo":

The coons they all acknowledge she's a wizard,
You'll cremate if around this gal you fool.

Some black women are made suspects before they ever enter the scene. The "angry black woman" comes to mind. Not unlike Peaches in Nina Simone's "Four Women," it is far too often presumed that a black woman will cut you. It should be understood that black women have great reason to do so, but this stigma helps no one. In fact, she has been dissected far too long by the larger society and within her own community. She has a hot temper because the world has been too cold to her.

In the second verse she is described as having a very hot body temperature. If in a January blizzard she has to fan herself, then she certainly is hot. Recall in the first verse she is referred to as "dis member." That could mean member of a community, but it could also mean something else. Regarding this kind of "temperature" reference there is great potential for her dismemberment.

Indirectly, this states that she has undeniable sexual prowess. There is potential in this scenario, however improper as deemed by polite society, for her empowerment. It appears that she may benefit from the prowess others assign her. Her lifestyle or approach to life is seen as carefree. Examine the following lyrics:

> Last January when we had a blizzard,
> She had to fan herself to take it cool,
> The pol'cy shops are broken by this hummer,
> She's luckier than a nigger with a hunch,
> She leads a life of everlasting summer,
> For she's the warmest baby in the bunch.

Looking more closely at the last four lines, her empowerment may be an inside job, no johns or sugar daddies involved. "She's luckier than a nigger with a hunch" could mean that she is on some sort of winning streak. She may lead a life informed by intuition and be clairvoyant about the result of any given roll of the dice in her life. "The pol'cy shops are broken by this hummer," says she follows no one's policy but her own. To have and follow a hunch that pays off is certainly a lucky experience. About what might she have a hunch that allows her to lead a carefree life, one "of everlasting summer?" A carefree approach to life, one inspired and informed by intuition, the understanding of signs, and the will or at least ability to attract synchronicities based on vibrations or ambiences informs the epistemology of many cultures. It is arguable that such knowing is indeed African.

In African culture it is fairly well understood that spirit or ethos is the truth of human experience. Deep spirituality is manifested in high vibrations, particularly through dance. The next song brings the "La Das [sic] Pas Malaise"—the Difficult Step—into the mix. We step down into layers of what "baby" can mean.

A nineteen year old white male composer John Raymond Hubbell wrote the song "Hea' Comes Ma Baby: A Coonville Episode," which tells the tale of a black man touting the graceful dancing abilities of his warm yellow-skinned black woman. As envisaged by the title, this song is replete with pejorative reference to blacks as coons.

The phrase "pas ma la" is a colloquialism that blends the words "possum" with the French dance term *Pas mele* meaning mixed dance. Reference to nature, especially animals, in the naming of dances, is not uncommon to African and African-derived dance. Connection with nature affords insight into pathways, into motion sensibilities found in African dance and the deep thinking such dance tends to reflect.

In particular there is one saving grace in the lyrics of the song. It is the gracefulness with which his "Baby" executes the Pas Ma La dance, like no other. The Cake Walk movements of the Pas Ma La resemble movements from the Ibeji dance of the Yoruba. In this case calling a black woman "baby" celebrates African dance. Her gracefulness is worthy of grand announcement. Since the lyricist of this song is likely co-opting black culture, he perhaps unwittingly promotes African culture. The "pamasla" dance and its spin off the "Pas Ma La" song were created in 1895 by an African American composer, Ernest Hogan.

Amidst the racist dehumanizing use of "coon" and the reference to a black folk dance—the Possum dance, "a dance seen as low-brow, and 'up-from-under'" (Lynn Abbott and Doug Seroff)—the mention of "baby" dancing the Pas Ma La so well is actually a dynamic cultural reference. He wants to show off the woman, his baby, because she so beautifully dances Africa. It is a moment in the sun like no other:

> But I'se got de warmest yaller gal dat ebber walked de floo'
> An a someday we'll show em' how
> When on de grand parade, we'll lay 'em de shade
> By dancin' de "Pas Ma La"

Here, "baby" as a reference to black women is a good thing because it points to gracefulness in the dancing of African deep thought. She is "graceful as Venus." Venus is a Western adaptation, at the least a parallel, of the West African, Yoruba goddess Oshun.[13] Hogan's song and dance employ transmutation and synthesis, thereby keeping African culture alive. Hubbell's youthful, read immature, co-opting of this cultural phenomena, not unlike too many white lyricists of that day, and of today, can be mined for some value.

The reference to dance, although co-opted by a white writer, sheds some light on the usage of "baby" as reference to a black woman. It can be positive. She brings joy through dance to her man and her community.

Conclusion: Not Tea Time but Honey Wine Time

Lyrics from the 1890s through 1922 that refer to women as "baby," "doll," or "baby doll" contain negative trends of objectification, dehumanization, belittlement, exile, and, reproach. Positive trends were also found. Most powerful were creative cultural exposition, black female spin on nomenclature, pride in black stylization of the feminine—the creative and intuitive—and praise for black women.

The exploration of some intersections in the usage of these terms was confounding and upsetting but ultimately empowering. For a black woman, it is necessary to build with the stones the world throws at you. It is necessary to appropriate your own culture in order to maximize the dynamism inherent in the culture. In a way, it and you must be tested. The explanation is actually simpler than the exploration. It is an African proverb, in fact: "A woman is like a bee: treat her well and she will make honey, treat her badly and she will go wild." The black woman as the "baby" and the "doll," when viewed through the lens of an African-centered cultural analysis, becomes an invaluable mirror for society at large. She can protect and provide for those she loves, who love her and love her not simultaneously. She often does so with a wildness that is serene.

Having developed context for the potential of cultural power that the Baby Dolls wielded, as it related to song lyrics, I found that a vast majority of the lyrics about women, black women, as "baby," "doll," or "baby doll" bore negative gender stereotypes. Our culture, however, was and is a powerful antidote to the poisons of the world. The race poison, race-gender poison, intra-race poison, and intra-race-gender poison that black women faced on a regular basis positioned us for certain debilitation. However, something in the cultural memory sustained us.

The only thing that we had was stock in our culture. It served as a lens through which we could filter the constant degradation that was thrown at us. There was no other real economic or political viability. When we came to the larger society through our culture, we wielded something mighty, even if it was in a brothel and on the streets, and as Baby Dolls.

NOTES

1. A major theme in that discussion: beliefs about women as some*thing* to be possessed by men—a possession.

2. Gerda Lerner, quoted in, Will Harris, "Early Black Women Playwrights and the Dual Liberation Motif," *African American Review* 28, no. 2 (Summer 1994). Lerner says, "The first step toward emancipation is self-consciousness of a distortion, a wrong: what

women have been taught about the world, what they see reflected in art, literature, phi-losophy, and religion is not quite appropriate to them." Emancipation—from patriarchal, read antiquated male and female's paternalistic definitions of females, girls, women, and the feminine—can be and is a basis for empowerment.

3. Empowerment here functions within African aesthetic ideals in creative expres-sion. What is bad or ugly has potential to be transformed into beauty and goodness. Lyrics that demean, objectify, or dehumanize, intentionally or not, can be contextually re-operationalized into lyrics that teach people not to demean, objectify, or dehumanize. If a creative expression does not uplift African people, in this case particularly African/ Black women, then it falls in the "ugly" spectrum and has no value.

4. Rape was common and, with the passing of this law, encouraged.

5. See Dona Richards discussion on the Kiswahili term Maafa or Great Disaster— one hundred million Africans were sold as chattel and treated like animals. Our ethos, however, is resilient and our spirituality enables us to recover from the pathos of such disastrous experiences.

6. As time moved forward, Africans were stripped of drums. To no avail, drums were simply replaced with fiddles whose strings could be rhythmically manipulated like the membranes of drums. The sound could not and would not stop.

7. That nomenclature promoted socio-economic constructs that worked against black and female advancement.

8. That "the lyrics of popular music not only reflect the attitudes of periods of history but also function, as do other media forms, to socialize attitudes," is a common sense proposition that fosters nonsensical contradictions such as virgin versus temptress. Far too often, the lyrics are particularly pointed in debasing women, especially black wom-en, further facilitating "conflict between men and women as they search for meaningful relationships." Virginia W. Cooper, "Women in Popular Music: A Quantitative Analysis of Feminine Images Over Time," in *Sex Roles* 13, nos. 9/10 (1985), 504. Also see Simone de Beauvoir, *The Second Sex*, H. M. Parshley, ed. and Trans. (New York: Alfred A. Knopf, 1952) for a discussion on the "virgin" and the "temptress."

9. Besides the fact that the sound quality of the nascent recordings was terrible, mass production was not yet massive because of costs, but the medium perpetuated racist and sexist ideology amongst the wealthy and "powerful." I first encountered and heard the song "My Little Zulu Babe"—a song that incites black American male antagonism toward continental Africans, particularly an African princess, whom he marries as a power move—on a compilation CD. On the back matter and in all caps it states, "CON-TAINS RACIALLY DEROGATORY LANGUAGE." Sadly the song promotes intra-"racial-cultural" discord by belittling continental Africans while simultaneously touting the takeover of Africa's riches by a black American male. See *Lost Sounds: Blacks and the Birth of the Recording Industry 1891–1922* (Champaign, IL: Archeophone Records, 2005). The compilation includes fifty-four songs written by African Americans.

10. This highlights the notion, perhaps the fact, that black women cannot be seen as beautiful unless they can live up to particular standards of female physical beauty, presumably white standards.

11. bell hooks, "Simple Living: An Antidote to Hedonistic Materialism," in *Black Genius*, ed. Walter Mosley (New York: W. W. Norton. 1999). Humans desire material goods; however, in this context where capitalists thrive off of race and gender-based denigration and Blacks and women are largely impoverished, that human desire is exac-erbated for the impoverished. In turn blacks and women are incentivized toward illegal acquisition of money; a game of go to jail fast follows. The prison industrial complex,

arguably the continuation of capitalism's use of free or cheap labor, profits from this vicious cycle while many of the impoverished are further politically and economically disenfranchised.

12. For a discussion on nkisi as living art, see Mary McCurnin, "From the Old to the New World: 9e Transformation of Kongo Minkisi in African American Art," 2010, *VCU Theses and Dissertations*, paper 78. Also see, Dunja Hersak, "There Are Many Kongo Worlds: Particularities of Magico-Religious Beliefs among the Vili and Yombe of Congo-Brazzaville," *Journal of the International African Institute* 71, no. 4 (2001), 621.

13. In Alan G. Vaughn's discussion on the archetypal, cultural musings of Jacob Lawrence's paintings, he relates Lawrence's receipt of the gift of art and music from Oshun. Vaughn leans on the work of William Bascom to situate archetypal connections between the Yoruba Oshun and the Greek Venus, that is, the Yoruba Venus. See William Bascom, "The Yoruba of Southwestern Nigeria" (Illinois: Waveland Press, 1984). Vaughn's use of Bascom's research unfolds, "Oshun is the Yoruba Venus, renowned for her beauty and for her meticulous care and appearance. . . . Because of her great beauty, Oshun is desired by all the gods and she takes many of them as husbands or lovers. Her amorous adventures complicate the divine genealogies, but her worshipers take pride in these adventures because they add to her reputation for beauty and desirability," (Bascom, 90), (2004, 29). This lends both a credence to artistic process and its direct cultural relativity to the beauty of a highly desirable, polyandry-practicing, West African female archetype, and to the honoring of a black woman as "baby" dancing the music of African heritage in the New World.

BIBLIOGRAPHY

Abbott, Lynn and Doug Seroff. *Out of Sight: The Rise of African American Popular Music, 1889–1895*. Jackson: University Press of Mississippi, 2002.

Berry, Jason. "Baby Dolls and Skeletons: Taking to the Streets on Mardi Gras." *New Orleans Magazine*, February 2014, 41. Accessed May 15, 2015.

Bratcher, Melanie E. *Words and Songs of Bessie Smith, Billie Holiday, and Nina Simone: Sound Motion, Blues Spirit, and African Memory*. New York: Routledge, 2007.

Britannica Academic, s. v. "Nkisi" (by Khonsura A. Wilson). Accessed July 3, 2015.

Brymn, James Timothy. "My Little Zulu Babe." Chicago, Ill: Windsor Music Co., 1900. Accessed July 2, 2015, Brown University Library Center for Digital Scholarship.

Cohan, George M. "The Warmest Baby in the Bunch: Ethiopian Ditty." New York: George L. Spaulding, 1897. Accessed July 2, 2015, Brown University Library Center for Digital Scholarship.

Cole, Bob. "You'll Have to Choose Another Baby, Now: Song and Chorus." New York: Howely, Haviland & Co., 1907. Accessed July 2, 2015, Brown University Library Center for Digital Scholarship.

Cook, Will Marion. "Brown-Skin Baby Mine." New York: Schirmer, 1902. Accessed July 2, 2015, Brown University Library Center for Digital Scholarship.

Cooper, B. Lee. "Images of Women in Popular Song Lyrics: A Bibliography." *Popular Music & Society* 22, no. 4 (Winter 1998): 79–89.

Cooper, Virginia W. "Women in Popular Music: A Quantitative Analysis of Feminine Images Over Time." *Sex Roles* 13, nos. 9/10 (1985): 499–506.

Davis, Angela Y. *Blues Legacies and Black Feminism: Gertrude "Ma" Rainey, Bessie Smith, and Billie Holiday*. New York: Pantheon Books, 1998.

Dorsey, Bruce. "A Gendered History of African Colonization in the Antebellum United States." *Journal of Social History* 34, no. 1 (Fall 2000): 77–103.

Downes, H. W. W. "De Coon Dat's Caught Ma Eye." Boston, Mass: Evans Music Co., 1899. Accessed July 2, 2015, Brown University Library Center for Digital Scholarship.

Edwards, Gus. "I Couldn't Stand to See Ma Baby Lose." Howley, Haviland & Co., 1899. Accessed July 2, 2015, Brown University Library Center for Digital Scholarship.

Harris, Will. "Early Black Women Playwrights and the Dual Liberation Motif." *African American Review* 28, no. 2 (Summer 1994). Accessed July 21, 2015.

Hersak, Dunja. "There Are Many Kongo Worlds: Particularities of Magico-Religious Beliefs among the Vili and Yombe of Congo-Brazzaville." *Journal of the International African Institute* 71, no 4 (2001): 614–40. Accessed March 7, 2015.

Holloway, Joseph. "The Origins of African American Culture." *Africanisms in American Culture*, ed. Joseph E. Holloway, 1–18. Bloomington: Indiana University, 1991.

hooks, bell. "Simple Living: An antidote to hedonistic materialism." *Black Genius*, ed. Walter Mosley, 125–44. New York: W. W. Norton. 1999.

Howard, Joseph E. "Hello! Ma Baby." New York: T.B. Harms & Co., 1899. Accessed July 2, 2015, Brown University Library Center for Digital Scholarship.

———. "I've Lost Ma Baby!" New York: T. B. Harms & Co., 1899. Accessed July 2, 2015, Brown University Library Center for Digital Scholarship.

———. "Ma Baby Girl." New York: T. B. Harms & Co., 1899. Accessed July 2, 2015, Brown University Library Center for Digital Scholarship.

Hubbell, John Raymond. "Hea' Comes Ma Baby: A Coonville Episode." Cincinnati: Goene Music Pub. Co., 1898. Accessed July 2, 2015, Brown University Library Center for Digital Scholarship.

Huggins. Mike J. "More Sinful Pleasures? Leisure, Respectability and the Male Middle Classes in Victorian England." *Journal of Social History* 33, no. 3 (Spring 2000): 585–600.

Jonas, Harry. "Vi'ginia Ma Baby: An Ethiopian Episode." New York: T. B. Harms & Co., 1897. Accessed July 2, 2015, Brown University Library Center for Digital Scholarship.

Kelly, John T. "Yer Baby's a Comin' to Town: Song and Chorus." New York: M. Witmark & Sons, 1896. Accessed July 2, 2015, Brown University Library Center for Digital Scholarship.

Lucas, Claude. "Ev'rybody Shout Fo' Ma Baby: The Latest Colored Commotion." Chicago: S. Brainard's Sons Co., 1897. Accessed July 2, 2015, Brown University Library Center for Digital Scholarship.

McCurnin, Mary, "From the Old to the New World: Transformation of Kongo Minkisi in African American Art" (2010). VCU Theses and Dissertations. Paper 78. Accessed June 6, 2015.

McMahon, T. Barrett. "I Got My Baby Back." New York: Primrose and West Music Pub. Co., 1898. Accessed July 2, 2015, Brown University Library Center for Digital Scholarship.

Metz, Theodore. "Baby Loo: A Negro Ditty of the Tenderloin." New York: Metz Music Co., 1898. Accessed July 2, 2015, Brown University Library Center for Digital Scholarship.

ParlorSongs.com. "The Parlor Songs Academy: Lessons in America's Popular Music History." Richard A. Reublin. 2002. Accessed July 8, 2015.

Perrin, Sidney. "That Brown Skin Baby Mine." New York: M. Witmark & Sons, 1898. Accessed July 2, 2015, Brown University Library Center for Digital Scholarship.

Reed, Dave. "My Hannah Lady, Whose Black Baby is You?" New York: Jos. W. Stern & Co., 1899. Accessed July 2, 2015, Brown University Library Center for Digital Scholarship.

Richards, Dona. *The Implications of African American Spirituality. African Culture: Rhythms of Unity*, ed. Molefi Asante and Kariamu Welsh Asante, 207–32. Trenton: Africa World Press. 1985.

Scheurer, Timothy E. "Goddesses and Golddiggers: Images of Women in Popular Music of the 1930's." *Journal of Popular Culture* 24, no. 1 (1990): 23–38.

Smith, Bessie. "Baby Doll." New York: Frank Music Corp., 1926.

Stone, Fred. S. "Ma'Rag Time Baby: Original Rag Time Song." Detroit, Mich: Whitney-Warner Pub. Co., 1899. Accessed July 2, 2015, Brown University Library Center for Digital Scholarship.

Thompson, R. F. "Idiom of clairvoyance, healing, and shared moral inquiry: a Kongo figures (nkisi lumweno)." *See the Music, Hear the Dance* (2004): 258–59. Accessed July 6, 2015.

Vaughn, Alan G. "Review: Analytical and Cultural Perspectives on the Life and Art of Jacob Lawrence." *The San Francisco Jung Institute Library Journal* 23, no. 1 (February 2004): 6–29. Accessed June 15, 2016.

Ward, Charles B. "She's My Warm Baby." New York: New York Music Co., 1897. Accessed July 2, 2015, Brown University Library Center for Digital Scholarship.

———. "I'm Happy When I'm by Ma Baby's Side." New York: Chas B. Ward Publishing Co., 1899. Accessed July 2, 2015, Brown University Library Center for Digital Scholarship.

Wilkins, Amy C. "Becoming Black Women: Intimate Stories and Intersectional Identities." *Social Psychology Quarterly* 75, no. 2 (June 2012): 173–96.

From the Bamboula to the Baby Dolls

Improvisation, Agency, and African American Dancing in New Orleans

—Jennifer Atkins

New Orleans has always been a dancing city where groups have clashed, challenged, and even complimented each other in ballrooms and on streets. The moving body has been a key factor in expressing New Orleanian identity, particularly in a city where people dance through the streets in world-famous parades, exuberantly displaying unique "stylings" on well-known social dances. Balls have also been popular since the early 1700s, when European immigrants—then their descendants—staged numerous celebratory balls throughout the year. Mardi Gras, of course, was the most popular time for dancing. Masked balls, operas, informal romps through the streets on the way to these events, and private soirees like the *bals de roi* peppered the landscape of revelry in New Orleans.[1] By the mid to late nineteenth century, formal organizations called "krewes" paraded through the streets, then retreated inside to private *bals masque*. At the same time roving bands of African Americans began their own festive rituals. Wearing Native American inspired costumes and calling themselves "Mardi Gras Indians," African American revelers took to the neighborhood streets to chant, dance, and face off rivals in ritual battles that marked their territory. The streets, in fact, have been particularly important in bringing New Orleanians together—notably for African Americans.

From the legacy of Congo Square to the emergence of jazz and beyond, New Orleans's sidewalks, neutral grounds, and other public thoroughfares have been energized with powerful bodily expressions rooted in improvisation and individuality, although ultimately the dances and dancers gained agency through the power of group solidarity. The Baby Dolls emerged from this tradition. The Baby Dolls—a mixed-sex group of maskers who costume as baby dolls, complete with short satin dresses, bloomers, and sometimes even pacifiers—parade on foot during Mardi Gras. These "babies" began in 1912 when a handful of African American prostitutes donned their doll costumes and took to the streets, dancing uptown to Storyville to rival their white counterparts. These women embodied the rambunctious ambulatory dance practices of New Orleans's African American community, playing with the dancing aesthetics of ragtime, a style created in part in New Orleans during the early years of the twentieth century. By tracing certain dynamics of movements and performative aesthetics, a clear lineage is revealed that connects the early Bamboula of Congo Square to the later Baby Dolls of Perdido Street.

Since colonial times, African American dance was a core contributor to New Orleans culture. The vibrant West African dances practiced in the colonies held movement retentions from the Old World, while simultaneously creating new forms as the dancers played with variations and extensions of traditions. In New Orleans, however, an added spatial generosity influenced the dancing. As the people celebrated various civic, religious, and community events throughout the year, dancers went outside to parade and ambulate through the streets.

An essential ingredient in colonial New Orleans dancing was Congo Square, an open area just beyond the city's formal limits where blacks (both enslaved and free) legally gathered to socialize, sell wares, make music, and dance on Sunday afternoons. New Orleans's population and geography as a French and Spanish port in America, a prosperous Catholic society with slaves, resulted in a more *laissez-faire* intermingling of diverse peoples and less stringent slave codes than those in effect in British America. These circumstances affected the African, African American, and Afro-Caribbean men and women. Demographics of early New Orleans reveal a high black-to-white racial ratio, which would have resulted in more restrictive policing of racial interactions and African American mobility in many of the American colonies. From the city's founding until the Louisiana Purchase in 1803, almost thirty thousand slaves from the West African Coast and the West Indies were forcibly translocated to New Orleans. Add to this subsequent generations of slaves, free people of color, and Creoles of color (people of African and French or Spanish lineage) born in New Orleans, as well as refuges from the Haitian Revolution—and by the early nineteenth century, more than 60 percent of the city's inhabitants were people of color (legally defined as negroes). They shared their respective traditions and formed new ones in Congo Square as they danced together in the Bamboula, the Calenda, and the Chica-Congo, among many other dances.

The bare-footed Bamboula was one of the most popular Congo Square dances. Similar to many West African dances, a few participants danced in the center of a moving circle of supporters, who kept up a continual chorus of clapping, shuffling, and singing. They did call-and-response singing with a drum (a *bamboula*) as they circled counterclockwise. "The feet scarce tread wider space than their own length," wrote Henry Didimus, "but rise and fall, turn in and out, touch first the heel and then the toe, rapidly and more rapidly, till they twinkle to the eye, which finds its sight too slow a follower of their movements."[2] What Didimus is describing is a bedrock of West African motion: the shuffle. According to MaryAnn Golden Christopher, who keeps alive the Bamboula practice in present day St. Thomas, another seminal Bamboula element is the sweeping motion that begins the dance. Christopher explains that women shake their skirts while moving forward to "send off the bad spirits, . . . then you shake your skirt and come backwards to bring the good spirits in."[3]

In writing about Louisiana life in the mid-nineteenth century, New Orleans journalist Henry C. Castellanos describes another essential West African movement, the "vibratory motions of the by-standers" while "the principal characters were going through the figures." Castellanos continues, "The performances were usually greeted by the vociferous acclamations and clapping of hands of all the assistants, and toward the close there followed such a whirling of the whole mass that one might have imagined a group of serpents interlacing one another, and casting a charm upon the throng of dancers and spectators."[4] What Castellanos describes is the characteristic shimming tremors that punctuate the dancing and the compelling, participatory nature of West African and African American dance events. The drum "calls" the bodies to move, and as the bodies shape the rhythms, the drum listens and responds.

The Calenda was another Congo Square favorite. According to New Orleanian novelist George Washington Cable, the Calenda—the most popular African dance in the West Indies and "a sort of vehement cotillion"—was so overtly sexual that it was banned from Congo Square in 1843. Cable wrote that it was "a kind of Fandango . . . in which the Madras kerchief held by its tip-ends played a graceful part."[5] As early as 1724, French clergyman Jean-Baptiste Labat (familiarly known as Père Labat) described the Calenda in his travelogue *Nouveau Voyage aux Isles de l'Amerique*:

> The dancers are arranged in two lines, facing each other, the men on one side and the women on the other. Those who are tired of dancing form a circle with the spectators around the dancers and drums. The ablest person

sings a song which he composes on the spot on any subject he considers appropriate. The refrain of this song is sung by everyone and is accompanied by great handclapping. As for the dancers, they hold their arms a little like someone playing castagnettes. They jump, make swift turns, approach each other to a distance of two or three feet then draw back with the beat of the drum until the sound of the drums brings them together again to strike their thighs together, that is, the men's against the women's. To see them it would seem that they were striking each other's bellies although it is only the thighs which receive the blows. At the proper time they withdraw with a pirouette, only to begin again the same movement with absolutely lascivious gestures; this, as many times as the drums give the signal, which is many times in a row. From time to time they lock arms and make several revolutions always slapping their thighs together and kissing each other. It can readily be seen by this abridged description to what degree this dance is contrary to all modesty.[6]

Martinique Creole colonist Moreau de St.-Méry, on seeing the Calenda in Haiti in the late nineteenth century, remarked, "When one has not seen this dance, one would hardly believe how lively and animated it is and how much grace it derives from the strictness with which the musical rhythm is followed. The dancers replace one another without respite, and the Negroes are so intoxicated with pleasure that it is necessary to force them to conclude dances of this sort, called *Kalendas*."[7]

Herbert Asbury described the third dance, the Chica-Congo, in his 1936 work, *The French Quarter: An Informal History of the New Orleans Underworld*. Though Asbury believed he was describing the Bamboula, dance scholar Lynne Fauley Emery asserts that it is actually the Chica-Congo he portrays.[8] Asbury wrote:

The movements of the Calinda and the Dance of the Bamboula were very similar, but for the evolutions of the latter the male dancers attached bits of tin or other metal to ribbons tied about their ankles. Thus accoutered, they pranced back and forth, leaping into the air and stamping in unison, occasionally shouting "Dansez Bamboula! Badoum! Badoum!" while the women, scarcely lifting their feet from the ground, swayed their bodies from side to side and chanted an ancient song as monotonous as a dirge.

He adds:

Beyond the groups of dancers were the children, leaping and cavorting in imitation of their elders, so that the entire square was an almost solid mass of black bodies stamping and swaying to the rhythmic beat of the bones upon the cask, the frenzied chanting of the women, and the clanging of the pieces of metal which dangled from the ankles of the men.[9]

Like Castellanos's Bamboula description, Cable's Calenda musings, and Asbury's illustration of the Chica-Congo, most Congo Square accounts were authored by white men, either New Orleanian, American, or European, but all tourists. Congo Square and its legalized status attracted many whites and high class Creoles to the site, even into its eventual dissolution in the 1850s. Throughout the decades, it lured vast numbers of white people who enjoyed (but were unfamiliar with) African food, music, and movement. The presence of whites seeking entertainment alludes to another aspect of Congo Square: surveillance. While the area is often touted as a free space for blacks to gather, it simultaneously functioned as a place where whites could monitor the scene. At the intersection of novel interest and policing, cultural misunderstanding was pervasive. This is obvious in another of Cable's depictions. After issuing a call to readers to see the "large and small lions of the place," describing the scene as "novel, interesting, and highly amusing," Cable writes that "in various parts of the square a number of male and female negroes assemble, dressed in their holiday clothes, with the very gayest bandana handkerchiefs upon the heads of the females, and, accompanied by the thumping of a banjo or drum, . . . perform the most grotesque African dances." He notes, "No devotee to the Polka or Mazurka in the most *recherché* ball room can enjoy the giddy mazes of the dance more than these sable performers. At one time there will be five or six upon the ground dancing and breaking down for dear life, and occasionally laughing and screaming with delight, while the companions who surround them find it difficult to sit or stand still, so infectious is the desire to dance among the blacks." Obviously fascinated by Congo Square, Cable concludes, "Until we saw these amateurs in Congo Square we thought that John Smoth and Picaninny Coleman [white minstrelmen who worked in blackface] were some [authentic dancers]; but if those worthy individuals could gaze upon the dark beauties of the square, they would beat their brains out with their own tambourines."[10] Whether in earnestly depicting the "infectious" and "grotesque" (in the nineteenth century, "grotesque" meant peculiar or eccentric) Congo Square events, or writing a critical commentary, Cable's account highlights what other spectators voiced. European tourists and white people, accustomed to the verticality and formally bound qualities of their own upright dancing, attributed the "frenzied," grounded nature and "lascivious" pelvic motions inherent in West African dance as portrayals of uncontrollable sexual behavior, effectively racializing blacks as highly sexualized and inferior.

Often African and African American dance styles and intentions were so foreign that white audiences often mislabeled them in travelogues, journals, and personal letters. Congo Square dances were called "Voodoo" rituals, which were, in fact, private affairs infrequently shared with outsiders. Despite its secrecy, Voodoo (voudon) spread throughout New Orleans, attracting both white and black practitioners. Revolving around danced ceremonies, the movement-centric spiritual rituals of Voodoo evolved from the intermingling of West African ancestral worship and Caribbean Catholicism. What separated the secular from the religious was function rather than form. The important totemic and ritualized paraphernalia and the sequencing of dance steps, which differentiated Congo Square dances from Voodoo practices, were carried out ceremonially behind closed doors, although in Africa, the distinctions between sacred and profane dances rarely existed.

The energetic corporeality of Congo Square dancers in particular intrigued and baffled white audiences. In opposition to the contained and restrained moving European body, where the torso works as a single unit, white viewers connected the spectacular undulations, tremors, and repetitious shuffling they saw in the black styles to what they heard rumored about possessed dancing in Voodoo. Some parts of Didimus's Bamboula descriptions, for example, expounded upon this correlation. "The head rests upon the breast, or is thrown back upon the shoulders, the eyes closed, or glaring, while the arms, amid cries, and shouts, and sharp ejaculations, float upon the air, or keep time, with the hands patting upon the thighs, to a music which is seemingly eternal."[11]

A dance of possession (a goal of some Voodoo worship) is loose and dynamic because it occurs during the physical and psychic transition in between being in the material world and entering a transcendent state. During possession, dancers are directly attached to the gods (loa), who speak to the community through the bodies in motion. St.-Mery, much like Didimus, remarked that Voodoo possession dancing looked as if "the upper part of the body, the head and the shoulders all move on springs."[12] The possessed body moves without the perceived limitations of normal body movements; its motions are driven by the spiritual, the mystical, by forces beyond the quotidian. Possessed dancers look unbalanced, with limbs dangling in the air or flying about, even as the feet shuffle in complicated patterns of quick agility. Most interestingly, a possessed body, for all its awkwardness, seems to levitate and glide as it moves. Though seemingly out of control, there is an eerie quality of manipulated suspension in each movement.

Memory of past spirits and the living memory of gods linked the individual worshipper to a cosmic importance and awareness of self. African

American choreographer, anthropologist, and Haitian Vodoun initiate Katherine Dunham captured this essence when she revealed how she felt during a *yonvalou* ceremony. As the pitch of the dancing became heightened in the moments before the gods "mounted" (or possessed) the dancers, Dunham recalled, "I felt weightless . . . but . . . weighted; transparent but solid, belonging to myself but a part of everyone else. This must have been the 'ecstatic union of one mind' of Indian philosophy, but with the fixed solidarity to the earth that all African dancing returns to, whether in assault upon the forces of nature or submission to the gods."[13] When observing a Trinidadian Shango devotional dance in the 1940s, anthropologists Melville and Frances Herskovits became cognizant of this element. While watching a priestess dance during possession, they remarked that, "though a large woman, she danced with consummate artistry, an artistry, in fact, characteristic of these large women, who astonish the more by their lightness of foot, and their supple use of the body."[14] Ironically, when the body is possessed and gods flow into this world through movement, the dancer is perhaps the most physically alive they have ever been. This mystical element intrigued and confused non-practitioners, leading to a multitude of fallacies about Voodoo. Around the beginning of the Civil War, one young woman, Julia LeGrand, commented in her 1862–63 diary:

> Heard to-day of the existence of a negro society here called the "vaudo" (I believe). All who join it promise secrecy on pain of death. Naked men and women dance around a huge snake and the room is suddenly filled with lizards and other reptiles. The snake represents the devil which these creatures worship and fear. The existence of such a thing in New Orleans is hard to believe.[15]

Julia LeGrand was not a New Orleans native, but a visitor. Her account emphasizes a telling point: many whites commodified black culture as an exotic, erotic, and dangerous spectacle.

In looking at some of the differences between black and white dancing aesthetics, the heritage of performance and motional dynamics seen in the dancing of the Baby Dolls becomes apparent. The aliveness of West African movement (in possession or not) was unlike anything whites had seen, demarcating their cultural values. In white ballrooms, performing minuets and later quadrilles, mazurkas, schottishes, waltzes, and more, the key to excellent performativity was an erect body that smoothly moved as a single unit. To contribute to the communal ethos, affluent French, Spanish, British, and American dancers literally stepped into patterned lines and figures that re-inscribed on the dance floor ideals of respectability, refinement, decorum, and demonstrated the individual's physical adherence to order and rules.

In West African culture, a stiff, erect body was a dead one that embodied *rigor mortus*. West African dances express aliveness through asymmetry and angularity, manifested in flexible torsos, spines, pelvises, and knees, and while everyone can dance together in unified patterns, each person has a slightly different style of delivery. As a sign of connection to the earth, West African dancing is grounded and deeply allied to the drum, sounding the deep-throated pulse and rhythm of life. West African dances are propulsive; the body carries polymetric rhythms through engaged or isolated body parts, which move in synchrony and harmony. Call and response (the backbone of improvisation) moves the group forward in linked conversations that shift as individual voices (dancing bodies) contribute new ideas. Part of this includes "looking smart," a display of virtuosity and even sexual attractiveness that never gets too hot (self-motivated) but instead enriches the community. Looking smart is coupled with an aesthetic of cool: a "masked" face that transcends the hard, physical work being performed, an alluring sense of luminosity, and meticulously subtle steps, gestures, and movement patterns that convey West African mastery—control and smoothness.[16]

These elements created a powerful stylistic foundation that enabled the aesthetics of West African music and dance to prevail despite transplantation from Senegal and Benin to New Orleans. These foundational aesthetics, first seen in Congo Square, have a phenomenal impact on groups like the Baby Dolls. Congo Square provided public space for black New Orleanians to express their cultural heritage, to absorb influences, and to collectively rally together through an intimate communal practice of bodily movement. The space enabled enslaved and free people of color to keep their past sacred and intact, and to honor generational knowledge and transmission, a transmission that needed less than a handful of generations to reach the first Baby Dolls. Through cultural preservation, Congo Square participants could adapt to the world around them. Additionally, through white spectatorship and interactions with European dance styles, a movement exchange began to shift the look of social dance in New Orleans, creating a truly American hybrid that foreshadowed late nineteenth century jazz innovations in music and dance.[17] And while Congo Square was but one element in jazz's birth, it did exemplify the innovation, survival, cultural strength, and aliveness that continued to define the spirit of music and dance that permeated both jazz and Baby Doll life.

When jazz did materialize in New Orleans, it was a vibrant force in dance halls, brothels, and, importantly, on the streets. Other important social and art practices at the turn of the century were the benevolent societies, essential in maintaining and keeping a public black jazz presence, and in cementing African American cultural continuity by sponsoring funerals with music. The turn of the century was an era of extreme hardship for most black New Orleanians who battled (among other things) poverty, bouts of yellow fever, and racial segregation, and by 1880, over 225 New Orleans benevolent societies supported various ethnic and racial communities. By 1900, eighty percent of New Orleans's black population belonged to at least one benevolent group.[18] African American benevolent societies sponsored funerals that continued West African burial traditions. There was a solemn march to the gravesite, followed by a lively, parading celebration of life on the return trip, all accompanied by music. In what became popularly known as "jazz funerals," these processions also garnered community participation in the form of "the second-line," the neighborhood dwellers, who joined the funeral as it passed by, dancing to the music as the funeral wound its way through community streets.[19] The ambulatory, participatory nature of jazz funerals not only underscored the connection between music and dance, but also between music, dance, and New Orleans African American traditions, including the Skulls and Bones practice of costuming as skeletons and walking through the streets making a racket to wake neighbors up at dawn Mardi Gras day (dating back to around 1819) and Mardi Gras Indians, who, like benevolent societies, gained momentum in the 1880s. From Congo Square and Voodoo to these turn of the century performances, creative interplay in the streets defined New Orleans dancing habits.

Such a publicly expressive emotional and cultural outlet was integral to African American identity, which reflected the indispensible connection of dancing to life (and death). At the heart of this experience was improvisation. For black dancers in the New Orleans streets and clubs, improvisation was the dialogue that moved the group forward collectively; it also functioned as a tool in the battle for individual distinction. The call-and-response nature of improvisation emphasizes personal power juxtaposed against the balance derived from interacting with (and being shaped by) the community. In times of oppression, improvisation offers hope and opportunities for growth. It affords people the chance to shape their own image while also playing with, even trumping, stereotypes and commenting on world around them. For New Orleans in the early decades of the twentieth century, this agency circulated from the streets to dance halls/cabarets and back, creating a specific regional context that was compatible with an emerging national phenomenon: ragtime.

A collection of stories and interviews from a Louisiana Writer's Project in the early 1940s alludes to the presence of ragtime, the "jazz age" dance and music craze. One story describes a jazz funeral: "When the procession was half a block from the cemetery, enroute [sic] home, the band burst into 'Just Stay a Little While,' and all the True Friends performed individual and various dances, and the sister, but lately unconscious with grief, was soon trucking with the rest of them."[20] Trucking, a little dance (almost a decorative dance phrase) popular from the 1920s to the 1960s, had continuous, gliding, or bouncy step-chugs below while above the torso and hips moved in isolated directions, creating a snakelike wave from the head to the airborne back foot, while the index finger pointed up, down or sideways, highlighting shimmying shoulders or swinging hips. From this description, it is difficult to determine: Does the above account refer to the *step* trucking or the general *quality* of trucking—a term used to denote a gliding, swinging feeling in use before the dance was named? The delineation is not clear, but the presence of ragtime in processional spaces is relevant to the distinct style of rag dancing that developed in New Orleans and the effect it had on the Baby Dolls.

For jazz funerals in the late nineteen teens, general ragtime dances may have been in vogue. But incorporated in them was a rambunctious individualism and improvisation that began to take over as more and more local musicians played it "hot." Jazz historian Burton Peretti explains that, in addition to New Orleans's unique African, European, and Caribbean cultural contexts, the abundance of trained musicians and "highly developed dancing and social traditions" led to a "more sensuous, 'dragging' instrumental kind of ragtime which featured a great deal of 'sliding' between notes."[21] Thus, the interplay between musicians and dancers in shaping New Orleans's jazz style was substantial. As historian Reid Mitchell argues, musicians adapted their style to the second-lining dancers.[22] Out in the open streets, participants occupied more space than the dance halls and clubs afforded. Swinging from curb to curb in parading fashion, dancers could make their movements bigger, include more flair, and participate with a bold, full-bodied commitment to the moment at hand. More space gave more time for improvisational dance boasting. Unencumbered, both the dancing and the music could swing with a grand, rollicking quality impossible in another setting. These specific physical contexts are, in part, what created an idiosyncratic music and dance culture in New Orleans; it is why New Orleans jazz was "more strongly accentuated, and, in a sense, wilder and more unrestrained," drawing as it did from Congo Square shuffles and movements to create a unique "hot number of dynamic rhythm" called the "stomp."[23]

Danny Barker provides us with another vignette: a rare glimpse of jazz funeral second lines before they became a target of media exploitation in the mid-twentieth century. He remembers: "No inhibition: everybody lets his self go out to his full physical extent. The old folks doing their old-time dance steps—cakewalk, turkey trot, shimmy, the wobble, Georgia grind, the peacock strut—and the youngsters doing the monkey, the twist, the dog: these are the same dance steps, but under different names for different periods."[24] The older dances Barker describes, especially the cakewalk and the turkey trot, were ragtime favorites during the early Baby Doll years. The cakewalk began as a strut dancing contest between slaves on Southern plantations where the best dancers earned actual cakes as prizes. It wound its way into minstrel and then vaudeville skits, where backward-leaning torsos satirized the highfalutin planter class promenades. Onstage, the cakewalk used high kicks and grand struts, with breakouts of glitzy improvisation. The turkey trot was another early 1900s dance amid a craze for "animal dances." Set to nimble upbeat ragtime music, the animal dances—like the bunny hug and the grizzly bear—used closed couple one-step movements and periodic jumps, interspersed with arm flailing and full-bodied, jerky motions (this became known later as the chicken or pecking). Animal dances incorporated steps that mimed the animal for which they were named, while incorporating shoulder shimmies, hip shakes, and dipping bodies. Above all, as part of the ragtime lexicon, animal dances were incredibly infectious.

Ragtime was a national music and a dance craze from the late nineteenth century until World War I. Waltzes and two-steps (and even mazurkas and schottisches) still existed, but they operated as relief from the faster rags and doubled as a tactic to divert dancers to the bar to buy a quick drink. In New Orleans, jazzmen still played the old-fashioned dances, but musicians quickly began to "rag" the fast polkas and quadrilles, and even add in some Joplin. The tunes they played and the dances they inspired largely reflected the "the occasion and the clientele."[25] Ragtime became a symbol of working-class leisure. As dancing couples entangled and whirled across dance floors to ragtime music, working-class youth, especially women, defied the mores of decorum imposed on them by middle-class values of domesticity, sobriety, and "passionlessness." Unlike the formal, more refined physical stances of middle- and upper-class dances, ragtime dancing brought men and women together thigh-to-thigh, chest-to-chest in sexually compromising arrangements.[26]

Ragtime dancing was raw, gritty, informal, flexible, intoxicating, and inextricably grounded in African American aesthetics. As dance historian Danielle Robinson outlines, ragtime "embodied an aesthetic of play, angularity, casualness, inventiveness, and abruptness." She clarifies: "Generally speaking, it had six key features: partners 1) held onto one another in intimate ways; 2) could both improvise; 3) made frequent use of gesture; 4) used boisterous movement qualities; 5) deployed angular body lines; and 6) engaged in a high degree of rhythmic play . . . a celebration of change, difference, discontinuity, and disruption."[27] For middle-class reformers, ragtime defined disruption and dance halls. Morality (or a lack thereof) was central to the reformers' platform. They feared what the intersection of growing female social autonomy and dance hall intimacy might produce. Yet, this was what made dance halls appealing for working-class youth. Chances to mingle with the opposite sex became increasingly popular as women began to test the limits of social acceptability through their bodies.

No law could prevent the youth, especially the "new woman," from dancing as they pleased and ragtime's freedom to experiment appealed across class lines. As a choice, working women saw themselves as justified in pursuing the dance hall leisure. What reformers condemned as "vice," working women termed "virtue," a definition steeped in self-reliance, independence, and the ability to choose their own fate. Cultural and gender historian Kathy Peiss points out that the "commercial culture of the dance halls meshed with that of working-class youth in a symbiotic relationship, reinforcing emergent values and 'modern' attitudes toward leisure, sexuality, and personal fulfillment."[28] Through social dancing, both men and women were less restricted by the strict moral standards of what constituted "acceptable" behavior. Working girls expressed liberation by dancing "lasciviously" and floating from one dance partner to the next. While these interactions seemed immoral to Progressive reformers, the freedom women maintained over their own bodies radically altered their social lives. Working girls no longer measured their worth by Cult of Domesticity standards. Now, women lowest on the social scale—prostitutes and groups like the Baby Dolls—gained agency when society began to embrace a wider spectrum of femininity, which included a toughness and resilient self-sufficiency that had long been necessary as a Baby Doll survival tactic. The strength and sexual boldness of the New Woman created a space of acceptability for the Baby Dolls, where those powerful, self-determining attitudes had been present for a very long time.

Accordingly, the ragtime dances most popular among the self-determined Baby Dolls were those from the fringes and displayed the most sexual content. Because of this, Baby Doll dancing carried with it a potent message of rebelliousness intermixed with creative spontaneity. They were very dynamic, vivacious dances (and women). One of the most popular provocative jazz dances, the Black Bottom, featured chugging forward and backward while slapping the buttocks, punctuated by salacious eye rolls and finger shaking, in addition to hip gyrations, shoulder shimmies, glides, shuffles, stomps, and swinging arms. Jazz dance historians Marshall and Jean Stearns trace the Black Bottom to composer Perry Bradford, who wrote "Jacksonville Rounders' Dance" in 1907. According to Bradford, Jacksonville, Florida, had been doing the dance for a while but the word "rounder" (which means "pimp") offended some people. So he changed the song's name to "The Original Black Bottom" and reprinted it in 1919.[29] Zora Neale Hurston, on the other hand, argued that the dance emerged from a rough and tumble Nashville, Tennessee neighborhood, while another source for the Stearns plugged Atlanta as the Black Bottom's birthplace.[30] Wherever its roots lay, it was a Southern dance[31] and, after being featured in Vaudeville skits and Broadway musicals in the early 1920s (like the wildly popular *Shuffle Along*), the Black Bottom, the Charleston, and other Southern jook-joint and dance hall favorites transitioned to the national limelight. Across America, however, the Black Bottom (only slightly less popular than the Charleston), succumbed to the fate of its fellow dances; it changed considerably as it migrated from Southern social dances to theaters and into Northern dance halls, then, once further refined, into ballrooms.

To some extent, the Black Bottom was one in a group of "shake" or "shimmy" dances. Not surprisingly, shake dances, which begin with rapid shoulder vibrations that emanate out to the entire body, have roots in West Africa (then Trinidad), but in America, the shake dances picked up exaggerated grinds and quivers.[32] Shake dances in their jazz form began, as with the Black Bottom, in the South; and, to a Congo Square visitor, shakes and shimmies were likely indistinguishable from the "possession" dances witnessed in the nineteenth century. The Shimmy, whose rumbling effects ranged anywhere from subtle trembles to full-bodied convulsions, supposedly won its name from New Orleans pianist Tony Jackson around 1900.[33] The Shimmy could involve any amount of mobility, from quaking in a fixed position to adding side-to-side slides or even elaborate acrobatics while shuddering. Often the Shake emphasized rolling the stomach (akin to belly dancing) and appeared in notorious Salome choreographies across the States under the name of "Hootchy-Kootchy." Society deemed both dances erotic.

Among the Baby Dolls, shakes and shimmies in general prevailed, but a subset also reigned: the naked dance. Mostly performed in Storyville brothels, the naked dance was a solo shake dance performed to a hot piano number. It was a device to rev up and entice male customers, alluding to the fun that would presumably come later. The Baby Dolls had their own spin on the naked dance. In keeping with the striptease fashion of the times, Baby Dolls instigated the naked dance by undressing one of their peers who then "started shakin' it on down." Sometimes, the naked dance went even further. According to Baby Doll Beatrice Hill, "Liberty and Perdido was red hot back in 1912 when that idea started. Women danced on bars with green money in their stockings, and sometimes they danced naked. They used to lie down on the floor and shake their bellies while the mens [sic] fed them candies."[34]

Other lewd dances in Storyville featured food, too. There was a "ham kick" dance where women without underwear kicked high in the air, aiming for a ham hanging from the ceiling. Winners of this "athletic contest" supposedly won the ham as the main prize, though spectators won another prize in watching the unclad women's attempts.[35] And, of course, in New Orleans there had to be "the oyster dance"—a specialty at Emma Johnson's House of All Nations bordello—that entertained men with dance and food. In the oyster dance, a naked woman shimmied an oyster from her head all the way down the contours of her body. Once the oyster rested on her foot, she kicked it into the air in an attempt to catch the aphrodisiac in her mouth. Alternately, a "quick kick" in this "lost art" could land the oyster back on the woman's head where, in all likelihood, the dance began anew.[36]

Another raunchy favorite, not only in New Orleans but across the country, was the Funky Butt. "The Funky Butt" was a music composition, perhaps drawn from popular melodies but made famous by infamous New Orleans native Buddy Bolden at the turn of the century. The song was so much a signature of Bolden's repertory that it was also known as "Buddy Bolden's Blues." Many versions of the song existed and Bolden and his collaborators often improvised (sometimes quite crude) lyrics on the spot to comment on the night's events or about the specific venue. It was a hit. Bolden was so famous for the ditty, in fact, and played so often at the Union Sons Hall, that people often referred to the space as the "Funky Butt Hall."[37] Purportedly, the song's name was even chosen as a comment on the smell that pervaded Union Sons Hall, a small space crammed with people dancing the night away. In an interview with jazz dance historians Marshall and Jean Stearns, blues singer and vaudeville performer Coot Grant describes the Funky Butt dance style: "Well, you know the women sometimes pulled up their dresses to show their pretty petticoats—fine linen with crocheted edges—and that's what happened in the Funky Butt." She continues:

> I remember a tall, powerful woman who worked in the mills pulling coke
> from a furnace—a man's job. And I can call her name, too. It was Sue, and

she loved men. When Sue arrived at my father's tonk, people would yell "Here come Big Sue! Do the Funky Butt, Baby!" As soon as she got high and happy, that's what she'd do, pulling up her skirts and grinding her rear end like an alligator crawling up a bank.[38]

Like other celebrated jazz dances, the Funky Butt focused on exposure, hip shaking, and gumption.

When it came to Baby Doll gumption, however, "walking raddy" was their signature mark. Walking "raddy" was the Baby Doll strut, a way of moving down the street, shaking their hips in a physically tantalizing manner to get men's (and women's) attention. As one Baby Doll remarked, "They liked the way we shook our behinds and we shook 'em like we wanted to"[39] Walking "raddy" was a flamboyant display of claiming one's space and body and using improvisational strategies to build an unforgettable character. Essentially, it was a well-danced boast, a contest between Baby Dolls for who reigned supreme. One Baby Doll disclosed: "We went on downtown, and talk about puttin' on the ritz! . . . Sho [sic], we used to sing, and boy, did we shake it on down. . . . We wore them wide hats, but they was seldom worn, 'cause when we got to heatin' we pulled 'em off. When them Baby Dolls strutted, they strutted. We showed our linen that day, I'm telling you."[40] Interestingly, this description is remarkably close to clarinetist Sidney Bechet's account of the jazz funeral's leader, the grand marshal:

The best strutter in the club, he'd be the Grand Marshal. He'd be a man who could prance when he walked, a man that could really fool and surprise you. He'd keep time to the music, but all along he'd keep a strutting and moving so you'd never know what he was going to do next. Naturally, the music, it makes you strut, but it's *him* too, the way he's strutting, it gets you. It's what you want from a parade: you want to *see* it as well as hear it. And all those fancy steps he'd have—oh, that was really something!—ways he'd have of turning around himself. People, they got a whole lot of pleasure out of just watching him . . . strutting and marching . . . gallivanting there in real style.[41]

In this sense, we can see that improvisational quick thinking, good dancing, and even superior strutting skills were prized aspects of performative identity for both Baby Dolls and grand marshals. Strutting, whether in Congo Square, Cakewalk, or jazz funeral style, exemplified one core movement lexicon of New Orleans's ever-present African American dance practices: ambulatory dancing that highlighted spontaneity and a spirited—even competitive—style that thrust the best of the best into the spotlight while acknowledging a sustained and influential communal presence. Walking "raddy" was but the Baby Doll way of mastering and adding to this heritage.

Shakin,' buttin,' and walking "raddy" were movement styles from the dance halls, brothels, or out in the neighborhood as Baby Dolls costumed for Mardi Gras and took to the streets to taunt, boast, and challenge each other and bystanders. Ragtime favorites—and especially the more ribald dances of the Baby Doll repertory—expressed the dynamism and spirit that the first Baby Dolls embodied. Significantly, the ingenuity involved in danced improvisations and call-and-response dialogues revealed a connection to a long-standing African American dance tradition in New Orleans: reaffirming life, safeguarding cultural ties, and activating a bodily (and internal) power despite oppressive circumstances. For the Baby Dolls this mitigated, even if only to a small extent, the racism and misogyny they experienced in daily life. Dancing became a meaningful tool that confronted and negotiated deeply embedded societal challenges. And it did this through upbeat celebrations and smart movement exchanges that expressed personal sentiments and attitudes. Through dancing, the Baby Dolls (and groups like them) defined the space they inhabited and used their bodies to generate a sense of collective survival. Struttin' down the street, ragging, or shaking, the Baby Dolls expanded possibilities for fullsome, womanly self-expression, engendering a strong sense of belonging. These moments were vibrant, no doubt, illuminating the power of the Baby Dolls as innovators within a rich, cultural tradition that left troubles behind as liveliness surged through their dancing processions.

NOTES

1. The first New Orleans ballroom built specifically to house public dances, La Salle Condé, opened in 1792. By the 1840s, there were over 80 ballrooms operating in the city; many had two to three balls a week during winter and some had as many as five dances a week during Carnival. See Henri Schinder, *Mardi Gras: New Orleans* (New York: Flammarion, 1997), 17; and Robert C. Reinders, *End of an Era: New Orleans, 1850–1860* (New Orleans: The American Printing Co., 1964), 154. The *bals de roi* (King's balls), on the other hand, were a colonial Creole tradition that highlighted family prestige. They originated in the European Twelfth Night celebrations, which featured *gateau des roi*, "king cakes," served to guests with a prized golden bean hidden inside. Whoever received a slice that contained the bean was dubbed the reigning king or queen for the next party (which they hosted) and where new "royalty" would be crowned. Henri Schinder, *Mardi Gras Treasures: Invitations of the Golden Age* (Gretna, LA: Pelican Publishing Company: Flammarion, 2000), 73.

2. Quoted in Rudi Blesh and Harriet Janis, *They All Played Ragtime* (New York: Oak Publications, 1971), 83.

3. CNN iReport, "Dancing for Freedom, Dancing for Identity." Posted February 28, 2013. Accessed April 15, 2014. http://ireport.cnn.com/docs/DOC-934943.

4. Henry C. Castellanos, *New Orleans as It Was: Episodes of Louisiana Life* (New Orleans: 1895), 297–98.

5. George Washington Cable, "The Dance in Place Congo," *The Century Magazine*, February 1886, 527. Cable also wrote, "The true Calinda was bad enough. In Louisiana, at least, its song was always a grossly personal satirical ballad, and it was the favorite dance all the way from there to Trinidad. To dance it publicly is not allowed this side the West Indies." In speaking of what he saw as a "vehement cotillion" nature inherent in the dance, Cable bemoaned that "the contortions of the encircling crowd were strange and terrible, the din was hideous." Writing in the late 1960s, African American dance scholars Marshall and Jean Steans point out that Cable's unfamiliarity with African-derived movement (like many other Americans in general at the time) shadowed the way he observed the Calinda:

> Finding nothing recognizable in the footwork—the activity that most Europeans associate with dancing—Cable turns to the African movements, which seem strange to a white person, accustomed to an erect posture. In the Dahomean shoulder movements (voodoo came from Dahomey), he was witnessing antecedent of the Quiver, Shake, Shimmy, and similar dances. Why he concludes that the dance is a "sensual, devilish thing" is not entirely clear. Perhaps it is as near as he cares to come to suggesting the simultaneous motions of the lower half of the body—the pelvic movements of the Congo—which surfaced in such dances as the Grind and most recently, and clumsily, in the Twist of 1960 and later rock-and-roll dances.

Marshall and Jean Stearns, *Jazz Dance: The Story of American Vernacular Dance* (New York: Da Capo Press, 1994), 20.

6. Quoted in Lynne Fauley Emery, *Black Dance: From 1619 to Today* (Hightstown, N.J.: Princeton Book Company, Publishers, 1988), 21–22.

7. Moreau de St.-Méry, *Danse* (Philadelphia: Font & Walnut Streets, 1796), 46–47.

8. Emery, 164. Additionally, Asbury, born in Missouri in 1889, was not old enough to see Congo Square dances for himself. Here, he is likely relying on reportage, interviews, and other research that he accumulated in assembling his history of the area when preparing his *The French Quarter* manuscript in the 1930s.

9. Herbert Asbury, *The French Quarter: An Informal History of the New Orleans Underworld* (New York: Basic Books, 2008), 243. The "bones upon the cask" here refer to general Congo Square gatherings as described by Asbury earlier on the page:

> At a signal from a police official, the slaves were summoned to the center of the square by the prolonged rattling of two huge beef bones upon the head of a cask, out of which had been fashioned a sort of drum or tambourine called the bamboula. As the dancers took their places, the rattling settled into a steady drumming, which the Negro who wielded the bones maintained, without a pause and with no break in the rhythm, until sunset put an end to the festivities.

10. *New Orleans Daily Picayune*, "Congo Square," March 22, 1846, 2.

11. See note 1 above.

12. Moreau de St.-Méry, 48.

13. Katherine Dunham, *Island Possessed* (Chicago: The University of Chicago Press, 1969), 136.

14. Melville J. Herskovits and Frances S. Herskovits, *Trinidad Village* (New York: Alfred A. Knof, 1947), 334.

15. Julia LeGrand, *The Journal of Julia LeGrand: New Orleans, 1862–1863*, ed. Kate Mason Rowland and Mrs. Morris L. Croxall (Richmond: Everett Waddey Co., 1911), 57.

16. These elements are derived from scholar Robert Farris Thompson's seminal work on West African dance. See, for example, "An Aesthetic of the Cool: West African Dance," *African Forum* 2, no. 2 (1966). Also see: Jacqui Malone, "'Gimme de Kneebone Bent': Music and Dance in Africa," and "'Keep to the Rhythm and You'll Keep to Life': Meaning and Style in African American Vernacular Dance," in *Steppin' on the Blues: The Visible Rhythms of African American Dance* (Chicago: University of Illinois Press, 1996), 9–36.

17. Even in the late eighteenth century, documentation of the very popular "tricolor balls" exists. These dances, which were frequented by whites, free blacks, and slaves, predated quadroon balls and "imprudently imitated" European habits. For more about mixed race dances in early New Orleans, see Henry A. Kmen, "The Quadroon Balls," in *Music in New Orleans: The Formative Years, 1791–1841* (Baton Rouge: Louisiana State University Press, 1966), 42–55.

18. Ardencie Hall, "New Orleans Jazz Funerals: Transition to the Ancestors," PhD dissertation, New York University, 1992, 72. Importantly, benevolent societies were fundamental to the survival of *many* different groups in nineteenth century New Orleans. An Irish benevolent organization formed as early as 1817 and new ones—catering to Germans, Jews, Creoles, and Italians, to name a few—continued to emerge during the ensuing decades. These organizations fostered community and social responsibility, provided health care, aided in charity efforts, and eased tensions surrounding acclimation and hardship. Ann Ostendorf, *Sounds American: National Identity and the Music Cultures of the Lower Mississippi River Valley, 1800–1860* (Athens: The University of Georgia Press, 2011), 118.

19. For more about the relationship between dancing and jazz funerals, see Jennifer Atkins, "Class Acts and Daredevils: Black Masculinity in Jazz Funeral Dancing," *The Journal of American Culture* 35, no. 2 (June 2012), 166–80. This essay not only highlights the importance of dance to jazz funeral practices, but also touches upon the fact that New Orleans funerals with music integrated homegrown musical developments into an existing funeral tradition that utilized brass band music (168). Brass bands became formal components of militias as early as the Revolutionary War, and by the Civil War, military bands were employed to play European inspired marches for parades, weddings, social parties, and funerals. Bands were also called upon to honor the death of famous politicians or members of the military. For an explanation of how brass band styles developed in New Orleans funerals, see John McCusker, "New Orleans Jazz Funeral History." Posted September 2, 2010. Accessed June 26, 2014. http://videos.nola.com/times-picayune/2009/10/video_new_orleans_jazz_funeral.html.

20. Lyle Saxon, Edward Dreyer, and Robert Tallant, *Gumbo Ya Ya: A Collection of Louisiana Folk Tales* (Gretna, LA: LA Writer's Project & Pelican Publishing Co., 1998 [1945]), 307.

21. Burton W. Peretti, *Jazz in American Culture* (Chicago: Ivan R. Dee, 1997), 19.

22. Reid Mitchell, *All on a Mardi Gras Day: Episodes in the History of New Orleans Carnival* (Cambridge, MA: Harvard University Press, 1995), 157.

23. Blesh and Janis, 166.

24. Danny Barker, *A Life in Jazz*, ed. Alyn Shipton (New York: Oxford University Press, 1986), 48.

25. Donald M. Marquis, *In Search of Buddy Bolden: First Man of Jazz* (Baton Rouge: Louisiana State University Press, 2007 [1978]), 107.

26. For an article addressing elite night dancing, see "Contemporary Dancing Has Evolved the Concave Man," *New York Times*, January 18, 1914, SM11. This humorous tale describes the tamer side of social dances prevalent among high society, where the environment is stuffy, champagne is the cheapest drink, and tough dances are considered out of date.

27. Danielle Robinson, "The Ugly Duckling: The Refinement of Ragtime Dancing and the Mass Production and Marketing of Modern Social Dance," *Dance Research* 28, no. 2 (November 2010), 182–83.

28. Kathy Peiss, *Cheap Amusements: Working Women and Leisure in Turn-of-the-Century New York* (Philadelphia: Temple University Press, 1986), 90.

29. Stearns and Stearns, 109–10.

30. Emery, 221, and Stearns and Stearns, 111.

31. Two synopses of the dance even name New Orleans as the Black Bottom's birth place, one generated for Dancetime Publications: "1920—Blackbottom and Charleston," http://dancetimepublications.com/resources/social-dance-timeline/1920-blackbottom -charleston/ and another in the Sonny Watson's StreetSwing database: "Black Bottom," http://www.streetswing.com/histmain/z3blkbtm.htm. Both accessed April 15, 2014.

32. The shake is known as the Shika (Nigeria), Banda (Trinidad), and Oleke (West Africa). Stearns and Stearns, 12.

33. Ibid., 105.

34. Saxon, Dreyer, and Tallant, 11, 13.

35. Al Rose, *Storyville, New Orleans: Being an Authentic, Illustrated Account of the Notorious Red-Light District* (Tuscaloosa: The University of Alabama Press, 1974), 115.

36. Rose, 85.

37. Marquis, 108–11.

38. Stearns and Stearns, 24.

39. Saxon, Dreyer, and Tallant, 15.

40. Ibid.

41. Sidney Bechet, *Treat It Gentle* (New York: Da Capo Press, 1975), 66.

Is the Unruly Woman Masker Still Relevant?

—Kim Vaz-Deville

Skelykins. . . . They'd dye union suits black, paint white bones on 'em and make paper mashey skulls. . . . That's all we knew 'bout Mardi Gras, jus' Zulus, Indians, Baby Dolls an' Skelykins.
—**Barbara Wallace,**[1] circa 1960s

In works such as *Fabulous New Orleans*, Lyle Saxon made readers feel that he was their personal escort to an exotic place. As they traveled with him across the page, the readers were lost in time and led to imagine the inhabitants of this intriguing city waiting to welcome them and reveal secret information for their amusement, amazement, and delight (Stanonis, 2001). Lyle Saxon oversaw the writers and editors of the depression-era Louisiana Writers' Project, which produced the *New Orleans City Guide*.[2] The book covered every inch of the city; mapped it out, annotated the attractions, and delivered it to readers with discretionary incomes to entice them to explore the hidden treasures of a magical land.[3] Lyle Saxon launched the publication of the *New Orleans City Guide* during the 1938 Carnival, since even then Mardi Gras was a major economic stimulus for the city.[4] The book would be introduced and available at the height of the tourist season. As a consequence, he also led a campaign to encourage more New Orleanians to mask for Carnival.[5] Business men approved and collaborated with his effort. Seymour Weiss, president of the Roosevelt Hotel's parent corporation congratulated Saxon on his vision, remarking that "the spirit of Mardi Gras can be kept only through promiscuous masking."[6] Nathan King, an employee of F. Strauss and Son, a wholesale liquor dealer, researched, wrote, and distributed annual guides to black carnival clubs, showcasing their members and season events. His devotion to Mardi Gras revelry was so intense that he made every ball in the black community, which could easily number several dozen.[7] He was honored for his devotion by his election to serve as King of Zulu Social and Pleasure Club parade in 1955.[8] His scepter had a coconut (the signature throw of the club) at its base and an old crow at the apex. Arthur Hardy, publisher of the *Arthur Hardy Mardi Gras Guide,* has for over three decades offered a sightseer's guide to the inner workings of krewes, their balls, their parades, and their historical narratives. A tireless reporter of the festivities as they happen, he broadcasts on local television, providing the soundtrack for the passing parades.

Rebecca Snedeker and Rosary O'Neill are docents of a different background. Both of them have deep family roots in the elite, private krewes in which their female relatives served as queens and members of the court and their fathers served as kings. Drawing on film, theater, and performing arts, Snedeker and O'Neill begin their tours of New Orleans Mardi Gras with their elite relative's enactments. O'Neill starts with Mardi Gras's birthplace in pre-modern Europe. She reveals the way rulers used the theater forms of the triumphal entry into the city and court masques to cement their power and authority. Through her coverage of Mardi Gras's past and present, she brings a perspective not often covered by other guides to Fat Tuesday customs: the continuing influence of the theatre tradition of the Medieval period to the formation of early Carnival customs in New Orleans and the persistence of these retentions to present day practices, performances, and productions. In so doing, she uncovers the psychology of city: the penchant for parties, pageants, and self-glorification. It is as though New Orleanians were children thrown out of the Garden of Eden who have been seeking reentry ever since. Carnival allows for the illusion of riches and royalty as available to everyman and everywoman, close yet so out of reach. Carnival is about abundance and excess, of having so much, there is enough to "throw" away to others.[9]

Born to the upper class of New Orleans, both Snedeker and O'Neill have been eye witnesses to the old-line krewes' productions of Carnival and its privileges and exclusions. Snedeker, in her film *By Invitation Only* (2007), and O'Neill, in her book, *New Orleans Carnival Krewes, the History, Spirit and Secrets of Mardi Gras,* expose the underbelly of the old-line krewes whose aims were to display, perpetuate, and consolidate white male privilege and power. Because of their prominence on business, municipal, and religious boards, councils, and commissions as citizen-kings, they could promote Mardi Gras to become an economic driver of the city's financial system, in which they stood to benefit the most.

Limiting the idea of Mardi Gras to elite male krewes with parades casts doubt on the value of other Carnival revelers: female krewes, working class, gay, and counter-cultural masking traditions. By consigning them to the margins as charming ancillary sidebars, the quest to shape the image of "real" Mardi Gras has been centered around krewe culture. The obvious aim is to publicly affirm their supremacy in both status and income, but it is not only that. The discounting of others points to elite male anxieties about the masking practices of women's and working class groups. Rendering the carnival activities of non-elite white men as happening in "dangerous" parts of the city (that is, black neighborhoods) or non-significant times of the day (daytime parading for women's krewes traditionally),[10] other revelers are characterized as being either violent or amusing, important to be differentiated from, but minor. It is not that non-elite white male masking is not part of Carnival festivities; it is that these are not as significant or as "real" as watching an elite male krewe's parade or being invited to an old-line ball.

That members of other Mardi Gras traditions have remained hidden, invisible, and outside the Mardi Gras economy has to do with the differences in their audience reach, their economic impact, and the social status of their members, but most importantly, it allows for powerful groups to ignore, minimize and disavow the claims these groups make about themselves. One early response came from a group of black friends who decided to invent an imagined Africa to satirically confront an imagined Europe. Around 1909, the Zulu Social Aid and Pleasure club asserted their right to ridicule Rex, an elite male krewe. Zulu created a street tableau that acted out the racist images old line krewes had been circulating for decades through their float themes and parading customs. Zulu's entry on the scene seemingly declared, "If you think our skin is black, we will make it blacker and if you think we are savages, we will come from the river and invade the city."[11] Promoting a view in which only old-line and parading krewes constitute "real" Mardi Gras is a way of disavowing the very humanity of those whom they feel superior to. They deny the desire of all people to be publicly adored, affirmed, and celebrated—simply put, to be "the toast of the town." Today, official Mardi Gras is kicked off on Twelfth Night at the old seat of city government, Gallier Hall, by the mayor and male krewes, Rex and Zulu.

Even though krewes and official Mardi Gras activities are nominally racially integrated, social class continues to be a standard of evaluation between old line elite men's parades, women's parades, black parades, and the Mardi Gras day truck parades. Factors include whether the beads are new or recycled; whether the floats are built for that specific parade and its theme or lent from a wealthier krewe; the quality of the construction of the floats and whether they were professionally designed or decorated by the riders themselves; and the percentage of the krewe members' income spent on throws and costuming.[12] Also obscured by a focus on male krewe masking are the enormous demands that it places on the men's female relatives and partners to arrange parties and favors, invitations to events, and to assist with costumes.[13]

Scholars warn that the city's continued and intensifying focus on using Mardi Gras to fund a third of its budget is jeopardizing the municipality's ability to develop a large middle class. Dependence on tourist purse strings diverts public administrators' and politicians' attention away from developing strategies and solutions to growing the economy in ways that resolve the city's many social problems. Attracting tourists to the city through bigger and more fantastic spectacles such as Mardi Gras only leads to increases in the number of those working in the poorly paid service sector, escalating crime, and a worsening of the wealth gap.[14] Mardi Gras activities for tourists also reveal and impose the intentions of the slave-era Black Codes and post-Reconstruction segregation, as an industry has developed for the production of videos where women "flash for beads." Writing about this localized phenomenon that occurs on a few blocks of the French Quarter, Vicki Mayer testifies that "the worst fights I have witnessed on Bourbon Street have occurred when an interloper, nearly always a local African-American male, reaches for a white woman's body in the video frame."[15] Men who are on the production team and bystanders police black men's hands on women flashers' bodies, conveying historical privileges of white men having unfettered access to women's bodies, both black and white.

Groups like the Mardi Gras Black Indians wear handmade costumes or "new suits" each year. They do not use preplanned parade routes. They see themselves as consciously opposing a society they believe has been hostile to their citizenship but quick to appropriate their image to sell the city to tourists. And though they have masked for over one hundred years, they are still seen as being outside krewe culture; that is, they fall under the label of "promiscuous" maskers. Carnival's essential elements, processions, competitions, feasting and spectacles of dance, music, staging, and masks are designed to give license to bodily needs and desires suppressed and outlawed in everyday living.[16] Scholars continue to discuss the limitations of ritual inversions for overturning the status quo even as they attempt to subvert it.[17] Masking by outsider groups, however, remains closer to the original conception of Carnival as a practice of using parody and satire to offer social critiques. In recent years, satirical parades have mushroomed. One of the most famous of these, Krewe du Vieux, bills itself as committed to the Mardi Gras parade as a vehicle for delivering their mocking observation in the form of "decorated mule-drawn floats with satirical themes, accompanied by costumed revelers dancing in the streets to the sounds of jazzy street musicians," dedicated to the mission of exhibition, "exposing the world to the true nature of

Mardi Gras—and in exposing ourselves to the world."[18] The women's carnival organization, Krewe of Muses, has been described by Virginia Saussy, a founding officer and chair of their theme and floats committee, as one joke with twenty-six punchlines (a reference to the number of floats in the parade).[19]

Merline Kimble has guided the twenty-first resurgence of her grandparents' social and pleasure club, called "The Gold Diggers," from its inception of a group of close friends, namely Wanda Pearson, Lois Nelson, Patricia McPherson, and sometimes Reza (Cinnamon Black) Bazile, to its current status as an expanding group of primarily women and a sizable contingent of "next generation" children and teens of the Kimble family. There is even a spinoff group called the Treme Baby Dolls created by her sister Janice Kimble, with Gold Digger members and invited guests. The Phillips' group emerged during the era in which Avery Hopwood's 1919 play *The Gold Diggers* came to dominate popular culture in the 1920s and 1930s, first on Broadway and then in a series of Hollywood films: *The Gold Diggers* (1923, silent film), *The Gold Diggers of Broadway* (1929), *The Gold Digger of 1933*, *The Gold Diggers of 1935*, and *The Gold Diggers of 1937*. The Baby Doll masking tradition was born almost a decade before women had the right to vote, and women's masking on the streets on Mardi Gras was not something "respectable" women routinely did.

Under Victorian standards, women belonged at home and never unaccompanied on the public streets.[20] Middle- and upper-class women shopping in areas London designed for them complained that it "seemed to entitle male pests to 'annoy' respectable women who tried to experience the freedom of the city."[21] Women were not supposed to walk the street alone. They could not, even if "tastefully dressed," "take pleasure in the city: to look, to ramble, to get lost in the crowd, to feel abandon and lack of restraint."[22] A woman alone in public was considered to be a "public woman," the object of the male gaze. As Walkowitz wrote, to be "open to public view" was to be open "to public access."[23] It was understood that public arenas were male, even though this idea was challenged by women of color in New Orleans.[24] Once the franchise was secured by American women, masculine construction of the national character and men's dominance over public space was challenged. The city's urban spaces began to be perceived as female, and filmic scenes prevailed where "unruly" women peered through windows and stalked men.[25]

The category of "Gold Digger," the woman who sexualizes her persona, flirts with men, and exchanges her time and body for the exclusive purpose of fleecing them, emerged shortly following the progressive era, when reform activity addressed a variety of social problems includ-

Merline Kimble seated with members of the Original Pinettes Brass Band and Baby Doll maskers: Janice Kimble, Dinah Dedmond, Dana Dedmond, Leslie Dedmond, and Shannon Paxton, October 1, 2015. Photo by Kim Vaz-Deville.

Merline in front of Meryt Harding's portrait displayed at the exhibit "Contemporary Artists Respond to the New Orleans Baby Dolls" at the George and Leah McKenna Museum of African American Art, May 21, 2015. Photo by Phillip Colwart.

Merline Kimble in white with Alfred Doucette Big Chief of the Flaming Arrow Warriors at Jazz in the Park, October 1, 2015. Photo by Kim Vaz-Deville.

Fabieyoun Walker (left), Kermit Ruffins, Merline Kimble (in purple with mask), Carol Harris, and Shannon Paxton at Jazz in the Park September 17, 2015. Photo by Kim Vaz-Deville.

ing prostitution. At that time, the "prostitute symbolized the failure of women to gain access to material benefits of industrial society due to low wages and a sexual double standard in the workplace."[26] During the 1920s, the appearance of the "flapper" growing out of the "new woman" discourses where both black and white women were determined to have greater opportunities, civil rights and the ability to fulfill their own dreams and desires, "anti-prostitution reform discourse moved away from policies embracing economic, social, and political issues. Instead, the discussion narrowed and shifted almost exclusivity to the character of the prostitute—her inherited traits, criminal tendencies, and psychological disorders—so as to define her sexuality and social position as deviant."[27] The Gold Digger characters of the 1920s were written as comedic foil. As the Depression moved in, the films transitioned from "linking gold digging not to the greedy acquisitiveness of prosperous times but to the economic concerns of women trying to survive in the Depression. It revitalized progressive era critiques of unfair labor practices and women's low wages."[28] The idea was entrenched as Gold Diggers portrayed circumstances in which working class women relied on feminine wiles not to acquiesce and submit to patriarchal values, but as a survival strategy.[29]

In the business of leading the Gold Digger Baby Dolls Merline Kimble expects compensation, but she embodies the conscious integration of the ludic nature of masking and being a black woman New Orleanian steeped in the culturally rich tradition of her Treme neighborhood. She epitomizes the playful black woman when masked; she is the unruly woman. The unruly woman is characterized by "excess, exaggeration, and comic incongruity,"[30] whether it is sitting on a sewer grate in her dainty satin dress, her favorite youthful pose of a putting her hand on her hip and the other on her knee a la 1970s fashion models like Maureen Flanagan; being sexually titillating with an elder male big chief as he lifts her skirt to expose her garter or putting her knee across the waist of a younger man, a popular musician.

Since the turn of the twenty-first century, the Baby Doll masking tradition has been enjoying a resurgence. Given the achievements of black women in New Orleans to enter the professions, run businesses, and to parade in organized krewes, are the Baby Dolls still relevant as unruly women? The late Antoinette K-Doe founded a highly popular and visible group of Baby Dolls named in honor of her late husband, the late Rhythm and Blues singer Ernie K-Doe. Geannie Thomas met Antoinette through the singer and became friends because of their similarities. Thomas grew up poor in Gulfport, Mississippi. She was unable to go to school very often because when it rained the mud would be just too thick to trek through. Lack of education made domestic work her primary occupation. K-Doe was also reared in poverty. She too missed opportunities for formal education and worked as a domestic. She also managed several lounges before encountering Ernie. It was at one of these lounges that Ernie came in 'sloppy drunk' for a drink. K-Doe had always been an ardent fan of his. She decided that if she could "clean him up," get him performing again, and get him to marry her, this feat would elevate her social status in her community. She believed it was her ticket out of domestic work. What is consistent throughout the history of the Baby Doll masking tradition is the low rate of literacy and the consignment of these maskers to the economic margins.

The 1912 Million Dollar Baby Dolls and the Ernie K-Doe Baby Dolls shared a desire to "be somebody." The 1912 Dolls existed in a milieu in which women could not vote, black children could not easily receive a public education beyond the fifth grade, jobs were scarce, dirty, and dangerous, segregation permeated education, religion, politics, housing and transportation, and black women's sexual violation was ubiquitous. Having grown up poor and poorly educated, few options were available for either group of women. Yet, they used the tools at hand: the culture, marriage and relationships, and grit to create a live art form that endured. Because of their Baby Doll masking tradition, K-Doe and Thomas became noted and celebrated by New Orleanians.[31]

The pre-Katrina-era poverty of New Orleans was created as in many cities with the vanishing industrial bases in urban areas. While housing projects were designed to be "way stations" on the path to upward mobility, this became truer for whites than for blacks. New Orleans resembled other urban areas in the development of a sizable number of chronically underemployed residents since

> racial segregation in housing affected the geographic location of black employment and reduced black job opportunities. Suburbanization of employment following World War II seriously aggravated the problem. The relationship flowed from housing discrimination to lack of access to employment.[32]

Hurricane Katrina revealed to the nation the results of the inequities facing poor and working class blacks in New Orleans.[33] Culture again would be used to showcase what was wrong structurally and institutionally that reinforced economic inequities and also as a vehicle to gain relief from those inequities. As Lipsitz wrote in 1988, "People fight with the resources at their disposal."[34] While Merline Kimble, Lois Nelson, Cinnamon Black, and their friends and relatives and Antoinette K-Doe and her Ernie K-Doe Dolls resumed their masking, in the Mardi Gras following Katrina, Millisia White, influenced by the late jazz musician and historian Eddie "Duke" Edwards, developed the Baby Doll Ladies as a response to coping with the storm and as a way to distinguish the newly formed company, the New Orleans Society of Dance.[35]

An ever-growing number of women's "walking" groups, which foregrounded their sexuality no matter what their age or body type, are taking root for Carnival season. Among the provocative sounding names, such as "The Bearded Oysters," "The Camel Toe Lady Steppers," "The Muff-A-Lottas," and "The Krewe of Drunken Whores," is one of the earliest: the "Pussyfooters." Founded by Camille Balassar, the group developed as she imagined the fun the high school girls appeared to have while they marched in the parades. Buoyed by conversations stemming from viewing Eve Ensler's *Vagina Monologues*, she started a group for women over the age of thirty. Sporting bustiers, dance routines, and spots in Mardi Gras parades, she offered women an opportunity to enjoy their own bodies in the same way she imagined high school girls did. Ann Marie Coviello, founder of the women-led Box of Wine parade, has asserted that "all the clubs owe a huge debt to the women-led social aid and pleasure clubs. . . . That image of women being able to be sexy and have a different body type really came from black Mardi Gras."[36]

The New Orleans Society of Dance's Baby Doll Ladies follows the character of these new groups: formal membership, staged performances, and choreographed dances. The point of reference for costume and performance for the Baby Doll Ladies is hyper-local. As they parade, the company chants bellicosely about their skill in the art of getting and ensnaring a lover and perform their perceived superiority over other Baby Doll groups in a way that mirrors the Black Indians of New Orleans's fierce proclamations that they "won't bow down" to any man and jockey over whose suits are "the prettiest." The company stops at various points on the route to form a tableau. According to Atkins, a tableau "freezes an entire narrative into a single, poised moment, but those chosen moments, also delivered key messages."[37] In the early years of secret, upper-class, all-white krewes like Comus and Rex, tableaus opened their balls at the end of their parade. Atkins suggests that these portraits served to assert male dominance in a population still reeling from the defeat of the Civil War. Through these sketches the men acted out their anxieties about nationality, wealth, entitlement, and masculinity. They often costumed as "marble men," a nod to the classics that staged not only a show of their virility, but also their sense of timeless domination. Notably, in comparison to the city's other Baby Doll groups, the company's members are younger and appear fitter. The exclusionary nature of

the organization ritualizes the rivalries of the tradition's mythical found-
ers over the oft-cited uptown-downtown divide and the relative value of
groups associated with each location. The Mardi Gras-themed ceramic
mask as souvenir object is the direct reference of the white painted faces,
the group's distinguishing look. The company's founder creates fictive
identities to accompany each mask akin to Blue Book (printed directo-
ries of the businesses in Storyville) descriptions of the ladies awaiting the
district's pleasure seekers. The mask signals the fantasy that a pretty and
enticing face can be purchased. It is the facade that brings the money.
In the district, the high price paid for "sex with a virgin"—a double for
a young girl—renders the Baby Doll masker as making a statement
through inversion and also identifying her as an attainable commodity.
The little girl in the progressive era was not off limits legally as a sexual
object, but it was a moral disapprobation for those outside the sporting
life. The company's "hot" dance is a play on the high-cultured style the
Blue Books touted of upper class refinement in dress and music to be
afforded brother patrons. In the pretention turned on its head what was
actually heard in the brothels most often was the new music of jazz.
Today, the company dances to its generation's new music of Bounce.
The early Baby Dolls appropriated popular culture in their group naming practices, street entertainment, attire, and alcoholic beverage and
tobacco consumption. Like tradition's foremothers, their objective of
achieving or identifying with fame and stardom are announced through
company produced shorts resembling popular culture's music videos.
The company's stock character of a "cigarette girl" carries a box of items
to smoke or candy to eat. Replete with sexual symbolism, the role recalls
the idea of stardom of cinematic elegance from a bygone era. As Blues
Queen, Bessie Smith would sing, "I want to be somebody's Baby Doll."

The company also resembles those social and pleasure clubs and
Mardi Gras Indian groups that perform second lines and masking outside their community and ritual settings. Rather than dismissing these
"for profit parades" as "'tourist' commodities," Regis sees these as opportunities for "cross-cultural communication." "Dismissing them as unau-
thentic only works to further silence groups that have few other venues
for representing themselves to the world." Instead, she adopts the view
that these are "culture making events in and of themselves."[38] Fred Myers
noted that the "rules of production and reception" of staged events are
yet to be determined, and ethnographic work has to be done to assess
the meaning of these productions to the performers and their audiences."[39] For Mardi Gras 2016, the New Orleans Society of Dance's Baby
Doll Ladies announced its newly established walking route along the
city's formal path for permitted walking groups slated to pass the may-

oral grandstand at Gallier Hall, a corridor most accessible to tourists. Regis notes that such staged shows conceal the "street-based expressions behind the iconic show," resulting in the perpetuation of "an effective secrecy through an apparent process of publicity." "Ironically," she notes, "they have been complicit in diverting serious attention away from community-based" expressions of American blackness.[40]

Women's Rites

Owing to the economic organization of enslavement, black women's reproductive capacities were commodities used by owners to create wealth. Either by demanding that women have intercourse with enslaved men or through the sexual violations of rape by overseers or owners, children were bred, slated for the slave market. A separate commerce developed, the fancy trade, for the sale of women, often light-skinned, as concubines.[41] These economic arrangements were accompanied by a scientific discourse developed by nineteenth-century European scientists that alleged that anatomical differences between white and African women proved the latter to be subhuman. Viewing them only as sexual beings who were impervious to rape served to excuse the pervasive sexual exploitation as part of the slave trade and slavery itself.[42] With emancipation, the claim was advanced to gain control over the black male population (whose wealth was increasing) to accuse them of a new crime: that of raping white women, a misconduct punished by lynching. The argument implicated the supposed promiscuous nature of black women (that is, their licentiousness and moral obtuseness), who needed hypersexual men to satisfy them. Freed from white supervision, black men were engaging in the "new Negro crime."[43] Black educated middle-class women fought back through formal organizational activism; some black women in New Orleans took advantage of the ritual opportunity for unruliness to lampoon these racists' myths.

Like women mystics during the Middle Ages, the early Baby Dolls did not attempt to escape their social position, but to play with it. The mystics gained a voice by focusing on having a relationship with God that was direct and embodied. They were excluded from ecclesiastic authority because clerics theologically defined them as too weak to resist sinful behavior. Since they were seen by male clerics as unable to control their sexuality rather than deny their bodies, they turned toward their "exorbitant physicality" as a source of spiritual authority. Their success was unsettling to the ecclesiastical leaders.[44] Some early Baby Dolls flaunted their monetized bodies, showing them off publicly in the way only girl babies could, exposing their drawers-clad genitals. In magnifying herself, determining the terms on which she is seen through showy, loud, boisterous speech, dress, and behavior, the unruly woman reveals what decorum conceals.[45] Comedy played out by unruly women calls attention to "permissible and forbidden desire" operating during their era.[46] Such behavior causes social panic because it occupies the space of liminality in what Russo terms "the perilous realm of possibility of 'anything may go' which threatens any social order."[47]

The appearance of the trope of unruly woman appears throughout New Orleans history in periods of political unrest. One of the principal players in the uprising of the Natchez Indians against the French colonists in 1792 was the wife of the Flour Chief. She was tortured and burned at the stake by the Tunica Indians, who carried out her punishment under the watchful eye of colonial authorities and the colonists who had been captured by the Natchez. Perishing by fire had been a warrior's way of dying. In the face of this anomalous execution of an Indian woman by fire, she is remembered as loudly defiant and proudly Indian, insulting the torturers as opposed to cowering in fear. During this revolt period, Marc-Antoine Caillot, of the Company of the West Indies, costumed as a female coquette to attend a wedding party, suggesting to Sophie White that the "topsy-turviness" of the Natchez insurrection destabilized the gender and race norms of the colonists. The men dressed as unruly women afforded the opportunity to see themselves as creating and controlling the disorder and assuaged the fears of the colonists that they would lose their French identity.[48] Framing the uprising as a ritual of misrule inevitably meant the normal order would be restored. Along this same line, many who saw or were accosted by the reconstruction-era Ku Klux Klan reported that the white vigilante group wore women's clothes: a woman's riding habit, dresses made from cotton or calico print cloth, and sometimes the dresses of their wives.[49]

The Baby Doll masking tradition was founded in the spirit of competition and in the desire to claim the attention of spectators as they processed through the streets. It had no intentional connections to African, Haitian, or European religious legacies that dominated the cultural background of New Orleans's people of African descent. Helen Regis (1999) uses the paradigm of the Haitian *lwa* Guede, not to argue for cultural retentions, continuities, or conscious adaptations, but rather to offer non-puritanical interpretations of the eroticism of second line dance practices.[50] Similarly, novelist Jesmyn Ward claims the right of black writers to align their texts to the classics because stories told by blacks tell universal human stories as well.[51] The black Mardi Gras traditions emerge from the fragments of diverse cultural heritage of the city, but also can best be understood in alignment with cultural productions of satire and parody of secular and religious rituals that offer subjugated people not only an outlet for critique, but a way to move their societies toward change by revealing through ludic play what is suppressed to maintain the social order. The female-centered Eleusinian mysteries and *Guede* theology provide a way of understanding the symbols that are contested and the meaning of existence asserted through the Baby Doll tradition.

> The Baby Dolls are historical, but they were seen as a way to mock the white prostitutes. My family was not involved because they felt ashamed. They did not want to be identified with the prostitutes or those pretending to be prostitutes. They did acknowledge them. My mother Odette Koller (age 93) grew up with them. I asked her today what she thought of them and she said they were bad women. They would get out there and shake and carry on. They were awful. My daddy, trumpeter Reginald Koller, played with all the brass bands from 1940s to 2004. He played with the Tuxedo, Olympia, Baptiste, Preservation Hall and had a hat band with the name of each band. He loved them because he liked to play the music for them and watch the people behind him who would gather and dance.[52]

The costuming and accessories of this tradition have changed over the years, but one aspect endures: the lifting of the skirt to display "drawers," or in today's parlance "bloomers." Stills from Mardi Gras circa 1928–1932 show a very happy crowd enraptured by the dance performance of the two Baby Dolls whose drawers are in full view. In the first, there is a little girl whose face seems to express joy at their performance. In a second still, when one dancer's backside is in her view, there seems to be a look of surprise, if not shock. In the third still, the little girl seems to be recovering from the performance.[53] For some maskers, the intention was to make money, and their little shows would entice a man to pay for more. Mary Thelma Pavageau Labat was born in 1907, masked as a Baby Doll in the early nineteen twenties, when she met her husband, who masked as an Indian on Mardi Gras. She and her sister left school to work to support the family. Her father was too ill to work, and on payday, her mother would say, "Here come my two husbands." At 14 or 15, in spite of her family's disapproval, she put on the short skirts, drawers showing. Once they married, her husband made her stop masking.[54]

The sensual dancing, bawdy singing, and showing drawers cracked people up. What they induced was the ordinary people's popular laughter, the humor that arises from applying satire and parody to the laws, customs, and pretensions of the ruling class. This laughter is filled with references to orifices and protuberances because as Mbembe suggests, "Defecation, copulation, pomp and sumptuousness are all classical ingredients in the production of power."[55] Mbembe notes that power operates intimately. In the New Orleans context, for example, Janice Cosey's great-grandmother Lula Williams Thomas worked as a maid in one of the French Quarter boarding or rooming houses.

> My grandmother Gertrude Thomas Maddison would stay with her some-
> times when she would come from the county. They were from Labadieville
> out by Napoleonville. She was about five years old. The boarders would give
> her a pail and a nickel and she would go get beer. The boarders would re-
> ceive it from the child at the door and pay her a penny. She could remember
> having the measles and being quarantined in the French Quarter watching
> the pretty ladies go by in their parasols and big dresses.[56]

McAlister observed the scene, applicable to many class-based societies, whereby poor bodies nurture, nurse, feed, pleasure, and protect richer bodies. "Sexual, emotional, and physical services are traded or exacted, and the body becomes a central site of power relations."[57] Mbembe points out that ordinary people live out their domination in quotidian prac- tices: "Social networks, cultures and secret societies, culinary practices, leisure activities, modes of consumption, dress styles, rhetorical devices, and the political economy of the body."[58] In these terms, ordinary people "perform their subservience."[59] Vulgar popular laughter, Mbembe sug- gests, is not necessarily directed at resisting the state or deconstructing inequities; it has a variety of other uses including "kidnapping" power and coercing it, "as if by accident, to contemplate its own vulgarity."[60] In this way, the ruled are able to "bear witness to the desire of the power- ful to disguise their own vulgar origins."[61] At times the laughter "drains the official universe of meaning and sometimes obliges it to function in emptiness or powerlessness." Another use comes in the form of appear- ing to "toy with" power rather than confronting it directly.[62] Instead of risking injury or death, in ridicule "they can tame it, or shut it up and render it powerless,"[63] or "modify it whenever possible."[64] The mecha- nisms the powerful used to create its subjects were aimed at disciplining the body, to steal its vitality and render it obedient, and to wrench as much productivity out of it as possible.[65] As such, identities were "con- cocted" for ordinary people that "allowed him/her to move in the kind of spaces where he/she was always being ordered around and where he/ she had to unconditionally put on show his/her submissiveness."[66] Ludic activities offer opportunities to diversify who oppressed people imagine themselves to be.[67]

The Mardi Gras Indian-based song recorded by Danny Baker in 1947, "Tootie Ma Is a Big Fine Thing,"[68] could have been describing the epitome of a Baby Doll in popular imagination. Tootie Ma "can shake that thing." The lyrics tell a story of a woman who appropriates masculine prerogatives via her sexuality. Lyrics such as "she does some things against the law" and "she took my maw right from my paw" do not deter this would-be suitor. In spite of her scheming behavior, he'll be looking to meet up with her on Mardi Gras day and declares that whatever crime she commits, he will bail her out, because "Tootie Ma sure is fine."

For women engaging in prostitution in such overt ways, this behavior would have been a routine part of their business. That the Baby Doll tradition has endured is no doubt made possible by the observation of bell hooks that "the black female body gains attention only when it is synonymous with accessibility, availability, when it is sexually deviant."[69] This is certainly borne out in the context of New Orleans. Janice Cosey's mother Odette Koller (b. 1922) recalled "performing" for white doctors in front of the segregated Touro Infirmary at the instigation of her grandmother, Gertrude Thomas Maddison, who worked there. When she was about four years old, having heard about her grandchildren's dancing so much, the doctors were eager to see the children for themselves.

> She brought them to the Infirmary and said, "Now I want you to shake for these doctors." She started humming and clapping. She was very proud of their dancing. It was a rite of passage. If you couldn't shake your behind, you couldn't proudly please your man.

But such showiness on the part of black women also offered them the ability to achieve a type of spectacular dominance.[70]

> The unruly woman points to new ways of thinking about visibility as power. Masquerade concerns itself not only with a woman's ability to look, after all, but also with her ability to affect the terms on which she is seen. . . . Visual power flows in multiple directions and that the position of spectacle isn't necessarily one of weakness. Because public power is predicated largely on visibility, men have long understood the need to secure their power not only by looking but by being seen, or rather, by fashioning—as subject, as author, as artist—a spectacle of themselves.[71]

The toughness that was a co-requisite for being a Baby Doll became a model of courage and performance for young black girls. Rosalind Theodore, who masks with the Gold Digger and Treme Baby Dolls, continues the legacy Ellyna Tatum, a woman in her neighborhood who was a

Rosalind Theodore in grand marshal tux and Janice Kimble in blue and white on Mardi Gras 2013. Photo by Phillip Colwart.

musician grand marshal. Each year she would don "fishnet stockings, bloomers or shorts, a traditional tuxedo top with tails, and a top hat. She would do a shimmy. Her legs shimmied and she would step as she shimmed. I loved that!"[72] While Theodore may wear a baby doll costume at events throughout the year, for most Mardi Gras days, she masked herself with the tuxedo top and "brings the Baby Dolls out like a grand marshal," because "that's tradition."[73]

Humor offers men a way of bonding that serves to exclude women. For Freud, the most successful of those jokes would force women to leave the room.[74] The Greek goddess of the belly laugh, Baubo, predates women's exodus from the arena of joke teller and punchline enjoyer. The goddess Demeter grieved the loss of her daughter through kidnapping (or willful yielding to seduction) to the god of the underworld, Hades. Unable to move past this trauma, Baubo lifted her skirt, showed Demeter her genitals (and in some interpretations, played with them as well[75]) and told her bawdy jokes. Merlin writes that not only did Demeter not bolt from the room, she laughed and was roused out of her despair. The Eleusian Mysteries observed for millennia reenacted the agrarian cycle from planting to harvesting and the essential bond of mother-daughter of life taken and reborn. The mysteries grand procession occurred during the middle period of the days-long ritual. Leading the way of the initiates, who were hilariously mocked by costumed jesters, was a "raucous old woman named Baubo or Iambe."[76] Women's Baby Doll masking is aimed at other women, to arouse their envy, their admiration, their competition, their recognition, and their laughter. They are playful and silly for each other, as much as they are coquettish and flirtatious with spectators.

At some point on Mardi Gras, the Baby Dolls process with the Skull and Bone gangs,[77] a tradition that begins Mardi Gras in black neighborhoods as they come out of the cemetery wearing a butcher's apron, with skeleton appendages passing for arms and legs, carrying bones and the warning "you next." They are meant to frighten children into living an educated, moral life; to remind the adults of their mortality, and to rouse the community into a day of frivolity, because in the end, there is death. The connection between the *lwa Guede* and the Skeletons of New Orleans has been consciously made by maskers and observers.[78] Although associated with the dead, when the *Guede* appear in ceremony, they do so because they know better than any force the pleasures of life and what it means to miss them.[79] The *Guede* exist at the crossroads of life and death and return with their antics of engaging people in irreverent and infectious bawdy songs, and, though they are incapable of having intercourse, they use lascivious gestures and jokes to mimic acts of copulation, with the aim to induce their followers to laughter and to call attention to their idea that life and death are fused.[80]

In recent years, Baby Dolls have been associated with death in several ways. Antoinette K-Doe, initiator of the resurgence of the Baby Doll tradition in the twenty-first century, commissioned Jason Poirier to construct a life-size statue of her husband as a stand-in for him at the lounge they managed and named in honor of his 1961 R&B hit song, "Mother-in-Law." The "debut" of the lookalike was staged at the Friends of New Orleans Cemeteries' Third Annual Mourning Glory Ball, held at a home of New Orleans native and gothic fiction novelist Anne Rice. Musicians who were owners of tombs in the city's fabled and famed historic cemeteries, Wanda Rouzan and Heather Twichell provided music. Local restaurants catered funeral food, guests were encouraged to wear mourning attire, and Ernie K-Doe (in absentia) was one of three "Gravie" award winners.[81]

The honoring of culture bearers (such as deceased members of Black "Indian" groups and social aid and pleasure club members) by Baby Doll maskers wearing their costumes and being visible during their jazz funerals' second lines has continued to increase. But the appropriation of masculine positions during funeral processions has emerged as a new focal point. The Ernie K-Doe Baby Dolls K-Doe, Geannie Thomas, Eva Perry, and Anita Bowers served as "honorary" pallbearers for the funeral of musician Lloyd Washington, whose ashes Antoinette stored at the lounge until his internment in the Musician's Tomb in St. Louis Cemetery No. 1.[82] The Black Storyville Baby Dolls were asked by the family of Gloria Leblanc Boutte (who was born in 1923 and died in 2015 and buried in a Baby Doll dress) to serve as an honor guard wearing their Baby

Black Storyville Baby
Dolls: Dianne Honore
and Joelle Lee. Photo by
Cedric Ellsworth.

Doll costumes. They led the mourners from the Catholic church as the family responded to the unfulfilled desire of Ms. Boutte to don a Baby Doll costume and dance with abandon on the streets of New Orleans. Her longing is captured in an interview with James Damaria:

> Prohibition, they had the dives and my idea was, I wanted to be a Baby Doll. . . . so I guess I had some of the dancing and wanting to be a little wild. Once I started having children, I couldn't turn out. . . . They would have groups: fat groups, skinny groups, black groups, white[83] groups and each one had enough in it to fill it. They would have short skirts, stockings, bonnets and wire masks. They would have a jazz band riding in a wagon. . . . They would be in there with their . . . home-brew in buckets . . . and they would stop on each corner. . . . I wanted to dance on the corner.[84]

Gold Digger Baby Doll Lois Nelson famously danced on top of the casket of her 17 year old son, Darnell (D-boy) Andrews when he was murdered. Dressed in a slacks or a tux, Nelson embodies the music through her trance-like dance gestures atop the coffin of the deceased culture bearers. Faced with the untimely death of another relative, 28 year old

Lois Nelson at Travis "Trumpet Black" Hill Funeral Second Line, New Orleans, Louisiana, May 23, 2015. Photo by Kim Welsh.

Lois Nelson and family at Travis "Trumpet Black" Hill Funeral Second Line, New Orleans, Louisiana, May 23, 2015. Photo by Kim Welsh.

Travis (Trumpet Black) Hill, who died when an infection resulting from a routine dental procedure spread to his heart,[85] she and her female relatives donned black tuxes and served as the pallbearers for his funeral.

Maskers are out to have a good time, but the form of the masking is constructed through "a work of holy bricolage"[86] consisting of popular culture, life circumstances, cultural memory, pervasive imaginings of women as either virgins or whores, and magic formulations of Hoodoo, religious practices from Voodoo where women actively appeal to supernatural forces to secure the love of men, to the invocations to the Catholic St. Ann.[87] Baby Doll masking, though not consciously, enters the realm of the Haitian *lwa Guede*. *Guede*, a spirit created by the black agricultural laborers of Haiti as a "god of derision," serves as a force that "could burlesque the society that crushed" them.[88] Like the Baby Doll maskers, *Guede* smokes cigars, displays obscene gestures, and prances about while indulging in alcohol and excessive truth-telling talk.[89] During the sacred calendar of late October and early November (corresponding to the feasts days of All Saints and All Souls), groups of *Guede* wear necklaces consisting of pacifiers and battle rattles[90] signaling their fondness for and protectiveness of children.

During one era, Baby Dolls were proud of "walking raddy," which was engaging in a muscular dance of hip and shoulder gyrations, movements that were extremely proactive. *Guede* dance the *banda*, a hip pulsating erotic move performed to its own sacred rhythms. The dancer holds a stick while the lower extremities circle it in a dance that reenacts reproductive sex to symbolize that "death and procreation are intrinsically linked, as one generation yields its presence in the world to another."[91] Banda is also considered "hot dancing." *Guede* is propitiated with objects and foods that are hot with peppers. This "hotness" of food and sex "raises life energy."[92] The Baby Dolls originated during an era of "hot music," and when they felt they were at their best, proclaimed that they were "red hot." McAlister writes that Haitian sexual songs, such as the *betiz* sung during the Easter season, "are a form of popular laughter that comprises the only public form of speech possible for the Rara *ti nèg* (small man)."[93] The realm of sex and satire is ruled by the *Guede* and allows for critique, parody, and laughter. "When you are not permitted to say anything else, at least you can swear, drink and sing vulgar songs."[94] Unless they are Vodou queens, women parading during Rara and singing lewd songs would be considered prostitutes. But

> queens sing as loudly as the men or louder in the spirit of competition. They may hike up their skirts and grasp them in their hands out to the side at waist level, displaying their white slips. When they are intent on collecting money at the height of Easter Week, the slips may come up too, to reveal *kilòt* (underpants) and the prized *pwèl* (pubic hair) that may show at the top of the thigh and will surely be enthusiastically remarked upon by male passersby.[95]

The Baby Doll tradition grew out of a "gate crashing" practice, whereby they imposed themselves on dances, parades and events where they showed up but may have not been invited. Tann writes of the *Guede* as "notorious gatecrashers . . . attempting to hijack a ceremony by leading the congregation in highly irreverent but catchy bawdy songs."[96] Just like second line dancers who attempt to steal the show from a social and pleasure club in the midst of their annual parade by performing on hoods of cars and roofs of houses,[97] Baby Dolls behaved similarly. The attire of *Guede* is a hat with a high crown, a worn black coat, and pants; the apparel of this god is in keeping with his people.[98] The attire of the social and pleasure club grand marshal resembles this uniform[99] and Rosalind Theodore's role model's adaptation of chorus girl and mortician's garb and Lois Nelson's habit of suiting up for funerals, though not conscious, aligns them with transcendent sexual meanings of *Guede*. Nelson's commanding presence atop the coffin recalls Ogun's control of iron, and she dances with his fierceness.

In her manifesto about the tradition posted on her Facebook page, writing of herself and her daughters, Resa Bazile invoked African-derived traditions to distinguish herself from "imitators" and "traditionalists."

> Some Dolls come in thru [sic] "private club invitations"; whereas others are "great imitators." They have no traditional training. They just do it. They do

it because they represent their New Orleans's communities as well as they must truly respect the culture. Allow me to reveal this unspoken act. Being a Doll is not just about butt shaking and being seen all the time. It's a special culture to be seen on special occasions, four to six times a year. It's part of an Egungun, an African procession. Can you step? When do you Dirge? When do you buckjump? What is a "monkeyshine?" It's in the craftsmanship of one building a suit every year. Every year it's carnival time, you get a new suit! Its women working together towards a common goal on projects in their own communities. We are cultural. It's uplifting our children and always honoring our elders. We are traditional.

As the Baby Doll tradition continues to reinvent itself, conscious connections are being drawn to African-derived spiritualties. Diana Garica Brooks, a priestess of *Yemaya* and *Oshun*, smoked a cigar as she donned a goldenrod colored satin dress during the 2014 funeral of the late former president of the Money Wasters' Social and Pleasure Club, Nelson Thomson. The Yoruba deity Obatala appeared in all white to bless the Gold Digger Baby Dolls before their second line parade down Claiborne Avenue on Mardi Gras Day 2016. Using no words, the ancient one conveyed her meaning to them through gestures. Some groups are aligning themselves with Mardi Gras Black Indian groups and coordinating costume colors and incorporating the signatory beadwork of the group. The Baby Doll tradition is experiencing a rapid growth. It remains relevant because it continues to excite women who mask and the new audiences that are embracing them. The practice provides an accessible means of participation in a topsy-turvy tradition where "women are on top,"[100] though they may not be in their everyday lives. What it is to become is not yet unknown. This reimaging of the tradition is in its infancy.

NOTES

1. Quoted in Samuel Kinser, *Carnival, American Style: Mardi Gras at New Orleans and Mobile* (Chicago: University of Chicago Press), 242.
2. Powell, 2011.
3. Stanonis, 2001.
4. Stanonis, 2001.
5. Stanonis, 2001.
6. Stanonis, 2001.
7. Medley, 2008.
8. Photo of King in 1955 http://www.nola.com/mardigras/index.ssf/2016/01/vintage _zulu_louis_armstrong_a.html#9.
9. Roach (1993) suggests the elite Anglo American male krewes threw trinkets at the crowds gathered to watch their parades just when the city outlawed throwing

flour on revelers, as was done by white working class youth. The ability of the elite to "throw" symbolized their being above the law as they were above the crowds on their elevated floats. The result was to "substitute" mirthful behaviors for actual physical confrontation.

10. In 2001, the women's carnival organization Krewe of Muses broke into the prestigious nighttime parade route in "uptown" New Orleans. Previously, in the founder's estimation few women had affordable opportunities for nighttime parading.

11. Martinez, 2008.

12. Roberts, 2006.

13. Roberts, 2006.

14. Gotham, 2002 and 2005, Stanonis, 2006, and Thomas, 2014.

15. Mayer, 2007, 86.

16. The above portion of this paper was originally published as a preface for Rosary O'Neill's *New Orleans Carnival Krewes, the History, Spirit and Secrets of Mardi Gras* (Charleston: The History Press, 2014).

17. DaMatta, 1979, Rowe, 2011, and Russo, 1986.

18. Krewe de Vieux website: accessed July 22, 2016: http://kreweduvieux.org/Mission .html

19. Quote from "Making Mardi Gras: Panel Discussion with the Architects of Some of New Orleans' Parading Organizations," Thursday, January 14, 2016, New Orleans Public Library.

20. The previous Victorian era promoted the social and legal position of women as children. The growing fashion industry began appropriating military inflected uniforms such as the sailor suit, children's clothing and girls' school garb to create trends for women's leisure wear. The height of the "'babysex' aesthetic" peaked in the 1930s with child star, Shirley Temple (Willis, 2001, 319). In the 1920s, these uniform inspired costumes and attire were considered sexy; but in the 1930s they came to be seen as more threatening as women's education and workplace presence increased significantly. A photograph of Merline Kimble's grandparents in the masking attire reflects these aesthetics (Vaz, 2013).

21. Walkowitz, 1998, 7.

22. Nord 1991, 373.

23. Walkowitz, 1998, 16.

24. Owens, 2015.

25. Willis, 2002, 322.

26. Robertson, 1996, 74.

27. Robertson, 1996, 75.

28. Robertson, 1996, 76.

29. Robertson, 1996, 78.

30. Glenn, 42.

31. Grimes, 2009.

32. Mahoney, 1990, 1251.

33. Lipsitz, 2006.

34. Lipsitz, 2006, 121.

35. While the dance company's "signature act" as the Baby Doll Ladies is generally accompanied by D.J. Hektik, the rise of the musical genre of bounce is not conterminous with the resurgence of the Baby Doll masking tradition. The musical performance collaborations of Antoinette K-Doe, Merline Kimble, Lois Nelson, and Resa Bazil who masked as Baby Dolls before 2005 were Rhythm and Blues and Brass Band.

36. Chelsea Brasted, January 28, 2016. "Women Krewes March, Dance into Mardi Gras History," *New Orleans Times-Picayune*, http://www.nola.com/mardigras/index.ssf/2016/01/mardi_gras_women_ladies_new_or.html

37. Jennifer Atkins, *New Orleans Carnival Balls: The Secret Side of Mardi Gras, 1870–1920*, Louisiana State University Press, 2017, 75.

38. Regis, 1999, 497.

39. Myers, 1994, 694.

40. Regis, 1999, 497.

41. Baptist, 2001.

42. Shaw, 2006.

43. Giddings, 1985, 27.

44. Judge, 2007.

45. Rowe, 2011.

46. Glenn, 2009, 49.

47. Russo, 1985, 41.

48. White, 2013. A clerk, Marc-Antoine Caillot, of the Company of the West Indies stationed in the Louisiana colony during the uprising, organized a Mardi Gras masking activity for the amusement of a bridal party.

49. Parson, 2005.

50. See also Fandrich, 2007, and Turner, 2006a and 2006b.

51. Ward, 2011.

52. Janice Cosey, personal communication, November 7, 2015.

53. See Vaz, 2013.

54. Helen Porche, daughter of Thelma Labat, personal communication, October 28, 2015.

55. Mbembe, 1992, 11.

56. Janice Cosey, personal communication, November 7, 2015.

57. McAlister, 79.

58. Mbembe, 23.

59. McAlister, 83.

60. Mbembe, 12.

61. Mbembe, 14.

62. Mbembe, 22.

63. Mbembe, 11.

64. Mebembe, 22.

65. Mbembe, 13–22.

66. Mbembe, 19.

67. Mbembe, 23.

68. Reissued on "New Orleans Jazz Man and Raconteur," GHB Records, 2015.

69. hooks, 1992, 117.

70. Mizejewski, 2007, and Shaw, 2006.

71. Rowe 2011, 11.

72. See Simmons's (2015) discussion of the geography of young black girls' pleasure in segregated New Orleans.

73. Rosalind Theodore, interview with the author, January, 2016.

74. Merlin, 2003.

75. Georgopoulos, Vagenakis, and Pierris, 2003.

76. Keller, 2009, 34.

77. Pierre Monk Boudreaux, 2005, Katie Mae on the album, *Mr. Stranger Man, Shanachie.*

78. Osborn, 2008; Turner, 2006; and Wehmeyer, 2012.

79. Tann, 2015.

80. Tann 2015.

81. *Preservation in Print*, September, 2000, 27, 7, 36. http://www.prcno.org/programs /preservationinprint/piparchives/2000%20PIP/September%202000/36.html.

82. Coclanis and Coclanis, 2005.

83. My research has not turned up any evidence of white women masking in this tradition until its resurgence under Antoinette K-Doe's leadership.

84. "Gloria Boutté: I Wanted to Dance," by James Damaria, https://www.youtube .com/watch?v=pRQtzoNEAIc&feature=share. Accessed November 18, 2015.

85. Alison Fenterstock, "Travis 'Trumpet Black' Hill, Rising New Orleans Trumpeter, Has Died at 28," May 4, 2015. http://www.nola.com/music/index.ssf/2015/05/travis_ trumpet_black_hill_risi.html.

86. Consentino, 1987.

87. Baby Doll masker Resa "Cinnamon Black" Bazile consciously connects her masking practices within the syncretic traditions of the religions that flowed through the Sixth ward, Yoruba *orisha* spirituality, New Orleans Voodoo and a special devotion to the Catholic saint Ann. In 1902 the Shrine of St. Ann was located in that neighborhood. As Estes has noted "matrimony is among the reasons for visiting the shrine, as suggested by this petition known to many Catholic women in New Orleans: 'Saint Ann, Saint Ann, give me a man'" (Estes, 2000).

88. Hurston 220.

89. Hurbon, 1993.

90. Brown, 362.

91. bookmanlit.com/banda.html. Accessed on March 15, 2016.

92. Brown, 1991, 374–75.

93. McAlister, 60.

94. McAlister, 61.

95. McAlister, 62.

96. Tann, 2015, 116.

97. Regis, 1999.

98. Hurston, 1990, 220.

99. Turner, 2006a and 2006b, and Wehmeyer, 2012.

100. Davis, 1965.

BIBLIOGRAPHY

Baptist, Edward. "'Cuffy,' 'Fancy Maids,' and 'One-Eyed Men': Rape, Commodification, and the Domestic Slave Trade in the United States." *The American Historical Review* (2001) 106 (5): 1619–50.

Bettelheim, Judith. "Ethnicity, Gender, and Power: Carnival in Santiago de Cuba." In Juan Villegas Morales (Ed.) *Negotiating Performance: Gender, Sexuality, and Theatricality in Latin/o America*. Duke University Press, (1994): 176–212.

Brown, Karen McCarthy. *Mama Lola: A Vodou Priestess in Brooklyn*. University of California Press, 2001.

Coclanis, Angelo P., and Peter A. Coclanis. "Jazz Funeral: A Living Tradition." *Southern Cultures* 11, no. 2 (2005): 86–92.

Cosentino, Donald. "Who Is That Fellow in the Many-Colored Cap? Transformations of Eshu in Old and New World Mythologies." *Journal of American Folklore* (1987): 261–75.

DaMatta, Roberto. *Carnivals, Rogues, and Heroes: An Interpretation of the Brazilian Dilemma.* Translated by John Drury. Notre Dame University Press, 1979/1991.

Davis, Natalie Zemon. *Women on Top.* Blackwell Publishing Ltd, 1965.

Estes, David. "The Saint Ann Shrine in New Orleans: Popular Catholicism in Local, National, and International Contexts." 2000. http://www.louisianafolklife.org/LT/Articles_Essays/SaintAnnShrine.html.

Fandrich, Ina J. "Yorùbá Influences on Haitian Vodou and New Orleans Voodoo." *Journal of Black Studies* 37, no. 5 (2007): 775–91.

hooks, bell. "Selling Hot Pussy: Representations of Black Female Sexuality in the Cultural Marketplace." *Black Looks: Race and Representation.* Boston: South End, 1992. 61–76.

Hoover, Elizabeth. "Jesmyn Ward on 'Salvage the Bones.'" The Paris Review, August 30, 2011. Accessed http://www.theparisreview.org/blog/2011/08/30/jesmyn-ward-on-salvage-the-bones/.

Hurbon, Laennec. *Discoveries: Voodoo: Search for the Spirit.* Harry N. Abrams, 1995.

Hurston, Zora Neale. *Tell My Horse: Voodoo and Life in Haiti and Jamaica.* Harper Collins, 1990.

Georgopoulos, Neoklis A., George A. Vagenakis, and Apostolos L. Pierris. "Baubo: A Case of Ambiguous Genitalia in the Eleusinian Mysteries." *Hormones* 2 (2003): 72–75.

Giddings, Paula. *When and Where I Enter.* Bantam Books, 1985.

Glenn, Susan . *Female Spectacle: The Theatrical Roots of Modern Feminism.* Harvard University Press, 2009.

Grimes, William. 2009. "Antoinette K-Doe, 66, Who Turned Club into Shrine to Husband, Dies." *The New York Times.* March 1, 2009, A18.

Judge, Jennifer. "Female as Flesh in the Later Middle Ages and the 'Bodily Knowing' of Angela of Foligno." In *The Catholic Church and Unruly Women Writers.* Palgrave Macmillan US, 2007.

Keller, Mara Lynn. "The Ritual Path of Initiation into the Eleusinian Mysteries." *The Rosicrucian Digest* 87, no. 2 (2009): 28–42.

Gotham, Kevin Fox. "Theorizing urban spectacles." *City* 9, no. 2 (2005): 225–46.

Gotham, Kevin Fox. "Marketing Mardi Gras: Commodification, Spectacle and the Political Economy of Tourism in New Orleans." *Urban Studies* 39, no. 10 (2002): 1735–56.

Lipsitz, George. "Mardi Gras Indians: Carnival and Counter-Narrative in Black New Orleans." *Cultural Critique* 10 (1988): 99–121.

Lipsitz, George. "Learning from New Orleans: The Social Warrant of Hostile Privatism and Competitive Consumer Citizenship." *Cultural Anthropology* 21, no. 3 (2006): 451–68.

Mahoney, Martha. "Law and Racial Geography: Public Housing and the Economy in New Orleans." *Stanford Law Review* (1990): 1251–90.

Martinez, Maurice. Cited in Royce Osborn (dir.) *All On a Mardi Gras Day*, Spyboy Pictures.

Mayer, Vicki. "Letting It All Hang Out: Mardi Gras Performances Live and on Video." *TDR/The Drama Review* 51, no. 2 (2007): 76–93.

Mbembe, Achille. "The Banality of Power and the Aesthetics of Vulgarity in the Postcolony." *Public Culture* 4, no. 2 (1992): 1–30.

McAlister, Elizabeth A. "Vulgarity and the Small Man." In *Rara!: Vodou, Power, and Performance in Haiti and Its Diaspora*. University of California Press, 2002.

Medley, Keith Weldon. "Tan Mardi Gras." In *Mardi Gras Guide*, Mandeville: Arthur Hardy Enterprises, 2008. 70–73.

Mizejewski, Linda. "Queen Latifah, Unruly women, and the Bodies of Romantic Comedy." *Genders* 46 (2007). http://www.iiav.nl/ezines/web/GendersPresenting/2008/No47/genders/g46_mizejewski.html.

Myers, Fred R. "Culture-Making: Performing Aboriginality at the Asia Society Gallery." *American Ethnologist* 21, no. 4 (1994): 679–99.

Nord, Deborah Epstein. "The Urban Peripatetic: Spectator, Streetwalker, Woman Writer." *Nineteenth-Century Literature* 46, no. 3 (1991): 351–75.

O'Neill, Rosary. *New Orleans Carnival Krewes, the History, Spirit and Secrets of Mardi Gras*. Charleston: The History Press, 2014.

Owens, Emily Alyssa. *Fantasies of Consent: Black Women's Sexual Labor in 19th Century New Orleans*. Harvard University, PhD dissertation, 2015.

Parsons, Elaine Frantz. "Midnight Rangers: Costume and Performance in the Reconstruction-Era Ku Klux Klan." *The Journal of American History* 92, no. 3 (2005): 811–36.

Powell, Lawrence N. *New Orleans City Guide*. Garrett County Press, 2011.

Regis, Helen A. "Blackness and the Politics of Memory in the New Orleans Second Line." *American Ethnologist* (2001): 752–77.

Regis, Helen A. "Second Lines, Minstrelsy, and the Contested Landscapes of New Orleans Afro-Creole Festivals." *Cultural Anthropology* 14, no. 4 (1999): 472–504.

Roach, Joseph 1993 "Carnival and the Law in New Orleans." *TDR* 37, 3 (T139): 42–75.

Robertson, Pamela. *Guilty Pleasures: Feminist Camp from Mae West to Madonna*. Duke University Press, 1996.

Roberts, Robin. "New Orleans Mardi Gras and Gender in Three Krewes: Rex, the Truck Parades, and Muses." *Western Folklore* 65, no. 3 (2006): 303–28.

Rowe, Kathleen. *The Unruly Woman: Gender and the Genres of Laughter*. University of Texas Press, 2011.

Russo, Mary. "Female Grotesques: Carnival and Theory." In Teresa de Lauretis (ed.), *Feminist Studies, Critical Studies*, Indiana University Press, Bloomington, 1986, 213–29.

Saxon, Lyle. *Fabulous New Orleans*. Pelican Publishing Company, 1989.

Shaw, Andrea Elizabeth. *The Embodiment of Disobedience: Fat Black Women's Unruly Political Bodies*. Lexington Books, 2006.

Simmons, LaKisha Michelle. *Crescent City Girls: The Lives of Young Black Women in Segregated New Orleans*. University of North Carolina Press Books, 2015.

Rebecca Snedeker, 2007. *By Invitation Only*. New Day Film.

Stanonis. Anthony. 2001. "'Always in costume and mask': Lyle Saxon and New Orleans Tourism." *Louisiana History: The Journal of the Louisiana Historical Association* 42 (1), 31–57.

Stanonis, Anthony. *Creating the Big Easy: New Orleans and the Emergence of Modern Tourism, 1918–1945*. University of Georgia Press, 2006.

Tann, Mambo Chita. *Haitian Vodou: An Introduction to Haiti's Indigenous Spiritual Tradition*. Llewellyn Worldwide, 2012.

Thomas, Lynnell L. *Desire and Disaster in New Orleans: Tourism, Race, and Historical Memory*. Duke University Press, 2014.

Turner, Richard Brent. "The *Gede* in New Orleans: Vodou Ritual in Big Chief Allison Tootie Montana's Jazz Funeral." *Journal of Haitian Studies* (2006a): 96–115.

Turner, Richard Brent. "The Haiti-New Orleans Vodou Connection: Zora Neale Hurston as Initiate-Observer." In *Vodou in Haitian Life and Culture*. Palgrave Macmillan US, 2006b.

Vaz, Kim. "How Wounded Healers Help: A Culture-Specific Response to Recovering from a Natural Disaster." Retrieved from http://counselingoutfitters.com/vistas/vistas11/Article_93.pdf

Vaz, Kim Marie. *The Baby Dolls: Breaking the Race and Gender Barriers of the New Orleans Mardi Gras Tradition*. Louisiana State University Press, 2013.

Walkowitz, Judith R. "Going Public: Shopping, Street Harassment, and Streetwalking in Late Victorian London." *Representations* 62 (1998): 1–30.

Wehmeyer, Stephen. "Playing Dead: The Northside Skull and Bones Gang." In Donald Cosentino, ed., *In Extremis: Death and Life in Twenty-First-Century Haitian Art*. Fowler Museum at UCLA.

White, Sophie. "Massacre, Mardi Gras, and Torture in Early New Orleans." *William & Mary Quarterly* 70, no. 3 (2013): 497–538.

Wills, Nadine. "Women in Uniform: Costume and the 'Unruly Woman' in the 1930s Hollywood Musical." *Continuum: Journal of Media & Cultural Studies* 14, no. 3 (2000): 317–33.

Memoirs
and
Musings

How the Baby Dolls Became an Iconic Part of Mardi Gras[1]

—Kim Vaz-Deville

reative her entire life, Clara Marcelin Camel, an early Baby Doll masker, spent her spare time crafting ornately decorated church hats for herself and her daughter, repurposed coats and dresses purchased from remnants, and had "an eye for nice things." Born in Erwinville, Louisiana, and residing in New Orleans for 76 of her 91 years,[2] she was an industrious worker, employed early on in a pecan-shelling factory and finally working into her eighties, she retired from her job cleaning and scaling fish from the Reuther's Seafood Company. She raised her only daughter Eunice as a single parent relying on her minister brother, "Buddy" Stevenson, and his missionary wife for childcare during her working hours. Mr. Stevenson had once ventured to assert that the couple should keep Eunice because Camel was "a little wild." Much of her life had been spent living in the uptown (above Canal Street) area of the city as a renter, always in a half of a double "shotgun" house, and once on Josephine and South Liberty Streets. She attended Ebenezer Missionary Baptist Church on South Claiborne Avenue and was a member in the Winter Capitol Temple No. 427 of the Order of Eastern Star. In retirement, Camel lived comfortably in the home purchased for her by her daughter and family, making her among the first black residents on Roosevelt Place and within walking distance of Bayou St. John.[3]

Born in the 1890s in Houma, Louisiana, Olivia Green left her small community in search of education, employment and fun in New Orleans. Considered a "traveler" by the family, Green enjoyed adult leisure activities and valued having a good time. She decided to forego raising her own family because it would reduce time for pleasure. When Green stopped

Clara Marcelin Camel. Reproduced with the permission of Janice Manuel.

Olivia Green. Reproduced with the permission of Joycelyn Askew Green.

Maskers Brave Chilly Winds To Climax Greatest Mardi Gras

"In a shot of these Baby Dolls, early risers like the Indians, were forced to keep their coats on while waiting for others of their clan to join them in making merry." Maskers Brave Chilly Winds to Climax Greatest Mardi Gras. Saturday, February 14, 1948, *Louisiana Weekly*. Reproduced with permission of *The Louisiana Weekly*.

masking, she increased her participation in the black Spiritualist church tradition that flourished in the first half of the twentieth century.[4]

There are striking similarities in the costuming and studio background of both their formal studio portraits. In their portraits, both women stood with a prop between a painted moon and classicized vase.[5] Both wear a garter at or near the knee and a bonnet with a deep brim far down the forehead, just over the eyes, with ribbon hanging rather than tied in a bow.[6] Their portraits could have been taken at the studio of one of the popular black photographers of the day: Florestine Perrault Collins, Arthur P. Bedou, or Villard Paddio. Olivia's family has speculated that this photo was taken around 1927. The T-strap peep-toe evening shoes were most popular in the 1930s, giving her a more adult look than the younger Clara.[7] These photos suggest that Clara and Olivia were contemporaries. The similarities do not stop with membership in the freedom-loving Baby Doll tradition. Both sought independence in dress-style, both increased their relationship with the divine and the church as they aged, both settled in to extended family life and both of their descents describe them as self-willed and self-defined women, not shy to put pleasure on equal par with the rest of their responsibilities.

In response to her question, "Who are these women and why do they dress like this?," *New Orleans Times Picayune* writer Lynette Dolliole Johnson's grandmother was to teach her about the Baby Doll masking tradition by sharing favorite memories.[8] Johnson described her grandmother who was a teenager in the late 1930s as a woman who loved to dance, attire herself in garish outfits, and to sing and move to her favorite phrases "sucki sucki" and "boogie woogie." She and her friends followed the Baby Dolls on Mardi Gras day and Johnson believed that she was "spurred on in the way she approached life with a sense of fun and confidence" by those who masked. "This tradition is about perseverance and rising above. It was harsh for them when Jim Crow was in full force. They set an example for us that we are, who we are. They were proud of who they are."

Lifelong New Orleanian Millie Charles, best known as the founding dean of Southern University in New Orleans's School of Social Work, was born in 1924. She and her friends used to wait with great anticipation for the costumed group of revelers known as the Baby Dolls to pass their way on Mardi Gras. They stationed themselves at Gertrude Geddes Willis Funeral Home. Travel writer Eleanor Early described this scene as follows:

> Zulu's Queen awaits her Lord on the balcony of the Gertrude Geddes Willis Funeral Home, where thousands have gathered to see her Majesty. The King's floats wind through the streets followed by black and white. Many Negroes are masked. Most of the women are Baby Dolls with blonde wigs and white faces. Many of the men are Indians with feathered headdresses and tomahawks.[9]

Millie Charles recalled that "the Baby Dolls would come with the Indians. They were large women [i.e., not skinny] who looked very serious. They wore beautiful well-made costumes that had layers of ruffles on the skirts. They needed the ruffles to show off their dance of shaking on down," she told me in 2013, as she playfully demonstrated their moves.[10]

Painter Charles Simms, a native New Orleanian, recalled the Baby Dolls as a "New Orleans special" in an interview on YouTube for his 2012 exhibition at the New Orleans African American Museum. "In my youth, a popular Carnival theme was the Baby Dolls, ladies of the night. Young ladies, old ladies used to dress like Baby Dolls. They wore what they called bloomers with fringe around it and a can-can skirt." Their accessories included a purse or basket, a baby bottle and or a sucker. "They would go tip-toeing down the street [singing] "Tra La La Boom Der É.""[11]

Origin of a Tradition

Just how the Baby Doll masking tradition came into existence is buried in many different stories of origin. Beatrice Hill worked as a prostitute in "black" Storyville, the few blocks around Gravier and Perdido Streets. There, gambling, drinking and sex for pay were readily available to both black and working-class white men. Hill said the Baby Doll tradition began as a result of a competition between her uptown (above Canal Street) gang and a downtown group of women working in Storyville itself.[12] Another woman who masked told WPA field investigator Robert McKinney that she always dressed as a Baby Doll and other women began to imitate her.[13] Miriam Batiste Reed dismisses ideas that Baby Dolls were prostitutes and maintains her view that the tradition started with her mother, Alma Trepagnier Batiste.

> "My mother started out with her club," she says. "They were the original Baby Dolls downtown, the first Baby Dolls that came out.
>
> The burgeoning Batiste clan was at the center of Carnival activities every year, Reed says, and open houses, impromptu concerts and festive parades were the norm. At 6 a.m. on Mardi Gras, the women would hit the streets in their bloomers and bonnets alongside the Dirty Dozen Kazoo Band, which consisted of the seven Batiste boys, family and friends. It wasn't abnormal, she remembers, for the gender divide to disappear.[14]

When Alana Harris, (Mama Pretty of the Creole Belle Baby Dolls) informed legendary restaurateur, Leah Chase, that she was going to mask as a Baby Doll, Chase simply said "Je n'aime pas ca." Chase attended St. Mary's Academy Catholic High School in New Orleans in the late 1930s. In those days, Creoles of Color disapproved of the practice. Classmate Ida Mae Thomas's mother, known for being a Baby Doll, raised the girls' ire because she seemed to have money. They whispered to themselves that "the nuns think she is 'hot stuff' but her mother is a Baby Doll." Referring to their costumes, Chase recalled that Ida Mae's mother, a svelte woman added padding to her derriere to add fullness while wearing her costume. Though they did 'nothing wrong,' they were considered 'low-life.' The Creoles also looked down on the Indians; but these groups made Mardi Gras.[15]

Regardless of the veracity of any claim, by the 1930s the Baby Dolls had become an iconic part of black Mardi Gras traditions alongside the Indian gangs, the Zulu Social Aid and Pleasure Club parade, and the Skeleton gangs. The best-known of these early groups were the Million Dollar Baby Dolls. Beatrice Hill said they had sign carriers and a male band consisting of a cornet, flute, drum, and banjo. They wore sexy costumes complete with garters stuffed with money. When the band played Beatrice boasted, "I'm telling you that when the Million Dollar Baby Dolls strutted, they strutted." They sang songs like "In the Evening when the Sun goes Down" that lamented a cheating and unrequited lover and a version of "When the Saints Go Marching in." A particular crowd-pleaser was "You Dirty M—F—, Your Momma Don't Wear No Draw-ers" probably sung to a vaudeville tune. That song lampoons a man who wants to pay for sex while denigrating the sex worker.[16] This particular song is still in the popular lexicon of local musicians and New Orleans hip hop artists known as Bounce rappers.

Memories of the Baby Dolls

The Baby Dolls may have also included men. Willis Rey grew up on Annette and Galvez Streets in the heart of the Seventh Ward. One Mardi Gras morning he heard singing and guitar playing. He looked out his window and there he saw a man playing and singing "I got a big fat momma, she call me her lollipop . . . She's a red hot momma, men love her both night and day. Well now I'm so scared my lollipop gonna melt away,"—a song by New Orleans-born Roy Brown. Another man danced to the music dressed as a Baby Doll. Though it was morning, they both were clearly drunk. Rey said he never saw a woman dressed as a Baby Doll. He had only seen men.[17] Similarly, J. Monique'D recalls "the first gang of Mardi Gras Indians I ever saw in my life was the Yellow Pocahontas. And in those days, they had this group of black men called The Baby Dolls. Here came the Indians, and then here came The Baby Dolls—all these guys that dressed up like babies and little girls. It was really funny to see all these grown up men. It touched something deep inside me."[18]

Maurice Martinez, a historian of New Orleans Creole culture, has a lingering sentimentality for a group of women who masked as Baby Dolls with Alfred Glapion, Arthur Hubbard, and others who formed an accompanying kazoo band. They were from the Seventh Ward on Villere Street near St. Bernard Avenue around the corner from Big Chief Alli-son "Tootie" Montana's home. These Baby Dolls were members of noted society groups: the Original Paramount Club and the Orchid Girls. A group of eight or nine would wear their pretty costumes and sing, "When the Saints Go Marching In" with the kazoo band. Their best-loved and theme song was "Pretty Baby"[19] composed by the black Storyville-era musician, Tony Jackson.[20]

Musician Gregory Davis saw the Baby Dolls on St. Philip Street between Marais and Robertson Streets, deep in the heart of the down-town Sixth Ward, now commonly known as Treme. His recollections date to the 1970s when there were different "factions" of Baby Doll groups masking in the SixthWard who performed dances characteristic of the type of group they were. That is, some groups' performances were more risqué than others. He witnessed his male relatives and their drinking buddies participating in the time-honored permissiveness of Mardi Gras, when they cross-dressed as Baby Dolls. As one of the founding members of the Dirty Dozen Brass Band, Davis was most familiar with the Batiste family's (Lionel and Miriam and their numerous siblings) revived tradition of wearing satin Victorian-era baby doll dresses, bonnets and bloomers. They were accompanied by men playing kazoos and making rhythm with common household items like spoons.[21] Lionel Batiste affectionately remembered that

> the baby Dolls were my momma, my aunt, and the older women in the Treme area. They came out masked at Carnival. They had the Baby Dolls, they had the Dirty Dozen, they had the Million Dollar Dolls. The night before Carnival, they would be drinking, playing the guitar costuming for the Dirty Dozen. . . . Baby Dolls would wear a nice hat, short dresses. They'd wear the leg stockings, put paper money in there. But if you go for the woman's leg, then you're in trouble. People lined up to see us come by; the Baby Dolls would dance and play tambourines.[22]

The Baby Dolls were known for their music, with some songs being chanted and sung in Creole. Lionel Batiste's sample of a Mardi Gras—a song captured in Royce Osborn's "All on a Mardi Gras Day,"—a film about black Carnival—whose lyrics:

> Hé lamizèr fé ma ka manjé pimen.
> Hé lamizèr fé ma ka manjé pimen, (pi mo sou?).
> Hé lamizèr fé ma ka manjé.

are roughly translated by a close friend of the family as "Oh, misery got me eating peppers. Oh, misery got me eating peppers, (and I'm drunk). Oh, misery has me eating." The context is that "the old people used to eat pepper (and or onions or garlic) to take the sickness away."[23] Leonard Huber wrote in *Mardi Gras: A Pictorial History of Carnival in New Orleans* that groups of Baby Dolls would chant repeatedly in Creole "Aye aye mo pé allé quitté" meaning "Hey, hey, hey, I'm going to quit my job."[24]

Eugenia Adams grew up in the Seventh Ward. Her aunt, Emily Bennett, was a modiste who sewed ball gowns for the members of the Venus and Pandora Carnival Krewes. Bennett had a close knit group of women friends. They were bonded by their love of music and parties. They frequented two important hubs of African American entrepreneurship: the

Ms. Lillian seated on the arm of the sofa next to Emily Bennett at a house party. Reproduced with the permission of Eugenia Adams.

Astoria Hotel on Rampart Street and the Pythian Temple on Gravier and Saratoga (today's Loyola Avenue) for parties and events. Bennett hosted an annual New Year's Eve party. One friend, Cadillac Lillian, described by Adams as heavy set and light-complexioned, owned a brothel on Bienville Street, but people regarded her as a successful business woman. She earned her moniker because she bought new Cadillacs frequently. Adams remembered there was another friend that she referred to as Ms. Lillian. Ms. Lillian was a domestic worker and seemingly without the disposable income of the other friends. But like the others, she was gregarious and fun-loving. Ms. Lillian liked to dance, drink home-brewed alcohol on holidays, and mask every Mardi Gras as a Baby Doll. Bennett made a new satin dress with an apron for her every year. The costume consisted of mesh stockings, Mary Jane shoes; a bonnet that was tied under the chin or with strings hanging loose, and a baby's bottle or a lollipop.[25] (See figure in Jerry Brock's essay, "Baby Doll Addendum and Mardi Gras '49.")

Baby Dolls were also uptown. Ms. Linda Green, also known as the "Yakamein Lady," recalled her aunt, Nettie Riley, was an Uptown Baby Doll who masked with Big Chief Robert Lee. On Carnival, they gathered at Jackson and Dryades Streets. Riley was of fair complexion and married to a man who worked on the riverfront. Riley was a sharp dresser, but also "she wasn't nothing nice."[26] Another notable example of an Uptown Baby Doll masker is Mercedes Stevenson, once, queen to the third chief of the Wild Tchoupitoulas Mardi Gras Indian gang when the group was founded. She masked with two of her friends for a couple of years before the gang's founder, George Landry, asked them to join him in the 1970s.

The Tradition Declines . . . and Revives

Over time, participation in the tradition declined, as some maskers grew older, and as time passed, the tradition was deemed old-fashioned, a similar issue experienced by diminishing participation in other black traditions such as the Zulu Social Aid and Pleasure club and the brass band organizations. In addition, when the interstate was built on Claiborne Avenue, the result was to destroy the epicenter of black Mardi Gras celebrations; hundreds of families were dislocated. Furthermore, in spite of the fact that the tradition had drawn participants in all walks of life, it remained tainted with the association to prostitution, making it unfashionable and embarrassing with the rise of the civil rights and black power movements from the 1950s–1970s.

The revival of the tradition began in the millennium with the efforts of Antoinette K-Doe, Geannie Thomas, Eva Perry, Prudence Grissom, Ann Bruce,[27] Charmaine Neville, Felice Guimont, and many others reaching out to Miriam Batiste Reed for guidance and legitimization.

These founding members of the Ernie K-Doe Baby Dolls sought to honor the late R&B singer. Prior to his death, Eva Perry, Geannie Thomas, and Antoinette sang back-up while he performed his old hits like "Mother-in-Law" and "Here Come the Girls" at revivalist events and at the Mother-In-Law Lounge that K-Doe and Antoinette managed on Claiborne Avenue. K-Doe was quite vocal in dissociating her group from the sullied reputation of the Baby Dolls, reminding everyone members of her group were women working in legitimate professions. For example, Denise Trepagnier, an accomplished dress designer and dressmaker, grew up near Elysian Fields Avenue and on Mardi Gras day she saw the women that masked as Baby Dolls.[28] Trepagnier began masking as a Baby Doll when the late Antoinette K-Doe decided to form her group, the Ernie K-Doe Baby Dolls. Under K-Doe's direction, the K-Doe Baby Dolls engaged in charitable works and her magnetic personality made the Baby Dolls attractive to many of the city's most noted women. Trepagnier recalled that Miriam Batiste Reed educated them about the Sixth Ward area Baby Dolls. Trepagnier learned from Miriam that housewives from the area made some of their dresses out of crepe paper. Denise

Denise Trepagnier's replica of a crepe paper Baby Doll costume with Peter Pan collar, puffed sleeves an empire waist carrying three large ruffles matching bonnet, bloomers, socks and umbrellas. Reproduced with permission of Mark J. Sindler/Louisiana State Museum.

replicated such a costume for display during the 2013 exhibit of the tradition, "They Call Me Baby Doll: A Mardi Gras Tradition" at the Louisiana State Museum's Presbytere.[29] Trepagnier prefers a "classic" baby doll style. Her costumes are replicas of the dresses worn by the dolls she played with as a child complete with hat, gloves, and jewelry. As she notes "since we are portraying a certain role, I add some burlesque: a garter and little more cleavage showing than is customary for me."[30]

Merline Kimble and Lois Nelson adopted the name of Kimble's family social and pleasure club tradition called the Gold Diggers. The original group started around Dumaine Street with their band, and carried hand-made baskets as accessories. Nelson brought the musical tradition of her R&B legend father Jessie Hill and the Andrews family's musical contributions. Today, the Gold Diggers, notably Kimble, Nelson, Wanda Pearson, Patricia McDonald, Sarah Brooks, Janice Kimble, Rosalind and Micah Theodore, Elizabeth Smoothers, and Bridget Valdery, can be seen performing with relatives James Andrews and the Crescent City Allstars or second-lining in the Treme with Jenard Andrews's New Breed Brass

Band and also at funerals for culture bearers and Stop the Violence parades. They continue the tradition of women cross-dressing during Carnivals and other ritual events most notably with Rosalind Theodore donning a tuxedo to act as their grand marshal. (See figure in Vaz-Deville's essay on the unruly woman.) At a benefit concert to help pay for the 2012 funeral expenses of "Uncle" Lionel Batiste, Big Chief Bo Dollis Jr. of the Wild Magnolias Mardi Gras Indian Gang invited the Gold Digger Baby Dolls to perform with him. The song he selected, "See See Rider Blues," was reminiscent of the risqué tradition of the Baby Dolls mourning the loss of one of their own. The lyrics bid farewell to a "honey," "baby child" who after a night of carousing comes home with clothes askew. They regret having to leave their honey; they "hate to say bye bye."[31]

When locals hum a tune about Mardi Gras, it is likely to be the song "Carnival Time" by Al Johnson. When residents are looking for Baby Dolls, they're often searching for Resa "Cinnamon Black" Bazile. It's no wonder these two meticulously coordinate their costumes with the rest of the Treme Million Dollar Baby Dolls—daughters Jay Wilon and JaVonee Bazile Chiszle, Natonja Gray, and Tammy Montana, other relatives and friends, and Spyboy Ricky Gettridge—in a style reminiscent of the of the sportin' men and women of the Storyville-era. They offer a tableau vivant that musician and jazz historian Danny Barker might have characterized as "beautiful fast women and well-dressed men having a good time."[32] Resa "Cinnamon Black" Bazile has been masking sometimes as a lone Baby Doll as the practice had waned by the time she began to participate and then with the Gold Diggers and the K-Doe Baby Dolls. After the storm, she became a 'renegade' Baby Doll because it became less possible to mask with any group.[33] Bazile's group, the Treme Million Dollar Baby Dolls, are featured in the annual Satchmo Salute, a second line parade during a festival highlighting the musician contributions of Louis Armstrong. (See figures in Ron Bechet's essay.) After the second line, they are ushered on stage to perform with a brass band and the Fi Yi Yi Mandingo Warriors to the surprise and delight of the crowd. Bazile will dress out for "traditional" events: funerals, second line parades, St. Joseph's night, and Super Sunday, a day Mardi Gras Indian wear their masks, parade through neighborhoods and ritually confront each other. On Mardi Gras Day, Bazile is both a Baby Doll and a Mardi Gras Indian Queen with the Fi Yi Yi Mandingo Warriors Mardi Gras Indian gang. Her masking practices are grounded in the spirituality of the Sixth Ward neighborhood that has come to be referred to as the Treme: Voodoo, devotion to the Catholic Saint Ann, and the Yoruba religion's goddess of sensuality and fertility, Oshun. Bazile participated in the drum circle on Sundays in Congo Square and works in the Voodoo

Museum in the French Quarter. Her devotion to St. Ann derives from the worship carried out at her shrine dating back to 1902. "Matrimony is among reasons for visiting the shrine, as suggested by this petition known to many Catholic women in New Orleans: 'Saint Ann, Saint Ann, give me a man.'"[34]

Controversies

According to Michelle Longino "there is a story that Big Chief of the Golden Eagles Indian Gang, Joseph Pierre "Monk" Boudreaux tells, that back in the day, everyone [the Baby Dolls, Skeletons, and Moss Men, ed.] came out together and making up the "101 Runners." He wanted to recreate that with the Golden Eagles and with many of us who are close friends of the family."[35] When "Monk" asked Longino to Baby Doll with his gang, she went to Antoinette K-Doe who gave Longino her costume to copy and return by Lundi Gras.[36] Prior to this time, men who masked as the Skull and Bone gangs had in the past accompanied him. Boudreaux affectionately calls them 'skeleton men.'

The Golden Eagles Baby Dolls were born in 2009 with women (including Kari Shisler, Jessie Gelini, Michelle Logino, Erika Goldring, Jennifer Johnson and her daughter Marli Jade Mason, Laura and Deborah Vidacovich, and Tiffany Lee Williams) who were fans of local music or who had worked as part of the Jazz and Heritage Festival crew or as advocates for black cultural traditions. They came together at Boudreaux's home after hurricane Katrina and bonded with each other and Boudreaux's family. These efforts were focused on raising money to secure the property that is the site of Boudreaux's home, and, in the case of Longino, working with Tamara Jackson of the Social Aid and Pleasure Club Task Force on an American Civil Liberties Union lawsuit against the city of New Orleans in 2006 for taxing these clubs excessively through charging exorbitant security fees for their parades, hampering their ability to enjoy their First Amendment rights.[37] The Golden Eagle Baby Dolls have been invited to mask for performances, but they confine their activity to masking with Boudreaux primarily for ritual occasions. Longino notes that as Baby Dolls they are not typical of the tradition of women being on the street on their own. As predominately white women, they recognize and appreciate their relationship to the tradition comes because of their connection to Boudreaux. They are not looking to grow their number and have tried to recruit within Boudreaux's circle, black women, to mask with them with little success. They have faced criticism from some who feel stridently that

Recreating the legend of 101 runners. Golden Eagle Baby Dolls on Mardi Gras Day 2011 with Big Chief Monk Boudreaux and the Golden Eagle Mardi Gras Indians. Left to right: Wynoka Boudreaux, Kari Shisler, Jessie Gelini, Michelle Longino, Monk Boudreaux, Mary Nelson, Erika Goldring, Jennifer Johnson and her daughter Marlie Jade Mason, Laura and Deborah Vidacovich, Tiffany Williams, and Joe Stern (Skull and Bones masker). Photo by Jerry Moran.

Golden Eagles Baby Dolls at the home of Big Chief Monk Boudreaux on Mardi Gras February 17, 2015, in New Orleans. Pictured are Jessie Wightkin Gelini, Christy Carney, Tiffany Pruett Williams, Erika Goldring, and Deborah Vidacovich. Photo by Erika Goldring.

white women should not be masking in this way. Criticisms include that these women are appropriating black local culture for their own enjoyment and rather than taking on the mantel of the moniker "Baby Doll" they should use a different referent, that they be an auxiliary group or more appropriately a nonprofit offering philanthropic support for the Boudreau family. The Golden Eagle Baby Dolls counter this criticism with the proviso that they were invited into the tradition by Antoinette

New Orleans Society of
Dance Baby Doll Ladies,
New Orleans Jazz and
Heritage Festival, 2017.
Photo by Kim Welsh.

K-Doe and Boudreaux; therefore it is impossible for them to be considered as usurpers. Yet, they have their defenders. A few Baby Doll maskers feel these traditions should be open to anyone, though paradoxically
those who espouse that view do not themselves have integrated groups.
Boudreaux has determined that it is with his family and these close and
trusted white friends masking as Baby Dolls, Moss Men, and Skeletons
that he wants to experience Mardi Gras and Super Sunday.

Boudreaux has composed a song titled "Katie Mae" about the Baby
Doll tradition that appears on his album *Mr. Stranger Man*. She is a
woman he recalls from his childhood who liked to shake and have a
good time hanging out at the local bar.[38] His song is a testament to the
powerful vector of sensual energy that embodies Mardi Gras's purpose:
to indulge the pleasures of the flesh as an aspect of the cycle of life. It
connotes the concentration of that energy in the character of the Baby
Doll. In the song, Katie Mae, Big Queen of the Baby Dolls, is pretty and
dances through the city with the aim of going to the cemetery to wake up
the skeleton, an important black Mardi Gras character who warns of the
death to come. In the song, her dancing is the means by which the dead
are called back to life: "Katie Mae was shaking them up."

Millisia White's company, the New Orleans Society of Dance, has a
signature act called The Baby Doll Ladies. The company's ribald chant,
"Fire in their Drawers," written by Eddie "Duke" Edwards, is performed
to a soundtrack provided by Calvin "DJ Hektik" Dyer, their "musical

ambassador" and White's brother. Edwards was a drummer, composer, and jazz historian whose aunt "Vanilla" masked as a Baby Doll during the tradition's heyday. His chant reflects the boldness that was the reputation of Baby Dolls as "tough" women. Every line is meant to highlight the transgressive behavior of women who through the power of their sexuality can "make their own laws." When Baby Dolls "crack the whip," women lose their men and men lose their minds. That's the meaning of the chant's bold assertion: "fire in their drawers." The Baby Doll Ladies' dances are set to contemporary New Orleans music, which blends brass band, funk, and bounce. To express resilience, in the 2011 Zulu parade the group performed to the Free Agents Brass Band's "We Made it Through That Water," a song that narrates the experience of people left in the city after the levees were breached during Hurricane Katrina and their determination to survive and rebuild. While Soulja Slim's song, "Make It Bounce" fits a patriarchal fantasy of women 'werking it,' the Baby Doll Ladies performance in the 2014 Macy's Day Parade appropriated the song to celebrate black women's bodies.

White's group is not without its controversies. Like the Golden Eagle Baby Dolls, White's group was born out of the recovery period in which she learned about the tradition from Duke and personalized it for use in her dance company. Her group is distinguished by the use of painted images using theatrical make-up to have each "doll" embody a different aspect of her interpretation of the carnival spirit. The idea is to present a tableau format with the porcelain mask that has come to represent New Orleans Mardi Gras krewe practices at their balls as a main feature. With the exception of the Golden Eagle Baby Dolls, those who mask as Baby Dolls also seek opportunities to work in the entertainment industry, often as Baby Dolls. But unique to this group, critics charge that the Baby Doll Ladies are disconnected from community-based masking, the traditional masking community where not all appearances are paid jobs but are opportunities to express the 'indigenous' art-form such as on Mardi Gras day in black neighborhoods and on St Joseph's night. Also at issue for some culture bearers is the use of the theatrical face paint. Some think it represents too far a departure from the tradition where in the early days, masks were worn and later masks were not worn at all. For other critics, the use of the face paint is a false consciousness reflecting the mimicking of adopting Eurocentric standards. Some women who once masked with her honorary Baby Doll unit have withdrawn their participation, citing a preference for young bodies that are svelte, a departure from the implicit community-based critique by middle-aged and older women unapologetically celebrating their bodies in whatever shapes these take.

A New Generation and an Expanded Interpretation

The Baby Doll tradition is spreading throughout the city once again. Like the Gold Digger Baby Dolls and the Batiste family's Happy House Social and Pleasure Club, Joycelyn Green is influenced by her family's past participation. Green's most recent costume is based on the circa 1927 photo of her great aunt, Olivia Green wearing her Baby Doll costume. It was made by a local modiste, Deborah Sylvest Martin, and according to Green "this dress represents three things: the kente cloth affirms my African heritage. Second, the *Gye Nyame* (meaning only God Almighty knows the beginning and the end) in the fabric symbolizes my spiritual journey. Third, the bonnet, dress, socks and shoes showcase the over 100-year culture and traditions of our ancestors in New Orleans."[39] (See figure in Phillip Colwart's artist statement.)

Dianne "Sugar Baroness" Honore has founded a group she calls Black Storyville Baby Dolls that is grounded in historical interpretation. In 2015 Honore ran Gumbo Marie's Creole Store located on Bayou Road. The store sponsored a costume exhibit, panel discussion, and film preview on the topic "From the Shackles to the Streets: Origins of Black Mardi Gras Traditions, a discussion on slavery, reconstruction, and Mardi Gras." (See figure in Kim Vaz-Deville's essay, "Is the Unruly Woman Masker Still Relevant?") The group stresses the origins of the tradition in the era of "the district," as it was popularly called. Events such as "A night in Storyville with the Black Storyville Baby Dolls at Julius Kimbrough's Prime Example Jazz Club" featured "a full dinner menu, full bar, short film, Ra Ta Te' with historians, early Jazz music, dancing, toasting, a good old fashion time." Honore makes explicit connections of her group with Afro-Creole culture such as using Creole terms like

> Ra ta té, according to my grandmother and mother, meant one who sits on the porch bragging and running their mouth! I can hear my Grandmother say "E's settin' out dere ra ta té -ing wit E's breta een law!" Translation: "He's sitting out there running his mouth with his brother-in-law!"[40]

Founding members include: Joell "Jo Baby" Lee, Anita "Magnolia Rose" Oubre, Lauren "Baby Blou" Blouin, and Arsene "Scarlett Monarch" DeLay.

Alana Harris, Omika Williams, and Fabieyoun Walker and Kadrell Batiste started a group they named the New Orleans Creole Belle Baby Dolls. (See figure in Phillip Colwart's artist statement.) While Harris (known as "Mama Pretty"), the group's founder has an Afro-Creole family background as well as relatives who were active in the civil rights movement. She incorporates the concept of "black power" into the group's

Black Storyville Baby Dolls and Royce Osborne's Skull and Bones Gang, Mardi Gras 2016 in front of Kermit Ruffins's Mother-in-Law Lounge. Photo by Kim Vaz-Deville.

New Orleans Creole Belle Baby Dolls with Big Queen of the Wild Magnolias, Laurita Dollis, Mardi Gras 2016. Reproduced with the permission of Alana Harris.

social mission. The group made its debut Mardi Gras 2016 with Bo Dollis Jr and the Wild Magnolia Mardi Gras Indians. Over time, the group members have included: Harris's daughter, Lyndee "Baby Doll Pinky" Harris, Karen "Baby Doll Rose" Williams, Saran "Baby Doll China Doll" Bynum, Cassidy "Baby Doll December" Ison, Demi "Baby Doll Dimples" Harris, Brandon "Baby Doll Lilly" Bigard, Aidan "Baby Doll Butterfly" Bigard-Sallier, Brenton "Little Police" Bigard-Sallier, and Deborah Taylor.

Maskers with Carol "Baby Doll Kit" Harris and the Wild Tchoupitoulas Mardi Gras Indians during the 2015 Katrina Walk and Pub Crawl commemorating the ten-year anniversary of Hurricane Katarina. Pictured are Dinah "Baby Doll Sassy" Dedmond, Donna "Baby Doll Panoonie" Dedmond, Shannon "Baby Doll Chocolate" Paxton and Leslie "Baby Doll Lollipop" Dedmond who are the Wild Tchoupitoulas Baby Dolls. Photo by Kim Vaz-Deville.

Carol "Baby Doll Kit" Harris began masking with Eva Perry and in August 2015 debuted her own group who accompanied the Wild Tchoupitoulas Mardi Gras Indians on a historic Katrina Walk, commemorating the destruction and resilience of the group and their community. She was being joined by new maskers with fanciful monikers: Dinah "Baby Doll Sassy" Dedmond, Donna "Baby Doll Panoonie" Dedmond, Shannon "Baby Doll Chocolate" Paxton and Leslie "Baby Doll Lollipop" Dedmond who have subsequently become the Wild Tchoupitoulas Baby Dolls. Baby Doll maskers' association with a particular Mardi Gras Indian group is a very current development whose longevity is yet to be tested.

By spring 2016, Baby Doll Kit had left the Wild Tchoupitoulas Baby Dolls to continue the independent tradition of the Baby Dolls, forming a group called Nawlins' Dawlins whose members include Janae and Monae Pierre, Sonji White among others Eva Perry has received a proclamation from Council of the City of New Orleans as a traditional culture bearer, which also recognizes her newly formed spin-off of the group she helped to found. Her new group is the Tee Eva Ernie K-Doe Baby Dolls with notable members being daughter Vanessa Thornton and granddaughters, as well as Gilda Lewis and Michelle Graham.

There is no need to name oneself or to attach oneself to a group. This is the tradition of free spirits. Kadrell Batiste now masks alone as Renegade Rebel, Baby Doll Mahogany. Anita Oubre has formed her own group of Mahogany Blue Baby Dolls with Vicki "Babydoll Lady Lotus"

Super Sunday, March 20, 2016 Mary K-Stevenson (right), second queen of the Wild Tchoupitoulas Mardi Gras Indians with Carol "Baby Doll Kit" Harris's Nawlins Dawlins Baby Dolls: "PJ" (left) and Sonji White (center) at their first masking appearance. Photo by Kim Vaz-Deville.

Carol "Baby Doll Kit" Harris and Wanda Pearson at tribute second-line for Mercedes Stevenson, August 20, 2016. Photo by Kim Vaz-Deville.

With Carol "Baby Doll Kit" Harris' Nawlins Dawlins Baby Dolls, Jane and Monae Pierre at Super Sunday, March 20, 2016. Photo by Kim Vaz-Deville.

Rhonda Washington of the Baby Doll with the Mohawk Hunters Mardi Gras Indians. Photo by Michael Neustadt.

Left to right: Baby Doll Katrice, Little Queen A'mil and Spyboy Radee of the Young Generation Warrior Indians, on Pauger and Rocheblave Streets on Mardi Gras 2017. Photo courtesy of Katrice Clark.

Gold Digger Baby Doll Janice Kimble's grandchildren, Armani, Elijah and Dwayne with their father, Leroy Amour and Merline Kimble's grandson Neko, Mardi Gras day. Photo by Phillip Colwart.

The newly formed Montana Dancing Baby Dolls joined in their family celebration of the Gold Digger Baby Dolls honoring their family tradition at the Backstreet Cultural Museum, Mardi Gras 2017. Photo by Freddye Hill.

Mardi Gras day 2016, Janice Kimble and her granddaughter second line on Claiborne Avenue. Photo by Phillip Colwart.

Wilson and Christina "Babydoll Gentilly Lace" Bragg. Rhonda Washington masks as the sole Baby Doll with the Algiers-based Mohawk Hunters Mardi Gras Indian Gang. Katrice Clark has joined her brother, Asmar Clark, a spy boy in the Young Generation Warrior Indians tribe, to mask as the group's Baby Doll. Denise Trepagnier calls herself a 504 Eloquent Baby Doll. Satin Mitchell who began in the tradition with Trepagnier now dubs herself the Satin Eloquent Baby Doll and frequently masks with Baby Dolls of various groups.

As for the future of the tradition, some maskers are training their young family members. The Gold Digger Baby Dolls have undertaken a concentrated effort to train the next generation in the art of the second-line, the grand marshal and the performance traditions of the Baby Dolls. The entrance of the very young into the tradition will ensure its continuation.

NOTES

1. A part of this article was originally published in the February 2015 issue of *OffBeat Magazine, New Orleans and Louisiana Music and Culture Publication*. Subscriptions are available at www.offbeat.com. Used by permission of publisher.

2. Her obituary appeared in the *New Orleans Times Picayune* on December 30, 1997. Accessed at http://files.usgwarchives.net/la/orleans/obits/1/c-02.txt.

3. Janice Manuel, personal communication, April 7, 2017.

4. Joycelyn Green, personal communication, 2011.

5. Thanks to art historian, Mora Beauchamp Byrd for the confirmation, personal communicataion, May 9 2017.

6. Wayne Phillips, Curator of Costumes and Textiles and Curator of Carnival Collections at the Louisiana State Museum, personal communication, May 11, 2017.

7. Ibid.

8. Lynette Dolliole Johnson, June 27, 2015, "From the Shackles to the Streets: Origins of Black Mardi Gras Traditions, a discussion on slavery, reconstruction, and Mardi Gras" sponsored by Gumbo Marie's Creole Store, 2513 Bayou Road, New Orleans, LA 70119.

9. Early, 1947, 275.

10. Millie Charles, personal communication, February 25, 2013.

11. The legend of the way that song became a Vaudeville hit is that it emerged from a singer, Mama Lou, at a brothel in St. Louis owned by Babe Connor, a black woman. The song was part of black folk music sung on the levees. It was heard many white men but Henry Sayers copyrighted it. During the song, it was reported that the women would lift their skirts to show their underwear or lack thereof (Stanfield, 1997). Babe was also said to have gotten black Creole women from New Orleans to work in her establishment leading me to wonder about a diaspora of sex trade among black madams with its attendant cultural exchanges.

12. McKinney, 1939.

13. McKinney, 1940.

14. Rally of the Dolls, Noah Bonaparte Pais, February 16, 2009. Gambit.com accessed July 16, 2016: http://www.bestofneworleans.com/gambit/rally-of-the-dolls/Content?oid=1256917

15. Leah Chase, personal communication, Wednesday, February 22, 2017.

16. McKinney, 1939.

17. Willis Rey, personal communication, November 29, 2014.

18. Scott, 1997.

19. Interview with Maurice Martinez, June 24, 2011.

20. Toni Jackson's originally lyrics for the song "Pretty Baby" were risqué (and some think it was penned with his male love interest in mind) and was sung in brothels and bars until becoming popular when in 1916 it was featured in a Broadway revenue called the *Passing Show of 1916* at the Winter Garden Theater in New York City.

21. Gregory Davis, personal communication, February 20, 2014.

22. Burns, 2006, 90.

23. Darlene Reed Roberts asked her mother Miriam Batiste Reed to translate, but she declined. Darleen asked a Creole speaking friend to translate and the result is recounted here. This was in March, 2013.

24. Huber, 69.

25. Eugenia Adams, personal communication, October 17, 2012.

26. Linda Green, personal communication, February 15, 2014.

27. See her artist statement in this volume.

28. Personal conversation, July 2015.

29. The dress has a Peter Pan collar, puffed sleeves an empire waist that carries three large ruffles. The bodice is adorned with pink and white buttons and a white satin belt and bow for accent. The collar is trimmed with a delicate white ruffle while the sleeves and hem has a larger one inch white ruffled trim. The "bonnet" is the brim of a hat that is fashioned out of cardboard covered with pink crepe paper and trimmed with pink ruffles. The pink and white satin sash is attached using fluffy bows that frame the face. The garter is made of pink and white paper, satin ribbon and a satin bow. The socks are also trimmed with pink and white crepe paper and fluffy bows for added accent. The umbrella is decorated with 458 sequins and 458 seed beads all hand tied and knotted three times. Thirty-five paper flowers resembling carnations, roses, peonies and camellias decorate the umbrella. Brown pipe cleaners are "stems" and green satin ribbon connects the flowers to the stems. Pink satin ribbon divides each panel of the umbrella and continues to the underside to create eight streamers for eight little flowers to dance, twirl and second line. The four inch pink ruffled trim and "flower garden" gives the umbrella a distinctly feminine look.

30. To make the fanned out skirt she uses twenty yards of toile. She gathers the toile and sews onto the petticoat and then attaches the petticoat to the dress. She hems the toile with fabric from the dress to prevent it from tearing her stockings. She makes a slip to wear under the dress from the same fabric as the dress so that when she flips her skirt while dancing or teasing an admirer, only finished work is visible. The bloomers are made like little girl panties with ruffles on the bottom and lace on the leg and bows. The hat is a brim that frames the face and ties under the neck. There is no back. The hat follows the pattern of the Batiste family. She makes ruffles to attach to her hat and umbrella from left over fabric from her dress. Her process to strengthen the cloth for use as ruffles is to treat it with fabric stiffener allowing it to soak and drip dry. She embellishes the entire costume with beads, sequences, rhinestones. Some embellishment are often hand made. For example, to make a flower to top the umbrella, she cuts three strips of

a fabric such as organza about an inch and a half. Scalloping the top of the fabric and spraying it with Fray Check to keep it from raveling, she gathers the fabric strips and hand stiches them while winding the fabric into a full blossom.

31. Second line for Lionel 414, July 15, 2012. Access at: https://www.youtube.com/watch?v=A2TV-wmrwag&feature=bf_prev&list=UUv_dLNMQKNCfYhRvu6mhVsQ.

32. Barker, 2001, 59.

33. Flynn, 2005.

34. Estes, 2000.

35. Michelle Longino, Kari Shisler, Tiffany Williams, and Erika Goldring, group interview, May 18, 2015. Founding members of the Golden Eagle Baby Dolls are Michelle Longino, Erika Goldring, Jessie Ritter Wightkin, Tiffany Williams, Jennifyah Johnson, Kari Shisler, and Deborah Vidacovich.

36. Michelle Longino, personal communication, July 25, 2015. Lundi Gras is a recent label for the day before Mardi Gras.

37. Lash, Jordan August 5,2015, End of the Line. *Slate*. Accessed July 16, 2016, at: http://www.slate.com/articles/news_and_politics/history/2015/08/katrina_anniversary_the_second_line_has_become_a_symbol_of_new_orleans_resilience.html.

38. Pierre Boudreaux, personal communication with Erika Goldring, May 18, 2015.

39. Jocyelyn Green Askew, personal communication, March 27, 2015.

40. Keith Weldon Medley (2016). "Healing through History: A Ra Ta Té with Dianne Gumbomarie Honoré." *The New Orleans Tribune*,32, 1. Accessed July 19 at: http://www.theneworleanstribune.com/main/healing-through-history-a-ra-ta-te-with-dianne-gumbomarie-honore/.

BIBLIOGRAPHY

Barker, D. 2001. *Buddy Bolden and the Last Days of Storyville*, A. Shipton (Ed.). New York Bloomsbury Academic.

Burns, M. 2006. A Note on the baby Dolls. In *Keeping the Beat on the Street: The New Orleans Brass Band Renaissance*, 93–94. Baton Rouge: Louisiana State University Press.

Cooperman, J. (September 19, 2014). Babe & Priscilla. *St. Louis Magazine*. Accessed at http://www.stlmag.com/table-of-contents-%28september-2014%29/

Early, E. 1947 *New Orleans Holiday*. New York: Rinehart.

Estes, David. The Saint Ann Shrine in New Orleans: Popular Catholicism in Local, National, and International Contexts." 2000. http://www.louisianafolklife.org/LT/Articles_Essays/SaintAnnShrine.html.

Flynn, K. (March 18, 2015). Baby Doll tradition remains a rich part of New Orleans' and Mardi Gras culture. NOLA.com|The Times Picayune. Accessed at: http://www.nola.com/arts/index.ssf/2015/03/mardi_gras_baby_doll_tradition.html.

Huber, L. 1976. *Mardi Gras: A Pictorial History of Carnival in New Orleans*, Gretna: Pelican Press.

Jordan, S. "Carnival Tales: Local Folks Remember Mardi Gras," *Offbeat Magazine*, February 1, 1997. Accessed at http://www.offbeat.com/articles/carnival-tales-local-folks-remember-mardi-gras/.

McKinney, R. 1939. "History of the Baby Dolls," Folder 423, Federal Writers' Project, Cammie G. Henry Research Center, Watson Library, Northwestern State University of Louisiana.

———. February 9, 1940. "A Real Baby Doll Speaks Her Mind," Folder 423. Federal Writers' Project, Cammie G. Henry Research Center, Watson Library, Northwestern State University of Louisiana.

Osborn, R. 2003 *All on a Mardi Gras Day.* New Orleans, LA: Spyboy Pictures.

Simms C. 2012. "Baby Doll" Accessed at https://www.youtube.com/watch?v=ibepBfx hOgM.

Stanfield, P. (1997). "An Octoroon in the Kindling": American Vernacular and Blackface Minstrelsy in 1930s Hollywood." *Journal of American Studies* 31, no. 3: 407–38.

Uncle Lionel Batiste, photo by Michael P. Smith.
Reproduced with permission of The Historic
New Orleans Collection.

In Memory: Uncle Lionel Batiste (February 11, 1932–July 8, 2012)

"Colorful in Life—Rich in Spirit"

—Jerry Brock

*L*ionel Batiste was the co-leader, a featured singer, and the bass drum player with the Treme Brass Band from its inception until he passed away in July 2012. He was an avid second liner, participant in the black parade culture of New Orleans, and a good friend. When he died, I was moved to write a memorial piece for his family. This article expands that work.

Perhaps the smartest thing Benny Jones did when he started the Treme Brass Band was to bring his uncle by marriage, Lionel Batiste, into the group. For Uncle Lionel, music was as natural as breathing air. When he entertained there was no pretense or burden of expectations, no lack of confidence or hint of arrogance. He was beyond good or bad taste. It was always about how we are in this thing called life together: "Would you care to dance?"

The marvel is that Uncle Lionel was born economically underprivileged during the Great Depression at the height of Prohibition (possibly the reason for his preference for home brew) in an era of intense segregation enforced by the notorious "White League" administration of Mayor T. Semmes Walmsley.[1] With the support of his immediate and extended family and friends, he bent a life burdened with inequality into a triumphant and uplifting personal expression of humanity, celebration, and kindness. That is the beauty of the New Orleans music culture that Uncle Lionel grew up in and embraced. As Louis Armstrong once said, "What we play is life and the natural thing."[2]

Music was a natural thing for the Batiste family from the cradle to the grave. They were not professional musicians; for decades only Lionel's family and the community that he lived in knew of his musical talent and modest allure. This was a family for whom community-based music, second line parade culture, and the Spiritual Church provided healing forces. In the face of racist oppression, these powerful outlets for creative expression nurtured a sense of freedom, positive self-identity, and benevolence, individually and collectively, albeit beyond mainstream social norms.

✦ ✦ ✦

On January 28, 1909, Walter Lewis Batiste married Alma Trepagnier.[3] Walter was born c.1890 and Alma c. 1892.[4] Their union birthed eleven children: Walter, Alma, Elvidge, Ferdinand, Henry, Rodney, Arthur, Norman, Lionel, Miriam, and Felecia. Fittingly, the name Walter from German means "leader of the army" and Alma from Spanish means "the soul."

Walter Batiste's ancestors are a bit of a mystery. Walter first appears in the historical record in Algiers living by the levee on Patterson Street at the age of seven with his older brother Arthur and their Uncle John and Aunt Mary.[5] John Batiste declared that he was a "Preacher of Gospel" and that his father (Lionel's paternal great grandfather) was born in Africa and his mother in Maryland. As a young man Walter worked as a stable man and blacksmith and later as a porter at various establishments.[6]

Alma was the daughter of Ursin (born c. 1871–75) and Marie Francois Trepagnier (born c. 1870–1875). Her siblings were Arthur and Marselette (later called Mercedes) and Gustave Mansion.[7] The Trepagnier family is one of the historical families of New Orleans and Louisiana. Claude Trepagnier, a French Canadian, traveled to the Louisiana Colony in 1699. He fathered seven children and founded a large, varied, and multi-ethnic clan of Trepagniers in Louisiana.[8]

Jean Francois Trepagnier II (b. 1747) established Trepagnier Plantation in St. Charles Parish and was one of two plantation owners killed in the Slave Revolt of 1811.[9] Ironically, there is a chance that Lionel had ancestors on both sides of that battle, as he did in the Civil War. Norbert Trepagnier (b. 1824, d. 1891), slave owner, business and landowner near Tunisburg (below Algiers), was a decorated Civil War Captain in the Confederacy, severely wounded in the failed defense of Baton Rouge. Before and after the war he was involved in politics and became Recorder of First District Court.[10] He marched along with John Treme and other dignitaries in a New Orleans reception parade for ex-President James Polk in 1849.[11]

Uncle Lionel's maternal grandfather Ursin was the son of Francois Trepagnier and Louise Daniel.[12] Ursin's paternal grandfather was also named Francois, and he resided in Treme's Fifth Ward as early as 1860.[13]

Ursin's father, Francois, mustered into the Confederate Army as an original member of the Louisiana Native Guards Militia on May 2, 1861, and, in turn, he volunteered in the Union Army on July 2, 1863, in Company A, Sixth Regiment, Louisiana Infantry (African Descent).[14]

As a soldier, Francois Trepagnier's duty was to learn drills and tactics that included formation of lines, marching, and battle formations; the most advanced likely being the first line and the second line. He did not see action in battle as did some soldiers of African descent, but he directly experienced and participated in the socio-psychological battle for black freedom, equality, and independence on the streets of New Orleans by marching in drills, parades, and in the funeral procession of a black Union officer Andre Cailloux on July 29, 1863.[15]

In 1887 a Marie Trepagnier was on a committee that organized a "Grand Dancing Festival" given by the Club du Foyer D'Amitié at the St. Angele & St. Alexis Hall on Bayou Road (Gov. Nicholls) between Villere and Robertson streets.[16] It is possible that this was Lionel's grandmother. Ernest "Nenesse" Trepagnier (1890–1968) played bass drum with the Excelsior, Onward, and Tuxedo brass bands, as well as drums with Clarence Williams, Manuel Perez, Armand J. Piron, the Olympia Orchestra and many others.[17]

Uncle Lionel did not necessarily know or have knowledge of any of the aforementioned Trepagniers, but he was related to them. Only Lionel's older brothers and sisters had direct contact with their grandparents Marie and Ursin Trepagnier. But, the multi-generational spiritual influence of their great uncle Jean Batiste and the experience of the struggle for freedom and equality manifested by marching in the streets as done by their great grandfather Francois Trepagnier were deeply rooted in Lionel's immediate family as deeply rooted as the trait that they spoke both French and English at home.

✦ ✦ ✦

Walter and Alma Batiste lived with Marie Trepgnier for at least the first twelve years of their marriage. In 1910 they resided at 936 St. Claude Street. The Treme neighborhood then included Germans, French, Hispanic and Latin Americans, Yugoslavians, Africans and Afro-Caribbeans, people of mixed heritage, and a preponderance of Italians.[18] Down from the Batistes lived the Tessitore family, who owned and ran a grocery and saloon at 942 St. Claude. The two families were close for many years. "I was born on the second floor above the Caldonia," Uncle Lionel once told me as we walked past the corner of St. Philip and St. Claude. "Man, they made some noise there. My mother used to cook for them."[19]

By 1932, when Uncle Lionel was born, the family had moved around the corner to 1215 St. Philip.[20] "When I was young, St. Claude had blacks on one side and whites on the other. St. Philip was mostly black, but on Ursulines Street it was mostly white—they were mostly Italians."[21] "[At 1300 Ursulines] there was a little store. That's where we'd go for ice cream. We couldn't go inside. We got served at the window. The Pericones had that. Down the block [1100] lived the Brocatos and Camporas. They owned sweet shops, bakeries—confectionaries, we called them."[22]

Lionel's father, Walter Sr., for a time worked at Routher's Bakery on Orleans Avenue, and his mother, Alma, took in wash at home. His mother and his oldest sisters Alma and Elvidge became active in the Spiritual Church. His mother was a charter member of the Three Star Temple Spiritual Church in 1941,[23] and active with the Channel of Faith Spiritual Church and the St. Joseph Helping Hand Spiritual Church of Love; as well as the Crescent City Temple No. 135 (Eastern Stars) and the Daughters of the Elks. She respectfully elevated to the position of Reverend Mother Sister Alma Batiste, as did her daughter Reverend Mother Sister Elvidge Batiste Colar.[24]

As a child Uncle Lionel, like many youngsters who grew up near the French Quarter, hustled money by shining shoes and tap dancing. Sometimes he joined the famed dancers Pork Chop and Kidney Stew on Bourbon Street. He followed in the footsteps of his family, carrying on their own down home musical entertainment and Mardi Gras traditions.

"My mom organized the Baby Dolls."[25] On Mardi Gras the Batiste women and friends wore bright colored satin baby doll outfits with bonnets, blouses, short skirts, and baby doll socks and shoes. In high satire they would strike an innocent, naive pose and then shake what their momma gave them, kick their legs high, and parade in the streets.

"My daddy played banjo and guitar. He mostly entertained us. He always kept instruments in the house. Guitars, banjos, ukuleles, kazoos; we didn't have any horns. We played to entertain ourselves and sometimes at backyard parties, fish fires, that sort of thing."[26] The Batiste men formed the Dirty Dozen Kazoo Band. They played banjos, guitars, ukuleles, drums, and kazoos. Parading together on Mardi Gras Day the Baby Dolls and Dirty Dozen Kazoo Band created a scene as surreal as any created by Guillame Appolinaire. "Sometimes the men wore diapers. They'd take mustard and put a stain down the back."[27] They played whenever the urge struck them but, above all, they paraded every year on Mardi Gras Day for decades.

Speaking the "dozens" or "dirty dozens" is a tradition of street corner verbal sparring, mostly done in fun, sometimes combining ribald language with the elocution of a recitation by Langston Hughes. Today this

The Baby Dolls and the Dirty Dozen Kazoo Band parading on a Mardi Gras Day. (l to r): Miriam Batiste Reed, tambourine; Norman Batiste, bass drum; Felicia Batiste Shezbie, baby doll; Uncle Lionel Batiste, banjo-ukulele and kazoo. In rear with sailor's cap is Ferdinand Batiste. Reproduced with permission of Maria Zuniga-Lott.

custom is acknowledged with lines like, "Your mama's so old that on her birth certificate it says it expired," or in return, "Your mama's so large that when she sits down she resides in four states." It is not a coincidence that Lionel's brother Rodney was known as "Mr. Precisely" simply for his ability and habit to deliver the word "P-R-E-C-I-S-E-L-Y" with perfect timing and finesse.[28] It was from this oral tradition that the Dirty Dozen Kazoo Band took its name.

The Baby Dolls and Dirty Dozen Kazoo Band performed songs associated with New Orleans, including "The Saints," "Margie," "Eh Las Bas," "Closer Walk With Thee," "The Second Line," and "Over in Gloryland." They did a comical version of the Ray Charles hit "I've Got a Woman." The men sang, "I've got a woman," the women responded, "I've got a man," respectively followed by "and she's good to me," "and he's good to me."

One song they called "The Pecker Song" was sung to the melody of "For He's A Jolly Good Fellow," and included multiple refrains of the lyrics:

The man played with his pecker,
The man played with his pecker,
The man played with his pecker-r-r-r-r,
His pecker don't peck no more.
His pecker don't peck no more,
His pecker don't peck no more,
The man played with his pecker-r-r-r-r,
His pecker don't peck no more.[29]

They created a heavy rhythmical blend of marching strings with snare and bass drum. The voices and kazoos carried the melody, and the rhythm

PRETTY MEMBER OF "BABY DOLL" CHORUS AT CASINO
THEATER DANCES HER WAY INTO HEART
OF THEATER OWNER.

—D. Perry Evans, Photo.
MISS VIOLET WOODS, WHO WAS SECRETLY MARRIED TO HAR-
LEY C. STEVENS AT ASTORIA AUGUST 8.

A vintage "Baby Doll" chorus girl in costume (Portland Oregonian, September 29, 1919). Source: the University of Oregon Libraries' Oregon Digital Newspaper Program (ODNP) and Historic Oregon Newspapers. oregonnews.uoregon.edu.

varied from military cadence to intense syncopation with stop time to multiple layers of rhythms, at times building into cacophony. When appropriate, the kazoos mimicked the horn section of a brass band.

On occasion Uncle Lionel referred to the kazoo as a mirliton; mirliton being the French word for kazoo, as a result of sixteenth-century French colonization of Western African regions. Mirliton classifies a body of instruments created on the African continent from which it is possible the American kazoo was derived, signifying an instrument made from a gourd, bone, or reed, with a membrane to vibrate when the player hums into it. Such instruments were utilized in various West African societies in ritual and religious ceremonies similar to those conducted by the Dirty Dozen Kazoo Band and Baby Dolls on Mardi Gras. Dissonance created by multiple vocalized kazoos blown simultaneously atop multiple rhythms abruptly engaged the mental and physical space of bystanders, allowing the procession to move easily through large gatherings.

The current origin story of blacks masking "Baby Doll" on Mardi Gras in New Orleans is derived from a single oral history collected by black journalist Robert McKinney from "Baby Doll" Beatrice Hill in 1940.[30] Hill's account of initiating the first group to mask as Baby Dolls in 1912 is a colorful tale of prostitutes, Storyville, and one-upmanship, but there is no direct evidence to support it; basing the history of the "Baby Doll" tradition on a single retrospective account is problematic and inconclusive.

By the late nineteenth and early twentieth century, in New Orleans and throughout the United States, the term "baby doll" was replete in ambiguity. Usage of "baby doll" encompassed multidimensional recognition and broad scopes of description, interpretation, and expression, blind of age, race, gender, religion, and social status. This was especially relevant during the latter decades of the women's suffrage movement, when "baby doll" could denote subservience or autonomy.

"Baby doll" as a black colloquialism is found in multiple songs, as well as in early vaudeville, minstrel, and burlesque performances black and white. In the spring of 1909 white blackface comedians Henry Armstrong and Billy Clark came to New Orleans on the strength of their new song "Baby Doll." On April 18, 1909, the announcement of a weeklong vaudeville revue at the Orpheum Theater contains, "Two celebrated song writers . . . whose latest success, 'Baby Doll,' is well known to Crescent Cityites."[31] On April 20 a reviewer noted, "Easily the best feature of the bill are Armstrong and Clarke, the songwriters who wrote 'Sweet Angeline' [*sic*, 'Sweet Adeline'], and 'Can't You See I'm Lonely?' and who are delightful entertainers. One of them [Armstrong] has a rich barytone voice, and the other [Clark] is a clever comedian. The latter's singing of 'Doll Baby' [sic, 'Baby Doll']—a bright and haunting coon song—alone makes the bill worth while."[32]

The Harry Von Tilzer Music Publishing Company of New York published Armstrong and Clark's "Baby Doll" in 1908. Before the end of that year, it was highlighted by black vaudeville and minstrel show performers throughout the South. Dunmore's Modern Minstrels reported from Macon Mississippi: "Miss Aldosla Myers, our clever soubrette, is making them scream with 'Baby Doll'";[33] at the Gem Theater in Memphis, Tennessee, there was "Madam Elnora Hunt, the lady with the phenomenal baritone voice, who takes two and three encores nightly featuring 'Down in Jungle Town' and 'Baby Doll' and setting the audience wild with her buck dancing;[34] and in Jacksonville, Florida, Miss Gertrude Williams was "cleaning up singing 'Baby Doll'" at the Exchange Garden Theater, while Mrs. Perkins was "'mopping up' with 'Down in Jungle Town' and 'Baby Doll'" at the Palace.[35]

"Baby Doll" is easily adaptable to a male or female perspective. The repeated chorus is:

> Of all the names I love to hear it is Baby Doll, Baby Doll
> Of all the names I love to be called that's the best of all, Baby Doll

Oh sweetie dear to me is mild, I don't care nothing bout y'ore Angel child
But if you want to set me wild call me Baby Doll—Doll—

On June 21, 1909, a writer for the Times-Picayune reported, "After
hearing Nina Seamans sing 'Call Me Baby Doll' you will realize that ditty
is a coon song epic. Miss Seamans has a pretty face and a pretty figure,
but her distinguishing quality in that tribe of soubrettes is an utter lack
of consciousness."[36] A 1913 report of burlesque at the Greenwall Theater in New Orleans informed, "'Tangled Up' the second burlesque is by
George Milton who has the leading part in it . . . 'The Baby Doll Chorus'
is one of the numbers."[37]

During the 1915 Carnival season, news from the black Iroquois Theater on South Rampart Street noted, "Seals & Fisher is the one big talk
of the Crescent City. The act is one of the best seen here. The patrons
and manager of the Theatre are more than pleased with the Seal's &
Fisher act."[38] Baby Franklin Seals was one of the most influential black
vaudeville performers of the day. His stage partner Baby Floyd Fisher
was widely known as "the Memphis Baby Doll."[39]

It was also in 1915 that local black composers and musicians Clarence
Williams and Armand J. Piron wrote, published, and performed "Brown
Skin Who, You For," which became enormously popular in the city. The
chorus starts with:

I'm going back to old Tennessee
Brown Skin come and go with me
Be my baby doll, two live as one, how happy we'll be . . . [40]

One of the most crowd-pleasing songs of the World War I era was
Shelton Brooks's "Darktown Strutter's Ball," which can still be heard in
New Orleans. The second verse is:

We'll meet our high-toned neighbors,
An exhibition of the "Baby Dolls,"—
And each one will do their best,—
Just to outclass all the rest,—
And there'll be dancers from every foreign land,—
The classic, buck and wing, and the wooden clog:—
We'll win that fifty-dollar prize—
When we step out and "Walk the Dog."[41]

The composer's grandson Geoffrey Brooks explained the inspiration
of the song: "there was a formal dance held in Chicago once a year for

those who you might say 'practiced the oldest profession in the world' and their associates. That was their night that they suffered no oppression and were not bothered very much if at all by the local authorities. . . . [I]t was a marvelous occasion looked forward to each year by thousands."[42]

Upon the publication of "Darktown Strutters' Ball" in 1917, music stores in New Orleans advertised the sheet music for sale, along with three different player piano rolls; one standard, one for four hands, and one with a lyric sheet included. That same year it was recorded by at least three musical groups, including the Original Dixieland Jazz Band.[43] On Friday, November 16, 1917, the annual Newcomb College Junior Party for the freshmen class included a minstrel show: "The music was furnished by the Sophomore orchestra . . . The minstrel performance was given in approved style except that the usual dusky gentlemen were assisted by 'colored girls' dressed in vivid colors. 'Call Me Shine' was the opening chorus; and 'You're a Pretty Doll,' 'I'm a Real Con [sic] Mamma,'

'Darktown Strutters' Ball,' and 'Robinson Crusoe' were sung during the performance."[44]

The grand reopening of the Jefferson Park racetrack in November 1917 was big news. One front page story, attributed to "The War Widow," states, "When we arrive there are fully 4,000 people swarming on the turf and grandstand, where a disconcerting band insists on getting every one to their feet with a bar or two from the national anthem, and then taking them joyously on to the 'Darktown Strutters' Ball.'"[45]

In 1917 John Robichaux orchestrated "Darktown Strutters' Ball" for his band, and it is likely they performed it at the Lyric Theater, "America's Largest and Finest Colored Playhouse," at Iberville and Burgundy Street during the period 1919–1926.[46] George W. Thomas, the black composer and performer who wrote "New Orleans Hop Scop Blues" in 1916, entered the fray in 1919 with "Sweet Baby Doll," which he co-wrote with Wilbur Le Roy and published from his office at 328 South Liberty Street. The King Oliver Jazz Band with Louis Armstrong recorded it in 1923, and Okeh Records released it in 1924.[47] The song includes the line, "I love this baby doll, indeed I do," and ends with "Come share your life with me sweet baby doll."[48]

In August 1920, black construction steel worker Phil Cooley drew attention for his fearlessness. He rode a chain-hoisted steel beam up and down fourteen floors in construction of the Whitney Bank Annex on Common Street, dancing and singing:

> Jazz Baby, Jazz Baby!
> Oh, you jazzy baby Doll!
> I love my girl, and she loves only me!
> I kiss for my girl, and she kisses for me!
> Oh, you jazz baby doll![49]

On February 20, 1922, it was advertised that, "The Child's Welfare association of Algiers will give a Baby Doll Ball at the Alhambra Club building Monday evening [Lundi Gras] at 8:30 o'clock to raise funds for a milk station."[50] On June 7, 1924, the Times-Picayune alerted the public: "Prizes Are Offered in Big Baby Dance: . . . in Tokio Gardens at Spanish Fort, Professor C. Eddie Morton, director of the dance pavilion announced . . . Prizes will be awarded for the biggest big baby, the best baby doll, the best bobbed baby, and the best baby dancers. The prizes will be awarded to participants over 16 years old."[51]

The first week of December 1926 the Lyric Theater featured Bessie Smith, "acclaimed the greatest negro stage star in the United States today."[52] The year she co-wrote, recorded and released the slow grinding and sensuous blues song, "Baby Doll."

I want to be somebody's baby doll
So I can get my lovin' all the time
I want to be somebody's baby doll
To ease my mind . . . [53]

An idea that may be overstated in the current literature about the tradition of masking "Baby Doll" is its relationship to prostitution and Storyville. Taking into consideration Alma Batiste's deep love and devotion to her family, when she "organized the 'Baby Dolls,'" as reported by Uncle Lionel, there existed a diverse cultural environment and ample opportunity for multiple exposures and experiences of "Baby Doll" roles for her to draw from.

For Alma Batiste to mask "Baby Doll," before or after her ascension to Reverend Mother Sister in the Spiritual Church, was for her to take possession of the character and to encourage an open mind to any observer's preconceived notions. Being "Baby Doll" was a means to acknowledge, accept, liberate, and celebrate womanhood, from innocent and virginal to down-to-earth and unrepressed, through joyous song, dance, fashion, and procession on Mardi Gras Day.

The parading of the Baby Dolls and Kazoo Band was one aspect of the tradition of marching and second line culture engrained in the Batiste family. Francois Trepagnier (Lionel's maternal great grandfather) learned the basics of the "evolutions of the line" as a soldier in the Civil War, as did the majority of enlisted men. In New Orleans, the term "second line" has come to represent a complete social subculture. It is used to identify a parade, funeral, music, dance, and the participants in this culture. As Danny Barker said, "This brass band music, the second line, should be preserved and taught in the schools because it is history. It is an important part of America's history."[54]

The "second line" originated as a military battle formation; the term was coined in ancient Rome from the Latin, "acies duplex."[55] In 1835 General Winfield Scott formalized the military terminology "line" and "second line" in the United States in his three-volume work, Infantry Tactics or Rules for the Exercise and Maneuvers of the United States Army.[56] A complete section of this work is titled "Evolutions of the Line."[57] In 1841 General Scott became Commanding General of the United States Army and held this post for twenty-two years. During the Civil War, "Evolutions of the Line," was adapted and revised in multiple Union and Confederate publications including the Union Army Officers Pocket Companion.[58]

The character, form, and music of the second line that Uncle Lionel played an integral role in during his life evolved directly from the era of the Civil War and Reconstruction in Louisiana. By the late 1860s black

Elks Parade, 1953—the first line. Photo courtesy of Hogan Jazz Archive, Tulane University.

YMOBA parade with the George Williams Brass Band, 1958—the first line is marching on the street and the second line on the sidewalk. Photo courtesy of Hogan Jazz Archive, Tulane University.

Benevolent and Mutual Aide societies were holding annual parades. The phrase "line of march" appears in print in 1887 in connection with a black social function held by the Unity Hope Circle: "two hundred ladies and gentlemen took up the line of march . . . The Crescent City Band . . . and W. M. Jackson as leader furnished excellent music."[59]

The term "second line" was propelled into American popular culture and New Orleans mainstream vernacular during World War I. In 1917 and 1918 rarely a day went by without news headlines and reports of "the line of battle" or "second line of defense." Citizen support for the war effort was encouraged as a "second line" of battle or defense. Soon schools, banks, insurance and medical companies began using such phrases in their advertising. Professional and amateur football teams adopted the terminology and formation in their plans and playbooks.

✦ ✦ ✦

When Louis Jordan sang "Saturday Night Fish Fry," or Smiley Lewis "Blue Monday," they could have easily been singing about the Batiste family. As black New Orleans and American music evolved, some black New Orleanians diversified their style by combining music labeled jazz, blues, boogie-woogie, gospel, brass band, and Latin and Afro Caribbean sounds into a new serving called rhythm and blues, later known as rock and roll, and Uncle Lionel feasted at the table.

By the mid 1940s the Batistes had moved to 1322 St. Philip. Across the street was the Nelson family at 1323 and the Guichard family at 1321.[60] The elder Alfred Guichard played saxophone and clarinet and sang with the Joe Robichaux Orchestra through the 1930s.[61] Walter Nelson Sr., a.k.a. "Guitar Black," played with many of the area jazzmen and with Smiley Lewis early in his career. He fathered Walter Nelson, Jr. ("Papoose"), who played guitar with Professor Longhair and Fats Domino; and Lawrence Nelson ("Prince La La"), who in 1961 scored a national hit record with "She Put the Hurt On Me."[62]

These three families—the Batistes, Nelsons, and Guichards—helped put the "monkey shine" into the "Monkey Puzzle," a popular good-time apartment house on the same block that composer and drummer James Black (who lived on Ursulines Street) immortalized in his composition of the same name.[63] "Old Man Nelson, Kid Howard, Slow Drag Pavageau, Alton Purnell, Sidney Brown, Chester Jones [Benny Jones's father] and his family, Old Man Picou [Alphonse], Burnell Santiago, Jim Robinson—some great musicians lived near us. Once, when I was just a kid, Jim Robinson was being mean and my brother and I filled a bag with horseshit, lit it on fire, and threw it on his porch. We rang the doorbell and ran off. He didn't say much to me after that."[64]

Down the street at 942 St. Claude, Michael Tessitore turned the family grocery and saloon into the Caldonia Inn. This is where Henry Roeland Byrd received the nickname Professor Longhair. Dave Bartholomew, Roy Brown, Louis Jordan, and many others played there. It was also the scene of infamous late-night drag queen shows. Caddy-corner at 1201 St. Philip was TBoys Shoe Shine. Dominique "TBoy" Remy led the Eureka Brass Band through the late 1930s and early 1940s. At the corner of Gov. Nicholls and Marais was Lucius Bridges Bicycle Repair, where Bridges, Brother Percy Randolph, Walter Nelson Sr. and Jr., Babe Stovall, sometimes Uncle Lionel, and others held impromptu jam sessions. Back in

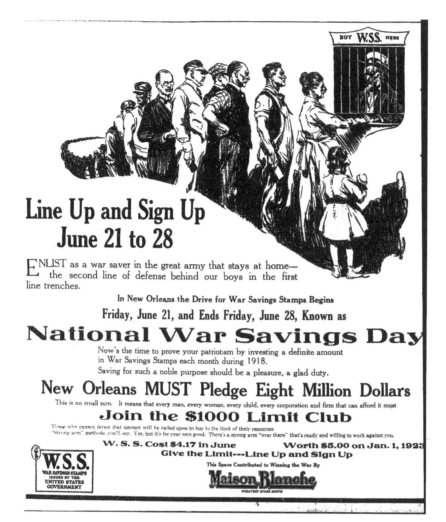

"The Second Line of
Defense Behind Our
Boys in the First Line
Trenches," *New Orleans
Item*, June 17, 1918.

those days Uncle Lionel's peers knew him as "Buddy Buddy." The Batiste family patronized their neighborhood music and cultural spots including Picou's Bar, the Gypsy Tea Room, Economy Hall, San Jacinto Hall, Mama Ruth's Cozy Corner, the Hi-Hat Club, Claiborne Theater, Prout's Club Alhambra, Municipal Auditorium, and others.

Community engagement played an important role in Uncle Lionel's life. He and his brothers Ferdinand, Rodney, Henry, and Arthur and sister Felecia joined social aide and pleasure clubs including the Square Deal, Golden Trumpets, Sixth Ward Diamonds, Treme Sports, Money Wasters, Mellow Boys & Girls, and Sixth Ward High Steppers. They participated in these organizations' annual parades, jazz funerals, fund raising events, and aide activities such as feeding the poor, burying the dead, sheltering the homeless, and visiting and caring for the sick and shut-in.

Equally significant was their involvement in the Spiritual Church, where individuality women's leadership, respect for ancestors, and

DIGGING THE SECOND LINE TRENCHES

Copyright, 1917, International News Service.

The Farmer Who Defends the Country from Famine Is as Truly a Hero as the Soldier Who Fights in the First Line Trenches.

"Digging the Second Line Trenches," *New Orleans Item*, April 15, 1917.

music was highly valued. Most of the Batiste family frequented the Calvary Spiritual Church, 1229 St. Philip Street, and the Helping Hand Spiritual Church, 1320 North Robertson.[65]

✦ ✦ ✦

In the 1960s, the brass bands that played the majority of downtown parades and funerals were the Eureka, the Olympia led by Harold Dejan, and, by the early 1970s, Floyd Anckle's Majestic Brass Band. Occasionally Uncle Lionel would play with the Olympia. Danny Barker, seeing a decline in young musicians, established, along with Rev. Andrew Darby, the Fairview Baptist Church Marching Band in 1970, led by Leroy Jones. The popularity of the Fairview Band contributed to new generations of brass bands. By the mid-1980s Uncle Lionel was playing bass drum and singing regularly with Anthony "Tuba Fats" Lacen and the Chosen Few

Benny Jones., Sr. photo by Michael P. Smith. Reproduced with permission of the Historic New Orleans Collection.

The Dirty Dozen Brass Band at a community picnic. Photo by Michael P. Smith. Reproduced with permission of the Historic New Orleans Collection.

In the Treme: Jim Robinson, Sidney Brown, and Benny Jones's older brother Eugene, sitting on Sidney Brown's stoop in the 1300 block of St. Philip Street. Reproduced with permission of Hogan Jazz Archive, Tulane University.

Brass Band. In 1986 he toured England and Scotland with Tuba Fats, and they returned to England in 1987.

Benny Jones played a pivotal role in the revival of the brass band tradition of the 1970s. As a founder of the Dirty Dozen Brass Band and as a drummer he kept the beat firmly in the New Orleans parade tradition: "I like to keep the beat in the pocket," he said. "That way, no matter what direction the horns take, we still keep the New Orleans sound in the music."[66] The Dirty Dozen Brass Band took their name from the Dirty Dozen Kazoo Band. The band grew organically from when Benny Jones and others began playing in the Kazoo Band and then formed the Dirty Dozen Brass Band that blossomed into an international success story.

When Benny formed the Treme Brass Band c. 1994 he combined music veterans with young, fiery players. Uncle Lionel, with his singing, dancing, and drumming, quickly emerged as a leading personality in the group. Uncle's syncopation, a throwback to his early days as a tap dancer and member of the Dirty Dozen Kazoo Band, was unique even among New Orleans drummers. His singing combined gospel and blues with 1920s and 1930s vaudeville standards. He was more of the vocal school of Ray Charles than, say, Louis Armstrong or Jelly Roll Morton.

With the Treme Brass Band Uncle Lionel recorded three CDs: "Gimme My Money Back" for Arhoolie Records; "New Orleans Music" for Mardi Gras Records; and a private recording with the Austrian banjo player Werner Tritta. He is the featured vocalist on the CD "Lars Edegran Presents Uncle Lionel" on GHB Records.

A chapter of Mick Burns's book *Keeping the Beat on the Street* is devoted to Uncle Lionel. He is featured in the film *This Ain't No Mouse*

Music, a documentary on the life of Chris Strachwitz, founder of Arhoolie Records. Following Hurricane Katrina, Uncle Lionel received national recognition featured in works by Spike Lee, the HBO TV series "Treme," and TV commercials.

The life of Lionel Batiste was "no accident," and neither are the history, culture, and socio-economic realities of the New Orleans that he lived in. The Batiste family and the second liners of Uncle Lionel's generation reshaped and enlivened the tradition of "the line" with inalienable and reclaimed African dance forms and spirit. The civil and human rights movement of the 1950s and 60s inspired and perpetuated new freedoms in the tradition.

To march in the streets like Uncle Lionel and his ancestors marched in the streets was a way to celebrate life and to create an experience and expression of personal and unified freedom. It was a way to actively participate in Reconstruction and stand against segregation and build momentum and motivation for change and perhaps to open doors to new possibilities, as did Homer Plessy when he boarded that train or when Martin Luther King Jr. and others marched on Selma. Uncle Lionel frequently said, "Take your time Neph. Take your time," not to encourage a laid-back, laissez-faire approach to life, but to encourage the patience required to "Get it right!" And Uncle Lionel sure did.

NOTES

Dedicated to the Batiste Family

Thanks to Lynn Abbott, Rick Coleman, Alaina W. Hebert, Alana Jones, Benny Jones, and Bruce Raeburn for help in the researching and writing of this article

1. "Races, New Orleans Sacrifice," *Time*, March 16, 1931: "Last week Mayor Walmsley, home from the capital, announced: 'As I am just as passionate an adherent to the cause of white supremacy as it is possible for any human to be'"; "That Anti-Negro Ordinance," New Orleans *Times-Picayune*, August 2, 1932, 1: "Personally, I am going to stand by the white man"; "Just As We Predicted," New Orleans *Times-Picayune*, August 12, 1932, 1.

2. Nat Hentoff, liner notes to "Satchmo the Great," Columbia Records CL 1077, 1956.

3. Louisiana, Orleans Parish marriage records, USGenWeb Project; 1910 U.S. Federal Census, Orleans Parish, New Orleans, Ward 5, Sheet No. 7A (Ancestry.com).

4. Every known document cites different birth dates for both Walter and Alma Batiste. Orleans Parish marriage records: U.S. WWII Draft Registration Card, 1942 (Ancestry.com); 1910 U.S. Federal Census, Orleans Parish, New Orleans, Ward, 5, Sheet, No. 7A (Ancestry.com); 1920 U.S. Federal Census, Orleans Parish, New Orleans, Ward 5 (Ancestry.com); 1900 U.S. Federal Census, Orleans Parish, New Orleans, Ward 15, Sheet No. 29 (Ancestry.com).

5. 1900 U.S. Federal Census, Orleans Parish, New Orleans, Ward 15, Sheet No. 29 (Ancestry.com).

6. Ibid.

7. 1900 U.S. Federal Census, Orleans Parish, New Orleans, Ward 5, Sheet No. 5 (Ancestry.com).

8. Stanley Arthur and George Huchet de Kerniou, "Trepagnier Family," *Old Families of Louisiana* (Gretna: Pelican Publishing Co., 1931), 284–88.

9. Albert Thrasher, *On To New Orleans! Louisiana's Historical 1811 Slave Revolt* (New Orleans: Cypress Press, 1996).

10. Norbert Trepagnier, age 25, 1850, U.S. Federal Census, Orleans Parish, New Orleans (Ancestry.com); Obituary, Norbert Trepagnier, New Orleans Daily Picayune, July 10, 1891, 2.

11. "Reception of Ex-President Polk," *New Orleans Daily Picayune*, March 20, 1849, 2.

12. New Orleans, Louisiana, Birth Record Index: Ursin Trapagnier born October 21, 1871, to Francois Trapagnier and Louise Daniel (Ancestry.com).

13. 1860 U.S. Federal Census, Orleans, New Orleans, Louisiana, Free Inhabitants, Ward 5, 113 (Ancestry.com).

14. "Records of Louisiana Confederate Soldiers and Louisiana Confederate Commands, volume 3, book 2" Andrew B. Booth, Commissioner of Louisiana Military Records, Published, New Orleans, LA, 1920, 868; Civil War Soldiers and Sailors Database (nps.gov).

15. Stephen J. Ochs, *A Black Patriot and a White Priest: Andre Cailloux and Claude Paschal Maistre in Civil War New Orleans* (Baton Rouge: Louisiana State University Press, 2000), 3.

16. "Rakings," New Orleans *Weekly Pelican*, October 1, 1887, 3.

17. 1900 U.S. Federal Census, Orleans, New Orleans, Ward 6, Louisiana, Sheet No. X (Ancestry.com); Al Rose and Edmond Souchon, *New Orleans Jazz: A Family Album*, 1967 (Baton Rouge: Louisiana State University Press, 1984), 123; Frank J. Gillis and John W. Miner, eds., *Oh, Didn't He Ramble: The Life Story of Lee Collins as told to Mary Collins* (Urbana: University of Illinois Press, 1974), 59; Samuel Charters, *A Trumpet Around the Corner: The Story of New Orleans Jazz* (Jackson: University Press of Mississippi, 2008), 225.

18. 1910 U.S. Federal Census, Orleans, New Orleans, Louisiana, Ward 5, Sheet No. 7A (Ancestry.com); 1920 U.S. Federal Census, Orleans, New Orleans, Louisiana, Ward 5 (Ancestry.com); *Soards' New Orleans City Directory*, 1921 and 1922; Ethnic data collected by the author from survey of 1900, 1910, and 1920 Census.

19. Lionel Batiste interviewed by Jerry Brock, August 2001.

20. *Soards' New Orleans City Directory*, 1932.

21. Lionel Batiste interviewed by Brock.

22. Ibid.

23. "Charters," New Orleans *Times-Picayune*, Thursday, June 19, 1941, 4.

24. "Deaths," Alma Batiste, Obituary, New Orleans *Times-Picayune*, Monday, June 23, 1952, 2.

25. Ibid.

26. Lionel Batiste interviewed by Brock.

27. Lionel Batiste interviewed by Geraldine Wyckoff, Donna's Bar, December 2002.

28. "Parade Fan Batiste Dead at 59," New Orleans *Times-Picayune*, August 25, 1983, Section 1, 23: "He acquired the nickname 'Mr. Precisely' because his frequent response to questions was the word 'precisely.'"

29. There is a history of many pecker songs in America. They are documented in the book "The Stag Party" published in Chicago in 1888. The best known recording of a pecker song, which there are only a few, is by blues artist Billy Mitchell titled "The

Song of the Woodpecker" in 1952 and this song is public domain because there is no copyright claim. This song also has no resemblance to the Batiste family bawdy little ditty. The Batiste family pecker song does have melody based on "For He's A Jolly Good Fellow" which itself is based on an almost ancient French song titled "The Bear Came Over The Mountain." There is no Batiste family claim. It's just a song that in the true folk tradition they had fun with. There exist no legal claim at the Library of Congress, nor at BMI, ASCAP or SESAC. *The Stag Party* can be accessed at http://www.horntip.com/html/books_&_MSS/1880s/1888ca_the_stag_party_(HC)/index.htm.

30. Beatrice Hill oral history collected by Robert Joseph McKinney (Robert Tallant Papers, Northwestern State University of Louisiana); Al Rose, *Storyville, New Orleans* (University, Alabama: University of Alabama Press, 1974), 177–81.

31. "Eva Taylor Is Orpheum Headliner," *New Orleans Item*, Sunday April 18, 1909, 19.

32. "In The Playhouses," "Orpheum Theater," *New Orleans Item*, Tuesday April 20, 1909.

33. "Dunmore's Modern Minstrels," Indianapolis *Freeman*, November 7, 1908, 5.

34. "Gem Theater, Memphis, Tenn.," Indianapolis *Freeman*, November 28, 1908, 5.

35. "The Profession At Jacksonville, Fla.," Indianapolis *Freeman*, December 26, 1908, 5.

36. "Summer Amusements," New Orleans *Times-Picayune*, June 21, 1909, 4.

37. "Yankee Girls Are At The Greenwall," *New Orleans Item*, Sunday, March 2, 1913, 17.

38. Lynn Abbott and Jack Stewart, "The Iroquois Theater," *The Jazz Archivist*, vol. 9, no. 2 (December 1994), 9.

39. "Bijou Theater, Greenwood, Miss.," Indianapolis *Freeman*, January 21, 1911, 5: "Baby Floyd Fisher, the Memphis baby doll, the smallest and the sweetest little thing on the stage."

40. Clarence Williams and Armand J. Piron, "Brown Skin, Who You For" (New Orleans: Dugan Piano Company, 1915) (Sheet Music Collection, Hogan Jazz Archive, Tulane University).

41. Shelton Brooks, "Darktown Strutters' Ball" (Chicago: Will Rossiter, 1917).

42. Tom Morgan, "Shelton Brooks: A Profile" (jass.com/sheltonbrooks/brooks), 1992.

43. Original Dixieland Jazz Band," "Darktown Strutters' Ball," Columbia A-2297, 1917.

44. Katherine Krebs, "Expenseless Party Given At Newcomb," *New Orleans Daily States*, November 17, 1917, 12.

45. The War Widow, "New 50-Cent Piece and Card Offered by War Widow Fail to Impress Old-Time Bookie," *New Orleans Item*, Friday November 30, 1917, 1.

46. Handwritten tenor and alto saxophone parts for "Darktown Stritters'Ball" can be found in the John Robichaux Sheet Music Collection at Hogan Jazz Archive, Tulane University.

47. King Oliver's Jazz Band, "Sweet Baby Doll" (instrumental), Okeh 8235, 1923.

48. Wilbur Le Roy, words, George W. Thomas, music, "Sweet Baby Doll," (New Orleans: Geo. W. Thomas Music Co., 1919) (Sheet Music Collection, Hogan Jazz Archive, Tulane University).

49. "Bold Ironworkers Dance Joy Step With Death High Above New Orleans Street," *New Orleans Item*, August 1, 1920, 7.

50. "Give Baby Doll Ball," *New Orleans Item*, Monday, February 20, 1922, 2.

51. "Prizes Are Offered In 'Big Baby Dance,'" New Orleans *Times-Picayune*, Saturday, June 10, 1924, 15.

52. "Lyric Midnight Frolic," New Orleans *Times-Picayune*, December 8, 1926, 14.

53. Bessie Smith, "Baby Doll," Columbia 14147-D, May 4, 1926.

54. Danny Barker interviewed by Jerry Brock for *In That Number! The New Orleans Brass Band Revival*, documentary film by Jerry Brock, Louisiana State Museum, 1986.

55. Ross Cowan, *Roman Battle Tactics 109 BC–AD 313* (Oxford: Osprey Publishing, 2007, 21.

56. Paddy Griffith, *Battle Tactics of the Civil War* (New Haven: Yale University Press, 1989), 99.

57. Winfield Scott, *Infantry Tactics or Rules for the Exercise and Maneuvers of the United States Infantry* (New York: George Dearborn Publisher, 1835), Title V., 7.

58. William P. Craighill, *Army Officers Pocket Companion* (New York: D. Van Norstrund, 1862).

59. "Unity Hope Circle," *New Orleans Weekly Pelican*, March 19, 1887, 3.

60. Polk's New Orleans City Directory, 1945, 106, 851.

61. Seagrams, "Solid, Man! Solid!" (clipping from unidentified journal, vol. 1, no. 9 (September 1953), 4, in Alfred Guichard vertical file, Hogan Jazz Archive, Tulane University.

62. Rick Coleman, *Blue Monday: Fats Domino and the Lost Dawn of Rock 'N' Roll* (Cambridge: Da Capo Press, 2006), 70, 215.

63. "Monkey Puzzle," Ellis Marsalis Quartet at the Music Haven, AFO Records 0001, New Orleans, 1963.

64. Lionel Batiste interviewed by Brock.

65. Obituary, Rev. Elvidge Batiste Colar, *New Orleans Times-Picayune*, November 3, 1967.

66. Benny Jones interviewed by Jerry Brock, June 1985, 1.

The author (right) with baby doll Ms. Lillian, Mardi Gras Day, 1984. Reproduced with permission of Maria Zuniga-Lott.

Baby Doll Addendum and Mardi Gras '49

—Jerry Brock

n my memorial piece to Uncle Lionel Batiste (*The Jazz Archivist*, vol. 27, 2014), I addressed the commonly accepted yet problematic and inconclusive origin story of black women masking Baby Doll as it related to Lionel's mother Alma Batiste. This brief addendum explores a bright moment in the baby doll tradition in New Orleans during the Carnival season of 1949.

Following Bessie Smith's June 1926 recording of "Baby Doll," the future movie actress Hattie McDaniel wrote and recorded "Brown Skin Baby Doll" in July 1926 for Meritt Records.[1] Earlier that same year Ethel Waters recorded "Sugar," foretelling the end of the baby doll trend in 1920s music:

> Found a word, just the one,
> That takes the place of one
> I use to call Baby Doll!
> . . . The name is Sugar![2]

However, the tradition and popularity of masking Baby Doll in New Orleans continued into the early 1980s, before its demise and subsequent twenty-first century revival. The New Orleans women's Afrocentric embodiment and expression of the baby doll persona outweighed and outlasted the national tendency.

Mardi Gras 1949 was unusually momentous. Louis Armstrong's reign that year as King Zulu created immense local excitement and generated national and international press. Local music clubs scrambled to present the biggest shows they could afford. The Caldonia Inn, corner of St. Phillip and St. Claude streets, promoted its Carnival season entertainment in the *Louisiana Weekly*:

> It's a new show again at the Caldonia Inn. This time it's "Baby Dolls of 1949." Last week's feature act, with the one-leg jitterbug dancer, Albert Bellvue, was such a success that the same routine will be repeated for the Carnival guests. Along with this teasin'—tossin' show will appear such stars as [baby dolls] Virginia Smith, Mary Anne Foster, Gloria Lopez and Myrtle Nightingale and the solid group the Hair Combo.
>
> Cha Cha Hogan, the versatile emcee will once again introduce those top performers of the show: Lloyd Ignicious, Mattie Campbell and Alma Lollypop Jones. . . . The two floor shows every week end begin exactly at 11:30 p.m. and 2 a.m. So for Carnival it's the Caldonia Inn.[3]

This line-up exemplifies the deep pool of down home talent that existed in and emerged from the culturally rich black New Orleans communities of the time, as Uncle Lionel Batiste and members of his family had done. Of the four featured Baby Dolls, there is no account that any of them pursued song and dance as a career; yet, to perform with the Hair Combo indicates talent. Also, the fact that they were promoted and presented as headliners attests to the popularity of the Baby Dolls and their potential to draw customers. Longtime Sixth Ward resident Henry Youngblood recalled, "Gloria Lopez was a Batiste Baby Doll. She went to Calvary Spiritual Church. You see back then, everybody had different names. There was Ruth Caldonia, Bo Weevil, Mule, Cutsie Babu, Steamboat."[4] Gloria Lopez continued to honor the New Orleans Baby Doll tradition, and she participated in downtown neighborhood parades and social organizations for decades.

This was possibly the first Carnival season performance of Henry Byrd, piano player in the Hair Combo, who was otherwise hustling day labor jobs. He began playing at the Caldonia in March 1948.[5] In November 1949 he made his first recordings as Professor Longhair, including "Mardi Gras in New Orleans," for the Star Talent label.[6] It is not too far a stretch to consider that this song, Longhair's ovation to Mardi Gras and the Zulu King, was inspired by Louis Armstrong's participation in that year's Carnival festivities. By the 1970s, Byrd had finally begun to achieve worldwide acclaim for his innovative contributions to American music.

The emcee, Sumter "Cha Cha" Hogan, was a New Orleans native, employed in 1949 as a driver for Ed's Cab Service, and residing at 606 North Johnson.[7] Around the time of Professor Longhair's first recordings, Hogan recorded "My Baby Loves Me" and "My Walking Baby" for the same label.[8] Huey "Piano" Smith remembered Cha Cha as a "blues

Within a year of appearing at the Caldonia Inn with the Baby Dolls of '49, Professor Longhair, Cha Cha Hogan, and Alma Mondy all launched recording careers, Vernon Winslow Collection of Recorded Sound. Reproduced with permission of Hogan Jazz Archive, Tulane University.

shouter" who was one of the people who inspired the term "rock n roll" and who stood up against race discrimination.[9]

Hogan moved to Detroit in the 1960s and continued to appear in bars and nightclubs as an emcee, comedian, and singer, opening for the Four Tops and others.[10] In the 1970s he made the funk instrumentals "Grit Gitter" and "Just Because You've Been Hurt" for Soulsville Records.[11] Some of his unexpurgated comedy routines, drawn in part from historic vaudeville, were collected on the X-rated comedy LP *Brother Eatmore and Sister Fullbosom*, as by "Cha Cha Hogan—The Black Foxx."[12] In the mid-1970s Cha Cha appeared on several episodes of the TV show *San-*

ford and Son, starring Redd Foxx.[13] Following the death of Bill Kinney, he became the lead singer with Stanley Morgan's revived Ink Spots and moved to Las Vegas.[14] There he continued his street-wise stage performances and passed away in November 1986.[15]

Albert Bellvue, the one-leg jitterbug dancer, was working in 1949 as a cobbler at Bean's Shoe Hospital uptown on LaSalle Street.[16] He later worked as a roofer and house painter, and in 1975 he opened the barroom Al's Place at 1738 North Galvez.[17] "One Legged Albert we called him. He could dance man. The jitterbug is high spirited and physical with a lot of moves. The way he'd turn was so fast the woman would get lost and another would jump in. I never saw a roofer like Al. He could walk up a ladder onto a roof with a full roll of felt paper on his shoulder like it was nothing."[18]

Of the show's three "top performers," Lloyd Ignicious was a "Golden Voice Crooner" and Mattie Campbell a "female mimic."[19] "Jump blues" singer Alma "Lollypop" Jones, wife of local comedian Lollypop Jones, recorded for Mercury in 1950 as Alma Mondy.[20] Their story deserves its own chapter.

NOTES

1. Hattie McDaniels, "Brown-Skin Baby Doll," Meritt 2202, June 1926.

2. Ethel Waters, "Sugar," Columbia 14170-D, February 20, 1926.

3. "'Baby Dolls of '49' Caldonia Carnival Theme," *Louisiana Weekly*, February 26, 1949.

4. Henry Youngblood interviewed by Jerry Brock, September 19, 2015; *Polk's New Orleans City Directory*, 1949, includes: Gloria Lopez, 2329 Ursulines; Virginia Smith, 538 N Rampart; Mary Anne Foster, 2753 St. Ann. It is possible that Myrtle Nightingale was also known as Myrtle Jones, who was a featured singer at the Caldonia during the late 1940s.

5. Rick Coleman, liner notes, *Mercury Records: The New Orleans Sessions 1950 & 1953*, Bear Family BCD 16804 BH.

6. Professor Longhair and his Shuffling Hungarians, "Mardi Gras in New Orleans," Star Talent 808.

7. *Polk's New Orleans City Directory*, 1949.

8. Cha Cha Hogan, Star Talent 810.

9. John Wirt, *Huey Smith and the Rocking Pneumonia Blues* (Baton Rouge: Louisiana State University Press, 2014) 44.

10. Imdb.com, Cha Cha Hogan.

11. Cha Cha Hogan, Soulsville 45 SV 1017.

12. Cha Cha Hogan, *Brother Eatmore and Sister Fullbosom*, Laff LP 147.

13. *Sanford and Son*, "Home Sweet Home for the Aged," Season 2, Episode 21, February 16, 1973; "Brother Can You Spare an Act? Season 6, Episode 93, October 17, 1975.

14. William Foy, "Ink Spots Appeal Evergreen," *Milwaukee Sentinel*, July 11, 1980, 4.

15. Sumter Joseph Hogan, *Social Security Death Records* (b. Dec. 8, 1920; d. Nov. 1986).

16. *Polk's New Orleans City Directory*, 1949.

17. "New Businesses," "Al's Place," *Times Picayune*, April 13, 1975.

18. Youngblood interviewed by Brock. Henry further stated, "We had a funeral for the Caldonia right before they were going to tear it down when they built the park. We had a small display casket that we got from Blandin Funeral Home and we marched to the 'Cal,' set the casket inside and set it on fire. We marched up the street as the Caldonia burned down."

19. Per Oldaeus, *Professor Longhair: A Scrapbook* (Stockholm: Pepper Pot Publishing, 2014), 221, 223.

20. See Coleman, liner notes, *Mercury Records: The New Orleans Sessions*, 40–45.

Dancing Women of New Orleans

Mardi Gras Baby Dolls

—DeriAnne Meilleur Honora

Many people can identify the icons of Mardi Gras: floats, bands, and even Mardi Gras Indians. But can that same group of people identify the Mardi Gras Baby Dolls? In the summer of 2012 while an undergraduate history major at Xavier University of New Orleans, I interviewed my family members and conducted research on these complex and beautiful women in search of more information about them. I focused on the identity of the Baby Dolls in the New Orleans's Seventh Ward, home to my family for generations.[1]

The Seventh Ward is located between the Marigny, Fairgrounds, Treme, and St. Roch neighborhoods. This neighborhood is a prime area to live because it is in the middle of the city which makes it easier to travel around to any area. According to various interviews conducted by Rachel Breunlin,[2] the Seventh Ward was an area, historically where creoles of color lived. Creole, means in this context, French-speaking Catholics whose ancestors were often Free People of Color. This area was historically set apart from other neighborhoods because of its creole culture. According to various interviews conducted by Breunlin, in the 1960s there was a distinct line between other black and white neighborhoods and the creole neighborhood. It was as if there was a large invisible wall dividing this neighborhood from the city.

The Baby Dolls are thought to have been black women who worked in the New Orleans Black Red Light District or as they called it "the District." These women used to drink alcohol and dance in bars and on the street during competitions between musicians, until one day they decided to mask Baby Dolls to mock the gender norms of the time. There were also men who masked as "Baby Boys" and wore diapers with mustard smeared on their bottoms. Years went by and the people taking up the tradition broadened to lower and middle class women. These women were ordinary people who were just looking for a great time during Mardi Gras.[3] They were women of various heights, statures, and personalities. Most were rambunctious and free spirited. They were of varying shades of skin color; just regular women who overstepped the boundaries of their time to have fun. They were someone's daughter, sister, cousin, aunt, and even mother. They were women who just enjoyed having fun while doing what they wanted. In the Seventh Ward these women would cook dinner for their families and do their regular duties; however, on certain holidays such as Mardi Gras and St. Joseph's night, these women would dress up, drink, dance in the streets, and have fun with other women just like them. According to Laurel Reimonenq "they were women who did what they wanted during that restrictive time, that's what made them stand out the most."[4]

During this time period women were expected to wear clothes that did not reveal much of their bodies. They were supposed to remain classy; however, when masking baby doll, those roles in society flew out the window. These women wore bright beautiful short dresses where short means above the knee. Some of the colors included baby blue, pink, yellow, white, and purple. They made sure they were seen no matter what. Depending on the weather, some of the women wore petite coats, white stockings, and tiny black baby dolls shoes with a black strap, bonnets. If they had long hair they wore it down, mostly in curls and if they had short hair they wore wigs. During that time these women grabbed what they had and put it on. Many of these lavish costumes were handmade and because some of the women worked in Haspels sewing factory the creation of these costumes was easy. When wearing these costumes the baby dolls felt alive and definitely portrayed it, especially in the way they acted and carried themselves.

The women who masked Baby Dolls were not a quiet group of women; they were loud and rambunctious. Unlike the common status quo of women being seen but not heard, they were seen and heard. In the Seventh Ward, these women walked throughout the neighborhood carrying a baby bottle full of alcohol, wine seemed to be the alcohol of choice. They were always followed by the Bone Gang, a group of men who dressed as skeletons, and they followed the Mardi Gras Indians. Many of these women paraded and danced on Claiborne Avenue before the interstate was developed. All those interviewed mentioned how the interstate ruined the black experience of Mardi Gras and how Claiborne Avenue was full of life on Mardi Gras with vendors, barbecue grills and trees. They mentioned how the women would dance in the street sashaying and buck jumping. Another place in the Seventh Ward where the women danced was through the neighborhood and in and out the neighborhood bars. One of the popular neighborhood bars was the Arceneaux Bar. Owned and operated by Alvin Arceneaux it was located near the corner of St. Anthony and Duels. This was a tiny brick box in which many people would go in and get a drink and stand outside to enjoy it. There was no way ten people would be able to drink and dance inside the place, so they mostly interacted in the street. The fate of this bar was sealed with the establishment of the Church of the Epiphany in 1948. Archbishop Joseph Rummel sent Alvin Arceneaux a letter in the mail demanding that he close his bar. The reverend's thinking was that it would not be good to have a bar located across the street from a church. What he really meant to say was he did not want the parishioners leaving church and going to the bar. After the closing of the Arceneaux Bar, the women sashayed a few blocks up the street to the Bon Ton where they resumed their festivities of drinking and dancing for the crowds.

My great-grandmother, Clea Desdune Gilyot, was one of the Baby Dolls who went to the Arceneaux and Bon Ton bars. She was a very outgoing, French speaking, Catholic Creole woman. She was fair skinned and small in stature. She began to mask Baby Doll in the 1950s. In speaking to my family members I found that she had a love for dance and defying rules. As a part of the neighborhood carnival club, she decided to mask baby doll. Her dream of masking baby doll did not actually happen until after her husband, Walter Gilyot died. As a Baby Doll she masked and frolicked through the streets of the neighborhood in her homemade costume. In order to create this piece she grabbed any material she had around and left everything else up to her creativity and everyone else's imagination.

Interview Summaries

Jacqueline "Aunt Jackie" Baham

"I did not like those women one bit." Aunt Jackie nor her mother or father believed what the women who masked baby doll were right. They believed in a classy Mardi Gras of clean fun with family and friends around. Aunt Jackie said that the Creoles did not dress as Baby Dolls because it was not a part of their culture. They all went to the Autocrat Club for Mardi Gras and some went on Claiborne. According to Aunt

Jackie, many of the women who masked baby doll were loose women who were drunkards and hung at bars. Her mother referred to these women as whores. At the age of 13 she was taught by her family that real women did not dress and behave in that manner. "Those women wore bright costumes with different colors of pink, blue, or yellow with high white stockings." She also said that they wore short dresses, bonnets, bloomers, and if they had hair it was in curls and if they did not have hair then it would be curly wigs. "They dressed that way because they wanted to be seen I guess." She also said that she didn't understand why they dressed that way and did not see the point of that. She recalls seeing these women on Claiborne Avenue near the Circle Food Store on Claiborne and St. Bernard Avenue. She recalls that the Baby Dolls hung near the Johnny Edmond Shoe Store. They were always carrying alcohol with men following them. She also recalled that the Baby Dolls were followed by Indians and Skeletons. She was frightened by the Skeletons when they would come around her. Many Blacks attended Mardi Gras on Claiborne Avenue and walked the street and socialized with friends and relatives. There was no violence like seen today. She referred to the Avenue as beautiful. She hated when the city decided to build an interstate in the middle of such a beautiful place. When asked if she would ever consider masking baby doll, her response was "hell no."

Celeste Robinson and Clea Williams (Mother and Daughter)

Celeste recalls seeing the Baby Dolls as a child, and she found them interesting. She said that they wore short dresses and danced around. "They were different from today's Baby Dolls. They looked like they grabbed what they could and just put it on." Many people today have stores that they can go and buy clothing to fit the persona of a baby doll; but then they had to work with the resources they had. Celeste said that many women who masked as Baby Dolls were from poor families and just sought out ways to have fun and enjoy the black experience. She believed that the black Mardi Gras was held on Claiborne in which the Indians, Skeletons, and Baby Dolls met and danced around and enjoyed themselves. Her mother Clea Gilyot (95) said that the women who masked baby doll just wanted to have a little fun. Celeste says that these women did this to escape the reality of the poor environment in which they lived. Many of her perceptions of the Baby Dolls she learned from her mother because she was an infant when the Baby Dolls were abundant and plentiful in the streets of New Orleans. However, there was always a small group that appeared. She said that there seem to be a strong interest in the Baby Dolls recently because she is now seeing them all over. "Even whites are dressing as Baby Dolls, which I don't agree with; those white people are always trying to take our black culture and claim it for themselves."

Lynn Reimonenq (71) and Jeanne Reimonenq (94) (Mother and Daughter)

Lynn says that the first thing she remembers about the Baby Dolls is that her grandmother masked as one, my great grandmother, Clea Gilyot. She said that my great grandmother masked with a group of Creole women from the Seventh Ward. Clea Gilyot was born in 1895 and she masked baby doll in the 1930s. Many of the women who masked worked as domestics and in sewing factories. As they were not very wealthy, they used to hand sew their costumes. They made them thigh high and above the knee and used old cloth. They carried bottles and wore pink or blue bonnets. They wore short skirts or dresses and showed plenty of leg. My great grandmother was always known for her long legs. Lynn believed that they dressed as Baby Dolls for fun and a way to relive childhood. They also had large pacifiers in which they carried around and occasionally sucked on. Lynn said that she personally did not have a problem with them. They were just regular women from all over New Orleans who were a part of organizations that sought out fun and wanted to dress up. She said she never really judged them or saw any problems with these women. She believed it was just the fun that women of the time were scorned for. When asked if she has ever considered masking as one, she replied "When I was young maybe, but now I'm too old." To Lynn, Mardi Gras is Claiborne. She recalls her early Mardi Gras days on Claiborne Avenue with people walking up and down the street with beautiful trees and vendors selling food from stands. "It's nothing like today." She remembers seeing people dressed up for a day "to become someone truly something different and truly original." She said that the Baby Dolls were followed by the Indians and the Skeletons. She said "Those were the days. You have to be careful now days, there is so much crime." She believed the Claiborne interstate contributed to the failure of the original black Mardi Gras. Now it is a sight to go there and not a place she would be caught. She also remember that the man that lived next door to her house on Pauger Street masked skeleton and she recalls being frightened of them because they were supposed to be dead. He created his outfit and shaped a skeleton head out of paper machete and also carried a large bone. He usually came out on Mardi Gras day.

Herbert and Laurel Reimonenq (75/76) (Husband and Wife)

Herbert Reimonenq remembered seeing them as a child around his Seventh Ward home. He said that his grandmother (nicknamed Gramou), my great grandmother had pictures of them masking around the house and he remembers being a little boy watching them drink and go in and out of the Arceneaux bar on St. Anthony and Duels Streets. He said these ladies were women in their middle-age and they were just parading around for fun and a way to get back at society. Gramou' began masking after her husband died of a heart attack. "She was a very feisty woman and didn't take no stuff" she was not the type of woman you could walk over. Many of the women drinking beer and hanging around that bar were like that. There were no prissy women who dressed that way. Many Creole women did not agree with the women doing this because it was apparently against their stature. But really they didn't know how to have a good time and were too uptight.

Laurel Reimonenq remembers seeing the baby dolls as a child on St. Claude Avenue while sitting with her father on his friend's porch. She remembers that they wore short pink laced baby doll dresses with curly hair and little black baby doll shoes with little black straps. Some even wore pink or white scarves. There were different types of women who dressed up but mostly they were regular women just looking for a good time. They used to dance around and have fun and drink their beer. Some of these women had dark skin and some had light skin. The women that masked Baby Dolls varied in many different ways: height, stature, and personality a result of the different social clubs and groups that masked. Different women came from different areas of the City had different styles depending on their taste and background. She said the crowds of people stood around and had fun watching these women dance, drink and have fun. They took pleasure in the moment and enjoyed this time because it was pure fun without crime and that is what Mardi Gras is all about. They did what they wanted against the time and that's why they stood out so much and people still remember them today.

They both recall the differences in the white Mardi Gras, St. Charles and Canal street further towards the river and the black Mardi Gras towards Claiborne Avenue. Before the I-10 construction in the 60s there was a beautiful neutral ground and with trees and people walking around having fun. After the construction, it created an ugly area where trash and drugs are plentiful. They believe the whites did this to destroy the black neighborhood and their Mardi Gras. You can see that today in limiting time and areas for people to mask Indian. After the I-10 was built many people stopped masking and the baby dolls were little to nothing. They believed the people did this as a rebellion against the I-10.

NOTES

1. "Seventh Ward Neighborhood Snapshot" Accessed June 2, 2017. http://www.gnoc dc.org/orleans/4/14/snapshot.html

2. Rachel Breunlin and Helen A. Regis. "Can There Be a Critical Collaborative Ethnography?: Creativity and Activism in the Seventh Ward, New Orleans." *Collaborative Anthropologies* 2, no. 1 (2009): 115–46.

3. McPherson, Natasha. "There was a Tradition among the Women: New Orleans's Colored Creole Women and the Making of a Community in the Treme and Seventh Ward, 1791–1930." PhD dissertation, Emory University, 2011.

Anthony, Arthe. A. "The Negro Creole community in New Orleans, 1880–1920: An oral history." University of California, Irvine, 1978

4. Author interview.

Reinvention

Miss Antoinette K-Doe and Her Baby Dolls

—Rachel Carrico

ntoinette Dorsey Fox K-Doe (1945–2009)—known to most New Orleanians as Miss Antoinette—played an important role in the history of the Baby Doll tradition.[1] In the last years of her life, she devoted herself to fostering a Baby Doll revival, helping to bring the practice back onto the streets at a time when many feared that it might become relegated to memory. Long before she donned a Baby Doll dress, Miss Antoinette's life had been dedicated to cultural preservation and innovation in multiple realms, and that work took on its most public face once she married rhythm and blues singer Ernie K-Doe.

When Miss Antoinette met Ernest Kador Jr., or Ernie K-Doe, in the early 1990s, his musical career had significantly dwindled and his life had become subsumed by alcohol. Miss Antoinette got him sober, booked him a new slate of gigs, and sewed the flashy outfits he wore onstage. Together they opened a popular music venue, the Mother-in-Law Lounge, in 1995. The lounge's name references Ernie K-Doe's 1961 chart topping single, "Mother-in-Law." This nationwide megahit ushered in a period of fame and success for K-Doe, but music industry winds shifted in ways that did not sustain his career. K-Doe resurfaced in the 1980s as an outrageous DJ on a local radio station, 90.7 WWOZ, but when he met Miss Antoinette, that gig had also ended. It is no overstatement to say that Miss Antoinette turned his life around, both personally and professionally. With Ernie, she transformed the lounge into a temple to his music and life. They covered the walls with photographs, stuffed the shelves with memorabilia, and stacked the jukebox with Ernie's records. On January 9, 1996, the two were married at the lounge, and on each anniversary, they reenacted their vows for their fans. As Miss Antoinette told a Jazz Fest crowd in 1998, "We did our wedding vows there and every year we recite our wedding vows over again. Same day, same time, wear the same clothes. So we like to welcome the fans. If you're in town January the ninth, please attend the wedding of Ernie K-Doe and I."[2] In this third period of his career, Ernie K-Doe dubbed himself "Emperor of the Universe" and named Miss Antoinette his Empress. They were a pair of royalty sitting on top of the world and ruling from their colorful castle, the Mother-in-Law Lounge.

As Ernie K-Doe's biographer Ben Sandmel reflects, in its heyday, the Mother-in-Law Lounge beckoned as a "walled oasis" in a "ravaged city."[3] The two-story building sits on North Claiborne Avenue, a thoroughfare that has long been a geographical focal point for black Mardi Gras traditions. In the 1960s, the construction of an elevated interstate eliminated Claiborne Avenue's grassy median and sliced historic African American neighborhoods in half. The interstate's construction ravaged, in Sandmel's terms, the economic, social, and cultural center of black New Orleans.[4] However, the Mother-in-Law Lounge remains a colorful oasis in the interstate's shadow. As Sandmel describes,

> Its outer perimeter was a parade of claw-foot bathtubs, painted and lined up end-to-end. This porcelain parapet suggested an esoteric art installation. But its primary function was to block drunk drivers from crashing through the wall of the inner sanctum: the small, two-story building that housed the Mother-in-Law Lounge and the K-Does' upstairs apartment.[5]

The Mother-in-Law Lounge's colorful décor extends to its façade, which is covered with Technicolor murals featuring larger-than-life renderings of Ernie, Miss Antoinette, and other local cultural icons, including the avant-garde musical duo Quintron and Miss Pussycat, and deceased Mardi Gras Indian Chief Allison "Tootie" Montana and his wife Joyce. These murals mirror the ones that appear on the interstate's support pillars, which picture the trees and traditions displaced by its construction. While Sandmel and many others have lamented the detrimental impact of the overpass on black Mardi Gras traditions, second line parades, and other African American cultural activities, Miss Antoinette was less pessimistic about the highway's presence. "Keep in mind what you had, don't lose that, but think about what you got now," she said. "If it rains on Mardi Gras day, that's a big umbrella."[6]

To enter the lounge when the K-Does still ran it, patrons would ring the buzzer and Miss Antoinette would answer by pressing a button behind the bar to unlock the front door.[7] Upon entering, visitors could never be sure of what they might encounter. One legendary episode occurred when Ernie suspected a *New York Times* reporter of boot-legging his live performance, and subsequently locked everyone inside while Miss Antoinette called the cops to report a robbery in progress.[8] When Ernie was still alive, his performances regularly graced the stage, along with Elvis impersonator Rico Watts and other local and traveling bands. Music journalist Alex Rawls surmised that, because of the "unique nature of Ernie K-Doe's fame—part musical hero, part cult icon—" the Mother-in-Law Lounge became a gathering place for musicians and music fans from different generations and backgrounds.[9] According to Sandmel, the lounge's "parade of picturesque patrons" included tat-tooed legions of alt-rock hipsters, Sixth and Seventh Ward neighbors, die-hard R&B fans on a musical pilgrimage, and those older, local fans who recalled K-Doe's 1960s stardom. When not pouring drinks, talking with visitors, or making announcements over her cab driver's micro-phone, the lounge's patrons might have found Miss Antoinette sitting at her sewing machine, where she stitched each of her husband's and her own ornate outfits. She drew upon the sewing skills learned from her grandmother—skills that she later put to use when fashioning Baby Doll dresses for herself. Stories of the lounge's eccentric goings on earned enough intrigue to become the subject of a play, *Burn K-Doe Burn: A Romantic Comedy from Another Dimension*, penned by Rob Florence in 2004, several years after Ernie's death.

When Ernie K-Doe died from cancer in 2001, at the age of sixty-five, his career had been on a comeback for about six years because of Miss Antoinette's savvy management. His celebrity status was confirmed by his legendary jazz funeral.[10] After her husband's passing, Miss Antoi-nette installed the most notable item amongst the lounge's surfeit of ephemera: Ernie K-Doe's effigy. Miss Antoinette commissioned Jason Poirier to make the statue, and he fashioned K-Doe's likeness from a department store mannequin. Much like the sentient K-Doe, the statue took on a vibrant public life. For example, every year on All Saints' Day, Miss Antoinette and friends commemorated Ernie's death at his tomb in St. Louis Cemetery Number Two. They arrived in Miss Antoinette's hearse—her personal vehicle, perfectly suited for carting the statue around town—decorated the tomb, positioned the statue outside of it, pitched a tent, and served gumbo to all passers-by and fans gathered there.[11] In between his frequent public appearances, the Ernie statue reigned on a wicker throne in a corner of the lounge, graced the cov-ers of local publications, and even earned the *Times-Picayune*'s satiric endorsement for mayor in 2010.

Miss Antoinette earned a fair amount of local fame as the stew-ard of her deceased husband's effigy, but she asserted herself as much more than an idiosyncrasy in New Orleans's vibrant cultural landscape. She turned the lounge into a community center and availed herself as a community organizer. Far more than a business, the Mother-in-Law Lounge became base camp used by various collectives, from social aid and pleasure clubs to Mardi Gras marching groups, as a place to hold meetings, fundraisers, sewing circles, and celebrations.[12] Many individuals also found a personal sanctuary in the lounge and comfort under Miss Antoinette's wing. Overall, Miss Antoinette embodied a unique brand of community organizing in New Orleans that centered on sharing stories, music, and meals.[13] In fact, when leading recovery efforts after Hurricane Katrina (2005), the aid organization Sweet Home New Orleans sought out Miss Antoinette right away—they knew that if they could help her to get back on her feet, then she would help a multitude of others to do the same.[14] The Mother-in-Law Lounge took in eight feet of water because of the levee failures following Hurricane Katrina, but it was rebuilt, thanks in part to volunteers from the nonprofit agency, Hands On New Orleans. When the lounge was finally ready to re-open, Miss Antoinette marked the occasion by constructing a Katrina effigy in the form of a witch. Patrons and friends assisted her in ceremoniously burying Katrina in the lounge's lawn.

As suggested by the Mother-in-Law Lounge's personified murals, the Ernie statue, and the Katrina witch, Miss Antoinette had an active history of constructing effigies, tributes, and monuments. Her efforts to revive the Baby Doll tradition can be seen in this context, as one effort in her commemoration work that both preserved the past and (re-) invented a present.

Miss Antoinette's Baby Doll group first emerged from the Mother-in-Law Lounge on Mardi Gras day, 2004. Members of the Miss Antoinette's Baby Dolls, which she dubbed the Ernie K-Doe Baby Dolls, cite several different factors motivating Miss Antoinette's desire to start the group. On one hand, Tee Eva Perry recalls that Miss Antoinette thought of the Baby Dolls as another way to keep Ernie's name alive. On the other hand, Geannie Thomas remembers that it all started with the murals. When Miss Antoinette commissioned a rendering of Chief Allison "Tootie" Montana on the lounge's façade, she began to wonder about the Baby Dolls. She recalled seeing groups of women dressed in short satin dresses parading with the Mardi Gras Indians in her youth, and got the idea to spearhead her own group.[15] Others attribute Miss Antoinette's and others' renewed interest in the Baby Doll tradition (at least in part) to the release of Royce Osborn's documentary film, *All on a Mardi Gras Day*, which debuted on public television in 2003. Osborn recalls, "After the movie first came out, we started really seeing a revival of the Baby Dolls. There were a couple dozen Baby Dolls in 2004. They all came out of the Mother-in-Law Lounge on N. Claiborne. After that year, they split into rival factions, so I knew it was gonna be strong."[16] In their inaugural march, Miss Antoinette and her Baby Dolls marched behind a banner and attracted a large number of followers. In one participant's estimation, the group exploded onto the Mardi Gras marching scene.

A key member of the Ernie K-Doe Baby Dolls was Miriam Batiste Reed, who paraded as a Baby Doll with her family in the first half of the twentieth century. Her first-hand knowledge was key to passing on the tradition to a new generation. According to Geannie Thomas, Miss Antoinette began forming her Baby Doll group by seeking out veterans, which led her to Reed, known to many as Ms. Batiste. In the weeks leading up to Mardi Gras, Ms. Batiste conducted a Baby Doll seminar for Miss Antoinette and her group inside the Mother-in-Law Lounge. She brought her handmade dresses and showed everyone how to cut a pattern for the bonnets out of newspaper. She also instructed the women on Baby Doll performance technique, showing them how to walk with a little shake, and reminding them that they could put anything they wanted in their baby bottles—Ms. Batiste claimed to prefer Scotch and milk.[17] Following Ms. Batiste's instructions, the Ernie K-Doe Baby Dolls would gather at the lounge every Sunday to work on their dresses and display their progress to the group. When the women discovered that the Baby Dolls' history had been linked to prostitution, Miss Antoinette declared that she wanted to distinguish her group from such associations. As a result, the K-Doe Baby Dolls took on a serious service role during the months between each Mardi Gras season. They visited nursing homes, sponsored Easter egg hunts, delivered food to needy families, and served as the pallbearers during the funeral for Lloyd Washington, singer and member of the Ink Spots.[18] They also made frequent public appearances around town, gracing the stages of Tipitina's, Rock 'n Bowl, the House of Blues, the Voodoo Festival in City Park, and marching in the Krewe of Muses Mardi Gras parade. Miss Antoinette and Geannie Thomas even performed as Baby Dolls with Al "Carnival Time" Johnson at a post-Katrina fundraiser in Boston.[19]

By Miss Antoinette's design, the K-Doe Baby Dolls was a diverse group, whose members were older and younger, black and white, born-and-raised New Orleanians and transplanted residents. As Miss Antoinette explained (in what was likely the last interview she ever gave):

> Half of us was from New Orleans, so whatever steps she [Ms. Batiste, the oldest living Baby Doll] was making, it was easy for us to catch on that day, because we had that music in us, you know what I'm saying? Older, younger, black, white. The reason we did black and white—we stressed we wanted white girls in there—because we're in a time now where black and white get together now. We didn't want that separation.[20]

Ann Bruce, a white woman who grew up in New Orleans, recalls the moment that Miss Antoinette invited her to join the K-Doe Baby Dolls. Bruce initially replied with hesitation: "Would it be OK, because these were black prostitutes?" Miss Antoinette replied, "This is the twenty-first century! This is the first group of integrated Baby Dolls!" That was all the encouragement Bruce needed.[21]

The multi-generational, multi-racial, and otherwise diverse group of K-Doe Baby Dolls demonstrates that music and dance can provide a meaningful language for people to communicate, and even to build meaningful relationships, across difference. Dance scholar Judith Hamera suggests that dance technique is a relational language for exchange, versus an object that dancers have and deploy. As a language that people use to speak to one another, dance technique has the potential to organize relationships "across culture and class to form affective environments, geographies of the heart."[22] In the case of the K-Doe Baby Dolls, speaking their dance language involved catching on to Ms. Batiste's steps. Dancing and marching together as part of the Baby Doll tradition enables New Orleans residents—black and white, young and old, native and newcomer—to find common ground, or a new terrain for exploring their differences, in an urban landscape that frequently divides residents by income, education, and race. It may seem remarkable that Miss Antoinette was able to gather such a diverse group of women to join the K-Doe Baby Dolls, but to those who knew her, it is no surprise. Throughout her various ventures, she was renowned for her unique ability to gather people together from all walks of life.

In the early hours of Mardi Gras morning, 2009, the first Baby Dolls arrived to the Mother-in-Law Lounge, prepared to come out the door as usual. However, they had to march without their leader. A few hours earlier, Miss Antoinette had suffered a fatal heart attack inside the lounge. She was sixty-six years old.

Ms. Antoinette's funeral was held the following Sunday, and it was a spectacle befitting of the cultural leader and community pillar that she was. Family, friends, and fans packed into St. James church for the service, sitting on the floor and standing in the back. Outside, a growing crowd waited patiently in the hot sun for the ceremony to end and the procession to emerge. By the time it did, hundreds of people—including photographers, videographers, and brass band musicians—had gathered on the church's lawn and beyond, blocking Ursulines Avenue. A vast cross-section of populations felt compelled to pay tribute to Miss Antoinette, reflecting the diverse allegiances that she so frequently facilitated. Uptown socialites walked alongside the lounge's neighbors from the Sixth and Seventh Wards. White hipsters turned out in droves from the nearby Bywater and Marigny neighborhoods. Chief among them was the avant-garde musician Quintron, who served as one of the pallbearers, wearing white gloves screen-printed with photographs of Miss Antoinette. Members of various social aid and pleasure clubs, including the Lower Ninth Ward Steppers and the Bayou Steppers, donned their colorful suits and streamers, pinned white doves to their shoulders, and hoisted their standards into the air. At least two Mardi Gras Indians in full regalia (one of them a white woman) joined the procession, while a line of suited Indians awaited the procession's arrival at the Mother-in-Law Lounge. And, of course, a few Baby Dolls donned their satin dresses and bonnets for the occasion. Many stalwarts of the local music community played the funeral, including members of the famed Tremé Brass Band and Preservation Hall Brass Band, while a whole cadre of self-styled percussionists beat on cowbells and tambourines.[23] People of all ages and races, residents of all kinds of neighborhoods, generations-old locals and brand new residents all danced together up the northbound lane of Ursulines Avenue; responded "Hey!" to the trumpet's call in the echo-friendly cavern under the I-10 overpass; and lingered outside the lounge for hours to share stories and sandwiches, play music, and dance with their children, all in her honor.

When the procession reached the Mother-in-Law Lounge, the pallbearers pulled the casket from its carriage. Miss Antoinette's daughter, Betty Fox, recalls that moment with wonder and reverence. The pallbearers lifted Miss Anoinette's casket into the air three times, as a form of tribute. Thinking about the massive crowd, the musicians, the documentarians, and the pomp and circumstance of her mother's funeral, Betty reflected, "That's like a queen that's gone to heaven."[24] Most who knew Miss Antoinette would agree.

NOTES

1. For more on Miss Antoinette's life, death, and cultural organizing activities, see Rachel Carrico, "On Thieves, Spiritless Bodies, and Creole Soul: Dancing through the Streets of New Orleans," *TDR: The Drama Review* 57, no. 1 (2013): 70–87.

2. Antoinette K-Doe and Ernie K-Doe, interview by Ben Sandmel, recorded at the New Orleans Jazz and Heritage Festival, May 3, 1998, MP3. New Orleans Jazz and Heritage Festival Foundation Archives, New Orleans.

3. Ben Sandmel, *Ernie K-Doe: The R&B Emperor of New Orleans* (New Orleans: Historic New Orleans Collection, 2012), 11.

4. For more on the I-10 construction and its impact on African American people and black cultural practices in New Orleans, see George Lipstiz, *How Racism Takes Place* (Philadelphia: Temple University Press, 2011), 224; Catherine Michna, "Hearing the Hurricane Coming: Storytelling, Second-Line Knowledges, and the Struggle for

Democracy in New Orleans," PhD dissertation, Boston College, 2011, 32–33; Kalamu ya Salaam, "Guarding the Flame of Life: The Funeral of Big Chief Donald Harrison Sr.," *Offbeat* (January 1999): 50–51; Matt Sakakeeny, "'Under the Bridge:' An Orientation to Soundscapes in New Orleans," *Ethnomusicology* 54, no. 1 (2010): 1–27.

5. Sandmel, *Ernie K-Doe*, 11.

6. Noah Bonaparte Pais, "An Original Passes," *The Gambit*, March 2, 2009, accessed March 21, 2011, www.bestofneworleans.com/gambit/antoinette-kandmdashdoe/Content?oid=1255710.

7. Following Miss Antoinette's death, her daughter, Betty Fox, moved back to New Orleans from Memphis to assume ownership and management of the lounge. After struggling to keep the doors open for a year and a half, she finally closed it in late 2010. New Orleans musician Kermit Ruffins assumed ownership and reopened the venue as Kermit Ruffins's Mother-in-Law Lounge in 2014.

8. Neil Strauss, "The Pop Life; Mother-in-Law of All Visits," *New York Times*, May 17, 2000, accessed June 29, 2015, http://www.nytimes.com/2000/05/17/arts/the-pop-life-mother-in-law-of-all-visits.html.

9. Alex Rawls, "Heartbeat Award: Antoinette K-Doe," *Offbeat Magazine* (January 2009): 42.

10. According to one source, Ernie K-Doe's funeral attracted 5,000 participants, and has been assessed as "the largest jazz funeral and second line New Orleans has ever seen. The grand celebration was quite in keeping with the style of the flamboyant K-Doe, proving that he was not just a legend in his own mind, but truly a respected legend by his many loving fans." Pat Jolly, *Ernie K-Doe: Emperor of the Universe—And Beyond!*, 2001, accessed August 30, 2011, http://www.itmustbejelly.com/Ernie-K-Doe/index2.htm.

11. Camille Hill-Prewitt, interview with the author, August 24, 2011; Ann Bruce, interview with the author, June 26, 2015.

12. Christilisa Gilmore, "It's a Darn God Shame: The Mother-in-Law Lounge Closes, For Real this Time," *Nola Defender*, December 7, 2010, accessed March 21, 2011, http://noladefender.com/content/its-darn-god-shame. George Lipsitz refers to the Lounge as the "Ernie K-Doe Community Center" in his chapter on New Orleans in *The Possessive Investment in Whiteness: How White People Profit from Identity Politics* (Philadelphia: Temple University Press, Revised and Expanded ed., 2006), 247.

13. Jordan Flaherty suggests that this sort of community organizing is particular to New Orleans. *Floodlines: Community and Resistance from Katrina to the Jena Six* (Chicago: Haymarket Books, 2010).

14. Jordan Hirsch, conversation with the author, October 16, 2009.

15. Tee Eva Perry and Geannie Thomas, interview with the author, October 18, 2009.

16. Helen A. Regis, "Introduction: Skeletons," in *The House of Dance and Feathers: A Museum by Ronald W. Lewis* by Rachel Breunlin and Ronald W. Lewis (New Orleans: Neighborhood Story Project, 2009), 178.

17. Noah Bonaparte Pais, "Rally of the Dolls," *Gambit, Blog of New Orleans*, February 16, 2009, accessed October 20, 2009, http://bestofneworleans.com.

18. The Ink Spots were an influential male vocal group during the World War II era. When the original group disbanded, numerous spin-off groups, composed of original and new members and also named the Ink Spots, continued to perform and record. Lloyd Washington was a frequent member of several of those groups. Marv Goldberg, "Group Members," *Ink Spot Evolution*, 2014, accessed July 16, 2015, http:// http://www.inkspotsevolution.com/groupmembers_page.htm.

19. Perry and Thomas, interview with the author, October 18, 2009.

20. Noah Bonaparte Pais, "R.I.P. Antoinette K-Doe," *The Gambit, Blog of New Orleans*, February 25, 2009, accessed December 23, 2010, www.bestofneworleans.com/blogofneworleans/archives/2009/02/25/rip-antoinette-k-doe.

21. Bruce, interview with the author, June 26, 2015.

22. Judith Hamera, *Dancing Communities: Performance, Difference and Connection in the Global City* (New York: Palgrave Macmillan, 2007), 60, 137.

23. The musicians at the funeral were Benny Jones, Sr., Lionel Batiste, Craig Kline, Woody Penouilh, William Smith, Kenneth Terry, Bruce Brackman, Steven Burke, Paul Robinson, Corey Henry, Kerry Brown, Seva Venet, James Andrews, Kevin Harris, and Robert Harris. The Grand Marshals were Oswald Jones and Jennifer Jones (Jordan Hirsch, correspondence with the author, October 22, 2009).

24. Betty Fox, interview with the author, October 14, 2009.

BIBLIOGRAPHY

Bruce, Ann. Interview with the author, June 26, 2015.

Carrico, Rachel. "On Thieves, Spiritless Bodies, and Creole Soul: Dancing through the Streets of New Orleans," *TDR: The Drama Review* 57, no. 1 (2013): 70–87.

Flaherty, Jordan. *Floodlines: Community and Resistance from Katrina to the Jena Six.* Chicago: Haymarket Books, 2010.

Fox, Betty. Interview with the author, October 14, 2009.

Goldberg, Marv. "Group Members." *Ink Spot Evolution.* Last updated 2014. Accessed July 16, 2015. http://www.inkspotsevolution.com/groupmembers_page.htm.

Hamera, Judith. *Dancing Communities: Performance, Difference and Connection in the Global City.* New York: Palgrave Macmillan, 2007.

Hill-Prewitt, Camille. Interview with the author, August 24, 2011.

Jolly, Pat. *Ernie K-Doe: Emperor of the Universe—And Beyond!* Last Updated 2001. Accessed August 30, 2011. http://www.itmustbejelly.com/Ernie-K-Doe/index2.htm.

K-Doe, Antoinette and Ernie K-Doe. Interview by Ben Sandmel, recorded at the New Orleans Jazz and Heritage Festival, May 3, 1998, MP3. New Orleans Jazz and Heritage Festival Foundation Archives, New Orleans.

Lipsitz, George. *The Possessive Investment in Whiteness: How White People Profit from Identity Politics.* Philadelphia: Temple University Press, Revised and Expanded Edition, 2006.

———. *How Racism Takes Place.* Philadelphia: Temple University Press, 2011.

Michna, Catherine. "Hearing the Hurricane Coming: Storytelling, Second-Line Knowledges, and the Struggle for Democracy in New Orleans." PhD dissertation, Boston College, 2011.

Regis, Helen A. "Introduction: Skeletons." In *The House of Dance and Feathers: A Museum by Ronald W. Lewis* by Rachel Breunlin and Ronald W. Lewis, 178–80. New Orleans: Neighborhood Story Project, 2009.

Perry, Tee Eva and Geannie Thomas. Interview with the author, October 18, 2009.

Salaam, Kalamuya. "Guarding the Flame of Life: The Funeral of Big Chief Donald Harrison Sr." *Offbeat* (January 1999): 50–51.

Sandmel, Ben. *Ernie K-Doe: The R&B Emperor of New Orleans.* New Orleans: Historic New Orleans Collection, 2012.

Sakakeeny, Matt. "'Under the Bridge:' An Orientation to Soundscapes in New Orleans." *Ethnomusicology* 54, no. 1 (2010): 1–27.

Adella Gautier illustrating that "The hands come off so I can take them across the street to get a manicure." Reproduced with permission of Rob Florence.

Antoinette K-Doe with the statue of Ernie K-Doe. Reproduced with permission of Rob Florence.

Harold Evans, Eva "Tee-Eva" Perry, and Rock N Bowl's John Blancher. Reproduced with permission of Rob Florence.

The World That Antoinette K-Doe Made

—Rob Florence

Antoinette K-Doe moved through life differently. Although that's a tremendous understatement, it's not nearly as sweeping as countless Ernie K-Doe-isms, starting with, "There are five great singers of Rhythm and Blues: Ernie K-Doe, James Brown, and Ernie K-Doe!" Antoinette didn't ask people to do things; she told you to do something. I wrote two full-length plays in response to directives issued by her. The first was *Burn K-Doe Burn!* whose opening line was something she actually said, a statement that reflected her singular world view. Referring to the legendary Ernie K-Doe statue, *Burn K-Doe Burn!* starts with Antoinette explaining, "The hands come off so I can take them across the street to get a manicure."

Burn K-Doe Burn! was peculiar on several levels. Actor Harold Evans didn't play Ernie K-Doe but rather the K-Doe statue come-to-life. Adella Gautier played Antoinette, while Antoinette played her mother Leola, Ernie's second mother-in-law. Therefore Antoinette was acting opposite her own life being depicted on stage in very personal detail at a time when she had not finished mourning her deceased husband. But Antoinette probably never did stop mourning Ernie, considering that she lived with him in the form of a statue until she died.

Antoinette brought wonderful, outside-the-box ideas to the production, such as audience-participation Ernie K-Doe-karaoke for the pre-show. One night Allen Toussaint performed this entire pre-show, which was of course completely made up of his songs. On another evening, Antoinette informed us that she might receive "a long-distance phone call" during the show but that her "double" would take over. She played her first scene, but for her second scene an identically dressed Eva

2004 cast with Baby Doll "Lollipop." Reproduced with permission of Rob Florence.

"Tee-Eva" Perry took the stage. When it was time for Antoinette's third entrance, she showed up again, her long-distance call completed.

Antoinette's crew, including Miriam Baptiste Reed, Eva Perry, Lollipop, and Geannie Thomas, would dress as Baby Dolls for the show. During scenes that broke the fourth wall, the Baby Dolls would enlist audience members to dance along with the action. One particular production challenge was how to convey Ernie K-Doe's epic funeral, which was attended by five thousand people. Our plan was to have Adella grieve Ernie's passing while seated under projections of the actual funeral, as a heart-wrenching funeral dirge played. That was as good as we could do in the confines of the theatre and of our budget. However, all the power and majesty of that grand event was unexpectedly transmitted by the unrehearsed movement of one Baby Doll. On opening night during this challenging scene, Lollipop spontaneously took the stage in her Baby Doll attire, ceremoniously brandishing a parasol to the dirge's stirring sway. Lollipop circled the entire playing area in classic jazz funeral style. Instantaneously birthed from this Baby Doll's sensibilities, the gesture's energy was breathtaking, while its economy was brilliant.

I worked closely with the K-Does on our cemetery preservation group, Friends of New Orleans Cemeteries (FNOC). Ernie was FNOC's grand marshal, making us the only preservation group in the universe with a grand marshal. As with everything else they did, the K-Does had their own approach toward mourning, and in essential New Orleans style, their approach toward things funereal was creative and celebratory. When Jessie Hill died, Antoinette K-Doe made outfits that identi-

Antoinette K-Doe addresses mourners including Geannie Thomas and Miriam Baptiste Reed (far right). Reproduced with permission of Rob Florence.

Hazel Washington holds cremated remains of her husband, Lloyd Washington. Reproduced with permission of Rob Florence.

Antoinette K-Doe, Tee Eva Perry (center), and "Lollipop," 'Baby Dolls as Pallbearers' at the interment of Lloyd Washington. Reproduced with permission of Rob Florence.

cally matched Hill's burial clothes. At the service, Antoinette, Ernie, and Hill's wife Doris wore black pants and jackets trimmed with gold at the shoulder and lapel, the very same uniform Jessie was wearing in his Holt Cemetery grave.

Antoinette K-Doe was a driving force behind the New Orleans Musicians' Tomb, a historic St. Louis Cemetery #1 final resting place whose use was donated by the New Orleans musical dynasty Barbarin family and whose restoration was paid for in part by benefits played by local musicians. The tomb now offers free burial to musicians. Vocalist Lloyd Washington of the Ink Spots was the Musicians' Tomb's first interment. One snag was that he died six months before the tomb restoration was completed. During those six months, Lloyd's cremated remains waited on a shrine Antoinette created at the Mother-in-Law Lounge. That August, Antoinette actually brought Lloyd to my 40th birthday party.

When it came time to inaugurate this first-of-its-kind grave with the burial of this celebrated singer, Antoinette decided to establish a precedent. "We've all seen second lines. Let's do something different for Lloyd and the tomb," she reasoned. So she conceived the idea of a "Baby Doll funeral," claiming there had not been one before. She should know, being the person who revived the Baby Doll tradition, which been gone dormant for decades.[1]

Moving forward from Lloyd Washington's 2004 funeral to Antoinette's in 2009, it was encouraging to see the presence of not only Baby Dolls but Mardi Gras Indians and Skull and Bones Gang members (along with the legions of Mother-in-Law Lounge regulars who seemed to have walked right out of a Fellini film). Prior to Antoinette's funeral, the typical streetscape had pretty much been brass bands and second lines. Antoinette must have been smiling down on the Baby Dolls out in full force for Trumpet Black's recent funeral.[2] This confluence of Baby Dolls, Indians and Skull and Bones Gang on Mardi Gras Day is a holy trinity consciously cultivated by Antoinette at the Mother-in-Law Lounge. It was as if Antoinette had arranged her own funeral, but this extraordinary scene emerged from the collective consciousness of thousands of people who knew that Antoinette would want it that way. In this town, which has given the world some of its most distinct and dazzling funerals, Antoinette K-Doe moved this needle forward even after she passed, similar to how she energized Ernie K-Doe's legacy after his death.

In 2011, the K-Doe-inspired mashup of New Orleans street traditions, the theatre, and historic aboveground cemeteries rolled on. We revived *Burn K-Doe Burn!* to commemorate the 50th anniversary of "Mother-in-Law" charting. This Allen Toussaint-penned K-Doe hit was the first New Orleans single to reach #1 on the Billboard pop charts. The Baby Doll

Baby Dolls Resa "Cinnamon Black" Bazile (left), Carol "Baby Doll Kit" Harris (center), Al Johnson, and Eva "Tee Eva" Perry (far right) at 2011 production of "Burn K-Doe Burn."

Statue in car when mistaken for a dead body. Reproduced with permission of Rob Florence.

presence expanded in the 2011 *Burn K-Doe Burn!* production, which after Antoinette's passing now featured Tee Eva as the mother-in-law character. We continued Antoinette's concept of pre-show Ernie K-Doe karaoke, which Al "Carnival Time" Johnson emceed every night. (Al had emceed several of the 2004–2005 pre-shows with Oliver "Who Shot the La La" Morgan.) In the 2011 pre-shows, there were more Baby Dolls who were more elaborately dressed, probably reflecting the increase of Baby Dolls on Carnival streets from 2004 to 2011.

Another difference in the 2011 version was that the Toussaint-penned Ernie K-Doe song "Here Come the Girls" had been recently released

Sylvia Barker, a Friends of New Orleans Cemeteries board member and daughter of Danny and Blue Lu Barker at interment of her husband's, Leonard Jones, remains. Reproduced with permission of Rob Florence.

because of the popularity of its use in the U.K. Boots television commercial. "Here Come the Girls" was the final pre-show song every night and Al Johnson went into the audience to make sure that every "girl" in the house was on that stage, throwing civilian theatre-goers together with Baby Dolls, probably recruiting some maskers in the process.

Something that occurred during this 2011 run with the statue falls squarely under the category of "only in Antoinette's universe." Her daughter Betty Fox allowed a rare public appearance of the actual statue at our closing performances. She told me I could come get the statue out of her closet, but that I'd probably have to kill a big spider first. I felt like I was in a Greek myth. I retrieved the statue without incident and we loaded it into my Ford Explorer. Shortly thereafter a neighbor called the police to report two people putting a dead body into a car.

I arranged two daytime events in conjunction with the *Burn K-Doe Burn!* revival. The first event was the unveiling of an historic marker I had made for Allen Toussaint's childhood home, where at a young age he wrote an astounding number of classic songs, including "Mother-in-Law." Ernie K-Doe, Irma Thomas, Aaron Neville, and many other legendary singers would go to 3041 College Court and wait while he wrote the songs on the spot at a remarkably fast pace. The second event tied up several loose ends, including the unveiling of a plaque for Antoinette on her tomb. This event started with the interment of Sylvia Barker's husband Leonard Jones's cremated remains, which had been in Rochester, New York, for a couple of years. Not only was Sylvia a Friends of New Orleans Cemeteries board member, but she's also the daughter of Danny and Blue Lu Barker, making her a family member of this Barbarin family tomb.

In characteristic Antoinette K-Doe style, this far-reaching event started in the mode of: "*This* has never happened before," and continued that way. After the interment of Sylvia's husband, Cinnamon Black and Tee Eva Perry led Baby Dolls before the brass band and second line from St. Louis Cemetery #1 to St. Louis Cemetery #2, probably also a first of its kind. *The Times-Picayune* ran a beautifully surreal photo of Cinnamon behind her parasol as she led the procession to the unveiling of Antoinette K-Doe's and Earl King's plaques on the Duval-Twichell family tomb. The idea for the Musicians' Tomb arose after Anna Ross and Heather Twichell had been so generous as to inter Ernie K-Doe in their tomb because K-Doe had said he wanted to be buried in St. Louis Cemetery #2, "Around all those great musicians like Danny Barker." K-Doe's funeral was followed six months later by interment of Antoinette's mother Leola (Ernie's second mother-in-law, the character in *Burn K-Doe Burn!*). Earl King was subsequently buried here, at which point Anna Ross reasoned that New Orleans needed a tomb to keep its postmortem musical community together, which led to the New Orleans Musicians' Tomb.[3]

A side note about Earl King's burial: Earl was the third nonpolitical figure to be laid in state at Gallier Hall (the first two were Danny Barker and Ernie K-Doe), from where his grand funeral proceeded to Congo Square. His family interred him in St. Louis Cemetery #2 the next day. Antoinette called me and asked me to go with her. I told her I didn't know Earl King personally so didn't want to attend this small family gathering. She then said, "I need your truck to carry the statue." So I picked up Antoinette and the statue at the lounge and drove them to the cemetery. Antoinette also brought a boom box, which I figured would be for playing hymns or maybe Earl King's music. After the interment, the King family, Antoinette, and tomb owners Anna Ross and Heather Twichell gathered around the tomb with the statue to visit and reminisce, and Antoinette played Ernie K-Doe songs on that boom box.

ANTOINETTE K-DOE
(February 3, 1943 - February 24, 2009)
Spouse of Ernie K-Doe, who added years to his life, and owner of the Mother in Law Lounge, a gathering place dedicated to perpetuating classic New Orleans R. & B. Antoinette breathed new life into Carnival traditions, especially the Baby Dolls, and All Saints' Day observances. She was a magnificent chef and clothing designer and did much to revive New Orleans following Hurricane Katrina.
Friends of New Orleans Cemeteries

Antoinette K-Doe grave plaque. Reproduced with permission of Rob Florence.

Back to the 2011 Earl King and Antoinette K-Doe cemetery tribute: when the procession arrived from St. Louis #1 led by Baby Dolls, the blaring brass band was greeted by Sunpie and the Sunspots playing Earl King songs. This was probably also a first: acoustic brass band music preceding a second line sonically merging with electric R&B in the open air of an historic New Orleans cemetery. Sunpie played Earl's classics to the King family, Baby Dolls, and second liners, after which we unveiled the two plaques on the tomb. I had written the text and didn't forget to note, "Antoinette breathed new life into Carnival traditions, especially the Dolls."

So as the tenth anniversary of Hurricane Katrina approaches, my second Antoinette-inspired full length play is in rehearsal: *Katrina: Mother-In-Law Of 'Em All*, a docu-theatre piece made up of true stories and set in the Mother-in-Law Lounge. As with *Burn K-Doe Burn!* the opening line of this play is something Antoinette actually said, which makes people say, "What?!" The Katrina play starts with Antoinette saying, "Yes, three pieces, in a garbage bag, in the closet!" This cryptic statement is in response to a newspaper article which reported that Ernie K-Doe drowned in the storm. She contacted the writer with a correction: "Ernie K-Doe did not drown in the storm. He was in a garbage bag, in three pieces, right here, in my closet." I hope the writer realized she was talking about the Ernie K-Doe statue.

When Antoinette told me that story in September 2005, it was the first time I had laughed since Hurricane Katrina. In the same conversation, she told me another anecdote, which made me laugh for the second time since Hurricane Katrina, and that story involved a Baby Doll. We were discussing the Katrina diaspora and the way it highlighted how New Orleans culture doesn't always translate elsewhere. She told me that Lollipop had ended up in the Astrodome with thousands of traumatized evacuees. Lollipop told Antoinette that because everyone was so sad, she decided to second line through the Astrodome in her Baby Doll outfit. (This struck me like a ton of bricks; most people forgot to bring a toothbrush and a change of clothes, yet Lollipop had the presence of mind to evacuate with her Baby Doll costume!) Lollipop the Baby Doll started to sashay through the tragic Astrodome, and a local person hollered at her, "Hey lady! Put some clothes on!"

Antoinette K-Doe did so much to perpetuate the legacy of deceased friends and loved ones who had created and defined New Orleans culture. Her efforts made clear that in the spirit world of this city, people can become even more of a presence after their passing. Just as Antoinette's life's work perpetuated so much brilliant culture that the rest of the world tends to overlook, the Ernie K-Doe Baby Dolls, author and curator Kim Vaz-Deville with co-curator and painter Ron Bechet, and McKenna Museum of African-American Art kept her spirit alive in the exhibit "Contemporary Artists Respond to the New Orleans Baby Dolls." At the exhibit's events, you could feel Antoinette's spirit in attendance, delighted to see so many young children carrying the torch. Without Antoinette K-Doe's Herculean efforts to connect the past to the present and future, those children might not have participated in that exhibit. For that matter, this fantastic exhibit might not have happened at all.

So as Antoinette kept the Baby Dolls alive, the Baby Dolls are now doing the same for Antoinette.

NOTES

1. Noah Bonaparte Pais, "Rally of the Dolls," *Gambit Magazine*, February 16, 2004. Access at http://www.bestofneworleans.com/gambit/rally-of-the-dolls/Content?oid =1256917.

2. Offbeat Staff (May 24, 2015) Photos: Trumpet Black Funeral Second Line, *Offbeat Magazine*. Travis Hill died unexpected while on tour in Japan. He is from the musical family of Jesse Hill. This family is closely aligned the Gold Digger Baby Dolls. Access at https://www.offbeat.com/news/photos-trumpet-black-funeral-second-line/.

3. Gwen Thompkins, "Beyond The Music In St. Louis Cemetery No. 2.," National Public Radio, Morning Edition, July 5, 2012. Access at http://www.npr.org/2012/07/05 /156252315/beyond-the-music-in-st-louis-cemetery-no-2.

Sass and Circumstance

The Magic of the Baby Dolls

—Daniele Gair

I am a native New Orleanian. I take a great deal of pride in having an insider's view of this magnetic city, and I enjoy being knowledgeable enough to educate a newcomer just a little, especially when it comes to *my* hometown. My city, however, is one with a complex history, one with a multitude of layers, meanings, and contradictions, and it yields up treasures of enlightenment and experience in the most surprising, unique, and joyous ways. One of these treasures presented itself to me as if by magic.

On the frigid Mardi Gras of 2015, I was given the opportunity to participate in a tradition that not many people, even the most in-the-know natives, are aware of. The masking custom known as the Baby Dolls has roots deep in New Orleans's Black Storyville neighborhoods. This tradition is one of the most vibrant ways in which African American women were able to exhibit power and agency throughout the Jim Crow era of segregation and repression. Yet, for years, it has either escaped common knowledge or has been, at best, ignored by many official histories of the city, and disparaged and maligned, at worst. As "loose women," those who started the Baby Doll tradition had little if any political or social power; their strength had a much deeper source, and in my opinion, an ancient and sacred one.

The day was monumental for me in a number of ways. In my mind, I separate it into three distinct parts, each one giving me a different perspective of being a Baby Doll. I was introduced to the Baby Dolls by Dr. Kim Vaz-Deville in the fall of 2014. I had recently joined Xavier University's staff as the manager of the university's art collection, and Dr. Vaz is, for lack of a better term, one of my fairy godmothers.

When she told me about the Baby Dolls and her incredible project in documenting the tradition and the lives of the women who mask, I was instantly intrigued. Who were the Baby Dolls and how had I never heard of them before? Storyville had fascinated me for years, and I knew that there were separate brothels for white, black, and mixed women, and that there were different establishments for black and white customers. But I had never heard of the women themselves having the amount of control and self-determination that the first Baby Dolls exhibited. What I discovered was that these qualities have been passed down to today's Baby Dolls, not only in the costumes and rituals, but in their response to adversity and sense of community.

It was my friend and colleague, Sarah Clunis, who suggested that she, Dr. Vaz-Deville, and I mask as Baby Dolls for Mardi Gras. As exciting as the prospect was, almost immediately, a baseline of apprehension ran steadily through my mind. My first concern was with my costume. Let me add that this suggestion was proposed and agreed upon just as the Carnival season began, barely a month before Fat Tuesday. The voice of worry in my psyche fretted that this wasn't nearly enough time to pull a proper costume together, especially for one so perennially costume-challenged as myself.

I've never felt that I've been good at costumes. I'm usually underwhelmed with my efforts, as a matter of fact. I remember one Mardi Gras when a friend and I dressed as teenyboppers from the 1980s. The different reactions we received as we bounced about the French Quarter that day were telling. She looked great, like she'd just stepped out of a Cyndi Lauper video, and I looked, well, maybe a little like a Tina Turner impersonator. Not a bad thing at all, just not on point, and definitely not attention-grabbing. Nevertheless, despite a slight nervousness that stirred automatically at the prospect of doing something so new and brazen, I agreed to join in, and was swept up in a whirl of planning. We strategized on color themes, debated about whether our dresses should match, and determined what sorts of accessories were absolutely necessary. We emailed one another links to different dresses, extolled the virtues of one style over another, and chose blush pink as our color. It was exhilarating and slightly terrifying, especially when we realized how last-minute we really were, but in the back of my mind, I was most hesitant about entering into what was, for me, new social territory.

As the big day approached, other logistical concerns took over. For one thing, cold is not something that one wants to be on Mardi Gras day. For at least a week before, my comrades-in-charms and I eyed forecasts with dread. Early reports were that the day would be extremely chilly, no higher than 40° F. We prayed for warmer temperatures, not merely for the sake of comfort, but because we had made a pact to costume that none of us was willing to break. Normally, I'm pretty good at skipping out on things, but this time, it wasn't an option. I had pledged myself to my friends and to this experience. I hastily procured tights and a matching sweater and pilfered my husband's thermal underwear.

Stepping Out

Allow me to take a moment to talk about the logistics of going out for Mardi Gras. The two hardest things to manage during Carnival are driving and other people. If one is not fortunate enough to live on or near a parade route, or if, like my comrades and I, one plans to be in another part of town, the day begins rather early. Traffic is usually nightmarish throughout the season thanks to road closures to make way for parades, and worst on Fat Tuesday most of all. Having a place to park is never a guarantee, either. Waking up late, as I did, is not recommended, as it only adds to one's stress level at the beginning of the day. Add to this a separate contingent of people, family or friends from out of town, for example, and you're asking for trouble.

We had decided to meet in the Marigny neighborhood, which is located a few blocks down river of the French Quarter. Here, we would join the boisterous Saint Ann Marching Krewe before venturing up into the Treme neighborhood, the home of the famous Mother-in-Law Lounge made popular by the late and legendary Ernie and Antoinette K-Doe. We were all being accompanied by our patient and accommodating husbands, who were, for the most part, dressing to match our outfits. Joining our core group were friends of mine who had come in from San Francisco. The ladies of the group had heard of our Baby Doll plans and were eager to dress accordingly.

Late start notwithstanding, my husband and I miraculously found a parking spot not far from Mimi's in the Marigny, one of my favorite bars and the official starting point (or as official as these things get) for the Saint Ann parade. I finished getting dressed in the car, and as we ventured out into the chilly morning, I texted furiously. The more people I manage to find during Carnival, the calmer I become. The Californians had met up with other friends at another bar, but I was desperate to find the other members of my triad, so my nervousness wasn't completely assuaged until we began to make our way to Mimi's. There the crowd thickened, making the temperature seem almost balmy.

The three of us had all decided to carry parasols, or in my case, a black pagoda umbrella, and it was with these that Sarah, Kim and I located one another in that massive crowd. Introductions were made, costumes admired, photos taken, and the sense of anticipation grew as we awaited the start of the parade. Someone even handed me a small, woven leather whip. I was sure it was an omen of some kind. My nerves gradually gave way to feelings of camaraderie, not only with my fellow Baby Dolls, but with all of the revelers. To be honest, it's an effect that Mardi Gras tends to have on me, and on others, I suspect. But for me, the idea of belonging is one that looms large; the question of acceptance, entry and being received without question is always in the back of my mind. As I think back on it, one of the things I admire about the Baby Dolls is the fact that they made their own space, both within the segregated theatre of Carnival in New Orleans and in everyday life. Belonging is not a question when you carve out your own place.

Our march toward the French Quarter continued, and our joviality increased exponentially. I suppose the free shots of King Cake vodka helped. Though the mood got lighter and lighter, it remained a bit difficult to keep up with everyone in our group. We convened at our friends' rental for a break, and gathered our strength, but I got the feeling that the Californians were interested in going a different way than we three had in mind. A popular stop for the Saint Ann krewe is the R Bar, and the crowd reached critical mass, making it harder for everyone to stay together. It was here that the decision was made for the three of us, plus husbands, to head toward the Mother-In-Law Lounge. I felt a twinge of guilt for abandoning our friends, but we were on a Baby Doll pilgrimage.

Paying Respects

As we ventured toward Claiborne Avenue and the Baby Dolls gathering there, the camaraderie that went with being a part of a throng gave way to something lighter. With this smaller fellowship, anticipation replaced my earlier apprehension. The closer we got to our destination, the more our costumes drew attention and recognition from people out on the street. We were greeted with shouts of "Hey, Baby Dolls," and I gradually got used to Being Seen.

The crowd that surrounded the Mother-In-Law was alive with color. Kim was instantly at home, greeting women she knew from her years of research. There were what seemed like several separate groups of Baby Dolls in attendance, as well as Mardi Gras Indians and Bone Men. This was my introduction to the relationship between these groups. We went inside to get drinks and were greeted warmly, asked about our costumes, and corralled for pictures.

The Baby Dolls converged with members of the North Side Skull and Bones Gang starting from the Ooh Poo Pah Doo Bar and going to the Mother-in-Law Lounge to join the Fi-Yi-Yi Mardi Gras Indian Tribe on Mardi Gras Day Tuesday February 17, 2015. Photos by Kim Vaz-Deville.

Resa "Cinnamon Black" Bazile

Micah "Pretty Face Baby" Theodore

Carol "Baby Doll Kit" Harris

Dianne Honore makes her debut as a Baby Doll with the Gold Digger Baby Dolls of Treme.

Resa "Cinnamon Black" Bazile (left) and Vanessa Thornton (right) dance in front of the Mother-in-Law Lounge on Mardi Gras Day Tuesday February 17, 2015. Photos by Kim Vaz-Deville.

Wanda Pearson, a member of the Gold Diggers Baby Dolls (left) and Tammy Montana, a member of Cinnamon's Treme Million Dollar Baby Dolls (right).

New Orleans Baby Dolls gather at the Mother-in-Law Lounge on Claiborne Avenue on Mardi Gras, 2015. Adults in the photo pictured in the first row left to right: Vanessa Thornton, Carol Harris, Rosalind Theodore. In the back row left to right are Janice Kimble, Eva Perry, Felicia Smith, Joell Lee, an unidentified reveler, Dianne Honore, Merline Kimble, and Wanda Pearson. The children are all relatives of the maskers.

As we stood outside, eyeing the pork chops being grilled on the curb, I tried to take in as much as I could about the Baby Dolls. It became obvious that it was all about them. The dresses were similar only in their vibrancy. Satin abounded, the hand-made beauty of each outfit equal to those of the Indians who were obviously there *in support* of the Baby Dolls, rather than the other way around. This was also not just a tradition reserved for women of a particular age. There were three to four generations present, from grand matriarchs to little girls still in diapers. This was a women's space.

This elevation of women may seem out of order in the patriarchal, male-centered society in which we live. However, its roots stretch out into antiquity with the worship of the Sacred Feminine. For millennia, the Divine was worshipped as a woman, one who embodied the life-giving force. In the regions of ancient Sumer and Assyria, she was known as Inanna, or Ishtar, and her worship involved an energetic expression of sexuality made sacred. Her rituals were rowdy celebrations of fertility, and besides making the "Hieros Gamos," or sacred marriage, with a king in order to ensure the fruitfulness of the land, her priestesses led the crowd in frenetic and suggestive dances. It was through these women that the people touched the Divine.

Kim Vaz-Deville, Albert Polite Jr., Sarah Clunis (middle) and Daniele Gair at the Mother-in-Law Lounge, February 17, 2015. Albert Polite Jr., spy boy for the Fi Yi Yi Mardi Gras Indians, wears a suit of pink feathers and elephants, to honor the passing of his wife from breast cancer. Courtesy of Kim Vaz-Deville.

There was a feeling of passing on the Baby Doll tradition to the next generation, as well, as the young girls followed their elders' lead, standing and talking, posing for pictures and walking in and out of the lounge. In fact, the babies were shown off as much as their mothers, grandmothers and aunties. And they weren't just cute curiosities; their voices were heard and welcomed in the singing and chanting. They were given space to dance and be who they were. So often children are told to be quiet, that their voices or opinions aren't significant in the adult arena, especially in the African American community, but this wasn't one of those times.

That the women were the focus does not mean that the masculine element was excluded from the revelry. The aforementioned Indians and Bone Men were present, as were younger men and boys, who participated in black pants and white shirts, and accessorized in the colors of the Baby Dolls with whom they were associated. And this is not a modern-day development. What may seem like a feminist spin on an old tradition is in fact *the* tradition. Men have always supported the Baby Dolls, not so much in a patriarchal sense, but by participating in a ritual that placed women at its center. I was amazed by the way in which these women owned this space and their rightful place in it, and by how the inclusion of young men served to seamlessly instill respect for women as a natural attitude. This also echoes through our earliest history. In her book *Seductress: Women Who Ravished the World and Their Lost Art of Love*, Betsy Prioleau calls seductresses "mistresses of misrule, carnival queens who cast off repressive shackles and declared a public holiday," and that, citing Shere Hite, men are instinctively drawn toward women who allow them to cut loose. Not only that, but prehistoric men, in worshipping the sex goddess, "cross-dressed, caroused, and let the deity *take possession of him*." (Emphasis mine.) Cross-dressing is another Baby Doll tradition, with men often wearing the finest ladies' garments that they could get their hands on.

The men that day exhibited reverence for the women in their lives in pain as well as joy. One of the most interesting people we spoke to was an Indian in a stunning pink outfit, Mr. Albert Polite. Of course, since we were in pink as well, we at first thought "Photo op!" But as we talked with him and got a better look at his costume, we noticed the pink ribbons. He had designed his suit for that year in honor of his wife who had succumbed to breast cancer.

The reaction to adversity is one thing that sets Baby Dolls apart. Illness, sudden loss of family and friends, violence and instability are parts of life for many, but the masking remains a way to express the joy of living. It's the spirit of the second line: at first, a mournful dirge is played and steps are slow and labored. The sadness is honored and faced. Then, the beat picks up, and mourning is transformed into a celebration, not only of the life of the one lost, but of life in general.

Into the Heart

Baby Dolls don't stay in one place for long on Mardi Gras. Like the Indians, they walk, strut and dance through the neighborhoods, stopping at designated spots or wherever the mood strikes them. So it was that the time came to move. We followed a group of Baby Dolls up Claiborne Avenue to Esplanade Avenue, then decided to head toward the New Orleans African American Museum in the Treme and the Backstreet Cultural Museum. The day had already transformed from hectic to spectacular for me, but it was during this walk, through a small part of town I had never even driven through, that the day began to be infused with a sort of magic.

The layers of history in New Orleans can be kind of like the pages of a book, flipping back and forth, and nowhere is this more apparent that in the Faubourg Treme neighborhood. As we strolled through on our way to the African American Museum, the pages seemed to turn back to another chapter. The Treme is home to one of the oldest black communities in the country, and one in which a certain level of autonomy not enjoyed by blacks in others states thrived. The neighborhood is one of the pillars of the city's cultural heritage, and its deep roots can still be felt. I had the sense that, even if the Baby Dolls weren't born here, this was sort of a spiritual home for them. It could have been the dresses, the incredible architecture, or the general high (alcohol content) spirits, but it felt marvelous just to be there. This feeling grew as we took photos at the Museum's Villa Meilleur, literally "the best estate," and marveled at its timeless beauty.

But we had magic, too, and it wasn't until we reached Backstreet, which is dedicated to documenting New Orleans's masking traditions, that we fully realized that we had Baby Doll Magic. Everywhere we went, we were greeted with smiles, every person we talked to genuinely loved Baby Dolls, wanted to reminisce about Baby Dolls in years past, and take pictures. Little girls looked up at awe at us, entranced by the frilly lace and fantasy hair. I was floating on air, as enchanted as everyone else by the love and good feelings that the Baby Dolls engender in those around them.

An Auspicious Ending

The day ended as Mardi Gras does for many: in the French Quarter. We emerged from the Treme as from a dream as we crossed Basin Street. I dragged my partners to a dance party on Chartres Street being hosted by one friend and deejayed by another. We ate jambalaya and danced in the street. There was something almost worshipful about the mood, as if we were back in ancient Assyria, dancing for the Divine Feminine. It was a fitting end to a day of joyous community that only this city could create.

BIBLIOGRAPHY

Prioleau, Betsy. *Seductress: Women Who Ravished the World and Their Lost Art of Love.* New York, NY: Penguin Books, 2003.

Visual Artists Respond to the New Orleans Baby Dolls

John McCrady's "Southern Eccentric" Regionalism

"Negro Maskers" from the *Mardi Gras Day* Series of 1948

—Mora J. Beauchamp-Byrd

n a 2005 publication called *The Ongoing Moment,* British journalist and novelist Geoff Dyer discusses several Depression-era WPA (Works Progress Administration) photographers.[1] The federal WPA and Farm Security Administration (FSA) were among numerous programs established by Roosevelt's New Deal legislation, a series of domestic economic programs enacted in the U.S. between 1933 and 1936 that were meant to address needs brought about by the Great Depression: relief for the unemployed and impoverished, national economic recovery, and reform of the nation's financial systems.[2] The WPA and FSA, distinct from other government-funded projects, employed artists to produce public works of art such as murals, and to document, through photography and other artistic means, the devastation caused by widespread economic depression. The FSA, in particular, marked a particular milestone in American photographic history; it was the sole historical moment in American history in which a government organization, in a highly expansive way, funded a large-scale visual documentation of American life.

Dyer's *Ongoing Moment* examines images that emerged from Roy Stryker's eight-year tenure as photography director of the historical section of the FSA, and their documentation of the social and cultural devastation arising from the Great Depression. The resultant photographs were meant to demonstrate, in a somewhat propagandistic manner, the intrinsic value of Roosevelt's New Deal policies. Stryker had been influenced by early twentieth-century images of New York City slums by Lewis Hine and similarly themed, late nineteenth century images by Jacob Riis. Hines and Riis's photographs would greatly impact child labor laws and spark other social reforms, initiatives that solidified Stryker's belief in the transformative potential of the photographic image. Under Stryker's direction, FSA photographers produced a virtual catalogue of imagery that documented the resilience of everyday Americans as they faced the seemingly insurmountable hardships of the Great Depression.

The seminal images by renowned American photographers Walker Evans, Dorothea Lange and others represent critical examples of works produced for the FSA during the mid to late 1930s. The FSA, initially known as The Resettlement Administration, was one of Roosevelt's New Deal agencies aimed at improving the lives of struggling, impoverished farmers and sharecroppers. By 1935, the FSA was led by Roy Stryker, and he was granted sole responsibility for producing a photographic record of the agency's policies and practices. Dyer's text notes that as Stryker's sense of his mission increased, he began issuing detailed 'shooting scripts,' divided by season as well as location. These itemized lists clearly outlined the ideal images sought by Stryker from FSA photographers. For example, Stryker's shooting script for "Summer" included the following:

> Crowded cars going out on the open road. Gas station attendant filling tank of open touring and convertible cars . . .
>
> People standing in shade of trees and awnings. Open windows on street cars and buses; drinking water from spring or old well . . . swimming in pools, rivers, and creeks.[3]

Photographers of "Small Town" life were instructed to find a "R.R. station-watching the train 'go through' . . . women visiting from porch to street."[4] In the city, photographers were asked to focus on "park bench-sitting . . . walking the dog . . . women with youngsters in parks or sidewalk . . . kids' games," while "General" shots included "Men Working," sign painters . . . crowds watching a window sign being painted . . . Parade watching: ticker tape; (people) sitting on curb."[5] In Stryker's view, such lists, in their poetic (and highly sentimentalized) cataloguing of elements, would together represent an expansive, all-encompassing documentation of Depression-era life in America.

In a similar fashion, American Regionalist painters and other artists producing work in this period (and in the decades immediately following the Depression), also sought to chart a new path for American art, one that, in many ways, celebrated the everyday strength of hardworking Americans despite Depression-era challenges. This essay focuses on a 1949 lithograph called "Negro Maskers" by New Orleans-based Southern Regionalist painter John McCrady (1911–1968). "Negro Maskers," a critical, mid-twentieth-century representation of New Orleans Baby

John McCrady, "Negro Maskers" (from *Mardi Gras Day*), 1948, lithograph on paper. Reproduced with permission of The McCrady Estate.

Doll masqueraders, was produced as part of *Mardi Gras Day*, a collaborative book project that McCrady completed with fellow artists Ralph Wickiser and Caroline Durieux in 1948. The Baby Doll masquerading tradition, as described by Kim Vaz, represented the "raddy-walking, shake-dancing, cigar-smoking, money-flinging" women who, around 1912, subversively inserted themselves into a largely male masquerading tradition in New Orleans.[6] Many of the Baby Doll masqueraders worked in entertainment or the red-light district. This essay will document the ways that McCrady, like Stryker and the WPA/FSA photographers, sought to capture a virtual catalogue of elements that rendered the southern US, in the decade following the Depression, a site of singular "folk" distinction, made unique by its eccentric compendium of picturesque rolling landscapes and bayous, African Americans laboring in fields, steamboats and dockside scenes along the Mississippi, and carnivalesque traditions such as Baby Doll masqueraders.

McCrady is best known for WPA War Services posters and enigmatic, American Regionalist-styled images of African American southerners,

Mississippi landscapes and New Orleans Mardi Gras scenes, as well as establishing an art school in the New Orleans French Quarter. This essay will begin with an overview of his life and work, then provide a detailed formal analysis of *Negro Maskers*, with its stylistic references to El Greco and Mannerism, the paintings of American Regionalist Thomas Hart Benton, and the dream-like aesthetics of Symbolism. "Negro Maskers" fits snugly into McCrady's cultivation of a "Southern Eccentric" aesthetic. In addition, this text represents an attempt to situate McCrady's image within the context of other early to mid-twentieth-century works, whether painting, photography or other media, that featured sentimentalized, yet often subversive, images of southern U.S. culture that engaged with race, class and gender-based identity construction and performance. Above all, this essay outlines how McCrady's works of the 1930s and 40s highlighted vernacular, Louisiana and Mississippi-based traditions that engaged with the "eccentric South" or "southern strange" as theme, thereby distinguishing his work from that of Midwestern US-centered American Regionalist painters.

Oxford on a Hill

McCrady is often considered the most well-known New Orleans-based artist of the 1930s, and is certainly one of the most recognizable twentieth-century artists of the southern US. His works, often featuring "cutaway" scenes that revealed the interior as well as exterior of houses, populated by scenes of dramatic human interaction and flowing city or landscapes, recall the paintings of American Regionalist (or American Scene) painters like John Steuart Curry, Grant Wood, and Thomas Hart Benton.[7] It is significant to note here that McCrady briefly studied with Benton in New York City in the early 1930s. Yet McCrady's work differed from American Regionalists' work in its geographical focus—all three of the aforementioned artists' works were centered on Midwestern scenes. McCrady's works, by contrast, focused primarily on the Southern US, with a particular emphasis on representations of southern African Americans.

McCrady was born in Canton, Mississippi, in 1911, the son of an Episcopalian minister, Edward McCrady, and Mary Ormond Tucker. The family resided in Greenwood, Mississippi, for a short time, then Hammond, Louisiana. In 1928, the McCradys settled in Oxford, Mississippi. There, Edward McCrady taught philosophy at the University of Mississippi (also called Ole Miss). After working as a crew member on a South American steamer, McCrady attended the University of Mississippi from 1930 through 1932. During the summers of 1931 and 1932, he

John McCrady, *Portrait of a Negro*, 1933, oil on canvas, 21" x 17", Gift of the Roger H. Ogden Collection, Ogden Museum of Southern Art. Reproduced with permission of The McCrady Estate.

completed coursework at the Pennsylvania Academy of Fine Arts, with frequent visits to Philadelphia's museum offerings, experiences that certainly expanded his pictorial vocabulary as an artist.

In 1932, at the age of 21, McCrady left the university and moved to New Orleans, planning to establish himself as a professional artist there. While living in a French Quarter apartment, McCrady began attending classes at the Arts and Crafts Club of the New Orleans School of Art. After a year of classes, in the Fall of 1933, McCrady won a one-year scholarship, along with nine other artists, to the Art Students League of New York by submitting an oil painting called *Portrait of a Negro Man* of 1933, an image of an individual who worked as a praline seller in front of the Presbytere building on Jackson Square.[8]

McCrady depicts his subject wearing a sport coat and white-collared shirt, a dignified image that was rarely seen in representations of African Americans during this period (with the exception of Harlem Renaissance imagery, often focused on an African American middle class).[9] *Portrait of a Negro Man* was critical to McCrady's development as an artist, providing him with an opportunity to study in New York, where he came into contact with Benton *and,* through his artistic guidance, became exposed to Benton's own sources of inspiration—El Greco, Diego Rivera and others. *Portrait of a Negro* must be considered a significant thematic precursor to a major body of McCrady works that focused on southern African Americans, as well as a key to McCrady's continuing interest in, and, largely sympathetic sentiments re: African American southerners. In addition, the image represents the initial stages of McCrady's life-long engagement with scenes of southern life, with a particular focus on Oxford, Mississippi, *and* New Orleans.

During this period, McCrady began to document (and, in a way, *catalogue*) those unique qualities that defined southern cities like New Orleans. With *Portrait of a Negro Man*, the city of New Orleans becomes signified by several of its central symbolic markings—its unique cuisine (whether pralines or produce) as well as an African American presence that had shaped a great deal of the city's culture. Indeed, what could be more quintessentially New Orleanian than a *praline* seller, or other a marketplace vendor (such as those found in the French Market, for example), in the *French Quarter*? Such a scenario appears to encapsulate all of the distinct and alluring qualities characterizing the image of New Orleans—its cuisine, Creolized architecture, histories of commerce, and a complex racial, ethnic and class-based heritage that has rendered the city distinct from every other urban area in the U.S.?

Also, McCrady's dignified vendor, produced in 1933, cannot be discussed without a consideration of WPA aesthetics. Such ideas, exemplified by Stryker's "scripts," often celebrated a hardy American work ethic, and McCrady's subject, a praline seller or other street vendor, documented an individual engaged in entrepreneurial endeavor, actively facing the challenges of the Depression.

The Midwest Triumvirate

When McCrady arrived at the Art Students League, he studied briefly with Thomas Hart Benton as well as Kenneth Hayes Miller. Benton was part of the "Midwest Triumvirate," three American Regionalist painters that also included Grant Wood and John Steuart Curry, whose images of hardworking, dignified rural folk and pastoral, rolling landscapes of America's Midwestern "heartland" celebrated what was viewed as a quintessentially "American" aesthetic. Their impact on his work was immediately discernible. McCrady's figures often revealed the impact of Benton's anatomical forms—elongated, sinuous figures, and his incorporation of turbulent skies, all reflecting the influence of EI Greco and Mannerism as well as Van Gogh and Symbolism.

For his part, Kenneth Hayes Miller, considered part of the "Fourteenth Street School" which included Reginald Marsh and Isobel Bishop, also had an impact on McCrady's work.[10] The Fourteenth Street School focused on "urban realism," burlesque shows, gritty cityscapes and a celebration of blue-collar workers that was, in many ways, a rejection of European modernism, with its abstraction-centered modes. Miller also introduced McCrady to a multistage (or underpainting) technique, utilized to paint oil transparencies over a tempera, often egg-based, underpainting, a process that McCrady would continue to employ for the rest of his life.[11] According to Teresa Parker Farris, "Miller introduced McCrady to the multi-stage technique (once used by Rembrandt, Da Vinci, Rubens and El Greco) to give their works an inner luminosity in which colorful glazes are painted over a layer of white "underpainting" on top of a transparent veil color."[12] Miller's initiatives with tempera were part of an early twentieth-century revival of tempera painting in American art. At the Art Students League in New York, beginning in the 1920s, Benton and Miller taught mural courses at the League and promoted tempera as an ideal medium for the grand themes and large-scale works that celebrated American life during this period. Benton and Miller would eventually inspire fellow colleagues and students such as John Sloan, Paul Cadmus and Jackson Pollock.

Certainly, McCrady's work reflected a stylistic transformation after his experiences in New York. In addition, his tremendous interest in the south as subject may be said to have increased after this period in the north. New York in winter, and the consistent appearance of NYC scenes in the work of faculty members and his fellow students, rendered him homesick and fatigued. McCrady began to relish the South in new ways, far beyond a mere desire for a warmer climate. During this period, he began to perceive of the South in an increasingly affectionate manner. McCrady wrote of this period in New York, stating that, "As the days grew longer and the snow got deeper . . . it all began to make me a bit homesick. I wanted the country, high rolling hills. I could see Oxford on the top of one of those hills . . . cotton fields where the Negroes were sweating in (sic) a boiling sun, laughing and singing songs about their work. . . . Then I began to paint . . . daydreams of home many miles away." He had attempted to paint NYC city scenes, the crowded clusters of people, but stated that "there was no reason for them."[13] With this turn to African American southerners, McCrady was provided with a *raison d'être*, a primary sense of purpose as the work took on a role of social commentary, albeit one that romanticized the southern past. McCrady, by all accounts, considered his images to be sympathetic ones, while critics, however, sensed varying degrees of paternalism in his images of African Americans.

After his studies in New York, McCrady returned to the French Quarter and taught at The Arts and Crafts Club, then located at 712 Royal Street. His work at this time centered on action-laden religious and rural scenes. In addition to influences drawn from Benton and other Regionalists, McCrady had also been influenced by Symbolist artists such as Albert Pinkham Ryder, most evident in McCrady's depictions of hazy, agitated skies that reflect an unsettling sense of foreboding or uneasiness.

In addition, although McCrady critiqued the work of Surrealists, his compositions reveal numerous stylistic affinities. For example, his works were often characterized by dream-like narratives that merged realism with the fantastic, and incorporated architectural elements in the vein of Giorgio de Chirico's Mediterranean cityscapes populated by solitary figures, Classicized architectural elements and statuary, all punctuated by ominous shadows.

In 1935, McCrady was included in a group exhibition entitled *Thirty-Five Painters of the Deep South*, a highly regarded exhibition at the well-established Boyer Galleries in Philadelphia. Later, in 1937, the NYC branch of the Boyer Galleries presented his work in a solo exhibition that included one of the artist's most well-known paintings entitled *Swing Low, Sweet Chariot* (1937). *Swing Low* is a nocturnal scene of African American mourners surrounding a deathbed, as seen through the open door of the cabin. Brown-skinned angels descend to transport the recently deceased soul to heaven via chariot while Gabriel blows his horn and an angel struggles to subdue the devil as he attempts to enter the home.

During this period, *Time* Magazine referred to McCrady as "a star risen from the bayous" who would "do for painting in the South what Faulkner was doing for literature."[14] The critic's reference to McCrady as a "star risen from the bayous" references how Louisiana functioned as a marker of legitimacy for his southern scenes. In 1939, *Life Magazine* commissioned McCrady to paint "the second in a series of dramatic scenes in 20th century American history." He chose to paint a depiction of the assassination of Louisiana's Governor entitled *Assassination of Huey Long*. It became one of his most widely reproduced images. Also, in 1939, McCrady received a Guggenheim Fellowship that supported his production of images representing "the life and faith of the southern Negro." Hence, McCrady's pointed focus on the southern US, and its inhabitants, should also be considered in light of its marketing potential and financially lucrative implications for the artist.

In the late 1930s, McCrady began producing murals and easel paintings for the Graphic Division of the War Services Office for the WPA, and in 1942, he completed a series of propagandistic posters including that revealed his skillful use of contour drawings, Surrealist influences and Symbolist-tinged overcast skies. Also, significantly, in 1942 the artist established the John McCrady School of Art in New Orleans's French Quarter, and administered the school alongside his wife Mary Basso McCrady. The McCrady School remained open for nearly forty years and its students included such notable American artists as Henry Casselli (b. 1946) and Ida Kohlmeyer (1912–1997).[15]

In 1949, McCrady joined the Associated American Artists, established in NYC in 1934, that marketed affordable prints to middle-class American audiences. As part of AAA, he was encouraged to work with the New Orleans-born artist Caroline Durieux to experiment with lithographic printmaking processes. Under the supervision of Durieux, MCrady produced four silkscreens that supported War efforts.

Other 1940s projects included McCrady's illustrations for Louisiana-born journalist Hodding Carter's publications *The Lower Mississippi* (1942) and *Floodcrest* (1947) as well as the illustrations for *Mardi Gras Day* (1948). McCrady's paintings were exhibited at the Associated American Artists Gallery in New York in 1946. Although the exhibition largely received favorable reviews, Marion Summers in *The Daily Worker*, a Communist newspaper, referred to McCrady as a "racial chauvinist," and deemed the artist's *Judgement Day* as "an outright slander of the Negro people."[16] Summers later queried, "Why should all these so-called religious painting have all-Negro casts?" In large part, the answer to Summers's inquiry may reside in McCrady's longstanding interest in African American gospel music. As the artist pointed out, "The music that surrounded me all my young life, and which was as natural to my environment as any other element of nature, was that which I experienced in the songs that came from the Negro, an expression of a religious philosophy that would startle and alarm, a philosophy acquired from the white man combined with a metaphysical heritage from the darkness of Africa."[17] McCrady's remarks, tinged with overarching tones of romanticized Primitivist sentiment, may also illuminate a potential source for his ongoing fascination with African Americans representations.[18] Indeed, in keeping with this notion of Primitivist thought, McCrady's incorporation of African American bodies engaged in dramatic enactments of biblical scenes, evokes stylistic as well as thematic linkages between works like Gauguin's *Vision after the Sermon (Jacob Wrestling with the Angel)* of 1888 and other Primitivist works centered on the religious fervor of Breton peasants.[19] In addition, McCrady's swirling, traumatized skies and emphasis on dream-like spirituality evokes a Symbolist aesthetic, certainly a reflection of McCrady's stated affinity for the work of Albert Pinkham Ryder.[20]

In many ways, prior to the Summers review, images of African Americans had come to be viewed as a signature component of McCrady's focus on Southern life, distinguishing his work from other American Scene or Regionalist painters' works. As Keith Marshall noted of McCrady's 1930s and 1940s works, in his exhibition catalogue essay for the New Orleans Museum of Art's 1976 McCrady retrospective, "When viewed within the context of American Scene Painting, these works stand out as the most vibrant and powerful images of the South."[21] It appears that for McCrady, the linkage of southern African Americans with religious ritual as well as a more generalized southern symbolism, provided him with a form of branding, or a distinct artistic identity that was inextricably linked to its geographical region. Marshall then points out a 1937 *Life* magazine review which described the works as "Tender, fully imagined . . . his Negro paintings appear as authentically melodious as the Kansas paintings of John Steuart Curry are authentically robust."[22] It is notable that the reviewer referenced an idea of authenticity in relation to place in assessing McCrady's works, further reiterating an idea of the artist as producer of a uniquely and definitively *southern* sensibility.

Disheartened by Summers's *Daily Worker* criticism, McCrady embarked on a lengthy phase of self-reflection, shifting his focus to teaching and writing rather than visual creative output. McCrady's disappointment may have been due, in large part, to the highly significant role that art criticism in publications like *The New Masses* and *The Daily Worker* played in shaping the visibility of leftist artists the time.[23] Whether he was actively involved in Communist activities remains to be explored in scholarship. Yet it is clear that McCrady held leftist sensibilities, evidenced by his consumption of *The Daily Worker* as well as by his stated visions for the American South, clarified in the artist's interviews and written correspondence.[24] Most significantly, progressive ideas are evident in a great deal of McCrady's work, providing an expanded vision of African American humanity and everyday life in works like *Repatriated* of 1946, which depicts the joyous return of an African American WWII veteran, and his rendering in the aforementioned *Portrait of a Negro*, described by a *Philadelphia Record* reviewer as having a "realism that does not preclude sensitive feeling and which reveals through characterization a strain of nobility . . ."[25]

From approximately 1963 to 1968, McCrady sharply lessened his focus on African Americans and undertook a renewed interest in Mardi Gras and the French Quarter, as well as scenes of rural Louisiana and Mississippi life. Soon after completing three murals for the Bank of Oxford in Oxford, Mississippi, he passed away on December 24, 1968, at 57, having been diagnosed with cancer three weeks earlier. His work is included in the collections of the Georgia Museum of Art, the Louisiana State Museum, the Morris Museum of Art, the Saint Louis Art Museum, and The Historic New Orleans Collection maintains many of McCrady's papers, as well as the records of the John McCrady School of Art.

McCrady's Themes

McCrady's work may be divided into a number of themes, including examinations of race in the South through depictions of the class and social status of African Americans in the South, as exemplified by the "cutaway" painting entitled *Evening Meal, Duck Hill, Mississippi* of 1934.[26]

An additional theme includes McCrady's focus on southern landscapes, as evidenced by the aforementioned El Greco–inspired *Oxford on a Hill*, and *Steamboat Round the Bend* (1945). Oxford, Mississippi, was critical to the development of the artist's Southern aesthetic in the years immediately after his New York-based studies and beyond. As he noted, "I believe one rather selects his home town . . . and I consider Oxford my home."[27] Southern cityscapes may also be viewed in McCrady's work, as seen in the cutaway entitled *I Can't Sleep* of 1933 and 1948. McCrady spent much of his youth residing in the small towns and rural areas of Mississippi. When he settled in the French Quarter of New Orleans in 1932, *I Can't Sleep* was produced, and appears to document the chaotic qualities of urban life. He produced an initial sketch for the

John McCrady (1911–1968), *I Can't Sleep*, 1933–48, Morris Museum of Art, Augusta, Georgia. Reproduced with permission of The McCrady Estate.

work in 1933, just after moving to New Orleans, then ceased working on it until completing it in 1948.[28]

Religion was also a major theme for McCrady, often merging with his interest in African American life. These include the aforementioned *Swing Low, Sweet Chariot, Eucharist Scene* of 1954 at Grace Episcopal Church in New Orleans, *Judgement Day* of 1938 (reminiscent of El Greco's Burial of Count Orgaz) and *Oh! Them Golden Slippers*, based on a nineteenth century African American spiritual sung by blackface performers, written by the African American composer James Bland, and later popularized by the Fisk Jubilee Singers. As noted earlier, the 1946 *Daily Worker* review was highly critical of these works, and subsequently, McCrady never painted an African American spiritual scene again.[29]

McCrady also produced a number of WPA-styled images of laborers, including *New Orleans Dock Scene* of 1939, executed in a Mexican Muralist style that often celebrated the efforts of laborers.[30] As previously noted, Thomas Hart Benton, with whom McCrady briefly studied in New York, was a great admirer of Diego Rivera, Jose Clemente Orozco and other Mexican Muralists, and taught their mural techniques to his students. During the Depression, murals were a key component of federal arts projects, and many American artists, including a large number of African American artists, found creative sustenance in the work of Mexican muralists as they produced murals that would address social issues while simultaneously beautifying the nation's post offices, libraries, parks and other public spaces.[31]

McCrady also focused on political commentary in the south in works like *Political Rally* of 1935, which depicted a speaker who is unsuccessfully attempting to capture an audience's attention. Together, all of McCrady's themes represent a concerted focus, or cataloguing, of southern US-based imagery, largely centered on New Orleans and Oxford, Mississippi, a fitting strategy for establishing a Southern Regionalist genre that would function in tandem with (and, in some ways, attempt to rival), the Midwestern focus of Benton and other members of the Midwest Triumvirate.

Mardi Gras Day and McCrady's "Negro Maskers"

Returning to McCrady's "Negro Maskers," as noted previously, the image is included in the 1948 publication entitled *Mardi Gras Day*, a satirical examination of the New Orleans festival through the artwork of artists McCrady, Caroline Wogan Durieux (1896–1989) and Ralph Wickiser (1910–1998), a native of Illinois who was then Chair of the Art Depart-

John McCrady, "Exhausted Merrymakers" (from *Mardi Gras Day*), 1948, lithograph on paper. Reproduced with permission of The McCrady Estate.

ment at Louisiana State University in Baton Rouge. The three artists produced a total of 30 drawings and lithographs, with each artist contributing a total of ten illustrations.

Mardi Gras Day is divided into five temporal periods of a standard *Mardi Gras* day, or Fat Tuesday: Morning, Midday, Afternoon, Evening and Night.[32] The format, and the illustrations' reliance on satire, may reference the "Times of Day," Seasons or "The Age of Man" traditions produced by eighteenth-century British painter and printmaker William Hogarth, a form of satire melded with, at times, moral instruction, Nicolas Poussin, Nicolas Lancret, and others.[33]

Each illustration is accompanied by text that briefly expounds upon each image in a paragraph of 4–5 sentences. The accompanying texts appear to *loosely* describe the proceedings depicted in each scene. Examples include McCrady's "Exhausted Merrymakers," an image of an exhausted (or drunken), cigarette-smoking couple, with shoes tossed to the floor, after a day of revelry. A woman, adorned in a wilted, star-accented headdress, is seated precariously on a stool while a man, with drink in hand, leans his head against her for support as he leans back on the wooden floor. A New Orleans rooftop cityscape may be seen from the expansive window view. The following text accompanies the image:

> The stoop of a studio is a good place to see the show that still goes on in the street in the lull before the Comus parade. These people are tired too, but a passing masker brings out the cry: Hey, look at that costume!"

Although the text represents an exterior stoop scene, McCrady has depicted his former revelers inside of the house, with a view of the city seen through a window. This dissonance hints at an additional example of McCrady's penchant for cutaway scenes that reflect both interior, intimate human drama while providing a glimpse of the distinct and equally intriguing cityscape outside.

Here, it may be helpful to ask, What exactly is the role of text in *Mardi Gras Day* in particular? The use of text associates it with the notion of an historical document, functioning, for example, in the manner of *Toussaint L'Ouverture* and other series produced by the American modernist Jacob Lawrence, who meticulously crafted narrative text to accompany each image in the series.[34] *Mardi Gras Day's* textual components lacked the somber, historically resonant narratives of Lawrence's chronicles regarding historical moments in the histories of African descendants. McCrady's juxtaposition of text and image functioned as humorous anecdotal text, in keeping with the celebratory tones of the Mardi Gras Day publication in general, and served as an integral component of the completed satirical whole.

In terms of composition, McCrady's "Negro Maskers" is clearly based on a 1938 photograph of Baby Doll masqueraders by the well-known *Life Magazine* photographer Bradley Smith (1910–1997), a founder of the American Society of Magazine Photographers (now called the American Society of Media Photographers, or ASMP).[35] A clear formal relationship exists between the composition of the Smith photograph of ten years earlier and the Mccrady lithograph. The work includes a central Baby Doll figure, with baton in hand, who prances forward at one side of the image, accompanied by a cluster of Baby Dolls who lift their skirts as they follow closely behind.

As Dr. Kim Vaz has noted, the Smith photograph (and additional images) were taken "most likely for Holiday: *The American Travel Magazine*, published from 1928 to 1977 as an organ originally of the American Auto Association."[36] Smith used these photos with his promotional materials and included this description: "the high spirit of jazz emerges as

Bradley Smith, *Baby Doll Masqueraders*, photograph, 1938. Inscription: "The high spirit of jazz emerges as these self-styled 'Baby Dolls' strut their stuff at the New Orleans Mardi Gras in the late 1930s. Their organization dates back to New Orleans' famed 'Storyville' of the pre-First World War days." Reproduced with permission of the Bradley Smith Estate. Copyright © The Estate of Bradley Smith.

these self-styled "baby Dolls" strut their stuff at the New Orleans Mardi Gras in the late 1930s. Their origins date back to New Orleans's famed "Storyville" of the pre-First World War days."[37] Smith links the baby doll masquerader with the "spirit of jazz," or, more pointedly, as a linkage between African American-derived cultures and the city of New Orleans.

Other works in *Mardi Gras Day* include Caroline Durieux's "Comus," featuring the King of Comus atop a massive float that is flanked by torch, or flame carriers called *flambeau* (traditionally men of African descent who illuminated nocturnal parade routes).[38] Durieux (1896–1989), a New Orleans native of white Creole descent, was a well-known Louisiana painter, printmaker and satirist who taught art courses at LSU in Baton Rouge and invented a print-making process that utilized radioactive ink.[39] A key figure in New Orleans's art scene of the 1930s and 40s, Durieux served as director of the (aforementioned) FAP for Louisiana, administered by the WPA.

Ralph Wickiser, who would later, in 1962, establish the fine arts graduate program at Pratt Institute in Brooklyn, produced an image called "Spasm Band" in *Mardi Gras Day*.[40] Like Durieux's flambeau carriers and McCrady's Baby Doll masqueraders, the work features primarily African American subjects and also appears to be based on an earlier photographic precedent. Wickiser's rendering of a spasm band, a group of young African American men who would skillfully create musical instruments from everyday objects and parade through the French Quarter to perform while accepting donations, is accompanied by the following text:

> Not in one of the parades, the Spasm Band goes, perhaps, down Royal Street and lingers near a crowd that looks happy. The leader gives a beat, and the washboard rhythm, from tin cans, wires and homemade percussion instruments, begins. These boys pass the hat too.

Wickiser's (somewhat paternalistic) text emphasizes the money-making aspect of these performers, just as he does in "Negro Maskers" (a point that will be further explored in this essay).

McCrady's "Negro Maskers" features a central figure, a slim African American woman in Baby Doll masquerade who is captured in the midst of a dance with baton in hand as she moves gracefully towards her right. Just beyond her is a taller, more rounded female figure who raises her skirt as she also grasps a baton. All wear black and white bonnets, white dresses with a sash at the waist, and white socks and shoes. At left, examples of New Orleans's distinctive architectural legacy looms behind the group.

By comparison, Bradley Smith's photograph, viewed side-by side with the McCrady scene, also features a triangular cluster of Baby Doll masqueraders. In Smith's image the rounded figure is just beyond the central figure, while in McCrady's version of the woman positions her at far left, set slightly apart from the central group. All wear white, with the exception of the central figure in McCrady's image. McCrady has provided her with a black skirt and a black mask. He also places a (presumably donation) cup in her hand, possibly after having difficulties in interpreting the tassel that is merely a flurry of movement in the Smith image.

On the right side of both images, a smaller figure of a woman is seen in profile, and we are provided with the only side-view of the black and white bonnet. McCrady, rather than distinguishing between the shadows of the women's faces, merely places masks on their faces rather than attempt to distinguish between the physiognomic elements of each woman's face. Other similarities may be seen in the placement of the feet on the figures in the front, a glimpse of an African American man's face in a bowler hat behind the women.

For authenticity, McCrady references a logo for the Double Eagle ale sign, loosely translating from the Regal beer sign visible in Smith's pho-

Dorothea Lange, "Nipomo, California. Destitute 'pea-pickers' in California; a 32-year-old mother of seven children. February 1936 (Migrant Mother)," 1936, (retouched version), LC-USF34-9058-C, Library of Congress Prints and Photographs Division, Washington, DC.

tograph. McCrady's *modus operandi* is largely focused on symbolism, and the codified *idea* of an object or concept. Smith's photograph provided McCrady with a starting point for a compelling Mardi Gras scene, and then he made it his own by modifying various details. McCrady employed Smith as a foundation to lay out the composition, then modified it because he sought to make his image distinct or because he didn't understand the codified meanings of what he saw and certainly appeared to have no knowledge of a distinct Baby Doll masquerading tradition. If so, he would have identified the tradition in the accompanying text. In all fairness, in the earlier photograph, Smith did not include descriptive text relating to the Baby Doll masquerade alongside his reproductions in *Holiday* magazine. McCrady changed purses and decorative batons into donation cups, and placed masks on the women's eyes (as mere symbol of masquerade), rather than closely or actively examining what was actually depicted in the Smith photograph. And, perhaps, McCrady merely sought to evoke a "carnivalesque" scene in New Orleans.

In addition, in the accompanying text, McCrady never identified them as Baby Doll masqueraders; they were simply "Negro Maskers." This simplistic and race-focused title appeared to be, for McCrady, descriptive enough. By his use of such a title, McCrady's subject is not fully explained, thereby entering the realm of the exotic and the semi-anthropological. While McCrady neglects to identify, or research, what *form* of "Negro maskers" they were, elsewhere in the *Mardi Gras Day* publication, groups are distinctly identified as "Zulu" or "Comus." Although, in fairness, the Baby Dolls masquerading tradition, in the 1930s and 40s, was perhaps less identifiably "named" (or as well-known) as a culturally and socially specific entity, for non–African American audiences, unlike the visibility of the Zulu Social Aid and Pleasure Club, for example.

It may be helpful to point out here how this relates to Gordon Parks' FSA images. Parks's work was largely distinguished by a critical element: he identified his subjects by name, a practice that was distinct from many WPA/FSA photographers. In considering the most widely circulated images that have come to represent WPA/FSA photography under Stryker's tenure, we know them by their "categorical titles" rather than the subjects' name: Dorothea Lange's image known as *Migrant Mother*, Ben Shahn's *Cotton Pickers* and Walker Evans's *Coal Miner's House*, for example.

"Negro Maskers," I am proposing, above all, engages with the idea of the "eccentric" southern US, a region characterized by unique (and often enigmatic) social and cultural traditions and narratives. For McCrady, New Orleans represents a compelling source of narrative content, although he had an earlier, stronger childhood connection to Oxford, Mississippi.

A major component of this romanticized southern symbolism includes the literal incorporation of an African American body—in a plantation setting, performing manual labor in both rural and urban settings, selling Crescent City-specific products on the streets of the French Quarter, congregating on porches, gathering at juke joints, and parading through the streets of New Orleans at Mardi Gras. For McCrady, all of these elements of southern particularity represented a form of southern stage set, exemplified by his exuberant *Parade* of 1950, completed two years after the publication of *Mardi Gras Day*. The Black corporal body punctuates the scene in *Parade* as limber flambeau carriers, deftly carry the heated flames during a nocturnal parade. Both the interior of the two-story house and the lively parade scene all culminate in a spectacle of dramatic revelry. In addition, in terms of race-based symbolism, the flambeaux accompany a massive float shaped like a watermelon, a fruit that, since the period of American enslavement, has long been stereotypically linked with African American consumption.

Returning to "Negro Maskers," it may be helpful to ask, "Why did McCrady base his image on Bradley Smith's photo? Perhaps he was seeking the implied authenticity of representation that comes with photography, and sought a reference point for his impressionistic scene.

"Negro Maskers" incorporates many of the uses of symbolism, or tropes, that mark McCrady's oeuvre as a whole—dramatic southern

John McCrady, *The Parade* (detail), 1950, multi-stage on canvas. A gift of the Roger H. Ogden Collection, Ogden Museum of Southern Art. Reproduced with permission of The McCrady Estate.

rural scenes and cityscapes, the inclusion of African Americans within these spaces, and turbulent skies overhead. For example, in McCrady's "Negro Maskers," and in much of his imagery, McCrady focused on African American southerners and their linkage to what art historian Richard Powell has called a "pictorialized folk past."[41] In this respect, we must consider *Self-Portrait on the Levee,* an early work from 1934, completed merely one year after the dignified portrait of the French Quarter vendor. *Self-Portrait* depicts McCrady being fanned by two African American youths. As described by Teresa Parker Farris, it was "one of the first works he painted upon his return to New Orleans. He's being fanned by two African American boys. Because he had been teased about being "a southern aristocrat with lots of Negroes to wait on me, so I thought I would carry on the joke."[42] Yet is this work merely satire, or does it reflect McCrady's own sense of comfort with such a scene? Several other McCrady works from the period, such as *Domestic Trouble*, actively traverse the realm of racial stereotype with a pointed degree of ease.

Acknowledging that *Self-Portrait on the Levee* is an early work, we still have to ask: How do such images compare with other African American representations of the period, particularly those produced by white American artists, during this period?[43] An example includes Doris Ulmann's well-known Baptism scene in the Carolinas that derives more from "folk" connotations than racial stereotype, and retains an overarching sense of dignity for its African American subjects.[44] Ulmann (1882–1934), the white American photographer best known for her portraits of rural Southern communities in the U.S., including Appalachian mountain communities and the Gullah populations of the Sea Islands, produced an image that fits squarely into the folk-themed images, linked to African Americans, that marked this period. With its sweeping expanse of trees and water, this outdoor scene of ritual deals with belief systems in an earthy, almost sentimentalized way.

By contrast, McCrady's images largely deal with a somewhat simplistic view of African American southerners. In considering his larger body of work, the images decidedly lack a great deal of range in terms of class level; the artist appears to have been wedded to a romanticized southern past in which seemingly content African Americans contentedly engaged in manual labor. Indeed, McCrady's scenes ignore the presence of a Black middle class, on view in great measure in the 1920s and 1930s works of Harlem Renaissance artists, writers and performers. The prolific body of middle-class representations of African Americans in James Van Der Zee's Harlem portraits and in New Orleans native Arthur P. Bedou's images of New Orleans-based African American Catholic populations, including Creoles of color, as well as Bedou's formal portraits of leading African American educator, author and activist Booker T. Washington, for example, provide a stunning counter to McCrady's often-monotone visions of African American lives.[45]

In addition, "Negro Maskers" includes an additional use of symbolism that is frequently employed by the artist—an incorporation of El Greco–like turbulent skies overhead, representing a form of drama that frames (and often envelopes) the scenes. These cloud-like forms, often ominous in their snake-like circuitry, appear to be more than just mere decoration; they endow these scenes with an overwhelming sense of foreboding. Race, ever-present in McCrady's work, may also be present in his use of unsettled skies. Might they be a commentary on the tenuous nature of race relations in the south? Here, the darkened skies appear to be a living, breathing *thing*, suffusing various scenes with turmoil like a massive creeping hand that appears to reference spirituality as well as psychological unease. It is significant to recall here that, as pointed out earlier in this essay, McCrady's father was a minister, and the artist had long produced works that referenced, in particular, African American spirituality in works like the aforementioned *Swing Low, Sweet Chariot* and *Oh Them Golden Slippers*.

To conclude, we must return to the central questions proposed earlier in this essay: What, exactly, was McCrady's appropriation of Smith's image about? Was *Negro Maskers* merely an example of the artist engaged in producing a form of "categorized list" (or "script") of elements that together documented an impression of New Orleans Mardi Gras culture for the 1948 publication? It is clear that McCrady quoted from Smith's photograph for his own aims—namely, to establish a complex genre of Southern Regionalism, marked by a reliance on highlighting the intriguing "eccentricities" of Southern life. For McCrady, the *Mardi Gras Day* publication was the perfect vehicle for envisioning the "southern strange," an idea that may be exemplified by Carnival as a spatio-temporal site of transformation, an environment in which a white Hollywood actor may become Zulu king for a day, or a working girl could become an exuberant and unhindered "Queen of Mardi Gras."

It is clear that McCrady was not fully committed to recording historical and cultural aspects of his southern scenes in great detail; his engagement was not a literal recording or documentation. To be fair, McCrady was *not* a documentary photographer hired by the FSA to address a gap in a "shooting script." He was far more concerned with depicting an impression, or a sensibility, that referenced various enigmatic southern traditions, employing a southern-based symbolism that was wholly distinct from Midwestern-specific American life. In this respect, McCrady's work may be viewed as an impressionistic narrative, shaped by his own enduring affection for the South and its storied inhabitants, and largely engaged with romanticized and simplified notions of Louisiana and Mississippi-based culture.

"Negro Maskers" and other McCrady works of the period reveal that his Baby Doll masqueraders and other southern-focused images were not fueled by a desire for historical, cultural, and anthropological accuracy. McCrady appeared to be far more concerned with constructing, and celebrating, an aesthetic distinguished by a strategic incorporation of southern, African American bodies, belief systems, and cultural traditions. In so doing, he produced American Scene paintings that, like those of his contemporaries, revered a folksy, post-Depression-era America— its people, its grand narratives and its natural vistas. Yet McCrady also succeeded, through Baby Dolls, French Quarter vendors and angels of African descent, in crafting a unique American Regionalist vision, one profoundly shaped by, and intimately located within, the illusory and carnivalesque realm of "the southern strange."

NOTES

I am extremely grateful to Dr. Kim Vaz-Deville, associate dean of the College of Arts and Sciences and professor of education at Xavier University of Louisiana, for both her groundbreaking work and enthusiasm for the New Orleans Baby Dolls masquerading tradition, as well as for her invitation to contribute to this important publication. Heartfelt thanks are also due to the following for providing images and much-needed discussions that assisted in my efforts to contextualize McCrady's life and career: Tulane University faculty member Matthew J. Martinez, who facilitated my communication with Blake McCrady Woods; Blake McCrady Woods (The McCrady Estate); Nicole McLeod, director of marketing and PR at the Morris Museum of Art; Bradley Sumrall, chief curator at the Ogden Museum of Southern Art; and Mara Vivat (Bradley Smith Estate).

1. See Geoff Dyer, *The Ongoing Moment* (New York: Vintage/Random House, 2007).

2. For detailed considerations of the New Deal and FSA photographers, see Beverly Brannan and Gilles Mora, *FSA: The American Vision* (New York: Harry N. Abrams, 2006), and Cara A. Finnegan, *Picturing Poverty: Print Culture and FSA Photographs* (Washington, DC.: Smithsonian Institution Books, 2003).

3. Dyer, 4.

4. Ibid.

5. Ibid.

6. See Kim Vaz, *The Baby Dolls: Breaking the Race and Gender Barriers of the New Orleans Mardi Gras Tradition* (Baton Rouge: Louisiana State University Press, 2013).

7. For a general overview of the work of American Regionalists and their impact, see Matthew Baigell, *The American Scene: American Painting of the 1930s* (New York: Praeger, 1974), and Marianne Berardi and Henry Adams, *Under the Influence: The Students of Thomas Hart Benton*, exhib. cat. (St. Joseph, MO: Albrecht-Kemper Museum of Art, 1993).

8. In a September 8, 2016, telephone discussion with the author, Bradley Sumrall, Chief Curator at the Ogden Museum of Southern Art, pointed out that art collector Roger Ogden had mentioned that McCrady's wife had sent *Portrait of a Negro* to the Art Students' League in New York without her husband's knowledge, thereby resulting in his scholarship award and acceptance to the historically significant educational institution.

Sumrall also noted that Ogden had recalled that the subject of the portrait may have been a fruit vendor. Ogden also told him that McCrady had befriended the man, after seeing him on a fairly regular basis at his stall. This relationship may explain McCrady's sensitive rendering of this highly significant portrait; it certainly appears to betray a heightened, or more engaged, sense of familiarity between the two individuals, although McCrady, in keeping with common practice, does not identify his subject by name.

9. See note 45 (and corresponding text in main body of essay) for a brief discussion of middle-class representations of African Americans by photographers James Van der Zee (1886–1983) and Arthur P. Bedou (1882–1966). Additional examples may be found in the work of the white, German-born artist Winold Reiss (1886–1953), exemplified by his 1925 portrait of Harlem Renaissance writer Langston Hughes.

10. See Amanda Beth Blake, *Images of Women Shopping in the Art of Kenneth Hayes Miller and Reginald Marsh, ca. 1920–1930*, MA thesis, Univ. of North Texas, 2006.

11. Miller, amongst other artists, had been influenced by the symbolist work of Albert Pinkham Ryder, as documented, for example, in the exhibition and catalogue entitled *Albert Pinkham Ryder: The Descendants*, organized in New York by the Washburn Gallery in 1989. Also, for additional details on the American revival in tempera painting, see Richard J. Boyle, ed., *Milk and Eggs: The American Revival of Tempera Painting, 1930–1950* (Chadds Ford, PA: Brandywine River Museum, 2002).

12. Teresa Parker Farris, *City on a Hill: John McCrady's Oxford, Mississippi*, MA thesis, University of Mississippi, May 2005.

13. Farris, 33.

14. "When the Dawn Breaks," *Time: The Weekly News-Magazine*, January 23, 1939.

15. Other students at the McCrady School included Alan Raymond Flattman and Rolland Harve Golden. The John McCrady School closed in 1983.

16. Marion Summers, "Studies in Contrasts: Chauvinism and Truth," *The Daily Worker*, May 29, 1946.

17. John McCrady, unpublished Letter I, April 14, 1967; see Keith Marshall, *John McCrady, 1911–1968*, exhib. cat., New Orleans Museum of Art, 1975, 42–43.

18. McCrady produced numerous images of African Americans throughout his career, including *Church Supper* (1934), *Domestic Trouble* (1934), *Self-Portrait on the Levee* (1934), *Woman Mounting a Horse* (1936), *Going to Town* (1937–8), *Leap Year* (1937), *Returning Home* (1937), *Swing Low, Sweet Chariot* (1937), *Judgement Day* (1938), *Heaven Bound* (1940), *Oh Them Golden Slippers* (1945), *Repatriated* (1946), *Still Life in La-Fay-Ette County* (1950), *Rural Symposium* (1964), *The Old Woman and the Pig* (1964–5) and *It's Phenomenal* (1965). Further scholarship remains to be produced on McCrady's complex and varied representations of African Americans.

19. See Gill Perry's essays on Primitivism in *Primitivism, Cubism, Abstraction: The Early 20th Century* (Yale University Press in association with The Open University, 1993).

20. See Marshall, 18.

21. Keith Marshall, *John McCrady, 1911–1968*, exhib. cat., New Orleans Museum of Art, 1975, 43.

22. *Life*, October 18, 1937.

23. Marion Summers was reportedly the pseudonym for the art historian Milton Brown, and he produced art criticism from March 1946 through May, 1947, for the *Daily Worker*. For a discussion of Daily Worker art criticism and its significance amongst leftist artists, see Andrew Hemingway, *Artists on the Left: American Artists and the Communist Movement, 1926–1956* (New Haven and London: Yale University Press, 2002), particularly pages 116–20 and 209–11.

24. Keith Marshall's essays in the 1975 *John McCrady* exhibition catalogue for the show at the New Orleans Museum of Art reproduces a substantial selection of excerpts from McCrady's personal letters as well as interviews.

25. *Philadelphia Record*, March 22, 1936.

26. As noted in the *Philadelphia Record* in 1936, one critic observed that his handling of "the Negro theme" is "sympathetic." See "John McCrady Puts Southern Soil into Paint," *Philadelphia Record*, March 22, 1936.

27. Farris, 1.

28. In 1936, McCrady wrote a letter to fellow artist Clyde Singer, describing *I Can't Sleep*: "I am cutting the building in two, showing the life inside as well as out . . . I'm showing myself on the ground floor, sitting up in bed with my hands over my ears trying to shut out the noise coming from a big party on the second floor. One of those parties given by Med. Students. On the top attic floor a woman walks a bawling brat while her husband snores. Outside, the moon, stars, chimneys, smoke, etc. Sounds like too much stuff for one picture, but I think I have it fixed so I can handle it all."

29. See Keith Marshall, *John McCrady, 1911–1968*, exhib. cat., New Orleans Museum of Art, 1975, 47.

30. See Sue Bridwell Beckham, *Depression Post Office Murals and Southern Culture: A Gentle Reconstruction* (Baton Rouge: Louisiana State University Press, 1989); Anthony Lee, *Painting on the Left; Diego Rivera, Radical Politics and San Francisco's Public Murals* (Berkeley, CA: The University of California Press, 1999); Karla Ann Marling, *Wall to Wall America, A Cultural History of Post-Office Murals in the Great Depression* (Minneapolis, MN: University of Minnesota Press, 1982); Richard McKinzie, *The New Deal for Artists* (Princeton, NJ: Princeton University Press, 1973); and Marlene Park and Gerald Marlowitz, *Democratic Vistas, Post Offices and Public Art in the New Deal* (Phil-

adelphia, PA: Temple University Press, 1984) for details regarding Depression-era mural painting in the U.S. and its roots in Mexican, Communist-centered public art.

31. For a comprehensive discussion on the impact of Mexican modernism on American artists, see Ellen G. Landau, *Mexico and American Modernism* (New Haven CT: Yale University Press, 2013).

32. Fat Tuesday is the English translation from the French-derived Mardi Gras. Also called Shrove Tuesday, it is the day before Ash Wednesday, and references the last night of consuming richer, or "fattier," foods before the ritual fasting of Lent.

33. For further examination of the times-of-day tradition, as well as earlier, Classical precedents, see Sean Shesgreen, *Hogarth and the Times-of-the-Day Tradition* (London and Ithaca: Cornell University Press, 1983).

34. The initial Toussaint L'Ouverture series by Lawrence was a series of 41 paintings, completed in 1937–38. A later series of 15 prints was completed in the 1980s and 1990s. The print series was much larger in scale than the earlier, relatively smaller gouache works. See Peter Nesbett and Michelle Dubois, *Over the Line: The Life and Art of Jacob Lawrence* (Seattle: The University of Washington Press, 2002).

35. Born in New Orleans in 1910, Bradley Smith became a photographer for *Life* magazine in the 1940s and also worked as a freelancer for *Time, The Saturday Evening Post, Vogue, American Heritage* and *Paris-Match.* Considered one of the earliest photojournalists, Smith also worked as an editor for *Time* magazine, and wrote and illustrated 23 books that covered a wide range of topics, from art history to erotica to the life of author Henry Miller. He photographed Helen Keller, Mahatma Gandhi and Harry S. Truman, but his most well-known portraits featured Billie Holiday and Louis Armstrong. In 1944, he gathered a group of photographers (including Philippe Halsman, John Adam Knight, Ewing Krainin, Nelson Morris and Ike Vern), and formed an organization devoted to photographers' rights, the American Society of Magazine Photographers, now called the American Society of Media Photographers.

36. Vaz, 3.

37. Ibid.

38. Comus parades, held from 1857 through the late 1980s, were organized by largely Protestant Anglo-Americans and would roll on Mardi Gras Night as the final parade of the carnival season.

39. Born in 1896, Caroline Wogan grew up on Prieur Street in New Orleans. She began studying art in 1912 at Newcomb College with the artist Ellsworth Woodward, founder of the Arts and Crafts Movement-inspired Newcomb Pottery movement. After securing a New Orleans Art Association scholarship, Durieux began studying at the Pennsylvania Academy of Fine Arts. In 1920, she married Pierre Durieux, an export merchant, and they traveled throughout the Caribbean in subsequent years. In 1925, after leaving Cuba for Revolutionary Mexico in 1926, she befriended Mexican Muralist painter and political activist Diego Rivera, who painted her portrait and influenced her interest in art and social satire.

In addition, in 1936, Lyle Saxon, then director of the Louisiana Writers Projects, arranged for Durieux to provide illustrations for the *New Orleans City Guide*. In 1938, she joined the Newcomb faculty at Tulane. In 1941, Durieux began working for the Museum of Modern Art in New York City, facilitating a series of cultural exchanges and a museum-sponsored exhibition of "democratic art" that traveled throughout Latin America. Later, she began teaching in the Art department at Louisiana State University, where she remained until her retirement in 1963. For additional details re: Durieux's work with the WPA Federal Art Project, see Kim Finley-Stansbury, "Caroline Wogan Durieux and the WPA Federal Art Project in Louisiana." *Regional Dimensions* 9 (1991).

40. Modernist painter Ralph L. Wickiser, best known for works inspired by trees and other aspects of nature, began his teaching career at Louisiana State University in 1937. In 1959, he began working at Pratt, where he oversaw an Art Department that included Franz Kline, Jacob Lawrence, Roy Lichtenstein and Philip Pearlstein as faculty members. In 1962 he founded the school's Graduate Programs in Art and Design, and also published two well-respected Art Education textbooks.

41. Richard J. Powell, *Black Art: A Cultural History* (London and NY: Thames & Hudson, 2003), 94.

42. Farris, 36.

43. Ullman's work, and McCrady's, are part of a lengthy trajectory of representations, frequently sympathetic, of African Americans by white American chroniclers during the 1920s through the 1940s. These include Harlem Renaissance–era images of Langston Hughes and others by the German-born artist and graphic designer Winold Reiss (1886–1953), the eroticized, homosocial male athleticism of artist and illustrator Robert Riggs (1896–1970), and photographer Walker Evans's *Girl in French Quarter* (1935), one of numerous images of African Americans produced by Evans and focused on the southern U.S., Harlem, NY and elsewhere. In addition, for a detailed, highly insightful exploration of American Scene painter Reginald Marsh's work of this period, see Carmenita Higginbotham, *The Urban Scene: Race, Reginald Marsh and American Art* (University Park, PA: Pennsylvania State University Press, 2015).

44. Significantly, in relation to McCrady's Louisiana-based images of African Americans, Ulmann also produced a large number of dignified, well-known and oft-reproduced portraits of members of the Sisters of the Holy Family (SSF), the second oldest Catholic religious order for women of color in the United States. The SSF was established in New Orleans in 1842, and founded St. Mary's Academy, Lafon Catholic Nursing Home and countless other missions throughout the world. In 1931, Ulmann produced a large body of group and single portraits of SSF members, as well as a number of children under their care, whether as part of the SSF's orphanage initiatives or educational institutions. One well-known image, Ulmann's portrait of Sister Mary Paul of the Cross Lewis (1876–1977) graces the cover of the Getty Museum's 1996 publication on Ulmann, part of the Getty's *In Focus: Photographs from the J. Paul Getty Museum* published series on influential photographers from the Museum's collection. In the Getty text, the image is identified, presumably, using Ulmann's title: *Member of the Order of the Sisters of the Holy Family, New Orleans, December 1931*, and, in the manner of numerous works produced in the period, like MCrady's *Portrait of a Negro Man*, does not specifically identify the picture's subject. In the context of conducting interviews and developing the exhibition and catalogue for *A Celebration of Faith: Henriette Delille and the Sisters of the Holy Family* (see note 45), the author was able to identify the sister as Sister Mary Paul of the Cross Lewis.

45. For an overview of James Van Der Zee's life and career, and his documentation of middle-class African Americans in Harlem, see Deborah Willis-Brathwaite, *Van Der Zee: The Portraits of James Van Der Zee* (New York: Harry Abrams Publishing, 1993). Bedou's work is discussed in Cynthia Beavers Wilson, "Chronicling Tuskegee in Photographs," in *To Conserve A Legacy: African American Art from Historically Black Colleges and Universities* (Andover, MA: Addison Gallery of Art and NY: Studio Museum in Harlem, 1999) and in the author's exhibition catalogue for an exhibition, also organized by the author, called *A Celebration of Faith: Henriette Delille and the Sisters of the Holy Family.* The exhibition was on view at the New Orleans African American Museum of Art, Culture and History NOAAM) in 2008 and included numerous works by Bedou. See Mora Beauchamp-Byrd, "Brides of Christ, Servants to the Poor: Tracing the Legacy

of the Sisters of the Holy Family," in Mora Beauchamp-Byrd, ed., *A Celebration of Faith: Henriette Delille and the Sisters of the Holy Family* (New Orleans: New Orleans African American Museum of Art, Culture and History, 2008). In addition, see several Bedou images discussed in additional texts by the author; see Mora Beauchamp-Byrd, "African Americans in New Orleans: A Visual History," an online Guest Editorial Photo-essay for Thematic Update/Community Spotlight re: New Orleans, Oxford African American Studies Center; Henry Louis Gates, Editor-in-Chief (Oxford University Press, 2015). See http://www.oxfordaasc.com/public/features/current/index.jsp.

Culture-Building and Contemporary Visual Arts Practice

The Case of "Contemporary Artists Respond to the New Orleans Baby Dolls"

—Ron Bechet

The significance of a call out for artists for the exhibit "Contemporary Artists Respond to the New Orleans Baby Dolls" is the opportunity it provides for artists to come outside of themselves as painters or textile designers and address their art from a different point of view. The significance of the exhibit is the opportunity to demonstrate how the community is an important part of grassroots culture and how community is significant to our development as a people. We cannot understand how to move forward until we are able to understand where we come from, but for the culture to survive, it has to change and evolve in the role of today's world. The exhibit is an example of how this process is unfolding.

The Street-Masking Culture of New Orleans and the Role of the Baby Dolls

There has persisted a lack of understanding of the Baby Doll tradition, not only by people who are not from here, but people who were born and raised here and do not grasp the significance of the tradition. I discovered this several years ago when I worked at The Porch, a Seventh Ward community center cofounded by artist Willie Birch. One year the young men were working on Mardi Gras Indian suits and traditions. We had worked with them the year before and all through the year on the masking traditions of the Mardi Gras Indians. And the girls thought that, "Well, the guys are getting to do this . . . what do we get to do? We kept trying to emphasize, "Well, it's not just a man's world, so to speak. It's not just a male tradition. There are a whole lot of ways they can be

Alma "Mama Goo" Borden, Last of the Baby Dolls, Treme, New Orleans, Mardi Gras 1992. Photos by Ed Newman.

involved." But, of course, all they saw was the emphasis on men and masculinity. And so, they were able to seek out the tradition of the Baby Dolls and said, "Well, you know, we want to do this tradition based on what we know from women." It was refreshing and enlightening to see these young ladies want to do this. But there was resistance from the board members against condoning the girls' masking because they did not want the girls "idolizing these kind of women." It led me to ask, "What do you mean by these kind of women?" and seek a better understanding.

I did my own research and I found its meaning in the sphere of social justice and the sphere of taking back what is rightfully theirs and ours. I thought it was wonderful that these girls wanted to find out about themselves through this masking tradition. Willie Birch came to a similar conclusion and he remembered it from growing up in the Magnolia

Dianna Garcia-Brooks, a Gold Digger Baby Doll and horse drawn hearse. Photo by Romain Beauxis.

Gold Digger Baby Doll Wanda Pearson. Photo by Romain Beauxis.

Youth participants at the Porch mask as Baby Dolls on Mardi Gras. Reproduced with permission of Ron Bechet.

Housing Project, literally across the street from the traditions of Mardi Gras and the traditions of the neighborhood. We felt strongly that this was something that was significant and important to continue, and that it was something that was important for young people to understand. We were able, when we came to some consensus about how they would mask and to pool resources together, to help them sew the costumes and to get things organized. Willie Birch played a major role, too, not only in the organization but also in organizing this group of young ladies to actually develop it.

It was important for us to continue this exploration—for young people especially—to understand and carry on with what this tradition means. The artists of this show offer a visual language to express and bring forward information.

Artists' Encounters with the Baby Doll Masking Tradition

The artists have been profoundly impacted by their meeting with the Baby Dolls. Painter Meryt Harding met someone she would have never anticipated meeting and has developed a friendship through the process of making a painting. It is very beautiful that she is able to understand someone from a culture different from hers and be able to get a relationship going. It seems like a relationship will continue and grow through this act of telling a story through painting. Harding's paintings, *Ernie K-Doe Baby Doll Tee Eva* and *Gold Digger Baby Doll Merline*, along with her mixed-media pieces of pillows with lace are typical of her style. (See figures in Meryt Harding's artist statement.) They are very realistic; but they also get the character of each woman, Merline Kimble and Eva Perry. But she also goes outside of herself by deciding to use something she has never used before—lace around a painting to frame it. In a way, she is starting to understand and bring in some the elements that she learned from these women. Kimble, Perry, and other women doing the actual masking, through their encounter with her, may begin doing something different, too, in their costuming or performance. This cultural exchange can lead to what will actually help this culture survive. This understanding of how we can blend and merge some of what she learned and some of the things that she has given the women may also manifest themselves in their performative practices in the future.

Keith Duncan's *Legacy of the Baby Dolls* represents in painting how the tradition has developed. (See figure in Keith Duncan's artist statement.) His awareness of the significance of the practice from the past through today is very direct. It is apparent what he is trying to say in

Rolling with the Dolls by Jamar Duval Pierre. Reproduced with permission of Jamar Duval Pierre. Photo by Phillip Colwart.

the way that he deals with the images of the Baby Dolls from the past, placing certain decorative elements behind them. Then, in the scene with the Baby Doll Ladies, a signature act of the New Orleans Society of Dance Company, he changes the decorative element behind them. This offers a blending between the space of the old and a new interpretation.

D. Lammie-Hanson's work is about the current condition in Baby Doll masking, but the way that she decided to use the gold in *The Golden Baby Doll Lady* is almost going back to the pre-Renaissance period in which something that is significant and important is golden. (See figure in D. Lammie-Hanson's artist statement.) Using the preciousness of the gold, she provides a way of talking about the significance and importance of the Baby Dolls, but she also painted the work on paper bags which tells the viewer something about the tradition itself. She is putting this precious gold on something that some have considered not to be so precious. A paper bag is something

Skeleton and Baby Doll by Jamar Duval Pierre. Reproduced with permission of Jamar Duval Pierre. Photo by Phillip Colwart.

that we consider transport, that we throw to the side. The importance being placed on something that is not so important is like what has been thought about the Baby Dolls tradition in general. The handles around the edge makes the viewer wonder about what they are there for. The handles are actually to move things around. I am led to think about how this culture that may be hard to handle may be out there waiting for everybody to handle. The handles and where she placed them-to the top and the bottom-offer a message about the ability for us to handle this culture that has been seen as a problem.

In *Top Hats, a Bonnet and Lace*, Lammie-Hanson is expressing a tradition, the new tradition of Baby Doll masking and how that works, but she still has a sense of the continuation of the tradition since she has placed the late Treme Brass Band drummer (whose family is known for masking as Baby Dolls) Lionel Batiste in the background. (See figure in D. Lammie-Hanson's artist statement.) He is pushing the women forward from the rear. The connection to the past becomes an important part of this painting as well. At the same time, Lammie-Hanson brings a different look in comparison to the paintings of Karen LaBeau, Peter Ladetto, Ulrick Jean-Pierre, Jamar Pierre, and Ruth Owens. Lammie-Hanson's Baby Doll Ladies have a different way of performing as well. They strike a different pose and posturing that is far more contemporary. I relate it to voguing, which now also has a new tradition popular in New York, the East Coast, and Miami, playing out in voguing contests. The Baby Dolls in her painting perform postures and poses more in line with those kinds of contests, whereas the poses and postures of the other painters seem to be more traditional.

Peter Ladetto's and Romain Beauxis's *Fiery Looking Baby Doll*, a dream energy painting that requires a cell phone to see the full effect, reminds viewers of the 1960s when the artist Andy Warhol made contemporary statements that were close to advertising. By actually using some of the techniques that were in advertising, he made it a part of contemporary world art culture. Ladetto, basing his painting on a photograph of a New Orleans Society of Dance Baby Doll Lady taken at the 2013 Treme Ladies Parade, uses colors that are so garish. He makes us look at beauty in the things that we do not necessarily find appealing in that piece. In the early days of the tradition, the intense application of cosmetics added to the way the Baby Dolls were making themselves seen through bright color.

Being seen is a major goal of vernacular expressions in New Orleans. Nobody exemplifies that better than Ernie K-Doe, who referred to himself as the "Emperor of the Universe" and once declared that all music started in New Orleans. K-Doe was a Rhythm and Blues singer whose

New Orleans Society of Dance Baby Doll Lady taken during the Treme United All Women Parade, October 2013. Photo by Romain Beauxis.

Based on a photograph taken by Romain Beauxis of one of Millisia White's New Orleans Society of Dance Baby Doll Ladies, taken during the Treme United All Women parade in October of 2013. Peter Ladetto's painting follows his Dream Energy series, a reversed color painting of the photography. The painting is best seen using a smartphone app (developed by Romain Beauxis) to reveal the hidden colors of the artwork, thus revealing two different sides and emotions associated with the artwork. With her fiery look and white face, both signature features of the Baby Doll Ladies, this artistic collaboration takes on the many complex and rich facets of the Baby Dolls culture.

A Fiery Looking Baby Doll, by Peter Ladetto. Reproduced with permission of Peter Ladetto.

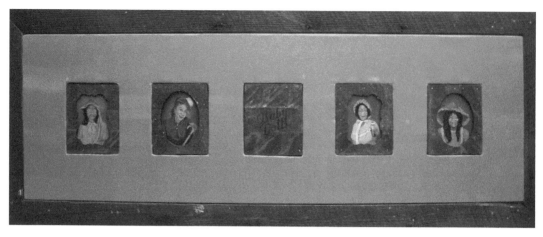

1961 number one hit, "Mother-in-Law," became the name of the lounge on Claiborne Avenue he managed with his wife Antoinette K-Doe. Karen Ocker's royal portrait represents K-Doe's ambition, but also her understanding of him as royalty in his community. Her painting reflects all of the things that he liked to use: crowns and scepters that set him apart. In this city, it is important to define yourself in your own way-that is, to set yourself apart. This is done through dress and performance. Whether it is dancing or just walking down the street, it is given as a performance for all to see. Ocker's four historically based paintings of real life Baby Doll maskers Olivia Green (circa 1927), an unidentified 1940s masker captured by a Louisiana Writers' Project photographer, Miriam Batiste, and Antoinette K-Doe reminds viewers about the tradition's past.

Using fabric and the technique of sewing support, Annie Odell's *Antoinette and Ernie K-Doe* and *Antoinette K-Doe*'s mixed media quilts challenge the viewer to deal with emotions that are elicited by the facts about their story. (See figures in Annie Odell's artist statement.) It comes across very strongly in the way she constructed the pieces, just as strongly as Ulrick Jean-Pierre's *"Celebrating the Culture of Life": New Orleans Mardi Gras Baby Dolls.* (See figures in Ulrick Jean-Pierre's artist statement.) Jean-Pierre's compositional technique, that satin leg in the satin shoes, sucks the viewer right into the painting. Directly in front of the viewer is the sensual element. Then he uses the church (St. Augustine Catholic Church, located in one of the oldest black neighborhoods in the country) as a base for tradition and then brings that forward to contemporary times. The three Baby Dolls bring in the trinity. The triangle diamond shape suggests the sacred feminine. The fact of the scene taking place early morning on a cloudy day is signaled by his use of El Greco style. The sun is behind clouds. The morning then brings a way of thinking about the tradition as experiencing a new beginning.

French sculptor Marielle Jeanpierre never saw the tradition in person, but was so impressed by it that she created *The New Found Pride, A Symbol of Resilience.* (See figures in Marielle Jeanpierre's artist statement.) The Baby Doll tradition has a universal appeal. People are able to understand it and communicate that understanding to the rest who know it and tell about its significance to them. A new understanding emerges through non-local eyes. Jeanpierre understands why these women began doing this a long time ago, and why they still do it today.

The Baby Doll in Steve Prince's *Bird in Hand: Second Line for Michigan* is that kind of individual who is so familiar with that tradition she comes into the second line and grabs the attention. (See figure in Steve Prince's artist statement.) Nathan Scott's *The Original "For Us By Us" P. O. S. S. E. (People Opposing Society's Segregational Entitlement)* is a second line accompanying a jazz funeral. (See figures in Nathan "Nu'Awlons Natescott" Haynes Scott's artist statement.) The face of each little figure tells much. The way that he has posed them and postured them in just the right way is one of the more significant ways of getting at the culture. Steve Prince's *Bird in Hand: Second Line for Michigan* emphasizes that big thing in New Orleans, the second line. It is not the first line. It is almost mandatory you participate. This is not a 'you can stand back and observe the culture' tradition. You have to participate in it. The Baby Dolls of New Orleans lead the participatory aspect in so many ways. Their practice is an important part of taking back what is yours. This is your neighborhood. This is your street. If this is your street, then you have to get out there and dance.

The Baby Dolls in the paintings of Ruth Owens have a particular attitude that comes forward in each. She gets into the psyche of who these women are especially with *Raddy Winner.* (See figure in Ruth Owens's artist statement.) Her pose resembles what we see on a day-to-day basis. It is what I grew up with. When women in my family had something that they really wanted to communicate, this is the posture that they took. If they really wanted you to listen, either their hands were folded or on the hips. The inherited posture can be seen in the Kongo power figure, the *Nkisi N'Kondi* of Mangaaka. It is considered "the preeminent force of jurisprudence. That power was represented as a presiding authority and enforcing lord or king. . . . The figure's posture and gesture, leaning forward with hands placed akimbo on the hips, is the aggressive attitude of one who challenges fearlessly."[1] In *Raddy Winner*, the delicate facial features are counter posed with the power stance. She is saying: "I'm important. I'm significant. I have something to tell you," but the face says, "I'm going tell it in a way that you understand."

Resa "Cinnamon Black" Bazile at the 2012 Satchmo
SummerFest. Photo by Kim Welsh.

Resa "Cinnamon Black"
Bazile's Treme Million
Dollar Baby Dolls at
the 2013 Satchmo
SummerFest. Photo by
Kim Welsh.

Resa "Cinnamon Black" Bazile and daughter Janine "Jay Pretty Green Eyes" Wilson as Treme Million Dollar Baby Dolls at the 2013 Satchmo SummerFest. Photo by Kim Welsh.

Ernie K-Doe Baby Dolls co-founder Geannie Thomas in front of the Mother-in-Law Lounge. Photo by Kim Welsh.

Finally and most important are connections formed because of the exhibit, between the women who mask and the artists. Some of the Baby Dolls and viewers of *Raddy Winner*, for example, began to circulate the idea that is was Treme Million Dollar Baby Doll Tammy Montana who was the source of the image. So, identified with the painting that at the closing of the show, Tammy came and stood by that painting, in that pose, and everybody thought, "That's Tammy Montana." Ruth Owens's model was a woman who plays roller derby locally. So the beauty of the show is that the maskers can recognize themselves within that structure even if it is not necessarily a portrait of them. The actual maskers see themselves in these images and feel empowered by them.

NOTES

1. Kongo Power Figure interpreted by The Metropolitan Museum of Art. Access at http://www.metmuseum.org/collection/the-collection-online/search/320053.

BIBLIOGRAPHY

Cooksey, Susan, Robin Poynor, and Hein Vanhee, *Kongo across the Waters*. Tallahassee: University Press of Florida, 2013.

Osborn, Royce. *All on a Mardi Gras Day*. Spyboypics.com, 2013.

Thompson, Robert Farris. *Aesthetic of the cool: Afro-Atlantic Art and Music*. Pittsburgh: Periscope, 2011.

———. *Flash of the Spirit: African and Afro-American Art and Philosophy*. New York: Random House, 1983.

Vaz, Kim. The *'Baby Dolls': Breaking the Race and Gender Barriers of the New Orleans Mardi Gras Tradition*. Louisiana State University Press, 2013.

Beyond Objectification and Fetishization

Telling the Story of the Baby Dolls through the Visual Arts

—Sarah Anita Clunis

> Our strategy should be not only to confront empire, but to lay siege to it. To deprive it of oxygen. To shame it. To mock it. With our art, our music, our literature, our stubbornness, our joy, our brilliance, our sheer relentlessness—and our ability to tell our own stories. Stories that are different from the ones we're being brainwashed to believe.
> —**Arundhati Roy**

Mardi Gras has long been a site for the flagrant and spectacular use of sexuality as well as negotiations of power between the sexes. Dressed in sexually revealing clothing and dancing provocatively in the streets of New Orleans, the first Baby Dolls emerged in 1912 in the Perdido and Gravier neighborhoods of Orleans Parish. Both shocking and titillating to the Carnival revelers, the performance of Baby Dolls, since this time, has continued to address conflicting issues of bodily exposure and containment.

The materials and aesthetics of the original New Orleans Baby Dolls are visualized in a myriad of ways by the contributions of the various artists to the exhibition, *Contemporary Artists Respond the New Orleans Baby Dolls*. The Baby Dolls' performance is collectively seen here as an activated, vibrant, kinetic site of empowerment for African American women. Through the eyes of these contemporary artists, the iconography of traditional Baby Doll performativity is examined as a pervasive body politic addressing specific concerns of representation for black women within the Carnival sphere. Additionally, the exhibit, as a whole, offers much needed examples of historical images of African American women in the throes of social performance. As Kim Vaz clearly suggests in her book, *The Baby Dolls: Breaking the Race and Gender Barriers of the New Orleans Mardi Gras*, Baby Dolls, in both traditional and contemporary manifestations, reflect a culture that understands Mardi Gras and its masquerade performance as a site for economic exchanges as well as gender negotiations.[1] The earliest Baby Dolls were prostitutes and were referred to as "baby dolls" in their trade. The performance of these early Baby Dolls continued the African masquerade tradition of a body in motion, this one representing the female body as an exchange-value, constructed and relative, "a relation constantly changing with time and place." A comparison of the historical stories and images of these earlier Baby Dolls with contemporary artistic documentation of the present-day Baby Dolls shows quite clearly that this identity has never been intrinsic but *produced and possessed* in accordance with time and place.[2]

The artist Ruth Owens gives us the signifier of the crossroads, the literal and metaphysical site where the worlds of the living and the ancestors converge, in her piece *Down by the Crossroads* and accompanying pieces *Raddy Winner*, *Strut*, and *Hey Y'all*. Owen's large-scale pieces represent contemporary Baby Doll maskers of a variety of age groups decked out in the sateen and tulle that has become the shape of Baby Doll identity. Here, a young, middle aged, and elderly woman (in different frames) gesticulate and demonstrate aggressive displays of sexuality and agency. (See figures in Ruth Owens's artist statement.)

Owens's Baby Dolls are coquettish, flamboyant, alluring, and seductive. They are represented as sexualized females, regardless of age. Here, the icon of the carnival costume becomes the female costume, the fake and false adornments of femininity, both historical and contemporary. The Baby Doll's antics are performed for the viewer, to entice and titillate, but in an ironic turn, they demonstrate a profound political commentary on the demolition of the "docile" body. *Raddy Winner* is a fitting example of how this display of power found itself inserted into this masquerade in the form of a coquettish and wanton "baby." Despite the delightful pink dress, white tulle and pink bow, the stance of *Raddy Winner* is anything but adorable. Vaz explains in her work the meaning of the word *raddy* as defining a kind of "strutting walk" that communicated "'not giving a damn'" about what others thought about one's behavior, art, and way of life."[3] The fact that Owens positions her work "down by the crossroads," can be read as a veiled reference to the inter-generational and ancestral component that is integral to the Baby Doll tradition.

In a roundtable discussion at the McKenna Museum of African American Art, Baby Dolls Merline Kimble and Diane Honore referred to the spiritual aspects of masking as Baby Dolls and to the importance of ancestral traditions as well.[4] This emphasis on ancestral traditions can be seen in the exquisite works of Karen Ocker, both in her homage to Ernie K-Doe and her mixed media work, *Baby Dolls*. (See figure in Ron Bechet's chapter.)

In *Baby Dolls*, Ocker combines pinewood, rusted tin, satin, oil paint, and nails to create a shrine-like work that honors some of the Baby Dolls that can be considered the "mothers" of the tradition. Ocker's incorporation of reclaimed architectural materials reference the subtle integration of historical bodies with historical buildings, re-creating ghost-like portraits of traditional Baby Dolls that reference an aged site as an important component of lived experience. Ocker's work is infused with both melancholy and magic by her use of old and used materials. Her Baby Doll becomes power object, an object of ritual and longing. These portraits, made more beautiful by the decomposition of wood and tin, seem tied in some way to the body, even to the slow process of aging.

Meryt Harding's iconic portraits of Baby Dolls Merline Kimble and Eva Perry (Tee Eva) are rendered with precise realism and delicate detail. While fitting neatly within the realm of classic portraiture, these works also suggest local notions of conformity and interchangeability while also referring to racial stratifications and stereotypes. This positing of the Mardi Gras African American female as raced, commodified, and ultimately sexualized (represented by the epitome of a vulnerable, playful, and innocent sexualized child or doll) is a telling political statement about how women's beauty has and is constructed in traditional and contemporary Carnival throughout the African Diaspora.[5] (See figures in Meryt Harding's artist statement.)

Yet, there is a tension and irony to these images of post-menopausal working class African American women adorned like pampered Uptown infants or precious china baby dolls. Harding's consideration of her subjects is respectful of their individual personalities and each Doll's individual stance is indicative of her agency. We learn from the artist's statement and the exhibition text that both of these women are powerhouse matriarchal personalities within their communities. Yet, here they are displaced as seemingly "docile" bodies.

Through their masquerade (and their subsequent rendering by Harding) both Kimble and Perry subvert a dominant paradigm of age and performance, while subtly addressing the work of the earliest Baby Dolls as sex workers. They accomplish this by displaying their bodies as alternate fetishized "identities" that can be created, used, circulated, and even discarded. Through their performance, identity becomes like a product to be consumed, a costume that can be constructed, distributed and exchanged. Harding's realism exhibits the way that both Kimble and Perry sculpt identities with the shapes of discipline and fetish, and display them so that their performance addresses the historical role of their Baby Doll ancestors.[6]

The photographs of Romain Beauxis, Ed Newman and Kathleen Flynn of Baby Dolls in the throes of public performance tackle similar issues of age and gender in performance arts. In the body of works on exhibit by all three photographers, post-menopausal women cavort, syncopate, and gesticulate in the midst of a multitude of people. Rites of passage, integral to the New Orleans black working class communities are highlighted in these photographs. In Ed Newman's 1992 images of Alma Borden in the Money Wasters' Parade, Ms. Borden shows us her satin pink bloomers while sucking on a pastel pink nipple bottle. (See figures in Ron Bechet's essay.)

In Kathleen Flynn's image of Carol Harris, Harris flaunts a matching gold baby bottle, bonnet and umbrella as she marches in front of her son Justin Harris (who is the flag boy for the Wild Tchoupitoulas tribe) on Super Sunday 2013.[7] In the works of Romain Beauxis, the ideal of the body of perfect proportions, the classic nude, the still life, and the beauty queen is dismantled and re-presented as a sensual, elderly, black female body, made simultaneously masculine and feminine with the juxtaposition of Peter Pan collars with cigars, tuxedos, and bonnets. Here the "docile" body is dismantled. What sense can the uninformed viewer possibly make of a baby doll with a cigar?[8] (See figures in Ron Bechet's essay.)

In a discussion of gender identity and masquerade, Amelia Jones discusses the photograph as an ideal medium to expose the visual determinations of identity as shifting and contingent. Jones goes on to describe "the visual as a realm in which gender is tenuously reinforced as unitary on the basis of surface attributes that work through opposition to signify sexual difference."[9] But Victor Turner reminds us that the "marginal position of women in the indicative world makes their presence in the subjective or possible world of the topsy-turvy Carnival "quintessentially" dangerous." Turner also suggests that what becomes dangerous is the female unruliness as "the mark of the ultra-liminal, of the perilous realm of possibility . . . which threatens any social order and seems the more threatening the more that order seems rigorous and secure."[10]

Beauxis's images provide the viewer with a glimpse into the liminal spaces, the in-betweens, places of dispossession, and the spaces that can be filled with a transgressive body. Meaning and identity occur at the actual process of inscription and are never determined or given. Carnival, second lines, and funerals in the New Orleans cultural sphere represent an essentially liminal sphere where there exists a temporary loss of boundaries and certain taboos concerning the female body are deployed. The unruly female is set loose, camped by either men or women—she takes the form of what Mikhail Bakhtin refers to as "the female grotesque": the pregnant, the elderly, the large or disorderly female, the seductress, the vulgar and sexually aggressive woman.

In his text, *Rabelais and His World*, Bakhtin in a discussion of the history of European Carnival traditions writes, "Carnival is not a spectacle seen by the people; they live in it."[11] Bakhtin argues that during Carnival there is a temporary suspension of hierarchies, barriers, and distinctions in general and that an ideal type of communication is established that is impossible in everyday life.[12] Bakhtin also discusses the grotesque as an integral part of Medieval, Renaissance, and Romantic-era Carnival traditions. The grotesque is described as images of the body in exaggerated form with a concentration on orifices, such as the genital organs, the anus, the mouth and the nose. Many times these orifices are inverted. Parts of the body that are open to the outside world, an emphasis on apertures, the parts from which the world enters and emerges from the body are stressed with the grotesque. Bakhtin writes:

> The grotesque image reflects a phenomenon in transformation, an as yet unfinished metamorphosis, of death and birth, growth and becoming. The relation to time is one determining trait of the grotesque image. The other indispensable trait is ambivalence. For in this image we find both poles of transformation, the old and the new, the dying and the procreating, the beginning and the end of the metamorphosis.[13]

In Bakhtin's analysis we can see a critical framework for understanding not just the performance of the Baby Dolls but also the documentation of this performance through the photographic image. In the photographs of Newman, Flynn, and Beauxis we see images of death and birth, old and new, dying and procreating in the juxtapositions of elderly women adorned as infants, the proliferation of phallic oral accouterments, and the feminine adorned as masculine (as in the case of Lois Nelson wearing a tuxedo and dancing on the coffin of Nelson Thompson during his funerary celebration).

The work of French sculptor, Marielle Jeanpierre, touches on similar issues of representing gender and age but focuses on the theme of resilience. Jeanpierre's bust of an elderly woman adorned like a New Orleans Baby Doll focuses on the "pride of having succeeded to exist wholly: without compromising her identity."[14] Jeanpierre's work is infused with a touchingly personal desire. She is self-fashioning, not just because she finds herself in a woman's body but also because she finds herself in an imperfect body. She states:

> For a long time, I have reflected on all that was expected from me, on behalf of my family, my company . . . etc, . . . to the point of being inhibited and intimidated.[15]

Jeanpierre's sculpture exhibits the invisibility of older women in academic feminism and the arts and the ageism that is prevalent in much of western culture. (See figures in Marielle Jeanpierre's artist statement.)

Kathleen Woodward in her essay *Performing Age, Performing Gender* makes the point that even feminism and cultural studies have not been immune to this ageism. Woodward states:

> We need to bring the representation of the older female body into focus, and we need to reflect on what we see and what we don't. How is the older female body represented and, more important . . . *performed* in visual mass culture? How have older women artists performed age? What might be said to constitute feminist aging in terms of the body?[16]

In many ways Woodward's questions can be answered by the multiple critical frameworks applied to understanding the phenomenon of the Baby Dolls: the historical documentation and analysis, the traditional and contemporary performance of the Dolls themselves, the artistic responses to the Dolls and the critical analysis of these artistic responses. The Baby Dolls are ironic in their performance and they shift the cultural paradigm of ageism and femininity in the process. Whereas western culture encourages women as they age to pass for younger and conceal their bodies in a masquerade of youth,[17] Baby Dolls take this paradigm to the extreme and mock and mime the idea of femininity as intrinsically youthful. By performing these shifts in identity the Baby Dolls demonstrate that women have choices in "creating" ourselves through image, object and language, through careful juxtapositions of both physical manifestation and idea. Each Baby Doll masquerader takes control of the self and dictates for that self a new purpose and function. Yet, her body continues to perform as a "body that matters." She performs a feminine ideal, a type, a female theatricality derived from melodrama that eventually facilitates a relationship with her audience.[18]

The multi-generational aspect of the Baby Dolls can be clearly seen in the works of Kim Welsh, D. Lammie-Hanson, and Lisa Dubois. In Welsh's photographs of Baby Dolls, a variety of age groups and family connections are highlighted. While all of Welsh's photographs communicate a profound history, of particular interest is *Like Mother, Like Daughter*. (See figure in Ron Bechet's essay.) In this image, renowned Baby Doll Cinnamon Black poses with her daughter in a sensual posturing that communicates volumes about feminine ideals and expectations. Welsh's photograph as well as Dubois's *New Orleans Society Baby Dolls 2012* addresses the spectacle of the black female body caught in endless circuits of production and reproduction, of appraisal and fetish.[19] And because Dubois and Lammie-Hanson's depictions are of the New Orleans Society of Dance Baby Dolls Ladies, who perform for profit, these Baby Dolls' bodies are an echo of their radical predecessors of 1912 Storyville.

Anthropologist Roger Lancaster appropriates the Marxist critique of political economy to suggest a "political economy of the body." A "political economy of the body" is "the sum of gender transactions and sexual exchanges that collectively constitute the social body" and all the supporting and supported power relations involved.[20] Lancaster refers to the body and the ideology of the body as the materials produced through this political economy. He argues that these, as products, constitute value and value systems. These values are then exchanged and circulated according to the rules of the power structures involved. In other words, humans are produced, by others and by themselves. What is produced is not a good but a value. If one is successful in the transaction she or he is validated and "valuable." If one loses in the ongoing exchange—failure.

We can see this "political economy of the body" addressed in the performances of the Baby Dolls in the early nineteenth century in New Orleans. When these prostitutes took to the streets on Mardi Gras Day with cigars in their mouths and garters stuffed with cash (that they would throw at unsuspecting men), they were addressing their position as commodities. For that day of Mardi Gras, men were groveling at their feet for money. As Baby Dolls, these women were standing in their power and at the same time acknowledging their objectification and fetishization. They were, in a sense, moving *beyond* these positions of disempowerment and transforming the male gaze in a way that subsequently empowered them as feminine and *dominant*. Still, remnants of this culture of performance, flirtation, masquerade, and exchange can be found embodied in the contemporary visual culture so eloquently exhibited in the works of Dubois, Welsh, and Lammie-Hanson.

Lammie-Hanson's work, elegantly rendered on brown paper bags, has the added dimension of making an insightful observation of the insidious way that skin color has worked its way into ideals of beauty for African American women. Lammie-Hanson admits that her use of brown paper bags is intentional and meant to communicate not only the myriad of skin tones to be found in the African American community but also to remind us of the history of our own internal segregation tactics. Lammie-Hanson references the historical brown paper bag test as a way that black Society organizations would effectively exclude individuals whose skin was darker than the brown bag. Lammie-Hanson reminds us that the material that she paints on was intentionally chosen as a reminder of its use as a historically divisive tool for African American women. (See figures in D. Lammie-Hanson's artist statement.)

In her 1998 essay, *Caribbean Bodies*, Caroline Allen discusses the female Caribbean body as it is displayed within and outside of the Carnival sphere. Allen suggests that the practices of masquerade in Carnival destabilize prescribed gender categorizations and an inverting or obscuring of gender, racial, and class identifications occur. In Carnival the body explodes out of its fixed self and intermingles with other bodies, defies societal codes for behavior and exhibits itself in multiple ways.[21]

Traditionally Baby Dolls have always worked to transform the female body as a site for edification and consumption into a site that can be displayed and admired, fashioned by women primarily for women. As Vaz argues in her work, the Baby Dolls were really about performing and dressing up for other women, as a form of competition along the same lines as the Mardi Gras Indians can be imagined as a site for competitive masculine performance and display.

Additionally, through the visual performance of Mardi Gras, ideals of conduct are inevitably transmitted and utilized as agents of social control. While considered stylish, playful, and fun by some, Baby Dolls were considered vulgar and uncouth by others. Vaz talks about the contradictory responses to the Dolls and recalls that, "Even today, those in the Baby Boom generation recall their mothers and grandmothers warning them against the rude and lascivious behavior evidenced by many a Baby Doll on Carnival day."[22]

The unruliness and "loose" behavior demonstrated by the Baby Dolls must have undeniably struck fear in the hearts of those committed to the policing of a "Black Respectability," especially as it related to women during the earlier part of the twentieth century.[23] Allen, in a discussion of the virgin/whore dichotomy that has plagued gender negotiations in the Western world, suggests that the sexual appetite of the whore challenges the construction of women as passive and defined by man. Because masculinity demands that there be a mastery of others as well as self, women who posit themselves as "in charge" of their sexuality inevitably challenge this masculinity. This virgin/whore complex and its exploitation can be observed in the portrayal of the Baby Dolls as representations of innocent babies in skimpy, thigh-baring costumes. The exhibitionism, vulgar behavior and sexually suggestive dance moves suggest immorality but in the package of an adorable child. Perfect examples of this dichotomy can be seen in the paintings of Jamar Pierre, Ulrick Jean-Pierre, and Karen LaBeau. While the three artists show a variety of techniques, the sensuality coupled with sweetness that defines the Baby Dolls is evident in their paintings.

The aggressive brushstrokes coupled with vibrant color of Jamar Pierre's work remind of luscious Haitian paintings. In his painting, *Rolling with the Dolls*, Baby Doll dancers gesticulate and undulate and almost seem to dance right off the canvas. (See figure in Ron Bechet's essay.) LaBeau's paintings are also reminiscent of Haitian works and document actual Baby Doll personalities cavorting in the streets. Here, the Baby Doll is imagined as the ultimate gadabout, frolicking in troupes, with her consort, or independently, all over LaBeau's canvases. LaBeau's tactic of painting personalities right up to the edge of the canvas, allows the viewer to anticipate that more "action" lies outside of the pictorial plane. (See figures in Karen T. La Beau's artist statement.)

In Ulrick Jean-Pierre's *Celebrating the Culture of Life,* Baby Doll Diane Honore is featured (also in Le Beau's *Cinnamon and Diane),* in multiple takes, dancing in front of St. Augustine Church in the Treme amidst a crowd of revelers. Honore's white-clad thighs takes center stage with her adorable yellow bonnet and cigar dangling out of her mouth. (See figures in Ulrick Jean-Pierre's artist statement.) But it is the thigh that, like *Raddy Winner,* holds the viewer's attention. Her hand lifts her short yellow satin dress to expose frilly white bloomers and we cannot escape her stance; that firm strong leg encased in shiny white. Jean-Pierre's exquisitely rendered work demonstrates that in both the historical and the contemporary New Orleans Mardi Gras sphere the phenomenon of masquerade, much like the emphasis on women's fashion and women's bodies, is strengthened by a conception of modern identity as a social performance that has always depended on a certain attention to costume and positioning. This social performance garners the most attention when it becomes a "spectacle," a display of attributes that are considered unusual, curious, and fantastic. Here, we see the relationship between clothing and the exploration of notions of comfort, discomfort, liberation, constraint, power, subservience, protection, violation, beauty, and sacrifice. And these have, of course, been the messages behind the ideals of fashion and beauty for centuries.[24]

Art Historian Chris Cozier, in a discussion on feminine performance during African Diasporic Carnival traditions, writes in a way that could describe Honore's performance and Jean-Pierre's documentation of it. Cozier states:

> Private obsession and public spectacle become entwined. The artwork as a record of an action or as documentation of an investigation that is simultaneously private, as in the way the child plays dress-up or how the individual imagines or constructs himself or herself in the mirror, is fused with the public ritual display of Carnival. . . . These images bring our attention to the roles and expectations with which women are confronted.[25]

Steve Prince's graphite drawing, *Bird in Hand: Second Line for Michigan* is a large scale work that is meant as a message for Detroit, a visual manual of possible ways to cope during the death of one phase of life and the rebirth of another. (See figure in Steve Prince's artist statement.) Seen as a cathartic, euphoric and transformative piece by the artist, *Bird in Hand,* makes connections between Detroit and New Orleans. The artist suggests the second line as a coping mechanism, a process which aids the transition from mournful to celebratory and from death to rebirth.[26] The Baby Doll dancer is of course in the middle of the action, pacifier necklace dangling suggestively from her neck. Her entire posture screams power. It is amazing how she accomplishes it—this being sexy without submission. She annihilates the male gaze, although it is a male artist that creates her, and explodes out of the canvas as an erotic and activated force. It is the Baby Doll and the other women in this work that "steal the show," reminding us of the imperative role of women of power in traditional African funerary traditions.

The Baby Dolls and the contemporary artistic responses to them confirm for feminist scholars what we already imagine: that the female body, through the mechanics of socialization, inevitably becomes a surface affected by an unconscious dependency on self-censorship. A perfect example is the statement—"She is making a spectacle of herself." This concept or danger of the "spectacle" is a specifically female issue. Little girls are often instructed that if one is not careful a loss of boundaries could signify carelessness, a kind of inadvertency. Mary Russo states:

> Although the models of course change, there is a way in which radical negation, silence, withdrawal, and invisibility, and the bold affirmations of feminine performance, imposture and masquerade (purity and danger) have suggested cultural politics for women.[27]

And in *Gender Trouble* Judith Butler writes:

> The reconceptualization of identity as an effect, that, as produced or generated, opens up possibilities of "agency" that are insidiously foreclosed by positions that take identity categories as foundational and fixed.[28]

The Baby Dolls' aggressive female sexuality coupled with a defiance of restrictions and values demonstrate the ways that, for women, artifice and display have come to represent the "real" in gendered performance. The Baby Doll mimes and mocks—performing a parody, a teasing masquerade. With every gesture or grimace she transforms her body with extravagance and exaggeration. Luce Irigaray discusses women's play with mimesis as a way to "make visible by an effect of playful repetition what was supposed to remain invisible: the cover up of a possible operation of the feminine in language."[29]

The works discussed here clearly posit the Baby Dolls as bodies of political action and criticism in both their traditional and contemporary manifestations. In her multiple incarnations the Baby Doll continues to be a figure of political agency that in the process of her revelry, offers us a paradoxical performance which combines issues of age, sexuality, innocence, vulgarity, and the commodification, objectification and fetishization of the Black female body. But Baby Dolls perform *beyond* these issues. They explode right out of the political sphere and into the liminal Carnival arena where they dance back and forth, transforming the urban space with generous realism and the vibrant colors of their personal fairytales. "For today, they are truly the prettiest thing."[30]

Through depicting their aggressive female sexuality coupled with a defiance of women's gender restrictions, the contemporary artistic response to New Orleans Baby Dolls is a body of work that creatively interprets an essential performance of struggle, of protection, of seduction, and of normative transformation for African American women.[31] But it is the Baby Doll, herself, that has the last word here, because she offers us a twist in the power dynamics always at play. And she does this by controlling her own body, relaxing the rules that govern it, changing its political economy, and subsequently making a spectacle of herself.

NOTES

1. Kim Marie Vaz, *The "Baby Dolls": Breaking the Race and Gender Barriers of the New Orleans Mardi Gras Tradition* (Baton Rouge: Louisiana State University Press, 2013).

2. General Marxian concept. See Karl Marx, "Capital, Volume One," in *The Marx-Engels Reader*, second edition, ed. Robert C. Tucker (New York and London: Norton, 1978), 294–438.

3. Vaz, 33.

4. A roundtable discussion at McKenna Museum of African Art that took place on May 21, 2015.

5. For a more in-depth discussion of the racialized female body in African Diasporic Carnival Traditions, see Phillip Scher, "Confounding Categories: The Global and the Local in the Process of Caribbean Art," *Small Axe* 6, September 1999, 50–54.

6. For a more in depth discussion of discipline, fetish, and docile and disciplined bodies see Michel Foucault, *Discipline and Punish: The Birth of the Prison*, trans. Alan Sheridan (New York: Random House, 1977).

7. Baby doll Kit or Carol Harris, stands in front of her son, flag boy Justin Harris of the Wild Tchoupitoulas Mardi Gras Indian gang. Photo by Kathleen Flynn. Access at http://photos.nola.com/4500/gallery/super_sunday_2013_gallery/index.html#/10.

8. In her discussion of the grotesque, Susan Stewart proposes that the grotesque scatters and redistributes body parts and becomes the antithesis of the body as machine, the disciplined, docile body. See Susan Stewart, *On Longing: Narratives of the Miniature, the Gigantic, the Souvenir, the Collection* (Durham: Duke University Press, 1993), 105.

9. Amelia Jones, *Postmodernism and the En-gendering of Marcel Duchamp* (Cambridge: Cambridge University Press, 1994), 183.

10. Victor Turner, "Frame, Flow, Reflection: Ritual and Drama as Public Liminality," in *Performance in Postmodern Culture*, ed. Michel Benamou and Charles Carmello, Center for 20th Century Studies, *Theories of Contemporary Culture* vol.I (Madison: Coda Press, 1977), 35–55.

11. Mikhail Bakhtin, *Rabelais and His World* (Bloomington: Indiana University Press, 1984), 7.

12. Ibid, 16.

13. Ibid, 24.

14. Marielle Jeanpierre, Artist's Statement, To Find One's Place After Crisis

15. Ibid.

16. Kathleen Woodward, "Performing Age, Performing Gender," in *NWSA Journal*, vol. 18, No.1 Spring 2006, pp.162–89, 162.

17. Ibid, 167.

18. Judith Butler, *Bodies That Matter: On the Discursive Limits of Sex* (London: Routledge, 1993).

19. Editor's note: Artists in the show who have featured or referenced them include Keith Duncan ("Legacy of the Baby Dolls"), Peter Ladetto/Romain Beauxis ("A Fiery Looking Baby Doll"), a dream energy painting and Karen LeBeau ("A Baby Dolls' Parade"). A photo of the Baby Doll Ladies at the New Orleans Jazz and Heritage Festival, 2017, by Kim Welsh can be found in Chapter 8 of this volume.

20. Roger Lancaster, "'That We Should All Turn Queer?': Homosexual Stigma in the Making of Manhood and the Breaking of a Revolution in Nicaragua," in *Culture, Society and Sexuality*, eds. Richard Parker and Peter Aggleton (London: UCL Press, 1999), 104.

21. Caroline Allen, "Caribbean Bodies: Representation and Practice," in *Caribbean Portraits: Essays on Gender Ideologies and Identities* (Kingston: Ian Randle Publishers, 1998).

22. Vaz, 62.

23. The phenomenon of the Baby Dolls gained popularity in New Orleans in the years after 1912 and simultaneously in other parts of the U.S. African American scholars, writers, and artists became increasingly politicized, citing the rise of "The New Negro." The New Negro Woman was posited as staid, refined, light skinned, and looking a lot like the Gibson Girl.

24. Ideas examined in Susan Dayal's, *Lips, Sticks and Marks*, ex. cat., 1998.

25. Chris Cozier, "Between Narratives and Other Spaces," in *Small Axe*, no. 6, September 1999, 19–36, 29–32.

26. Steve Prince, Artist Statement for Bird in Hand: Second Line for Michigan

27. Mary Russo, "Female Grotesques: Carnival and Theory," in *Feminist Studies/ Critical Studies*, ed. Teresa de Laurentis (Bloomington: Indiana University Press, 1986), 213–29.

28. Judith Butler, *Gender Trouble: Feminism and the Subversion of Identity* (London: Routledge, 1990), 147.

29. Luce Irigaray, *The Sex Which Is Not One*, trans. Catherine Porter (Ithaca: Cornell University Press, 1985), 76.

30. Adapted from Maurice Martinez's discussion of the Baby Dolls in Vaz, *The Baby Dolls*, 75.

31. Ideas borrowed from Kim Vaz.

Contemporary Artists Respond to the Baby Dolls

Artists' Statements

Ann Bruce

"A New Orleans Farewell and a Heavenly Welcome"

I am a native of New Orleans, educated at Miss Aiken's School for Little People, Louise S. McGehee School, Newcomb College, The University of Florence, and at the New Orleans Academy of Fine Arts. For as long as I can remember I have been drawing "funny" little things that amuse me.

Looking Down on the Mother-in-Law Lounge, 2006. Reproduced with permission of Ann Bruce. Photo by Phillip Colwart.

Mardi Gras Indians, Skeletons, Brass Band, Weenie Man, and Baby Dolls, 2013. Reproduced with permission of Ann Bruce. Photo by Phillip Colwart.

A New Orleans Farewell and a Heavenly Welcome. Reproduced with permission of Ann Bruce. Photo by Phillip Colwart.

In the 1970s, I began painting my version of landscapes with buildings and little blue and green trees. In the 1980s, I added my version of little people into the landscapes. And in the 1990s, I began incorporating New Orleans characters into my paintings. Among my favorite local characters are the legendary Ernie K-Doe (The Emperor of the Universe), Fats Domino, Ruthie the Duck Girl, Keith Sam, Lucky Dog vendors, and those who appear at Mardi Gras—the Zulus, Skeleton Men, flambeaux carriers and the irrepressible, fun loving Baby Dolls.

In 2005 Antoinette K-Doe invited me to join the Ernie K-Doe Baby Dolls. We marched in the Krewe of Muses parade and had a wonderful time struttin' down the street showing off our "linens." I love New Orleans, its traditions, and the magic of Mardi Gras. In my pictures, my Baby Dolls do all the things I do and all the wild, crazy things I don't dare do—I love them and have so much fun with them! And, since 2005, I appear in their pictures. I am not hard to find!

Pillow "throw" of Ann Bruce. Photo by Phillip Colwart.

Pillow "throw" of Antoinette K-Doe. Photo by Phillip Colwart.

Pillow "throw" of Miriam Batiste Reed. Photo by Phillip Colwart.

Pillow "throw" of Eva Perry. Photo by Phillip Colwart.

Pillow "throw" of Jeannie Thomas. Photo by Phillip Colwart.

Pillows made to "pass out" or "throw" during the 2005 Muses Parade by the Ernie K-Doe Baby Dolls. Reproduced with permission of Ann Bruce. Photo by Phillip Colwart.

Phillip Colwart

"Portraits of the Baby Dolls"

The Baby Dolls are such a unique phenomenon. Everything happens on the streets, and for a photographer, this means candid photos with no posing, unrepeatable events, and uncontrollable backgrounds. My method of capturing the beauty, emotion, and artistry of the Baby Dolls is to use as wide a visual perspective as possible without distorting their features, and to get as close as possible to the subjects in order to create an intimacy between the viewer and the artists. It is important for me to convey to my subjects the respect I have for them as artists, and to transfer to the viewers of these images the joy and excitement I feel while photographing the Baby Dolls.

Armani, Gold Digger Baby Doll, Mardi Gras Day 2015. Reproduced with permission of Phillip Colwart.

Omika Williams and Joycelyn Green at the opening of "Contemporary Artists Respond to the New Orleans Baby Dolls." Reproduced with permission of Phillip Colwart.

Vanessa Thornton in the Treme, with St. Augustine Catholic Church in the background, Mardi Gras Day 2015. Reproduced with permission of Phillip Colwart.

Wanda Pearson

Janice Kimble

Merline and Janice Kimble

Rosalind and Micah Theodore

Vanessa and Bradleigh Thornton and Satin Mitchell

Alana Harris, Omika Williams, Fabieyoun Walker, and Kadrell Batiste

Studio Portraits taken at the George and Leah McKenna Museum of African American Art by Phillip Colwart, Craftsman Photographer, Certified Professional Photographer. Reproduced with permission of Phillip Colwart.

Keith Duncan

"Legacy of the Baby Dolls"

My origin is narrative and my images with familiar signifiers embody everything that is unique, diverse, and "creolized" in the manner of storytelling. Undoubtedly, I am a storyteller testifying and signifying on the human condition in the Old South and most importantly, in a post-Katrina era. I use pattern in my background as a means to connect with my roots and my heritage in the Mande and A'kan regions of the Kongo (in West Africa) and the African American women quilters in the South. Indeed, the connection is far beyond the South. Ultimately, I am doing something "ancestral." My paintings of Southern culture, through the use of traditional motifs and post modern language in the realm of Afro-American narratives' "signifying," along with social street art, have created an aesthetic that is both current and yet aware of its historical past.

Legacy of the Baby Dolls. Reproduced with permission of Keith Duncan. Photo by Phillip Colwart.

Marielle Jeanpierre

"'Little Queen of the Night"

One day, a rumor arrived in Paris that something great was being prepared in the South of the States.

So, carrying my poetry as my only identity document, I took the migrants' boat, crossed the Atlantic, sailed up the Mississippi, and landed in a beautiful country that greeted me with open arms like a distant cousin: Louisiana.

A tram named "Marielle's Desire" dropped me in New Orleans: IT WAS CARNIVAL TIME!

There, springing out from the dark holes of the city like multicolored pond lilies, an army of raddy-walking street-sweet ladies were dancing, shaking to the sound of trumpets and drums with the pandemonium of a traumatic delivery. It was not exactly Parisian style; I was even a little taken-aback by their sticks and their cigars. Yet, I had to admit, they were invested with compelling strength and unwavering faith.

They wanted to exercise their freedom, to restore their reputation, to rattle the brains secluded in the penitentiary of their clichés: we are neither decorative vases nor playthings for all games. Like the young woman's movement that started in the mixed suburbs in France: *"Ni putes ni soumises"* (that is, neither whores nor submissive).

Under their bonnets, they revealed not empty or deranged heads, but rather witty ones, spirited and strong: iron ankles in white velvet socks, yielding thighs in embroidered bloomers, assumed illiterate mouths pacified with rubber teats.

These women, miracles of risky, rough lives, who were themselves marvels of dire straits, turned out to be adorable monsters, or saints, or hybrids.

The one that came to me like a vision in the middle of fireworks, was a saint, and she was so gentle—so obvious that she emerged from the earth through my hands, in a night's labor.

Like Pinocchio, so loved by the carpenter that created him, my "Little Queen of the Night" could take her place in the wake of these emancipated women, flourishing with stories of battles, romance and conspiracy . . .

In that fabulous night, they were followed by the "Indians" with their giant purple, gold and green feathers. Detecting my ignorance, a tall Bacchus on a float told me with an ironic smile, that the rainbow of red wine, champagne and absinthe were the icons of New Orleans.

Strengthened by the alcohol fumes, I overcame my resistance and tried to gate-crash into the Baby Dolls' rows.

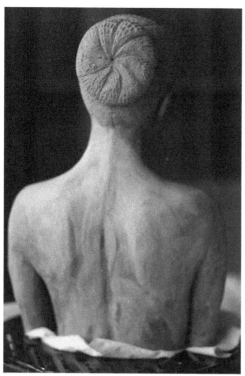

Unfired back view of *Little Queen of the Night*. Reproduced with permission of Marielle Jeanpierre.

Completed work *Little Queen of the Night*. Reproduced with permission of Marielle Jeanpierre.

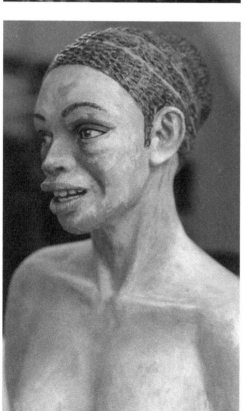

Side view of *Little Queen of the Night*. Reproduced with permission of Marielle Jeanpierre.

I felt for them. And I felt like them. I, too, have had to face tragedy and despair. Yet I keep my story to myself, wary of opening Pandora's box.

They greeted me naturally and even persuaded me to have dinner together in a famous seafood restaurant.

The "Crawfish à l'étouffée" were a real treat but suddenly my body itself—I am as big as a lobster—became stifled and steamed!

Too much emotion for me! I am not bold!
I would be unable to act collectively.
A mother of six; no longer a wife; I have no energy to rebel.
It is too late for me.
My weapon is my art. But not for weaklings.

I admit that I can be wrong. I confess that I could not return to New Orleans recently and that I had to make do with my memories, photos, and academic studies.

But we don't care for the details.

Each year for Mardi Gras, people dress up and go out on higher stilts, with replenished feathers, crazier hair-dos, stranger coats, double-clicking skeletons, and two flamboyant eyes, orchestrated by rejuvenated brass bands wound up like old alarm clocks.

Popular traditions, as unbridled as they can be, help to keep one's balance.

Ulrick Jean-Pierre

Celebrating the Culture of Life: New Orleans Mardi Gras Baby Dolls

As a New Orleans artist, my creative expression is a mirror of my own observation, memory and experience. Living and breathing in the heart of this rich culture is an ongoing inspiration. My art is a tangible representation that comes from the depths of my creative consciousness. At the same time, it allows me to share with the world my vision of how I see the world. Through my artistic lenses, I consider my painting of the New Orleans Mardi Gras Baby Dolls as an open window of endless celebration of life in the past, present and future. The painting embodies New Orleans's colorful spirits as the cultural treasure and melting pot that encompasses African, Native American, and European cultures.

For me, the creation of this painting of the Mardi Gras Baby Dolls is a way to document New Orleans's authentic cultural traditions and

Celebrating the Culture of Life: New Orleans Mardi Gras Baby Dolls. Reproduced with the permission of Ulrick Jean-Pierre. Photo by D. Eric Bookhardt.

Celebrating the Culture of Life: New Orleans Mardi Gras Baby Dolls close-up. Reproduced with the permission of Ulrick Jean-Pierre. Photo by D. Eric Bookhardt.

aesthetic beauty in another dimension. New Orleans is not only an exciting place to live but also a continuous source of inspiration for me as a Haitian-American artist. There is a well-known connection between the revolutionary period of Saint-Domingue (Haiti) and the socio-political development of Louisiana, especially New Orleans. My work on the Haiti-Louisiana connections is an overflowing river of endless inspiration and a source of creative energy. My painting *Celebrating the Culture of Life: New Orleans Mardi Gras Baby Dolls* is one of the various paintings in my series depicting the Haiti-Louisiana connections. Symbolically, this painting represents a tribute to the people of New Orleans, particularly to the countless artists of all kinds—be they musicians, writers, folk artists, composers, dancers, filmmakers, etc. who contribute their love, passion and creative souls to preserve New Orleans's unique cultural identity.

Karen La Beau

"A Historic Group of Women"

I have chosen to tell my story through visual art. To me, telling my history on canvas, vinyl albums, and wood is far more interesting then writing it down on paper. Since my history primarily revolves around the culture of New Orleans, my life in Shreveport, as well as my encounters across the state, it's my goal to exhibit "My Life on Canvas" across the state of Louisiana.

Cinnamon Black and Sugar Baroness. Reproduced with permission of Karen La Beau.

Baby Dolls Parade. Reproduced with permission of Karen La Beau.

I am a native of New Orleans and now reside in Shreveport, LA. I am a self-taught artist and began professionally painting in 2007. I was inspired to create my first Baby Doll piece two years ago. I captured the "New Orleans Society of Dance Baby Doll Ladies" on canvas. I noticed the resurgence of the Baby Doll presence in New Orleans and felt compelled to capture the spirit of this historic group of women. I am attracted to the bright colors that the women sport as well as the confidence that exudes from them as they sashay down the street. I also painted a few of the Baby Doll scenes on vinyl records, but only on those records that are music or dance related. It seemed a natural fit to add the ladies onto vinyl since they are normally dancing down the street.

D. Lammie-Hanson

Top Hats, a Bonnet, and Lace, A Golden Baby Doll

Top Hats, a Bonnet and Lace is a representational abstract portrait painting of the New Orleans Baby Doll Ladies. Each subject is depicted in my personal style in the fashion of my One Eyed Tulips series of various dresses in a procession. Like most ancient Greek and Roman sculpture, over time, features are lost. Remove one eye and you can still see deep within the soul of the subject and the original beauty. Focusing on the mouth, imagine that the lips are like petals of the flower, tulips. Only once the petals open to expose what's inside the flower can the cycle of giving life and nourishment begin. Now imagine the "tulips," the mouth opening to communicate what is deep inside the subject. The beginning of the healing, love and trust can begin. This series breathes validity to the mute words through delicate, vulnerable, and luscious lips.

The Golden Baby Doll Lady stems from my series "Beyond the Brown Paper Bag." The project takes the everyday item like the brown paper bag which gets used and tossed by millions worldwide and transforms it into beautiful works of fine contemporary art in the form of paintings. It is an innovative and unconventional approach to a healing dialogue, recycling and repurposing. The paintings are made up of various sizes of brown paper bags that I have been collecting from donated sources. The series includes individual paintings on smaller bags like the wine bottle brown bags. The larger brown bags like shopping bags (such as from Whole Foods or Rouses) are dissected, weaved, primed and transformed into tapestry-style paintings. These larger paintings can consist of 100 to over 150 brown paper bags each. The Golden Baby Doll Lady references the

Top Hats, a Bonnet and Lace. Reproduced with permission of D. Lammie-Hanson.

Golden Baby Doll Lady. Reproduced with permission of D. Lammie-Hanson.

infamous "paper bag test." This test, once used at certain black Creole social events, involved comparing a person's skin color to a brown paper bag. Those with skin lighter than the bag were granted admission. Those with darker skin were turned away. I see vestiges of this color caste system at work today and uses art as an intervention.

Meryt Harding

"Two Strong Women"

Born in England, I have spent most of my adult life in the United States. I studied visual arts at Savannah College of Art and Design, majoring in painting. For the last 15 years I have based my paintings on the many trips I have taken to Africa. Recently, I have wanted to switch my focus to my culturally rich hometown of New Orleans, where I have lived for the last 17 years. When I saw the call to artists by Xavier University and the McKenna Museum to document the Baby Dolls, I knew I wanted to participate. I did not know much about the Baby Dolls although I had taken photographs of them on a couple of occasions at second line parades and delivered photographs to Tee Eva's (Eva Perry) Pies and Pralines. When the call to artists came, I immediately went back to Tee Eva, a member of the Ernie K-Doe Baby Dolls, and asked if she would agree to have her portrait painted. I wanted to paint Perry because at 80 years old she was one of the oldest Baby Dolls and had such an amazing spirit and energy. The following day she put me in contact with Janice Kimble and other Gold Digger Baby Dolls. They invited me to meet and take photographs of them while they were collecting money for the funeral of a little girl that had recently been shot. There, I was introduced to Janice's sister Merline Kimble: she was passionate about the Baby Doll culture and shared all of her family's rich tradition of masking as Baby Dolls since the 1930s. I knew I wanted to include her in the project.

I researched as much as I could about the Baby Dolls, including reading Kim Vaz-Deville's book *The Baby Dolls*. I met with Kimble and Perry many times, learning more about their lives, personalities, and their history with the Baby Dolls. In painting these portraits I did not want the paintings to be solely about capturing a likeness. I wanted the essence, individuality, and personality of these two strong women to come through.

I began the paintings with a burnt sienna grisaille, or under painting, laying down the shapes and tones of the figures. Next, I built up the

Baby Dolls Eva "Tee-Eva" Perry and Merline Kimble.
Reproduced with permission of Meryt Harding.

Gold Digger Baby Doll Merline Kimble. Reproduced with
permission of Meryt Harding.

Ernie K-Doe Baby Doll Eva "Tee-Eva" Perry. Reproduced with permission of Meryt Harding.

painting with many layers of colored oil paint, working back and forth developing the colors and tones. I chose a white background so that the figures would stand out in an iconic way. After the portraits were completed I felt that I needed to add something significant to the pieces and I found inspiration one night whilst visiting the Baby Dolls at the Oop Oop a Doo Lounge, where I saw Perry selling her pies and pralines and small pillows with her printed image surrounded by ribbon and lace. The next day I started to attach lace and ribbon to the outside of my canvases. For the show I also made some small pillows that I hung near the paintings. Each pillow was signed by the Baby Dolls and had historic significance relating to them.

The whole nine-month experience has been a wonderful journey. I have learned about the Baby Doll masking tradition and met a wonderful group of people who have great pride and passion about their Baby Doll culture. I have enjoyed painting the portraits of Kimble and Perry and it has been a real pleasure getting to know and become friends with these interesting, smart women, who work hard in their communities, have boundless energy, and are fun to be with.

Annie Odell

Antoinette K-Doe

My work is a fashion statement as well as an environmental one, to renew, reuse and recycle. My primary materials are men's neckties, cummerbunds, vintage buttons, and costume jewelry. I acquire these items at thrift shops and garage sales and as donations from friends. The majority of the sewing I do is on my 1976 Pfaff sewing machine. Although it is 38 years old, it is an old friend and workhorse with many utility and decorative stitches that I can mix and match to create textures and bind my pieces together. I create mixed-media quilted portraits of Louisiana's cultural icons from recycled textiles and trinkets. I keep a box of special items that remind me of individuals for portraits that are yet to be made. I had stashed away for several years a red velvet white lace little girl's dress with the intention of using it in a portrait of Miss Antoinette K-Doe as a Baby Doll.

Miss Antoinette is dressed as a Baby Doll in the red dress with a bonnet created from pieces of it. Her facial features and skin are quilted and embroidered in pleather. Her braids are embroidered as well. The

Antoinette K-Doe quilt. Reproduced with permission of Annie Odell. Photo by D. Eric Bookhardt.

Antoinette K-Doe quilt close-up. Reproduced with permission of Annie Odell. Photo by D. Eric Bookhardt.

Antoinette and Ernie K-Doe. Reproduced with permission of Annie Odell. Photo by D. Eric Bookhardt.

portrait is embellished with Mardi Gras beads and other trinkets. Miss Antoinette's efforts spearheaded the revival of the Baby Doll tradition in 2004. Sadly, she passed away in 2009 on Mardi Gras Eve, while preparing to parade the next day. She will forever live on in the hearts of many to be remembered for her generous and kind spirit, and her dedication to preserving so many traditions and epic memories that help to make New Orleans a special place.

Ruth Owens

"Baby Doll Series"

The Baby Doll marching groups of New Orleans have a legacy that dates back to 1912. They began in the black vice district of the city and represented the most disenfranchised segment of society: poor, black, female sex workers. A common epithet used by clients in addressing these women was "baby doll." Seizing upon the irony of this nickname, the women masked as baby dolls with short skirts, bloomers, pacifiers, etc. during Mardi Gras and St. Joseph's Day. Their appearance was where the

Hey Y'all, oil on canvas, 2015. Reproduced with permission of Ruth Owens.

Raddy Winner. Reproduced with permission of Ruth Owens.

Down by the Crossroads. Reproduced with permission of Ruth Owens.

Strut, Baby Doll. Reproduced with permission of Ruth Owens.

similarity to the innocence of a child's plaything ended, however. They boldly displayed a fierce streetwise attitude when marching through town, and most of all they danced.

My "Baby Doll" paintings are a dynamic depiction of these women, and show the movement and energy associated with walking "raddy," and dancing the "black bottom" in the streets. The exaggerated poses, the loose paint and the composition on the crossroads make reference to the self-possession, and confidence of the Baby Doll groups dancing the jazz in the streets in the early 1900s. The paintings: *Raddy Winner, Down by the Crossroads, Strut Baby Dolls*, and *Hey Y'all* are an unapologetic display of prowess and sexuality by women that on most days suffered the degradation of poverty, racism, and sexism. They show an enduring strength of spirit in the face of overwhelming day-to-day hardships.

Nathan "Nu'Awlons Natescott" Haynes Scott

The Original "For Us By Us" P. O. S. S. E.
(People Opposing Society's Segregational Entitlement)

Nearly a half of a century after President Abraham Lincoln issued the "Emancipation Proclamation," many Americans still held on to, practiced, and lived according to the ignorance that is racism. This poison was allowed to freely flow through the veins of every aspect of our life, especially here in the Deep South. Racism influenced where we lived, where we worked, where we worshiped, our use (or lack of use) of public systems and places. Racism even influenced how and where we socialized, even at Carnival time.

Though Carnival practices began early in the founding of the Louisiana colony, it wasn't until 1901 when an organized group of black men known as the Tramps marched on Mardi Gras Day, adding to the even earlier custom of blacks and Afro Creoles who used Native American Indian costumes to express their adapted African masquerading practices. This bold and entertaining form of self-expression cleared the path for many to follow. From the Tramps, Zulu was born in 1909. And, a short time later, around 1912, the Baby Dolls became a part of the celebration. The Baby Dolls may, on the surface, seem like the introduction of just another carnival marching club. However, in that day, as is now, America struggled with the fact that people of color, especially people of African descent, are an essential part of our existence as a human race. We (especially women of color) were largely excluded from political and judicial processes. Women of color were not even represented fairly in the women's suffrage movement in 1912. The economy was depressing and the Titanic even sank in that year. The emergence of an organized group of black women in a white-male-dominated and controlled venue conveys historical significance. The strutting out of this group of courageous black men and women in this social and economic climate was a bold statement of determination and self-entitlement. *The Original FUBU P.O.S.S.E.* is a statement of a people's determination and faith. The 1912 Baby Dolls did not wait for anyone to give them permission to enjoy life. There creative celebration was a unique, fun and, entertaining method of self-empowerment.

The Original "For Us By Us" (FUBU) P. O. S. S. E. (People Opposing Society's Segregational Entitlement) is one body of work consisting of 50+ pieces hand-carved from driftwood (driftwood, integral to our ecosystems, but by many considered debris) representing a people that give life in so many ways to this world, yet are so de-valued by man. The

The Original "For Us by Us" P. O. S. S. E. (People Opposing Society's Segregational Entitlement). Reproduced with permission of Nathan Scott. Photo by D. Eric Bookhardt.

The Original "For Us by Us" P. O. S. S. E. (People Opposing Society's Segregational Entitlement) close-up. Reproduced with permission of Nathan Scott. Photo by D. Eric Bookhardt.

processional attendees represent persons that are at different stages of growth from those that are still sighing: "Woe is me," to those that are celebrating the gift of life. It features a renowned jazz band of musicians both past and present, revelers, second-liners, moaners, a coffin, a grand-marshal, baby dolls, flambeaux carriers, Black Apaches (Mardi Gras Indians) and more. The funeral procession symbolizes the putting away or burying of society's segregation practices as an excuse for complacency or failure. It is a statement to others as well as to ourselves that we will "not be conformed to this world, but be transformed by the renewing (born again) of our mind." Changing the way we think, and therefore changing the way we perceive and are perceived.

This creative use of common materials (such as fabric, plastic cups, glue, wood, nails, and so on) is a visual definition of "folk art." Each piece is hand-painted using acrylic paints to achieve unique coloring and texture. Figures stand 7" to 12" tall. They are secured to a wooden platform by screws and glue. The entire project is a stand-alone piece that is approximately 12" x 38" x 50".

Gailene McGhee St.Amand

Rebirth of the Baby Dolls: A New Awareness in New Orleans

Coincidence, I don't believe in that term. I am referring to the historical performance of the New Orleans Society of Dance's Baby Doll Ladies in the Macy's Thanksgiving Parade in 2014, the book *The Baby Dolls: Breaking the Race and Gender Barriers of the New Orleans Mardi Gras*

Dancing Baby Doll. Reproduced with the permission of Gailene St.Amand.

Black Mask. Reproduced with the permission of Gailene St.Amand.

Golden Mask. Reproduced with the permission of Gailene St.Amand.

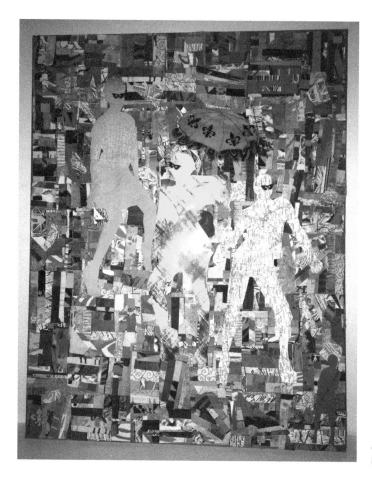

Mardi Gras Madness. Reproduced with the permission of Gailene St.Amand.

Tradition, and the exhibit, "Contemporary Artists Respond to the New Orleans Baby Dolls."

The Baby Dolls book shines a very bright spotlight on the group of high-spirited dancers, an important group of creative women. After living in New Jersey for 10 years, I returned to New Orleans three years ago, and had forgotten this old tradition. My earliest memories of the Baby Dolls were in my childhood neighborhood in the '60s. I remember the Baby Dolls parading in the black neighborhoods. Their origin is quite interesting as independent women. A truck with a flatbed passed with several older woman dressed in little girl dresses and bonnets. They were shaking with cigars in their hands and some had a baby bottle. I had no idea, who these women were, but they were having a great time.

Charles Lovell

"The Baby Dolls of New Orleans"

After moving to New Orleans during the summer of 2008, I immediately began photographing in a solely digital format. Formerly I worked in traditional black and white photography. Since my move to New Orleans, I have taken tens of thousands of photographs of subject matter including second line parades, jazz funerals, social aid and pleasure clubs, New Orleans cemeteries, Mardi Gras, Baby Dolls, and other processional parades, and scenes of the street and the unique cultural atmosphere or "roux," that makes up the verve of the Crescent City. My current works are in the tradition of documentary photography, as practiced by European artist Henri Cartier-Bresson and New Orleans historical documentarian Michael P. Smith.

In my photographic works, for the past seven years I have documented the rich and unique history of the African American cultural traditions that include second line parades, social aid and pleasure clubs, Mardi Gras Indians, brass bands, jazz funerals and Baby Dolls. The Baby Dolls tradition, according to Sylvester "Hawk Mini" Francis in the publication *Keeping Jazz Funerals Alive*, published by the Backstreet Cultural Museum in 2011, "Baby Dolls in the early years, groups in Mardi Gras Processions of woman use to dress up like Baby Doll's and the men used to cross-dress like women. . . . They also beat on homemade

Treme Million Dollar Baby Dolls Resa "Cinnamon Black" Bazile and Ricky Gettridge at a second line for "Uncle" Lionel Batiste. Reproduced with the permission of Charles Lovell.

instruments and this led to the founding of the Kazoo Band." While the immediate origin of this Carnival tradition is said to date from the early twentieth century and was influenced by the notorious New Orleans Storyville-era culture, these traditions also have strong roots in African and Caribbean traditions.

In a recent lecture in June 2015 at the New Orleans's Contemporary Art Center, "In Conversation with Nicolas Dumit Esteves," the Bronx-based artist who hails from the Dominican Republic showed men and women dressed as Baby Dolls. Their accessories included pacifiers also used by New Orleans Baby Dolls that I photographed during New Orleans's Satchmo Fest. My recent work from the back streets of New Orleans offers surreal depictions of masking typically out of view of urban centers and more tourist-oriented settings. The Baby Doll tradition is rife with surrealism and echoes the early twentieth-century photographs of European artist Hans Bellmer and American artists such as Man Ray and Frederick Sommer.

In photographing the New Orleans Baby Dolls, my hope is to engage and impress the importance of this artistic and cultural tradition rooted in African American life, to researchers, scholars, historians and a larger national and international audience.

Steve Prince

Bird in Hand: Second Line for Michigan

The image titled *Bird in Hand: Second Line for Michigan* symbolically utilizes the jazz funerary tradition from New Orleans to revive the failing economy of Detroit, Michigan. The 'jazz funeral' is broken up into two parts. The first portion is called the dirge, and the musicians conspire to play mournful music for the people present at the funeral to assist in the mourning process. Once the person is laid to rest, the music transforms from mournful to celebratory music, and the participants are encouraged to dance because the deceased does not have to suffer any longer, they are forever nestled in the arms of God in the afterlife.

In the top right hand portion of the composition four Horsemen of the Apocalypse carry a 1950s Chevy Coupe away from the gravesite as to revive it from its murky grave. The Horsemen walk the crossroads and process into the community of mourners. Three horn players blow in cadence, as a woman/Baby Doll, adorned with a pacifier, dances a lament barefoot. A woman professes to her Lord with her hand upraised, while

Bird in Hand: Second Line for Michigan. Reproduced with the permission of Steve Prince.

a man in the foreground lays a handkerchief upon the ground as if to lay it to rest. The handkerchief conspicuously has an "x" on the tip, which symbolizes death. In the center of the composition is a white male bass drummer. He represents the commingling of African and European traditions to create the original musical form created by African Americans called jazz. European marching band traditions are linear-based, while African traditions are circular-based. Adorning his drum is the name Treme, which represents one of the oldest African American neighborhoods in the nation, and home to many of the musicians creating the new music, jazz.

The drum acts as a counterpoint for the composition to transition the music from the dirge to the second line. Three women feverishly dance in celebration because that which has died is alive again in us all if we collectively work to grapple with the issues of our community. In the woman's hand in the left of the composition is a white handkerchief. During funerals the cloth would be used to wipe away tears, but it also symbolically represents the Holy Spirit. The woman animates the cloth by the movement of her hand and body to mimic the movement and path of a white dove. The handkerchief that has an "x" on it on the ground has been revived and an eye is on the cloth in the air. The Bird in Hand also refers to the nickname for the mainland and Upper Peninsula of Michigan. If you ask a person who is from Michigan to describe where they are from, they oft-times will reply by showing you the palm of their hand for the mainland and the opposite hand as a bird for the upper-peninsula to indicate where they live. So, this piece makes a symbolic connection between two distinct cultures that are in need of a revival of the spirit in the face of trying times. That which is dead and dying in our community can be revived through our collective imagination.

Vashni Balleste

Transforming Identity: The New Orleans Baby Dolls

Within my work I search for the truth in people.

I began observing the Baby Doll tradition in New Orleans as a student at Xavier University of Louisiana. Quickly, I recognized that masking for them was not just simply throwing on a costume. There was a defiant transformation here: the air lighter, a switch in step, and a noticeable sass. The woman I saw pre-costume was not the woman before my eyes. She was unbound, fearless, proud and free of society's expectations/standards—she was Baby Doll. I depicted Baby Doll dualism by photographing each woman as they were and then with costume. The transformation couldn't have been more beautiful.

Merline Kimble of the Gold Digger Baby Dolls poses in front of the Sycamore tree in Congo Square. Her grandmother was one of the early Baby Dolls to mask. Photo by Vashni Balleste.

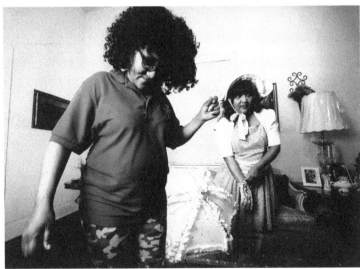

Carol Harris, known as "Baby Doll Kit," 2016. Photo by Vashni Balleste.

Alana "Mama Pretty" Harris, leader of the New Orleans Creole Belles, 2016. Photo by Vashni Balleste.

Lyndee "Pinky" Harris represents next generation Baby Dolls of the New Orleans Creole Belles, 2016. Photo by Vashni Balleste.

Kadrell "Mahogany Doll" Batiste masked for the first time in 2016 and started her own group known as the Renegade Rebel BabyDolls, 2016. Photo by Vashni Balleste.

Afterword

I arrived in New Orleans in August 2015 after living in Trinidad and Tobago for more than 8 years. In Trinidad, I played 'mas' during the Carnival season, where thousands of revelers dress in bright colorful feathers and scant beaded costumes. Rum and Soca music are essential elements of a Trini Carnival, and like its cousin, Mardi Gras, there are tons of parties and an influx of tourists. As a new transplant to New Orleans, I wanted to experience what it is like to mask during Mardi Gras.

Dr. Kim Vaz-Deville, my colleague at Xavier University of Louisiana, learned about my eagerness to be a part of Mardi Gras group and invited me to an event where a group of African American women where making their debut as the New Orleans Creole Belle Baby Dolls. I pictured myself as a baby doll, adorned with a short satin dress, ruffled bloomers and an oversized hair bow. Cute. The Baby Dolls' costumes had more fabric that I was accustomed too 'playing mas' in Trini Carnival, but the ruffles and stockings added sensuality and flair that appealed to me. It seemed like hours had passed before the Baby Dolls would take the stage. I heard someone from the back of the hall yell, "Here Come the Baby Dolls!" and four impeccable Baby Dolls sashayed onto the stage unfazed by the glaring stares, from the mostly White crowd. The Creole Belles were sassy, flirty and adorned in the brightest yellow I had ever seen. It was obvious that Mama Pretty aka Alana Harris, was their leader, as she unapologetically positioned herself center stage and demanded attention from every human in attendance. She twirled her jeweled umbrella playfully and the crowd rushed in like paparazzi.

The Baby Dolls were like rock stars. I realized that I couldn't just join a Baby Doll group. I couldn't buy my way into this experience. The Baby Dolls were something special and were doing a whole lot more than just masking. I don't know if it was my experience as an ethnographer, or my gut, that signaled to me that my desire of being a Baby Doll was out of order. I was accustomed to paying to play mas in Trinidad Carnival, where having the financial ability to pay satisfied the vetting requirement. The Trinidad Carnival allows for tourists to access carnival culture for a price, while the history, rituals and tradition were learnt by the most curios mas player. I had the privilege of being a resident of Trinidad and Tobago and my Trini friends and colleagues and I would often engage in stories about the history of traditional Carnival and how it has changed over the years.

While Trinidad and Tobago has opened space for tourist participation in Carnival celebration, African American Mardi Gras traditional masking culture was not as accessible. There is an intimate living history associated with the African American masking tradition that is passed on from generation to generation. Careful attention is given to teaching their children the meanings behind the meticulous sewing of the suits, the ornate dresses, and the vibrant colors that adorn the maskers. Because of this, tourists only participate in African American Mardi Gras traditions as temporal onlookers. And, even though I am an African American woman, I am an outsider to this cultural tradition. Therefore, I was uncomfortable with the idea of asking to just join this group of women without little experience in understanding how they reached 'rock stardom' status.

I had another idea to respectfully engage with the Baby Doll life. To understand how the Baby Dolls help shape the culture of New Orleans, I would make a great documentary. I shared my idea with Dr. Vaz-Deville, who put me in touch with various groups of Baby Dolls that she interviewed for her book. I assigned a cohort of my Mass Communication students at Xavier University to participate in the process. The students would gain hands on experience in ethnographic media filmmaking as researchers, interviewers, and videographers. With no budget, the students and I set out on an ethnographic journey in documentary film.

Gaining Access

The process of getting the footage for the film was not unlike traditional ethnographic research. Ethnography is a process whereby researchers immerse themselves within a culture. This immersion is to gain spatial, social and cultural understanding of cultural norms and values. This type of understanding can be achieved through participant observation, in-depth interviews, and general observation. Though all of these methods are integral to ethnography, none can be possible without having access. So before the students and I set out in the field to film interviews, we had to be introduced by someone whom the baby dolls trusted—Dr.

Vaz-Deville. Ethnographic research requires time to develop trust with a community. This is especially necessary when the ethnographer is an outsider, a non community member. Although a handful of students were native New Orleanians, none had any intimate experience with the Baby Dolls. They knew contemporary Mardi Gras as parades, krewes, and riding on floats. Students that were not from New Orleans had an understanding of Mardi Gras as represented in the media. Having Dr. Vaz-Deville as an intermediary allowed the students access to a community of Baby Doll voices.

As the director of the film, I wanted to invite as many voices of Baby Dolls to share lived experiences. Black women's voices are often marginalized and poor black women's voices go unheard. So it was extremely important to me, as a black woman, to be as inclusive as possible and to ensure a fair representation of diverse voices had an opportunity to tell their truth on their own terms. I asked Dr. Vaz-Deville to list baby doll groups that may be willing to be interviewed and then I would contact them only after Dr. Vaz-Deville alerted them.

Following the course of traditional ethnography, I did not have fixed ideas about the film. I understood this experience to be a journey and that themes would emerge and become more salient as we interviewed various Baby Doll groups. However, the students had little experience with ethnography and the unpredictable nature of ethnographic film triggered much frustration among the students. Students were accustomed to scripted media, with specific direction, timing and outlines that alerted them to what would likely happen next.

They had to readjust their expectations and learn extreme patience while waiting for Baby Dolls to arrive at a venue to be filmed or interviewed. There was not a script and students had to adjust quickly and become flexible. Because students were already frustrated by the unpredictable nature of ethnography, it was difficult for them to fully engage with some of the older groups of Baby Dolls. They fell into the background as 'production crew' and were disengaged from the experience.

This changed when they met the Creole Belle Baby Dolls. Perhaps it was the laid back and sassy nature of Mama Pretty, leader of the Creole Belles that first resonated with the students. She is funny, sassy, no-nonsense and heavily opinionated. Students were drawn to her energy and playful spirit. The other members of the Creole Belles were equally relatable to the students. After interviewing the Creole Belles, students were less frustrated and more patient with the ethnographic experience. They decided to spend more time with the Creole Belles and film their 'coming out' on Mardi Gras Tuesday.

Protectors of Culture

My gut didn't fail me; the story of Baby Dolls is very rich. In the film, *Baby Dolls: Preserving Culture in New Orleans*, the Baby Dolls recollect memories about the history and culture of Baby Dolls as entrepreneurs and community organizers. They share stories about how they are fighting to protect the tradition amid gentrification and the changing landscape of New Orleans. Baby Dolls shared stories about inequity in housing, raising rents, economic disenfranchisement and a struggling school system. They shared anger about feeling pushed out of New Orleans by White transplants to the city and how the baby doll tradition needed to be preserved as an act of resistance to preserve culture.

They worried that the authenticity of the baby doll tradition is under fire as outsiders, (there is a group of predominately white women Baby Dolls, organized by the Big Chief of the Golden Eagles Mardi Gras Indians) are finding their way in as participants. White women masking as Baby Dolls was not popular among five Baby Doll groups we interviewed. All expressed concern about the culture changing too much and shared concerns that White women lacked the understanding of the tradition and were 'taking' their culture because they did not have one of their own. We did interview two members of the Golden Eagles Baby Dolls to learn why they wanted to participate in the culture and they noted that they were invited by Joseph Pierre "Big Chief Monk" Boudreaux. However, some felt that being invited to participate and vetted is not the same thing as taking a culture that is not theirs and making it their own.

Lessons Learned

I walked away with having learned three things from this journey. First, as a teacher, I learned that making an ethnographic documentary takes a lot more time than is available for a class assignment. Though students bonded with the Creole Belles, their commitment to complete the film did not extend beyond the timeframe of the class. Only one student, Vashni Balleste[1], felt so connected to the project that she was inspired to assist and see it through to completion. In total, we filmed over the course of 8 months, conducted 11 interviews and filmed countless of hours of footage.

Second, as a researcher, I learned to be sensitive in my understanding of the nature of culture and change. Sometimes change is progressive, though, may not always be welcomed. Who does the change impact? Who is inconvenienced by change? Who makes the decisions about change? Who has the right to speak? Who speaks? These questions must be considered, especially when seeking to a critically nuanced understanding of culture and preservation.

Finally, as a Black woman, I learned that my being black and being woman does not always equal complete understanding of every black woman's lived experience. We are much too complex to be oversimplified. There is diversity in our experience even as we share a commonality. We can't all mas in the same way, and that is what makes us so beautiful.

—Tia L. Smith

NOTE

1. See her artist statement in this volume.

Acknowledgments

I would like to thank the contributors to this anthology for accepting my invitation to delve into the world of the Baby Dolls of New Orleans from their respective positions as scholars, writers or artists. I appreciate Ron Bechet's willingness to walk with me on faith as we planned and ultimately produced the exhibit "Contemporary Artists Respond to the New Orleans Baby Dolls." Much gratitude is due to those who contributed funding to the show and all those who donated to the crowd-sourcing initiative. I am grateful to Sarah Clunis and Daniele Gair who oversaw the show's installation and to Pamela Franco and Mora Beauchamp-Byrd for jurying the show with them. I also thank Daniele for proofreading two manuscripts. Cheryl Dejoie-LaCabe produced eye-popping graphics in the form of flyers, signage, mini-catalogs, and certificates of appreciation for the artists. I thank Beverly and Dwight McKenna, owners of the Leah and George McKenna Museum of African American Art in New Orleans, and Jennifer Williams, former museum director, for accepting the exhibit into their rotation of shows. Leeandra Nolting, Xavier University of Louisiana's Writing Resource Center Coordinator, spent many hours proofreading the final draft of the manuscript and undertaking the mammoth task of ordering the images into consistent labeling throughout the text. I am grateful to Herbert W. McGuin, Xavier University of Louisiana's Head of Reference, Research, and Instruction, for tracking down the copyright sources for hard-to-identify sources. Right when this manuscript was sent to go to press, I was fortunate to meet Jenestaer Hayes Horne. She entrusted me with the scrapbook she made of Hernietta Hayes Warrick's documents and lovingly told me everything I needed to know could be found there. I thank her and family for their embrace of this work. I am grateful to Elizabeth Frank, Eugenia Adams, Joyelyn Green, Janice Manuel, Helen Porche and Alvarez Labat and their families for generously sharing memories and cherished family photos with me. I thank everyone who has come out to the events associated with this project, for spreading the word and generously engaging in its social media identity. I applaud the Baby Dolls of New Orleans for their seizing of the tradition from its fate of descending into obscurity and reinvigorating it with new life and new meanings.

Contributors

Jennifer Atkins is an associate professor in the School of Dance at Florida State University. She earned an MA in American dance studies and a PhD in history at Florida State University. Her research interests delve into the relationships between American social dance and cultural identity, especially related to her hometown of New Orleans. She is the author of *New Orleans Carnival Balls: The Secret Side of Mardi Gras, 1870–1920* (Louisiana State University Press, 2017), which won the Jules and Frances Landry Award for 2017 and is co-editing two anthologies about dance in American culture. Atkins teaches courses in dance history, research, and theory.

Vashni Balleste is from upstate New York and studied broadcast journalism at Xavier University. She has been a freelance photographer for *Ebony Magazine* and written for tennis.com. Balleste is a UNCF grant recipient and documented political issues at the borders of Haiti for American Friends. She has directed music videos, contributed to publications such as *Sofar Sounds, BalconyTV,* and *Data News Weekly*. A black culture enthusiast and documentarian, Balleste's goal is always to build platform for often silenced voices.

Mora J. Beauchamp-Byrd is an art historian, curator, and arts administrator specializing in the art of the African Diaspora (including artists engaged with feminist theory and African American cartoonists); curatorial studies; eighteenth-century British art (with an emphasis on William Hogarth's graphic narratives); and contemporary British art with a particular focus on British artists of African, Asian, and Caribbean descent. She is a visiting assistant professor of art history at Oklahoma State University. She has also taught at Duke University, Spelman College, and Xavier University of Louisiana. Beauchamp-Byrd completed a BA in art history and an MA in visual arts administration at New York University. After earning an MA in art history from Columbia University, she completed a PhD in art history at Duke University in the Department of Art, Art History, and Visual Studies.

Romain Beauxis is originally from France and is an avid explorer of New Orleans and southern Louisiana culture. Through his photos, he tries to capture some of the richness, joyfulness, and fascination that he has witnessed during his adventures.

Ron Bechet, MFA, is a native of New Orleans and a relative of the early jazz pioneer Sidney Bechet. He began drawing in the fourth grade, studied art at the University of New Orleans and went on to earn a graduate degree from Yale University. His art teaching career began at Delgado Community College, then at Southern University in New Orleans and, since 1998, at Xavier where he holds the Victor H. Labat Endowed Professor of Art Painting. Even though he is a celebrated and accomplished artist, he feels he learns as much about himself and his art while teaching as his students do in their own studies. One of the biggest influences on his recent work was fellow art professor at Xavier, the late renowned sculptor John T. Scott.

Melanie Bratcher is president of Maatic Empire, LLC, and MelangeVibe. She has served as an associate professor at the University of Oklahoma. Bratcher received her doctorate in African and African American studies from Temple University in 2005. Her research focuses on Africana aesthetics—philosophy of art—with a specialization in Africana performance. Having coined the term "sound motion," she applies Africana philosophy to the study, explanation, description, and evaluation of Africana artistic process and production. She is the author of *The Words and Songs of Bessie Smith, Billie Holiday and Nina Simone: Sound Motion, Blues Spirit and African Memory* (Routledge, 2012).

Jerry Brock is a member of the Cherokee Nation. He is the co-founder of WWOZ 90.7 FM radio station in New Orleans, a Grammy Award–winning record producer, independent researcher, writer, and documentary filmmaker. He is a life-long advocate for human rights and environmental sustainability.

Ann Bruce is a native of New Orleans. In 2005, Antoinette K-Doe invited Bruce to join the Ernie K-Doe Baby Dolls. They marched in the Krewe of Muses parade and had a wonderful time struttin' down the street showing off their "linens." Bruce loves New Orleans, its traditions, and the magic of Mardi Gras. Her work has been shown in the Ogden Museum of Southern Art.

Violet Harrington Bryan is a professor emeritus of English at Xavier University of Louisiana. She has her BA from Mount Hòlyoke College and her PhD from Harvard University. Her book, *The Myth of New Orleans in Literature: Dialogues of Race and Gender* (U of Tennessee P, 1993) has been read widely. She has contributed a literary biography of Lorenzo Thomas and an entry on African American poetry collectives to the *Encyclopedia of American Poetry*, edited by Jeffrey Gray, James McCorkle and Mary Balkun (Greenwood, 2005); she has also published an analysis of the writings of the New Orleans writer Marcus Christian in *Creole: The History and Legacy of Louisiana's Free People of Color*, edited by Sybil Kein (LSU Press, 2000); and a discussion of the twentieth-century African American literary community in *Literary New Orleans in the Modern World*, edited by Richard Kennedy (LSU Press, 1998). She has published essays on a number of African American and Louisiana writers and is currently writing a book of comparative critical analysis on the writings of two Jamaican sisters, Velma Pollard and Erna Brodber.

Rachel Carrico holds a PhD in critical dance studies from the University of California Riverside and an MA in performance studies from NYU. Her research explores the aesthetic, political, and social histories of second lining, an African diaspora dance form rooted in New Orleans's black parading traditions. Carrico was the 2015–16 Mellon Postdoctoral Fellow in Dance Studies and the Humanities at Stanford University. Her scholarship has been published in *TBS: The Black Scholar* and *TDR: The Drama Review*, awarded the Society of Dance History Scholars' Selma Jeanne Cohen Award, and supported by grants from such entities as the UC President's Dissertation Year Fellowship Program; the UC Center for New Racial Studies; and the Center for Gulf South Research at Tulane University. Carrico is also a contributor to New Orleans's *Data News Weekly* and a consultant for the forthcoming documentary film, *Buckumping*, on New Orleans vernacular dance. She parades annually with the Ice Divas Social and Pleasure Club.

Sarah Anita Clunis is the director of the Xavier University of Louisiana Art Gallery and assistant professor of art history at Xavier University of Louisiana. She received her PhD in art history from the University of Iowa. She specializes in arts of Africa and the African diaspora from traditional to contemporary. She has worked for over twenty years with private collections of African and diaspora art in Europe, the U.S. and the Caribbean. She has done extensive work with university collections both with university museums (including Xavier's art collection and galleries) and with collections management of smaller endowments for growing institutions. Clunis has also taught art history for over twenty years at a various public universities and HBCUs including Xavier and SUNO. Her research has included looking at the history of African art and display of African objects in Western museum settings, as well as looking at the influence of African aesthetics and philosophy on the arts, religious rituals, and cultural identities of the African diaspora. Clunis is originally from Kingston, Jamaica.

Phillip Colwart was born in Baton Rouge and raised in New Orleans. He is a Hammond-based professional photographer who contributes his time and photography to the Mardi Gras Indian, Baby Doll, and Skull & Bones community. Having grown to appreciate and value this culture, Colwart gives back to these groups through his images and thus helps to preserve and perpetuate these traditions.

Keith Duncan is an artist and fine-arts educator. His focus is on local sub-cultures, folk cultures using traditional motifs, the postmodern language of Afro-American "signifying," as well as social street art. He has exhibited at the Taller Boricua Gallery in New York; Danny Simmons Corridor Gallery in Brooklyn; the CUE Art Foundation in New York; and the GSL Arts project in New Orleans.

Rob Florence is a New Orleans playwright, author, preservationist, documentary filmmaker, and tour operator. He has written two books on New Orleans cemeteries and curated several museum exhibits on the subject, as well as created a permanent *Plessy v. Ferguson* exhibit in the Cabildo's Sala Capitular where the case was first heard. He holds an MFA in playwriting (with distinction) from the University of New Orleans and is the Dramatists Guild's first Gulf Coast Regional Representative. His plays include *Burn K-Doe Burn, Holy Wars*, and *KATRINA: Mother-in-Law of 'Em All*. Florence's first film *Zack and Addie* won awards in festivals worldwide. He is currently working on a documentary about Cosimo Matassa's recording studios.

Pamela R. Franco is a native Trinidadian who earned a PhD in art history from Emory University in Atlanta. She was an assistant professor of art history at Tulane University, an executive associate to the provost and vice president of academic affairs, interim director of the Institute of Black Catholic Students, and chief of staff of the president of Xavier University of Louisiana. She has served as a member of the Newcomb Gallery Advisory Board. Her work on carnival arts has been published in *Small Axe: A Caribbean Journal of Criticism, African Arts*, and *Trin-*

idad Carnival: The cultural politics of a transnational festival (Indiana University Press, 2007).

Daniele Gair is the manager and registrar for the Xavier University Art Collections. Gair received her BA in English, with a minor in women's studies, from Newcomb College of Tulane University. A writer by trade, she has spent many years researching art and antiques and is thrilled to be able to apply her talents and expertise to the care and study of Xavier's exceptional collection of African and African American art. A New Orleans native with roots in beautiful St. Charles Parish, Gair enjoys reading many books at once, winning at trivia, and spending time with her family and friends.

Meryt Harding was born in England and uses photography to tell a story. Her paintings are derived from photos captured while traveling and are inspired by her sketch book and a diary. Recent exhibits in New Orleans include the Ashe Center's *Martin Luther King Show*, *NOLA NOW-Figurative* at the Contemporary Art Center, and *Los Invisibles* photography exhibit at Barristers Gallery and the New Orleans African American Museum.

Megan Holt is the executive director for One Book One New Orleans and the CEO of Words & Music: A Literary Feast in New Orleans. Raised in Muscle Shoals, Alabama, Holt received a BA in English and Spanish from the University of Alabama in 2003 and a PhD in English/comparative literature from Tulane University in 2013. She currently teaches freshman composition in the English Department at Tulane University. Holt is a member of the board of directors for the Literacy Alliance of Greater New Orleans, a member of the board of directors for the Tennessee Williams Literary Festival, and a member of the advisory board for the Lower Ninth Ward Street Library. Her husband, Jermaine Smith, and their sons, Jefferson and Abel, inspire her to work toward making New Orleans a better place.

DeriAnne Meilleur Honora is a lifelong New Orleans resident. She grew up in the Gentilly neighborhood, receiving her high school diploma from Cabrini High School in 2009, and was awarded the Sister Thea Bowman Scholarship from the Black Catholic Educational Foundation. She earned her BA in history with a concentration in education from Xavier University of Louisiana in 2013. Currently the college and career counselor at St. Augustine High School, Honora met and married fellow Xavier University of Louisiana graduate Jarred Honora in

2015. Honora is a parishioner at Blessed Trinity Catholic Church in New Orleans.

Marielle Jeanpierre was born in the port city of Lorient, in Brittany, France. A former business executive and mother of six, she is a self-taught ceramist. She has pursued further study in figurative sculpture at Terre et Feu in Paris, under Christian Siméon. Her work on the Baby Doll tradition is a personal reflection of the possibility of radiating bliss after overcoming difficulty and achieving a new status. She chooses to illustrate the theme of resilience.

Ulrick Jean-Pierre is renowned for his creation of Haitian historical paintings. His painting *Celebrating the Culture of Life: New Orleans' Mardi Gras Baby Dolls* is one of the various paintings in his series depicting the Haiti-Louisiana connections, which include *Marie Laveau Invoking the Spirit of Love*, a commissioned painting entitled *The Life of St. Katherine Drexel* on display at the Church of St. Katherine Drexel in New Orleans, and the official portrait of Henriette Delille for the Sisters of Holy Family in New Orleans.

Jessica Marie Johnson is an assistant professor in the Center Africana Studies and Department of History at the Johns Hopkins University. She is the author of *Practicing Freedom: Black Women, Intimacy, and Kinship in New Orleans Atlantic World* (University of Pennsylvania Press, forthcoming) and co-editor of *Black Code: A Special Issue of the Black Scholar* (2017). Her work has appeared in *Slavery & Abolition*; *Black Scholar*; *Meridians: Feminism, Race and Transnationalism*; *Debates in the Digital Humanities*; *Bitch! Magazinei*; and *Black Perspectives* (AAIHS)."

Karen La Beau comes from a line of "natural" artists that began with her grandfather. In New Orleans, he was known as "Abe the Sign Painter." He did all the sidewalk ads for all the local groceries from the 1950s until the 1980s and influenced her persistence as an artist. The majority of her art is a direct memory, history, or link to the past. She calls it "My Life on Canvas." She began to paint professionally to cope with her relocation from New Orleans to northwest Louisiana after Hurricane Katrina.

Peter Ladetto is a self-taught artist from Massachusetts. Romain Beaux-is's photograph, which inspired Ladetto's *Fiery Baby Doll*, is one in a series of paintings he calls "dream energy." These paintings involve an interactive experience for the viewer. He has shown his work in New Orleans at the Louisiana Pizza Kitchen, Byrdie's Art Gallery, DNA

Art Gallery, and Lucky Pierre's Show Bar. In 2014, he was featured on "WGNO News with a Twist." He is co-owner with Daphne Britton of Shinola Consignment Gallery.

D. Lammie-Hanson has shown with the Jazz and Heritage Foundation Gallery as a participant in the Women's Caucus of Arts (Louisiana Chapter) "Femme Fest" and with the New Orleans's African American Museum "Pop-Up" show. She has also exhibited at the Contemporary Arts Center and with the Arts Council of New Orleans. Her latest work focuses on the infamous "paper bag test." She sees vestiges of this color caste system at work today and uses art an intervention.

Karen Trahan Leathem has served as a historian at the Louisiana State Museum for more than sixteen years. A Louisiana native, she began researching New Orleans carnival while earning her PhD at the University of North Carolina at Chapel Hill. Each Mardi Gras, she assumes a new identity and dances on the streets with all the other joyful revelers.

Charles Lovell has taken over ten thousand photographs of Second Line Parades, Baby Dolls, Jazz Funerals, Social Aid and Pleasure Clubs, Mardi Gras and other processional parades, and scenes featuring the unique social atmosphere of the Crescent City. He is a member of the Backstreet Cultural Museum and regularly attends and documents the cultural events and parades that include the procession of the Baby Dolls.

Ed Newman worked with the legendary New Orleans documentarian Michael P. Smith, whom he considers his mentor. He has photographed New Orleans's jazz funerals, second line parades, and musical performers. Newman's work has appeared in a number of American and European publications, including the *Oxford American* and *OffBeat* magazine. His photography also appeared in the HBO television series *Treme*.

Karen Ocker first gained notoriety for her political satire in *The George W. Bush Coloring Book* (Garrett County Press, 2005) and *The Ray Nagin Coloring Book* (New Basin Press, 2009). Her work appeared in *Day for Night*, the 2006 Whitney Museum Biennial Catalogue, and was recently featured on the cover of *OffBeat* magazine's "Jazz Fest Bible" and Louisiana Cultural Economy's *Cultural Connections*.

Annie Odell makes skirts, dresses, purses, belts, and headbands out of recycled neckties and quilted pleather portraits of Louisiana musicians. Their portraits are highly detailed quilted pieces with embroidered features and hair. She incorporates ties, trinkets, and background materials reflective of the subjects' lives and music, paying homage to their accomplishments.

Ruth Owens was born in 1959 to a young German woman and a black serviceman from Georgia. The nomadic military lifestyle of her childhood was complicated by restrictions to mixed families in many communities and laid the basis for the formation of her cultural identity. She will graduate with a Masters of Fine Arts from the University of New Orleans after quitting her medical practice of twenty-five years and will continue her artistic pursuits as a member of an artist collective called "The Front," located in the St. Claude art corridor in New Orleans. Notable solo shows include "Conspiracies" in 2017 at Barrister's Gallery in New Orleans and "Stepin' Out" at Xavier University Chapel Gallery in 2016. Ruth Owens has also participated in numerous group shows including "Currents, 2018," at A.I.R. Gallery, Brooklyn, New York; "Image and Text," 2017, at Site: Brooklyn Gallery, Brooklyn, New York; "LA Contemporary, 2015" at the Ogden Museum of Southern Art; "Contemporary Artists Respond to the New Orleans Baby Dolls," 2015, at the McKenna Museum of African American Art; "Imago Mundi: New Orleans: Repatriation," Prospect.3 Adjunct at the New Orleans Museum of Art; "True Colors," 2014, at the Ashe Cultural Center; and "NOLA NOW: The Human Figure," 2012, at the Contemporary Art Center in New Orleans.

Jamar Duvol Pierre is a celebrated painter, illustrator, and designer. His works are widely lauded for capturing the *joie de vivre* of New Orleans. A short list of some of Pierre's commissioned work include Beyoncé Knowles, Tina Knowles, Wendell Pierce, Anthony Mackie, Maurice Brown, 2007 Official Essence Music Festival Poster, Time Warner Entertainment, album covers for Straight Out the 6th Ward Brass Band, and Treme Allstars.

Steve Prince received his BFA from Xavier University of Louisiana and his MFA in printmaking and sculpture from Michigan State University. He is an assistant professor of art at Allegheny College in Meadville, Pennsylvania. Prince is concerned with the conditions of humanity and the challenges we face in a society that erodes our sense of true community and communal togetherness. His art explores these challenges and solutions to life's moral, ethical, and spiritual dilemmas. He is represented by Eyekons Gallery in Grand Rapids, Michigan, and is the owner of One Fish Studio, LLC.

Nathan "Nu'Awlons Natescott" Haynes Scott grew up in and around New Orleans's housing developments. Over the years, he has painted posters, canvas, and anything else that was available. He considers art his gift and hobby. The artistic pieces from driftwood that evolved from this sponta- neous flow of creative energy were so unique and beautifully decorated that they immediately caught the attention of celebrities, politicians, and fellow artists.

LaKisha Michelle Simmons is assistant professor of history and women's studies at the University of Michigan, Ann Arbor. She received her PhD from the University of Michigan in the Joint Program in History and Women's Studies in 2009 and held postdoctoral positions at Davidson College (History Department) and at the Center for the Study of the American South at UNC Chapel Hill. Her research exists at the produc- tive intersection between African American gender history, the history of sexuality, and cultural geography. As a scholar, she works to unveil the inner lives and everyday concerns of black women and children. Her book, *Crescent City Girls: The Lives of Young Black Women in Segregated New Orleans* (University of North Carolina Press, 2015) explores black girls' coming of age through the lenses of sexuality, space, and affect and was awarded the 2016 Julia Cherry Spruill Prize from the Southern Asso- ciation for Women Historians for best published book in southern wom- en's history, broadly construed.

Tia L. Smith joined the Mass Communication Department at Xavier University in 2015 as department head. Smith received her bachelor's in mass communication, speech, and theater from Bennett College for Women. She earned a masters of arts in international telecommu- nications with a concentration in women's studies, and a PhD in mass communication from Ohio University's coveted Scripps College of Com- munication. She has collaborated and consulted with her colleagues on many research projects, conferences, films, and academic papers. She trained journalists and media professionals throughout the Caribbean and Latin America on covering taboo topics such as child sexual abuse, domestic violence, and human trafficking. Her research interests focus on intersections of gender, media, and sexual culture. Smith has lived and worked in diverse cultural and learning environments in the United States, Zimbabwe, Swaziland, Brazil, and Trinidad and Tobago, giving her first-hand knowledge of the sensitive nature and challenges associ- ated with issues of media, diversity, and inclusiveness.

Gailene McGhee St.Amand is a collage and fabric artist from New Orleans. Her work has evolved from painting in oils and watercolor to ceramic glazes on bisque tiles, collages of handmade and found papers, and assemblages and textile or fabric arts creating soft sculpture busts with

Voodoo symbols and Mardi Gras themes. Her works are in collections such as at Ochsner Medical Center.

Kim Vaz-Deville grew up in New Orleans and attended St. Mary's Academy and Tulane University. She is a professor of education and associate dean of the College of Arts and Sciences at Xavier University of Louisiana. She is the author of *The "Baby Dolls": Breaking the Race and Gender Barriers of the New Orleans Mardi Gras Tradition* (Louisiana State University Press, 2013), the Young Leadership Council's One Book One New Orleans's 2016 selection. Her book served as the basis for a 2013 major installation on the Baby Doll tradition at the Presbytere unit of the Louisiana State Museum as part of the museum's permanent display on the history of Carnival in Louisiana. She co-curated with Ron Bechet "Contemporary Artists Respond to the New Orleans Baby Dolls" in 2015 at the George and Leah McKenna Museum of African American Art in New Orleans.

Kim Welsh is a retired psychologist and a photographer who advocates for cultural preservation and aims to understand the unique world view of her subjects and to respectfully translate that using visual imagery. For Welsh, New Orleans's diverse, vibrant, and spectacular cultural traditions should always be protected and encouraged as they are a treasure, which enriches lives and often goes unappreciated.

Index

Page numbers in *italics* refer to illustrations.

A

Adams, Eugenia, 147–48

Adams, Margaret, 25

African Americans: culture of, 95; economic margins of, 21–25, 79–80; men, rape accusations against, 120; middle class, in art, 254; narrative and jazz, 52; religious ritual in McCrady's work, 244; and vaudeville/minstrel shows, 173–74

African culture: in New World, 63; spirit in, 81, 84n5

Afro-Creole culture, xx, 22, 48–49

Alexander, Loyce, xxviin2

All on a Mardi Gras Day (Osborn), 147, 206

All Saints' Day death commemoration, 205

Allen, Caroline, *Caribbean Bodies*, 279–80

American Civil Liberties Union, 152

American Missionary Association, 25

American Regionalist painters, 236

American South, An (Kein), 49

A'mil, Little Queen, *160*

Amour, Armani, *161*

Amour, Elijah, *161*

Amour, Leroy, *161*

Amsterdam, Morey, 70, 74n31

Anckle, Floyd, 181

Andrew Sisters, 70

Andrews, Darnell (D-boy), 127

Andrews, James, 151

Andrews, Jenard, 151

Andrews, Lois, 3

Andrews family, 150

Antoinette and Ernie K-Doe (Odell), 268, *302*

Antoinette K-Doe (Odell), 268, *301*

Arceneaux, Alvin, 197

Arceneaux Bar, 197, 200

Arhoolie Records, 144–45, 183–84

Armani, Gold Digger Baby Doll (Colwart), *288*

Armstread, Viola, xi–xii

Armstrong, Louis: at 1949 Mardi Gras, 189, *190*; as King Zulu, 189; recordings by, 176; and Satchmo Salute, 151

Art Students League of New York, 239

Arthur Hardy Mardi Gras Guide (Hardy), 110

Arts and Crafts Club (New Orleans), 242

Asbury, Herbert, *The French Quarter: An Informal History of the New Orleans Underworld*, 92–93, 105n8

Assassination of Huey Long (McCrady), 242

Associated American Artists, 243

Astoria Hotel, 147–48

Atkins, Jennifer, 118

Autocrat Club, 197–98

Avila, Eric, xv

B

"Baby Boys," 195–96

"Baby Doll" (Smith), xxi, 176–77, 189

Baby Doll Ladies: musical choices of, 132n35; as response to Katrina, 117–20

Baby Doll Masqueraders (Smith), 248–49, *249*, 250–51, 254–55

Baby Dolls, xi–xxvii; associations with, 149, 173; Balleste's photos of, *312–13*; Batiste family involvement in, 170, 177; Black interview, 7–18; as caring mothers, 69; commercialism of, 13; controversies, 152–56; in costume, *172*; cross-dressing by, 147, 151, 231, 309; dancing, 38, *39*, 40, 95, 100–101, 103–4; early years of, 284n23; and ecclesiastical leaders, 120–21; economic margins of maskers, 117; emergence of, 89–90; expanded interpretation of, 156–62; formation of, xviii; at funerals, 126–31, 209, 216; future of, 13–18; Harding on, 298, 300; incarceration of, 67; interviews, 195–97; Kimble interview, 3–5; as legacy, 27–28; low opinion of, 197–98; in Macy's Thanksgiving Parade, 307; and Mardi Gras, 141–44, *143*, *171*; masking, 89–90, 198, 263 (*see also* Maskers, women); McCrady's representation of, 236–37, *237*; meaning of, 173; memories of, 146–49, 197–200; men as, 3–4, 11–13, 146–47, 231, 309; origins of, 144–46; as pallbearers, 126; participant experiences, 223–32; passing on tradition, 16, 18, 230, 261–64; political action by, 283; resurgence of, 5; revival of, ix, 8–9, 149–52, 189, 206–7; sexy ("babes"), 67; stigma of, 9–11; toughness of, 124; walking raddy, ix–x, 67, 103, 129; white women as, 11–13, 152–54, 199, 207–8
Baby Dolls: Preserving Culture in New Orleans, 318
Baby Dolls, The (Ocker), *268*, 274–75
Baby Dolls, The (Vaz-Deville), ix, xix, 273, 300
"Baby Dolls of 1949," 190
Baby Dolls of Perdido Street, 90
Baby Dolls Parade (La Beau), *295*
Back o' Town, 69
Backstreet Cultural Museum, 8, 231–32
Baham, Jacqueline "Aunt Jackie," 197–98

Baker, Danny, 124
Bakhtin, Mikhail, *Rabelais and His World*, 276–77
Balleste, Vashni, *311–12*, *312*, 318
Balls, 89, 104n1, 106n17
Bank of Oxford murals, 244
Barbarin family, 216
Barker, Danny, 99, 177; in Fairview Band, 181; lying in state, 219
Barker, Sylvia, *218*, 219
Bascom, William, 85n13
Bastardy Ordinance, 70, 74n28
Batiste, Alma Trepagnier, 145, 170, 177
Batiste, Ferdinand, *171*
Batiste, Kadrell "Mahogany Doll," 156, 158, *289*, *313*
Batiste, Lionel, 3, 147, *166*, 167–68, 184; childhood, 170; community engagement of, 180–82; Dirty Dozen Kazoo Band, 170–72; family background, 168–69; funeral of, 151; "Gimme My Money Back," 183; in Lammie-Hanson's painting, 266; "Lars Edegran Presents Uncle Lionel," 183; at Mardi Gras, *171*; "New Orleans Music," 183; in New Orleans music scene, 172–79
Batiste, Miriam. *See* Reed, Miriam Batiste
Batiste, Norman, *171*
Battle of Liberty Place (1874), 26
Battle of New Orleans, men of color in, 24
Baubo (Greek goddess), 125
Bazile, Resa. *See* Black, Cinnamon
Bazley, Tony, 38
Beauty, standards of, 79, 84n10
Beauxis, Romain, *263*, *267*, 275–76
Bechet, Ron, 221
Bechet, Sidney, 103
Bedou, Arthur P., 143, 254
Bellvue, Albert, 190, 192
Bennett, Emily, 147–48, *148*
Benton, Thomas Hart, 238, 239–40
Big Chief of the Flaming Arrow Warriors, *115*
Bigard, Brandon "Baby Doll Lilly," 157
Bigard-Sallier, Aidan "Baby Doll Butterfly," 157
Bigard-Sallier, Brenton "Little Police," 157
Big-Baby Dance, *175*, 176

Birch, Willie, 261–62, 264

Bird in Hand: Second Line for Michigan (Prince), 269, 281–82, *311*

Bishop, Isobel, 241

Black, Cinnamon (Resa Bazile), 7, 8–11, 13–18, 219; on Baby Dolls, 130–31, 151; in *Burn K-Doe Burn*, *217*; as Gold Digger, 113; after Katrina, 117–18; at Mother-in-Law Lounge, 227–28; musical choices of, 132n35; on religious influences on masking, 134n87; at Satchmo Summer-Fest, *270–71*

Black, James, 179

Black Foxx, The. *See* Hogan, Sumter "Cha Cha"

Black Indians. *See* Indians (Mardi Gras); Mardi Gras Black Indians

Black Indians of New Orleans, The (Martinez), xviii, xxviin13

Black Mask (McGhee), *307*

"Black Respectability," 280

Black Storyville. *See* Storyville

Black Storyville Baby Dolls, 126–27, *127*, 156; at Mother-in-Law Lounge, *157*

Black women: bearing children of white males, 76; as concubines, 120; court challenges by, 22–23; denigration of, through music, 78–81; empowerment of, 75, 85n3; reclaiming female bodies, 61–62, 65–66; white male violation of, 69. *See also* Women of color

Blouin, Lauren "Baby Blou," 156

Blue Books, 27

Bolden, Buddy, "The Funky Butt," 102

Bon Ton, 197

Bone gang. *See* Skeletons; Skull and Bones Gang

Borden, Alma "Mama Goo," *262*, 275–76

Boudreaux, Joseph Pierre "Monk," 152–54, *153*, 318; "Katie Mae," 154; *Mr. Stranger Man*, 154

Boudreaux, Wynoka, *153*

Boutte, Gloria Leblanc, 126–27

Bowers, Anita, 126

Box of Wine parade, 118

Bradford, Perry, "Jacksonville Rounders' Dance," 101

Bragg, Christina "Babydoll Gentilly Lace," 158, 162

Brass bands, 106n19, 183, 220; decline of, 149; revival of, 177. *See also* *individual names*

Breunlin, Rachel, 195

Brooks, Diana Garica, 131

Brooks, Geoffrey, 174–75

Brooks, Sarah, 150–51

Brooks, Shelton, "Darktown Strutter's Ball," 174

Brothels, 27; Emma Johnson's House of All Nations, 102; music in, 119, 163n20; naked dancing in, 101–2; segregation of, 224; US military personnel and, 70. *See also* Storyville

Brother Eatmore and Sister Fullbosom, 191

Brown, Milton, 257n23

Brown, Sidney, *183*

"Brown Skin Baby Doll" (McDaniel), 189

"Brown Skin Who, You For" (Williams and Piron), 174

Bruce, Ann, 285–86, *287*; in Ernie K-Doe Baby Dolls, 149, 208, 286; *Looking Down on the Mother-in-Law Lounge*, 285; *Mardi Gras Indians, Skeletons, Brass Band, Weenie Man, and Baby Dolls*, 286; *A New Orleans Farewell and a Heavenly Welcome*, 286

Bryan, Violet Harrington, *The Myth of New Orleans in New Orleans Literature*, 45

Burn K-Doe Burn (Florence), 205; early production of, 213–14; revival of, 216–19, *217*

Burns, Mick, *Keeping the Beat on the Street*, 183

Butler, Judith, 35; *Gender Trouble*, 282

By Invitation Only (Snedeker), 110

Bynum, Saran "Baby Doll China Doll," 157

Byrd, Henry Roeland. *See* Professor Longhair

C

Cable, George Washington, 45–46, 91, 93, 105n5; *Doctor Sevier*, 46; *The Grandissimes*, 46; on New Orleans's pleasure economies, 26; *Old Creole Days*, 46

Caillot, Marc-Antoine, 121, 133n48

Caldonia Inn: Carnival season entertainment, 189; funeral for, 193n18; as night spot, 179; recording careers launched from, 191

Calenda dance, 91–92, 105n5

Call-and-response singing, 91, 96, 97

Callis, Arthur, 48

Camel, Clara Marcelin, 142, 143; and Eunice, 141

Camel Toe Steppers, 13

Campbell, Mattie, 192

Caribbean Bodies (Allen), 279–80

Carney, Christy, *153*

Carnival: Caribbean, 279–80; enslaved blacks, options for, 63, 73n7; in Europe, 276–77; masking for, 109; mulatta's role in, 47; segregation and, 10; in Trinidad, 64, 72, 73n7, 315

"Carnival Time" (Johnson), 151

Carter, Hodding, 243

Casselli, Henry, 243

Castellanos, Henry C., 91

Caucasian Baby Dolls, 13

Celebrating the Culture of Life (Jean-Pierre), 268, 281, *294*

Charles, Millie, 144

Chase, Leah, 145

Child support, 68, 69–70, 71

Chiszle, JaVonee Bazile, 151

Chopin, Kate, *A Night in Acadie*, 46

Chosen Few Brass Band, 181, 183

Christopher, MaryAnn Golden, 91

Church of the Epiphany, 197

Cinnamon Black and Sugar Baroness (La Beau), 281, *295*

Civil War, 25, 168–69, 177

Claiborne, W. C. C., 24

Claiborne Avenue, 196, 199, 204

Clark, Asmar, 162

Clark, Katrice, 162

Class: color caste system, 279, 298; colored-middle, 73n7; high, 63, 65, 66

Clunis, Sarah, 224, *230*

Coal Miner's House (Evans), 252

Cohan, George M., "The Warmest Baby in the Bunch: Ethiopian Ditty," 77–79

Coleman, Picaninny, 93

Colfax Massacre (1873), 26

Collins, Florestine Perrault, 143

Colwart, Phillip, 288; *Armani, Gold Digger Baby Doll*, 288; studio portraits by, *289*

Comité des Citoyens, 26

Company of the West Indies, 121, 133n48

"Comus" (Durieux), 249

Comus (krewe), 118; parades, 258n38

Congo Square, 89–94, 96, 101, 105n9

Contemporary Artists Respond to the New Orleans Baby Dolls, ix–x, xvii, 273

Cooley, Phil, 176

Cosey, Janice, 123, 124

Cotton Pickers (Shahn), 252

Couvent, Marie, 24

Coviello, Ann Marie, 118

Cozier, Chris, 281

Crawford, Ralston, *36–37, 37–38, 39–40, 40–41*

Creole: The History and Legacy of Louisiana (Kein), 49

Creole Ballads and Zydeco (Kein), 49

Creoles: as Baby Doll maskers, 199; preservation of culture, 48–49; women, 197, 200

Creoles of Color, 145

Crescent City Allstars, 151

Curry, John Steuart, 238, 240

D

Daily Worker, 243, 244, 246, 257n23

Damaria, James, 127

Dances, 62–64, 67; animal, 99; Bamboula (drum), 90–91, 105n9; banda, 129–30; "beggin mas," 68; Black Bottom, 101, 107n31; cakewalk strutting, 99; Chica-Congo, 92–93; Funky Butt, 102–3; and high society, 107n27; oyster, 102; shake, 4, 101, 105n5, 107n32; shimming tremor, 4, 91, 101, 105n5; shuffle, 91; the "stomp," 98; trucking, 98; turkey trot, 99

Dancing, *39, 40*; in brothels, 101; and

Jim Crow, 36–37; naked, 101–2; in New Orleans, 89–95, 105n5; in night spots, *36–37*; posture during, 95–96; as response to social ills, 64, 72

Dancing Baby Doll (McGhee), *307*

"Darktown Strutter's Ball" (Brooks), 174–76

Dauphine, Perine, 22

Davis, Gregory, 146–47

Davis, Natalie Zemon, 66

Davis, Quint, xviii

de Chirico, Giorgio, 242

Dedmond, Dana, *114*

Dedmond, Dinah "Baby Doll Sassy," *114*, 158, *158*

Dedmond, Donna "Baby Doll Panoonie," 158, *158*

Dedmond, Leslie "Baby Doll Lollipop," *114*, 158, *158*

Dejan, Harold, 181

Dejoie, C. C., Jr., 35

DeLay, Arsene "Scarlett Monarch," 156

Delille, Henriette, 24

Delta Dancer (Kein), 49

Demeter (Greek goddess), 125

Desegregation: of Baby Dolls, 11–13, 152–54, 199, 207–8; of schools, 25. *See also* Segregation

Dew Drop Inn, *36*, 38

Didimus, Henry, 91, 94

Dieudonné, Elizabeth, 24–25

Dirty Dozen Brass Band, 147, *182*, 183

Dirty Dozen Kazoo Band, 170–71, *171*, 183

Doctor Sevier (Cable), 46

Dollis, Big Chief Bo, Jr., xviii, 151, 157

Dollis, Laurita, *157*

Doucette, Alfred, *115*

Down by the Crossroads (Owens), 274, *303*

Dress style: *a la jupe*, 65, 73n11; of Baby Boys, 147, 195–96, 231, 301; of Baby Dolls, xvii–xviii, 8–9, 143, 144, 147–49, 196, 198; of Black Indians, 112; bloomers (drawers), 11, 17, 122; burial clothes matching, 214, 216; clothing construction, 18, 163n30, 207, 315; crepe paper costumes, 150, *150*; diapers with mustard, 170,

195–96; fabric purchases for, 13; *foulard* (scarf), 73n11; *la grande robe*, 65, 73n11; military-inspired, 132n20; to rival white counterparts, 90; in sartorial body masquerade, 64–65; for shake/shimmy dances, 4; in Trinidad, 64–68, 71–72

Dunbar, Paul Laurence, 45, 47

Dunbar-Nelson, Alice, 45–48; "Brass Ankles," 48; *Give Us Each Day: The Diary of Alice Dunbar-Nelson*, 48; *The Goodness of St. Rocque and Other Tales*, 45; *An Hawaiian Idyll*, 47–48; *Violets and Other Tales*, 45; *The Works of Alice Dunbar-Nelson*, 48, 54n2

Duncan, Keith, 290; *Legacy of the Baby Dolls*, 264–65, *290*

Dunham, Katherine, 95

Durieux, Caroline Wogan, 258n39; "Comus," 249; *Mardi Gras Day*, 237, 246; McCrady's collaboration with, 243

Dyer, Calvin "DJ Hektik," 154–55

Dyer, Geoff: *The Ongoing Moment*, 235; on Stryker, 236

E

Edwards, Eddie "Duke," 118; "Fire in their Drawers," 154–55

El Greco, 240

Eleusian Mysteries, 125

Elks Parade, *178*

Emancipation, 21–22, 23–24, 25, 84n2

Emery, Lynne Fauley, 92

Emma Johnson's House of All Nations, 102

Ensler, Eve, *Vagina Monologues*, 118

Ernie K-Doe Baby Doll Tee Eva Perry (Harding), 264, 275, *299–300*

Ernie K-Doe Baby Dolls, 206–8; drivers for, 116–18; as K-Doe (Antoinette) legacy, 221; as resurgence, 5; Trepagnier's memories of, 149–50

"Ethiopian ditties," 78

Eureka Brass Band, 179, 181

Europe, 110

Evans, Harold, 213

Evans, Walker, 236; *Coal Miner's House,*
    252; *Girl in French Quarter,* 259n43
Evening Meal, Duck Hill, Mississippi
    (McCrady), 245
"Exhausted Merrymakers" (McCrady),
    247–48, *247*

F

Fabulous New Orleans (Saxon), 109
Fairview Baptist Church Marching Band,
    181
Farm Security Administration (FSA),
    235, 252
Farris, Teresa Parker, 241
Fat Tuesday. *See* Mardi Gras
"Faubourg Study No. 3: The Seven Sisters
    of New Orleans" (Osbey), 52–54
Faubourg Treme neighborhood, 231–32
Federal Aid Highway Act (1956), xiv
Fi Yi Yi Mandingo Warriors, 151
Fido, Elaine Savory, 69
Fiery Looking Baby Doll (Ladetto and
    Beauxis), 266, *267*
"Fire in their Drawers" (Edwards), 154–55
First Amendment rights, 152
Fisher, Baby Floyd, 174
Flaherty, Jordan, 210n13
Flaming Arrow Warriors, *115*
Flattman, Alan Raymond, 256n14
Florence, Rob: *Burn K-Doe Burn,* 205,
    213–14; and fortieth birthday par-
    ty, 216; *Katrina: Mother-In-Law of
    'Em All,* 220
Flour Chief, wife of, 121
Flynn, Kathleen, 275–76
"For Us by Us" P. O. S. S. E. (People
    Opposing Society's Segregational
    Entitlement), 269, *306*
Foucault, Michel, 65
"Four Women" (Simone), 80–81
Fourteenth Street School, 241
Fox, Betty: effigy loan by, 218; on K-Doe
    (Antoinette) funeral, 209; and
    Mother-in-Law Lounge, 210n7
Francis, Sylvester "Hawk Mini," 8; *Keep-
    ing Jazz Funerals Alive,* 309
Frederick Douglass High School, 25
Free Agents Brass Band, "We Made It
    through That Water," 155

*French Quarter: An Informal History of
    the New Orleans Underworld, The*
    (Asbury), 92–93
French Revolution, 67
Friends of New Orleans Cemeteries, 126,
    214
FSA (Farm Security Administration),
    235, 252
Funerals: Baby Dolls at, 17, 126–31, 151;
    for Caldonia Inn, 193n18; free
    burial, 216; of K-Doe (Antoinette),
    208–9; of K-Doe (Ernie), 205,
    210n10; of Lloyd Washington, 126,
    207; West African burial tradi-
    tions, 97. *See also* Jazz: funerals

G

Gair, Daniele, *230*
Gait, 66; walking raddy, ix–x, 67, 103, 129
Gallier Hall, 111
Galvez Street, 34
Garcia-Brooks, Dianna, *263*
Gaudin, Juliette, 24
Gautier, Adella, 213
Gelini, Jessie Wightkin, 152, *153*
Gender: Baby Doll mockery of, 195; in
    music, 78, 83, 84nn8–9; and racial
    violence, 32–34
Gender Trouble (Butler), 282
George Williams Brass Band, *178*
Gertrude Geddes Willis Funeral Home,
    144
Gettridge, Spyboy Ricky, 17, 151
Gilyot, Clea Desdune, 197, 198
Gilyot, Walter, 197
"Gimme My Money Back" (Batiste), 183
Girl in French Quarter (Evans), 259n43
*Give Us Each Day: The Diary of Alice
    Dunbar-Nelson* (Dunbar-Nelson),
    48
Glapion, Alfred, 146
Gold Digger Baby Doll Merline Kimble
    (Harding), 264, 275, *299*
Gold Diggers (Baby Dolls), 8; Kimble on,
    3–5; at Mardi Gras, 4, *161*; mem-
    bers of, 150–51, 228; resurgence
    of, 113
Gold Diggers, The (Hopwood), 113
Golden, Rolland Harve, 256n14

Golden Baby Doll Lady (Lammie-Hanson), *297*
Golden Eagle Mardi Gras Indians, *153*, 154, 318
Golden Eagles Baby Dolls, 152–54, *153*, 318
Golden Eagles Indian Gang, 152
Golden Mask (McGhee), *307*
Goldring, Erika, 152, *153*
Gombo People (Kein), 49
Goodness of St. Rocque and Other Tales, The (Dunbar-Nelson), 45
Graham, Michelle, 158
Grandissimes, The (Cable), 46
Grant, Coot, 102–3
Gray, Natonja, 151
Great Depression, 235
Green, Joycelyn, 156, *288*
Green, Linda, 148–49
Green, Olivia, 141, *142*, 143, *268*
Grissom, Prudence, 149
Guede, Iwa, 126, 129–30
Guerand, Charles, 34
Guichard family, 179
Guimont, Felice, 149
Gumbo Marie's Creole Store, 156
Gye Nyame, 156

H

Hades (Greek god), 125
Haitian Revolution, 23
Hamera, Judith, 208
Hands On New Orleans, 206
Harding, Meryt, 298–300; *Ernie K-Doe Baby Doll Tee Eva Perry*, 264, 275, *299–300*; *Gold Digger Baby Doll Merline Kimble*, 264, 275, *299*; painting style of, 275
Hardy, Arthur, *Arthur Hardy Mardi Gras Guide*, 110
Harlem Renaissance, 48
Harris, Alana "Mama Pretty," 145, 156–57, *289*, *313*, 315
Harris, Carol "Baby Doll Kit," *115*, 158, *158–59*, 227, *289*, *312*; Flynn's image of, 276, 283n7; and Mother-in-Law Lounge, 229
Harris, Demi "Baby Doll Dimples," 157
Harris, Justin, 276, 283n7

Harris, Lyndee "Pinky," 157, *313*
Hawaiian Idyll, An (Dunbar-Nelson), 47–48
Hayes, Sherman, xi–xii
"Hea' Comes Ma Baby: A Coonville Episode" (Hubbell), 81–82
Hearn, Lafcadio, 67
"Here Come the Girls" (Toussaint), 149, 217–18
Herera, Rose, 24–25
Herskovits, Melville and Frances, 95
Hey Y'all (Owens), 274, *303*
Highgate, Edmonia, 25, 29n15
Hill, Beatrice: on Baby Dolls' origin, 144–45, 172; on brothels and US military, 70; on naked dancing, 102; in Storyville, 144–46
Hill, Jessie, 150; death of, 214, 216
Hill, Travis "Trumpet Black": death of, 221n2; funeral of, *128–29*, 129
Hine, Darlene Clark, 26
Hine, Lewis, 235–36
Hogan, Sumter "Cha Cha," *191*; "Grit Gitter," 191; "Just Because You've Been Hurt," 191; "My Baby Loves Me," 190; "My Walking Baby," 190
Hogan Jazz Archive, 37–38
Hogarth, William, 247
Honore, Dianne "Sugar Baroness": on ancestral traditions, 274; as Black Storyville Baby Doll, *127*, 156; with Gold Diggers (Baby Dolls), 228; in Mother-in-Law Lounge, 229
Hoodoo, 52–53
"Hootchy-Kootchy," 101
Hopwood, Avery, *The Gold Diggers*, 113
Horne, Jenestaer Hayes, xii
Hubbard, Arthur, 146
Hubbell, John Raymond, "Hea' Comes Ma Baby: A Coonville Episode," 81–82
Huber, Leonard, *Mardi Gras: A Pictorial History of Carnival in New Orleans*, 147
Hughes, Langston, 32, 259n43
Humor: defanging power with, 123; male bonding with, 125; racism in, 80; satire/parody, 122–23; for social control, 78

Hunter, Tera, 31
Hurricane Katrina: and Baby Doll Ladies, 117–20; in effigy, 206; government payments after, 14–15; music reflecting, 155; play commemorating, 220; recovery efforts, 206; ten-year anniversary of, 158, *158*
Hurston, Zora Neale, 101

I

I Can't Sleep (McCrady), 245–46, *245*, 257n28
"I Want to Be Somebody's Baby Doll" (Smith), 119
Ignicious, Lloyd, 192
Inanna, 229
Indians (Mardi Gras) , xiii–xiv, 97, 121, 145, 264, *286*; Baby Dolls with, 9, 15–17, 226, 227; costumes of, 112; at funerals, 209, 216; Mardi Gras Indians, 89, 97
Ink Spots, 192, 210n18, 216
Interior Scroll (Schneemann), 61
Interstate highway, 149; impact on black New Orleans, xiv–xv, 204; impact on Mardi Gras, 149, 199
Irigaray, Luce, 282
Ishtar, 229
Ison, Cassidy "Baby Doll December," 157
"It's Carnival Time" (Johnson), 17
Iyer, Vijay, 52

J

Jackson, Tamara, 152
Jackson, Tony, 101; "Pretty Baby," 146, 163n20
"Jacksonville Rounders' Dance" (Bradford), 101
Jamestown Colonial Law (Virginia), 76, 85n4
Jazz: and African American narrative, 52; Danny Barker on, 99; emergence of, 96; funerals, 18, 97, 106n19, 310–11, *311*; New Orleans–style of, 98
Jazz in the Park, *115*
"Jean and Dinah" (Mighty Sparrow), 70–71
Jeanpierre, Marielle, 291–93; *Little Queen*

of the Night, 277, 292; *The New Found Pride, A Symbol of Resilience*, 269
Jean-Pierre, Ulrick, 293–94; *Celebrating the Culture of Life*, 268, 281, 294
Jefferson, Janine "Jay Pretty Green Eyes," *271*
Jim Crow era, 31–35; and Baby Dolls, 223; escape from, 35–41; streetcars, 32. *See also* Segregation
John McCrady School of Art, 243, 256n14
Johnson, Al, 217–18; *Burn K-Doe Burn*, *217*; "It's Carnival Time," 17, 151
Johnson, Jennifer, 152, *153*
Johnson, Lynette Dolliole, 143–44
Jones, Alma "Lollypop," 192
Jones, Amelia, 276
Jones, Benny, 167, 183
Jones, Benny, Sr., *182*
Jones, Beulah, 34
Jones, Eugene, *183*
Jones, Leonard, *218*, 219
Jones, Leroy, 181
Judgement Day (McCrady), 246

K

Kador, Ernest, Jr. *See* K-Doe, Ernie
"Katie Mae" (Boudreaux), 154
Katrice, Baby Doll, *160*
Katrina: Mother-In-Law of 'Em All (Florence), 220
K-Doe, Antoinette (Miss Antoinette), 126, 203–7, *215*, 287; Baby Doll revival by, ix, 149, 203; in *Burn K-Doe Burn*, 213–14; with effigy, *212*; of Ernie K-Doe Baby Dolls, 116–18; funeral of, 208–9, 211n23; as honorary pallbearer for Lloyd Washington, 126; legacy of, 213–21; musical choices of, 132n35; performance for Bush, 17; plaque for tomb, 219–20, *220*
K-Doe, Ernie, 126, 266; effigy of, 205–6; as FNOC grand marshal, 214; funeral of, 205, 210n10; on great R&B singers, 213; "Here Come the Girls," 149; lying in state, 219; marriage of, 116–17, 203; "Mother-in-Law," 149; at Mother-in-Law

Lounge, 205; performance for Bush, 17; as royalty in community, 268

Keeping Jazz Funerals Alive (Francis), 309

Keeping the Beat on the Street (Burns), 183

Kein, Sybil, 48–49; *An American South*, 49; *Creole: The History and Legacy of Louisiana*, 49; *Creole Ballads and Zydeco*, 49; *Delta Dancer*, 49; *Gombo People*, 49; *Maw-Maw's Creole Lullaby and Other Songs for Children*, 49; *Serenade Creole*, 49

Kidney Stew on Bourbon Street, 170

Kimble, Janice: as Gold Digger, 150–51, 289; at Mardi Gras, 125, 161; in Mother-in-Law Lounge, 229; with Original Pinettes Brass Band, 114; and Treme Baby Dolls, 113

Kimble, Merline, 3–5, 132n35, 289, 299, 312; on ancestral traditions, 274; as Baby Doll elder, 17–18; with Doucette, 115; as Gold Digger, 113, 116, 150–51; at Jazz in the Park, 115; after Katrina, 117–18; in Mother-in-Law Lounge, 229; with Original Pinettes Brass Band, 114

King, Earl, burial of, 219–20

King, Grace, *New Orleans: The Place and the People*, 46

King, Nathan, 109

Kline, Franz, 259n40

Kohlmeyer, Ida, 243

Koller, Odette, 122, 124

Koller, Reginald, 122

Kongo power figure (*Nkisi N'Kondi*), 269

Krewe du Vieux, 112–13

Krewe of Muses, 113, 132n10

Krewes, white male elitist, xix, 110–11, 118, 131n9

K-Stevenson, Mary, 159

Ku Klux Klan, 121

L

La Beau, Karen, 280–81, 295–96; *Baby Dolls Parade*, 295; *Cinnamon Black and Sugar Baroness*, 281, 295

Labat, Jean-Baptiste (Père Labat), *Nouveau Voyage aux Isles de l'Amerique*, 91–92

Labat, Mary Thelma Pavageau, 122

Labor, post-slavery by women of color, 22, 24, 26–27

Lacen, Anthony "Tuba Fats," 181, 183

Ladetto, Peter, *Fiery Looking Baby Doll*, 266, 267

Lammie-Hanson, D., 279, 296–98; *Golden Baby Doll Lady*, 265, 297; *Top Hats, a Bonnet and Lace*, 266, 297

Lancaster, Roger, 279

Lancret, Nicolas, 247

Landry, George, xix, 149

Lange, Dorothea, 236, 252; *Nipomo, California. Destitute 'pea-pickers' in California*, 251

"Lars Edegran Presents Uncle Lionel" (Batiste), 183

Lawrence, Jacob: McCrady compared with, 248; at Pratt Institute, 259n40; Toussaint L'Ouverture series, 258n34; Vaughn on, 85n13

Le Roy, Wilbur, "Sweet Baby Doll," 176

Lee, Big Chief Robert, 148–49

Lee, Joell "Jo Baby": as Black Storyville Baby Doll, 127, 156; at Mother-in-Law Lounge, 228–29

Legacy of the Baby Dolls (Duncan), 264–65, 290

Legitimation Ordinance No. 8 (1927), 70

LeGrand, Julia, 95

Lemelle, Jaqueline, 22

Leung, Stephen, 68

Lewis, Gilda, 158

Lichtenstein, Roy, 259n40

Liddell, Janice Lee, 69

Like Mother, Like Daughter (Welsh), 278

Lillian, Cadillac, 148

Lillian, Ms., 148, 148, 188

Lipsitz, George, 117

Little girl Dolls ("the toy"), 67

Little Queen of the Night (Jeanpierre), 277, 292

Lollypop: Baby Doll clothes in Astrodome, 220–21; in *Burn K-Doe Burn*, 214, 214; at funeral, 215

Longino, Michelle, 152, 153

Looking Down on the Mother-in-Law Lounge (Bruce), 285

Lopez, Gloria, 190

Lord Invader, "Rum and Coca-Cola," 70, 74n31

Louisiana Creole culture, preservation of, 48–49

Louisiana Purchase, 23

Louisiana State Museum, Baby Doll exhibit, 150, *151*, 163n29

Louisiana Weekly, The, 34

Louisiana Writers Projects, 258n39

Lovell, Charles, 309–10; *Uncle Lionel Second Line Baby Doll*, *309*

Lurie, Alison, 66

M

Macy's Thanksgiving Parade, 307

Maddison, Gertrude Thomas, 123, 124

Mahogany Blue Baby Dolls, 158, 162

Majestic Brass Band, 181

"Make It Bounce" (Slim), 155

Mannerism, 240

Mardi Gras, 196, 199, 225, 273; in 1949, 189–90; Comus parades, 258n38; as economic stimulus, 109; as Fat Tuesday, 258n32; guides to, 109–10; and Jim Crow, 37–38; masked balls, 89; as satire/parody, 122; theater tradition in, 110; white, 200

Mardi Gras Black Indians, 112, 131. *See also* Indians (Mardi Gras)

Mardi Gras Day (McCrady, Durieux, and Wickiser), 237, 246–50, *247*

"Mardi Gras in New Orleans" (Professor Longhair), 190

Mardi Gras Indians. *See* Indians (Mardi Gras)

Mardi Gras Indians (Smith), xix

Mardi Gras Indians, Skeletons, Brass Band, Weenie Man, and Baby Dolls (Bruce), *286*

Mardi Gras Madness (McGhee), *308*

Mardi Gras Records, 144

Marginalization: of men, 72; of minority krewes, 110–11; by patriarchal society, 61

Marsh, Reginald, 241

Marshall, Keith, 244

Martin, Deborah Sylvest, 156

Martinez, Maurice, 146; *The Black Indians of New Orleans*, xviii, xxviin13

Martinican (sartorial body) 64–66, 71–72

Martiniquian, 73n7

Mas, 73n1

Maskers, women, 89–90, 198, *263*; Baby Doll origins, 121; contemporary, 71–72; as reality escape, 198; sartorial body (Martinican), 64–66, 71; in Trinidad, 61–64; unruly (Baby Doll), 66–71; white, 152–54

Mason, Marlie Jade, 152, *153*

Maw-Maw's Creole Lullaby and Other Songs for Children (Kein), 49

Mayer, Vicki, 112

Mbembe, Achille, 122–23

McAlister, Elizabeth A., 123, 130

McCrady, John, 235–38, 256n14; early period, 238–40; later period, 240–45; political commentary of, 246; themes, 245–55

Works: *Assassination of Huey Long*, 242; *Evening Meal, Duck Hill, Mississippi*, 245; "Exhausted Merrymakers," 247; *I Can't Sleep*, 245–46, *245*, 257n28; *Judgement Day*, 246; *Mardi Gras Day*, 237; "Negro Maskers," 236, *237*, 246–48, 250–53, 254–55; *New Orleans Dock Scene*, 246; *Oh! Them Golden Slippers*, 246; *Oxford on a Hill*, 245; *Parade*, 252, *253*; *Political Rally*, 246; *Portrait of a Negro*, 239, 256n8; *Repatriated*, 244; *Self-Portrait on the Levee*, 253; *Steamboat Round the Bend*, 245; *Swing Low, Sweet Chariot, Eucharist Scene*, 246; *Swing Low, Sweet Chariot*, 242

McCrady, Mary Basso, 243

McCray, Hattie, 34

McDaniel, Hattie, "Brown Skin Baby Doll," 189

McDonald, Patricia, 150–51

McKenna Museum of African-American Art, ix–x, 221

McKinney, Bill, 192

McKinney, Robert, 145, 172–73

McPherson, Patricia, 113

Mechanics Hall Riot (1866), 26

Men: as Baby Dolls, 3–4, 11–13, 146–47, 231, 309; cross-dressing by, 147, 231, 309; marginalization of, 72; public shaming of, 68, 72; rape accusations against, 120

Mendieta, Ana, *Untitled (Rape Scene)*, 61

Mercury Records, *191*, 192

Meritt Records, 189

Merlin, Lara, 125

Midwest Triumvirate, 240

Mighty Sparrow, "Jean and Dinah," 70–71

Miller, Kenneth Hayes, 240; in Fourteenth Street School, 241; influences on, 256n11

Million Dollar Baby Dolls, 67, 68; birthing of, 117; formation in 1912, 27; and Jim Crow, 37–38, 40–41; music of, 145–46; as response to segregation, 31

Milon, Gerald "Jake," xviii

Mintz, Sidney, 63

Miro, Esteban, 42n24

Miss Pussycat (Panacea Theriac), 204

Mitchell, Reid, 98

Mitchell, Satin, *289*; costume of, 229; as Satin Eloquent Baby Doll, 162

Mohawk Hunters Mardi Gras Indians, *160*, 162

Mondy, Alma, *191*, 192

Monque, James, 146

Montana, Allison "Tootie," xviii, 12, 204, 206

Montana, Joyce, 204

Montana, Tammy, 151, *228*

Montana Dancing Baby Dolls, *161*

Moore, Alice Ruth. *See* Dunbar-Nelson, Alice

Moore, Consuela Marie. *See* Kein, Sybil

Moreau de St.-Méry, Médéric Louis Élie, 92

Morgan, Stanley, 192

Motherhood, Caribbean image of, 69

"Mother-in-Law" (Toussaint), 126, 149, 216, 219

Mother-in-Law Lounge, 203–5; effigy at, 126; K-Doe performances at, 149; during Mardi Gras, 227; recovery from Hurricane Katrina, 206; reopening of, 210n7; in Treme, 225

Mr. Stranger Man (Boudreaux), 154

Murals: courses in, 241; of cultural icons, 204; Mexican muralists as inspiration, 246

Music, 171–72, 190; "Baby Doll" as hit tune, 173–74; of Baby Dolls, 145–46, 147; in brothels, 119, 163n20; call-and-response singing, 91, 96, 97; coon songs, 78; dance rhythms, 96; dehumanization in, 78, 80, 83; denigration of Baby Dolls, 78–81, 83; drums, 84n6; ethnic characterizations in, 78; fiddles, 84n6; intra-racial-cultural discord from, 84n9; "minstrel songs," 78; objectification in, 78, 80, 83; positive use of baby, 82–83; racism in, 78; as religion, 13–14; stigmatization in, 80–81. *See also* Jazz

Musicians' Tomb, 216, 219–20

"My Baby Loves Me" (Hogan), 190

"My Walking Baby" (Hogan), 190

Myers, Fred, 119

Myth of New Orleans in New Orleans Literature, The (Bryan), 45

N

Natchez Indians, 121

Nawlins' Dawlins Baby Dolls, 158, *159*

"Negro Maskers" (McCrady), 236–37, *237*, 246–48, 250–53, 254–55

Nelson, Lois: at funerals, 127, *128–29*, 129–30, 277; as Gold Digger, 113, 150–51; after Katrina, 117–18; musical choices of, 127

Nelson, Mary, *153*

Nelson, Robert J., 48

Nelson family, 179

Neville, Charmaine, 149

Neville Brothers, xix

New Breed Brass Band, 151

New Deal economic programs, 235

New Found Pride, A Symbol of Resilience, The (Jeanpierre), 269

New Masses, The, 244

New Orleans: and American Civil Liberties Union lawsuit, 152; as city of interracial vice, 26; demographics of, 90; French control of, 21–22; refugee influx into, 23; Spanish control of, 22; US control of, 23–28

New Orleans: The Place and the People (King), 46

New Orleans African American Museum, 231

New Orleans Baby Dolls, 229, *297*

New Orleans Carnival Krewes (O'Neill), 110

New Orleans City Guide, 109, 258n39

New Orleans Creole Belle Baby Dolls, 156–57; at Mardi Gras, *157*; Smith at debut of, *315*; student interaction with, 317–18

New Orleans Dock Scene (McCrady), 246

New Orleans Farewell and a Heavenly Welcome, A (Bruce), 286

New Orleans Jazz and Heritage Festival, xix, *154*

"New Orleans Music" (Batiste), 183

New Orleans Musicians' Tomb, 216, 219–20

New Orleans School of Art, 239

New Orleans Society of Dance, 118–20, 154–55; Baby Doll Ladies, 265, *267*; in Macy's Thanksgiving Parade, 307; at New Orleans Jazz and Heritage Festival, *154*

Newcomb Pottery movement, 258n39

Newman, Ed, 275–76

Nicaud, Rose, 24

Night in Acadie, A (Chopin), 46

Nipomo, California. Destitute 'pea-pickers' in California (Lange), 251

Nkisi N'Kondi (Kongo power figure), 269

North Claiborne Avenue, xi, xii, xiii. *See also* Claiborne Avenue

Nouveau Voyage aux Isles de l'Amerique (Labat), 91–92

O

Obatala (Yoruba deity), 131

Ocker, Karen, *The Baby Dolls*, 268, 274–75

Odell, Annie, 301–2; *Antoinette and Ernie K-Doe*, 268, 302; *Antoinette K-Doe*, 268, *301*

Oh! Them Golden Slippers (McCrady), 246

Okeh Records, 176

Old Creole Days (Cable), 46

Olympia Brass Band, 181

O'Malley, Lurana Donnels, 47–48

O'Neill, Rosary, *New Orleans Carnival Krewes*, 110

Ongoing Moment, The (Dyer), 235

Ooh Poo Pah Doo Bar, 227

Orchid Girls, 146

Original Paramount Club, 146

Original Pinettes Brass Band, 114

Osbey, Brenda Marie, 51–54; "Faubourg Study No. 3: The Seven Sisters of New Orleans," 52–54; "Why We Can't Talk to You about Voodoo," 51

Osborn, Royce: *All on a Mardi Gras Day*, 147, 206; at Mardi Gras, *157*

Oshun (Yoruba goddess), 82, 85n13, 152

Oubre, Anita, 158

Oubre, Anita "Magnolia Rose," 156, 162

Overton, Bonnie, 35

Owens, Ruth, 302–4; *Down by the Crossroads*, 274, *303*; *Hey Y'all*, 274, *303*; *Raddy Winner*, 269, 271–72, 274, *303*; *Strut, Baby Doll*, 304

Oxford on a Hill (McCrady), 245

P

Paddio, Villard, 143

Pandora Carnival Krewes, 147

Parade (McCrady), 252, *253*

Parks, Gordon, 252

Paxton, Shannon "Baby Doll Chocolate," 14, 18; at 2015 Katrina Walk and Pub Crawl, 158, *158*; at Jazz in the Park, *115*; of Original Pinettes Brass Band, *114*

Pearlstein, Philip, 259n40

Pearson, Wanda, 263, *289*; as Gold Digger, 113, 150–51; at Mardi Gras, 228; in Mother-in-Law Lounge, 229; at tribute for Mercedes Stevenson, *159*

"Pecker Song, The," 171, 185n29

Peiss, Kathy, 100
Pennsylvania Academy of Fine Arts, 239,
    258n39
Peretti, Burton, 98
Performing Age, Performing Gender
    (Woodward), 278
Perry, Tee Eva: at 2015 Katrina Walk and
    Pub Crawl, 158; in Baby Dolls,
    17, 149, 206; at funerals, *215*, 219;
    as honorary pallbearer for Lloyd
    Washington, 126; as K-Doe stand-
    in, 213–14; as mother-in-law char-
    acter, 214, 216–17, *217*; in Mother-
    in-Law Lounge, 229; paintings of,
    299–300; pillow throw of, *287*
Philadelphia Record, 244
Phillips, Louise Recasner, 8
Pierre, Jamar Duval: *Rolling with the
    Dolls*, 265, 280; *Skeleton and Baby
    Doll*, 265
Pierre, Jane and Monae, 158, *159*
Piron, Armand J., "Brown Skin Who, You
    For," 174
Plessy, Homer, 26
Plessy vs. Ferguson, 31
Poirier, Jason, 126, 205–6
Police brutality, 34–35
Polite, Albert, Jr., *230*, 231
Political Rally (McCrady), 246
Porch, The, 261
Pork Chop (dancers), 170
Portrait of a Negro (McCrady), 239, *239*,
    256n8
Potter, Eliza, 24
Poussin, Nicolas, 247
Pratt Institute (Brooklyn), 249, 259n40
Preservation Hall Brass Band, 209
"Pretty Baby" (Jackson), 146, 163n20
Price, Richard, 63
Prince, Steve, 310–11; *Bird in Hand:
    Second Line for Michigan*, 269,
    281–82, *311*
Prioleau, Betsy, *Seductress*, 230–31
Prison industrial complex, 84–85n11
Professor Longhair: at Caldonia Inn, 179;
    "Mardi Gras in New Orleans," 190;
    recording career of, *191*
Prohibition, 167
Prostitution: Baby Dolls association with,

68–69, 90, 144–45, 149; and black
    madams, 162n11; Chicago dance
    for, 174–75; as commodity, 279;
    desegregation of, 70; distancing
    from, 4, 10, 12, 14, 207; K-Doe
    distancing from, 207; as survival,
    75–76, 116; twentieth-century, 69;
    white, 122. *See also* Storyville
Pussy Footers, 13

Q
Quintron (Robert Rolston), 204, 209

R
R Bar, 226
Rabelais and His World (Bakhtin), 276–77
Race: in Dunbar-Nelson's writing, 46–48;
    in masking styles, 63
Racism: in humor, 80; in music, 78,
    84nn8–9. *See also* Segregation
Raddy Winner (Owens), 269, 271–72,
    274, *303*
Radee, Spyboy, *160*
Ragtime, 97–100, 104
Rape: for breeding slaves, 120; and James-
    town Colonial Law, 84n4; and
    Mendieta painting, 61
Rawls, Alex, 205
Reconstruction, 25–26
Red Beans and Ricely Yours (Saloy), 50
Red Light District, Baby Dolls in, 195
Reed, Clarita, 32
Reed, Miriam Batiste, 149, *215*, 268; in
    Baby Dolls, 8, 17, 145, 207; in *Burn
    K-Doe Burn*, 214; costume in
    Mardi Gras exhibition, ix; pillow
    throw of, *287*
Regis, Helen A., 119, 121
Registration act of 1830, 24
Reiss, Winold, 259n43
Religion: in masking, 134n87; in Mc-
    Crady's work, *245*; of spirit from
    African culture, 81, 84n5; from
    Spiritual Church, 168, 170, 180–81,
    190; of spiritualism, 52–53; of
    Treme: Voodoo, 151–52
Repatriated (McCrady), 244
Resettlement Administration. *See* Farm
    Security Administration

Rex (krewe), 111, 118

Rey, Willis, 146

Rice, Anne, 126

Riggs, Robert, 259n43

Riis, Jacob, 235–36

Riley, Nettie, 148–49

Rivera, Diego, 240, 258n39

Robichaux, John, 176

Robinson, Celeste, 198–99

Robinson, Danielle, 99–100

Robinson, Jim, *183*

Rohlehr, Gordon, 69

Rolling with the Dolls (Pierre), *265*,
    280–81

Rolston, Robert (Quintron), 204, 209

Ross, Anna, 219

Rouzan, Wanda, 126

Ruffins, Kermit, *115*, 210n7

"Rum and Coca-Cola" (Lord Invader),
    70, 74n31

Rummel, Joseph, 197

Russo, Mary, 121, 282

Ryder, Albert Pinkham, 242, 243, 256n11

S

Sacred Feminine, 229

Saint Ann, 152

Saint Ann Marching Krewe, 225

Saloy, Mona Lisa: on death, 51; *Red Beans
    and Ricely Yours*, 50; *Second Line
    Home*, 50

Sandmel, Ben, 204–5

Sanford and Son, 191–92

Satchmo Salute, 151

Satire: in Mardi Gras, 112–13; of subjugat-
    ed people, 122–23

Saussy, Virginia, 113

Saxon, Lyle: *Fabulous New Orleans*, 109;
    and Louisiana Writers Projects,
    258n39

Schneemann, Carole, *Interior Scroll*, 61

Scott, Nathan Haynes, 305–7; "For Us by
    Us" P. O. S. S. E. (People Opposing
    Society's Segregational Entitle-
    ment), 269, *306*

Scott, Winfield, 177

Seals, Baby Franklin, 174

Second line: adaptations for, 98; as
    coping mechanism, 282; in jazz fu-

nerals, 97, 99; in military, *180*, *181*;
    in Prince's painting, 269; as social
    subculture, 177–79, *178*

Second Line Home (Saloy), 50

Seductress (Prioleau), 230–31

Segregation: and Baby Dolls, 223; black/
    white/Creole, 195; of brothels,
    224; and Carnival, 10; of housing,
    117; internal, 279; Lionel Batiste
    experience with, 167, 170; post–
    Civil War, 26–27; Separate Car
    Act, 26, 31; violence of, 33. *See also*
    Desegregation; Jim Crow era

Self-Portrait on the Levee (McCrady), 253

Senegal, 22

Separate Car Act (1890), 26, 31

Serenade Creole (Kein), 49

Seventh Ward, 195

Sex workers. *See* Prostitution

Sexuality: in dancing, 62–63; at Mardi
    Gras, 273; sacred, 229

Shahn, Ben, *Cotton Pickers*, 252

Shezbie, Felicia Batiste, *171*

Shisler, Kari, 152, *153*

Simms, Charles, 144

Simone, Nina, "Four Women," 80

Singer, Clyde, 257n28

Sisters of the Holy Family, 24

610 Stompers, 13

Skeleton and Baby Doll (Pierre), *265*

Skeleton gangs, 145

Skeletons, 196, 199

Skeletons of New Orleans, 126

Skull and Bones Gang: Baby Dolls with,
    227; costuming of, 97; at funerals,
    216; during Mardi Gras, 126, *157*

Slavery: children kidnapped for, 24–25;
    codes, 90; restrictions after, 25;
    revolt against, 23–24; and sexual
    exploitation of, 120; slave ships,
    21–22; trading, 22, 23; of women,
    21

Slim, Soulja, "Make It Bounce," 155

Smith, Bessie: "Baby Doll," xxi, 176–77,
    189; "I Want to Be Somebody's
    Baby Doll," 119

Smith, Bradley, 258n35; *Baby Doll Mas-
    queraders*, 248–49, *249*, 250–51,
    254–55

Smith, Felicia, 229

Smith, Huey "Piano," 190–91

Smith, Michael, *Mardi Gras Indians*, xix

Smoothers, Elizabeth, 150

Smoth, John, 93

Snedeker, Rebecca, 110

Social Aid and Pleasure Club Task Force, 152

Soulsville Records, 191

"Spasm Band" (Wickiser), 249–50

Spiritual Church, 168, 170, 180–81, 190

St. Amand, Gailene McGhee, 307–8; *Black Mask*, 307; *Dancing Baby Doll*, 307; *Golden Mask*, 307; *Mardi Gras Madness*, 308

St. James church, 208

Stalberte, Dwayne, *161*

Star Talent label, 190, *191*

Steamboat Round the Bend (McCrady), 245

Stearns, Marshall and Jean, 101, 102, 105n5

Stern, Joe, *153*

Stevenson, "Buddy," 141

Stevenson, Mercedes, 149

Storyville, 69; Baby Dolls impact on, 4; Blue Book guides to, 27; as racially divided, 26, 223; World War I servicemen in, 70. *See also* Brothels

Stouck, Jordan, 47

Strachwitz, Chris, 183–84

Straight College, 33

Strut, Baby Doll (Owens), *304*

Strutting: cakewalk dance as, 99; images of, *274*; walking raddy, ix–x, 67, 103, 129

Stryker, Roy, 235–36

Suffrage, 23, 48

"Sugar" (Waters), 189

Summers, Marion, 243, 257n23

Sunpie, 220

Sunspots, 220

Super Sunday, *159*

Super-T-Art (Wilke), 61

Surrealism, 243

"Sweet Baby Doll" (Le Roy and Thomas), 176

Sweet Home New Orleans, 206

Swing Low, Sweet Chariot (McCrady), 242

Swing Low, Sweet Chariot, Eucharist Scene (McCrady), 246

T

Tann, Mambo Chita, 130

Taylor, Deborah, 157

Taylor, Dorothy Mae, xix

Tee Eva Ernie K-Doe Baby Dolls, 158

Temple, Pythian, 147–48

Temple, Shirley, 132n20

Theodore, Micah "Pretty Face Baby," *289*; as Gold Digger, 150, 227

Theodore, Rosalind, *289*; attire of, 124–25, 130; as Gold Digger, 151; at Mardi Gras, *125*; in Mother-in-Law Lounge, 229

Theriac, Panacea (Miss Pussycat), 209

They Call Us Baby Dolls: A Mardi Gras Tradition, ix

Thirteenth Amendment, 25

Thirty-Five Painters of the Deep South, 242

This Ain't No Mouse Music, 183–84

Thomas, Geannie, *215*; Baby Doll revival by, 149; in *Burn K-Doe Burn*, 214; as honorary pallbearer for Lloyd Washington, 126; limited opportunities of, 116–17; at Mother-in-Law Lounge, *271*; performance for Bush, 17; pillow throw of, *287*

Thomas, George W., "Sweet Baby Doll," 176

Thomas, Ida Mae, 145

Thomas, Lula Williams, 123

Thomson, Nelson, 131

Thornton, Bradleigh, *289*

Thornton, Vanessa: at Mardi Gras, *289*; at Mother-in-Law Lounge, 228, 229; in Tee Eva Ernie K-Doe Baby Dolls, 158

Tignon law (1786), 42n24

Tijuana Club, *37*, 38

"Tootie Ma Is a Big Fine Thing," 124

Top Hats, a Bonnet and Lace (Lammie-Hanson), 266, *297*

Toussaint, Allen: "Here Come the Girls," 217–18; "Mother-in-Law," 219; preshow performances by, 213; song writing process of, 219

Toussaint L'Ouverture series (Lawrence), 258n34
"Tra La La Boom Der É," 144, 162n11
Treme: Voodoo, 151–52
Treme, Mother-in-Law Lounge in, 225
Treme Baby Dolls, 113, 124–25
Treme Brass Band, 167, 183, 209
Treme Million Dollar Baby Dolls, 151
Trepagnier, Denise: crepe paper costume replica by, *171*; as 504 Eloquent Baby Doll, 162; replica of, *150*
Trepagnier Plantation, 168
Trinidad: Carnival, 62, 63–64, 66–72; sex work in, 70; Shango devotional dance in, 95
Turner, Victor, 276
Twichell, Heather, 126, 219

U

Ulmann, Doris, 253–54, 259n43; and Sisters of the Holy Family, 259n44
Uncle Lionel Second Line Baby Doll (Lovell), *309*
Union Sons Hall ("Funky Butt Hall"), 102
Unruly women: Merline Kimble as, 116; relevance of, 109–20, 131; in Trinidad Carnival, 64, 66–72; twenty-first century resurgence of, 116; and women's rites, 120–31
Untitled (Rape Scene) (Mendieta), 61

V

Vagina Monologues (Ensler), 118
Valdery, Bridget, 150
Van Der Zee, James, 254
Van Gogh, Vincent, 240
Vaughn, Alan G., 85n13
Vaz-Deville, Kim: as Baby Doll participant, 223–24; *The Baby Dolls*, ix, xix, 273, 300; on contradictory responses to Baby Dolls, 280; K-Doe (Antoinette) influence on, 221; in Mother-in-Law Lounge, 230; on "quasi red light" district, 69; on Smith photos, 248–49
Venus (Greek goddess), 82, 85n13
Vidacovich, Laura and Deborah, 152, *153*
Vincent, Rosalie, 24–25

Violets and Other Tales (Dunbar-Nelson), 45
Voodoo, 51–52, 94–95, 105n5

W

Walker, Fabieyoun, *289*; at Jazz in the Park, *115*; in New Orleans Creole Belle Baby Dolls, 156
Walking raddy, ix–x, 67, 103, 129
Walkowitz, Judith R., 113
Ward, Jesmyn, 121
"Warmest Baby in the Bunch: Ethiopian Ditty, The" (Cohan), 77–79
Warrick, Henrietta Hayes, xi–xvi, *xii–xiii*, *xvi*, xxviin2
Warrick, Joseph, xiii, xv
Washington, Booker T., 254
Washington, Lloyd: cremains at Florence's fortieth birthday party, 216; Ernie K-Doe Baby Dolls as pallbearers for, 126; interment of, *215*, 216
Washington, Rhonda, *160*, 162
Waters, Ethel, "Sugar," 189
Watts, Rico, 205
"We Made It Through That Water" (song), 155
Weiss, Seymour, 109
West Africa: burial traditions, 97; dance movements, 90–96
White, Lulu, 27
White, Millisia, 117–18, 154–55
White, Sonji, 158, *159*
White Eagles, xviii
"Why We Can't Talk to You about Voodoo" (Osbey), 51
Wickiser, Ralph, 259n40; *Mardi Gras Day*, 237, 246; "Spasm Band," 249–50
Wild Magnolia Mardi Gras Indians, 151, 157
Wild Magnolias, xviii–xix, *157*
Wild Tchoupitoulas, xix
Wild Tchoupitoulas Baby Dolls, 18, 158, *158*
Wild Tchoupitoulas Mardi Gras Indians, 149, 158, *158–59*
Wilke, Hannah, *Super-T-Art*, 61
Williams, Clarence, "Brown Skin Who, You For," 174

Williams, Clea, 198–99

Williams, Hattie Louise, 33

Williams, Karen "Baby Doll Rose," 157

Williams, Niquan, *161*

Williams, Omika, *288*, *289*; in New Orle-
    ans Creole Belle Baby Dolls, 156

Williams, Tiffany Lee, 152, *153*

Williams, Tiffany Pruett, *153*

Wilmington Advocate, 48

Wilon, Jay, 151

Wilson, Vicki "Babydoll Lady Lotus," 158,
    162

Winters, Lisa Ze, 42n24

Women, 229–30; decorum defiance by,
    99–100; and morals/ethics, 69; as
    male possession, 75, 83n1; Victori-
    an standards for, 113, 132n20

Women of color: abuse of, 32–33;
    resistance to racial dominance,
    22–23, 42n24; support for, 24; and
    Victorian standards, 113. *See also*
    Black women

Wood, Grant, 238, 240

Woodward, Ellsworth, 258n39

Woodward, Kathleen, *Performing Age,*
    Performing Gender, 278

Works of Alice Dunbar-Nelson, The
    (Dunbar-Nelson), 48, 54n2

Works Progress Administration (WPA),
    235, 240

World War II, 3–4

Y

Yellow Pocahontas, xviii, 146

Yonvalou ceremony, 95

Yoruba goddess (Oshun), 82, 85n13, 152

Young Generation Warrior Indians, *160*,
    162

Youngblood, Henry, 190

Z

Zulu Social Aid and Pleasure Club, xix;
    decline of, 149; parade by, 145;
    respectability of, xviii; ridicule of,
    111; and Warrick family, xiii